Case Studies on Digital Government

Bruce Rocheleau
Northern Illinois University, USA

IDEA GROUP PUBLISHING

Hershey • London • Melbourne • Singapore

Acquisitions Editor:	Kristin Klinger
Development Editor:	Kristin Roth
Senior Managing Editor:	Jennifer Neidig
Managing Editor:	Sara Reed
Assistant Managing Editor:	Sharon Berger
Copy Editor:	Amanda Appicello
Typesetter:	Amanda Appicello
Cover Design:	Lisa Tosheff
Printed at:	Yurchak Printing Inc.

Published in the United States of America by
    Idea Group Publishing (an imprint of Idea Group Inc.)
    701 E. Chocolate Avenue, Suite 200
    Hershey PA 17033-1240
    Tel: 717-533-8845
    Fax: 717-533-8661
    E-mail: cust@idea-group.com
    Web site: http://www.idea-group.com

and in the United Kingdom by
    Idea Group Publishing (an imprint of Idea Group Inc.)
    3 Henrietta Street
    Covent Garden
    London WC2E 8LU
    Tel: 44 20 7240 0856
    Fax: 44 20 7379 0609
    Web site: http://www.eurospanonline.com

Library of Congress Cataloging-in-Publication Data

Case studies on digital government / Bruce Rocheleau, editor.
    p. cm.
  Summary: "This book includes cases from local, state, Federal, and international governments, covering a wide variety of technologies such as geographic information systems, enterprise resource planning, Web-based customer response systems, and cross-agency shared systems, among others. The practitioners' in-depth knowledge brings a reality to the cases that readers will find stimulating as well as instructive"--Provided by publisher.
    Includes bibliographical references and index.
    ISBN 978-1-59904-177-3 (hardcover) -- ISBN 978-1-59904-179-7 (ebook)
    1. Internet in public administration--Case studies. 2. Public administration--Information resources management--Case studies. 3. Public administration--Information technology--Case studies. 4. Electronic government information--Case studies. I. Rocheleau, Bruce A.
    JF1525.A8C36 2007
    352.3'802854678--dc22
                        2006033763

British Cataloguing in Publication Data
A Cataloguing in Publication record for this book is available from the British Library.

Case Studies on Digital Government

Table of Contents

Foreword

By now, we are all familiar with the pervasive impact of information systems on the administration of government. Accessing local, state, and national Web portals for access to information is now commonplace for most citizens of advanced industrial societies. In the academic discipline of public administration, the study of information technology is now a mandated topic, required for the accreditation of degree programs in the field. More and more governmental operations, from applying for driver's licenses to paying taxes, are now accomplished electronically with greater convenience to the citizen and with greater efficiency for government.

Yet, in spite of the pervasiveness of public information technology, much of the literature available to the student or the interested reader has fallen into one of two genres: dull and excessively uncritical governmental reports on the one hand, and on the other hand, highly generalized academic treatments of the expansion of information technology (IT) in the last few decades. By providing extensive case treatments of important topics and issues in the public management of IT, Bruce Rocheleau has gone a long way toward filling an important gap in the literature.

The cases which Rocheleau has brought together, taken as a set, provide a comprehensive view of managing information technology in the public sector: contract management, control issues, customer orientation, ethics, evaluation, funding and fees, implementation, intellectual property, intergovernmental coordination, interorganizational dynamics, IT governance, outsourcing, political leadership, political participation, portal strategies, project management, systems acquisition, and vendor relationships are among the topics treated. Moreover, treatment is not at an airy and generalized level but is put into the more useful context of actual recent cases which have challenged practitioners in the field.

Case study research is a time-honored, traditional approach to the study of topics in public administration and management. Case study research has the capability of uncovering causal paths and mechanisms, and through richness of detail, identifying causal influences and interaction effects which might not be treated within the technical parameters of statistical studies. And these very research advantages are pedagogical advantages as well, drawing students into the interesting processes and issues of managing public information systems.

There has been a dearth of good case studies up to now, and this volume makes an important contribution to the field by helping to fill the gap. The contribution is enhanced by involvement of many practitioners in the writing of detailed case studies which help bridge theory and practice. The kinds of problems and issues dealt with by these case studies are a healthy sampling of issues faced by IT practitioners and academics, whether studying IT at the local, state, or federal level. In summary, case studies represented in this volume contribute in important ways to learning about public-sector information management and will help students of public administration understand and prepare for the coming era of digital government.

G. David Garson
North Carolina State University
July 15, 2006

G. David Garson *is a full professor of public administration at North Carolina State University. He is the author of more than 50 articles and the recipient of both the Donald Campbell and Aaron Wildavsky awards from the American Political Science Association. He is the author of Public Information Technology and E-Governance: Managing the Virtual State (2006), editor of Public Information Systems: Policy and Management Issues (2003), and co-editor of Digital Government: Principles and Practices (2003). He is the author, co-author, editor and/or co-editor of more than 20 other books. He is the editor of the Social Science Computer Review and is a member of several other journal editorial boards.*

ption

Preface

I was at the Conference of the American Society for Public Administration in Portland, Oregon in 2004, at a panel concerning the teaching of information management in Master of Public Administration programs. This particular session was attended by a host of professors engaged in teaching information technology. The one point of consensus of all of the panel members and the audience was the need for a book of case studies of information management in government. There exist many case study books concerning private sector management of technology but none dedicated to case studies of public sector information management. It was agreed that students need richly-detailed case studies to convey to them the complexities of management of technology and to allow them to see how proposed prescriptions and theories apply in real life. This book is intended to fill this gap.

I knew that it would not be easy to put together such a book. A good, richly-detailed case study is difficult to write. It requires deep knowledge of the organization involved. Such knowledge requires a basis of long-term participation observation and/or extensive interviews with organizational staff. It requires that the organization give access if such a case study is to be done by outsiders such as academic researchers. Such access can be difficult to obtain and necessitates a long-term commitment on the part of the researcher. As a consequence, I have found few richly-detailed case studies done by academics in the literature. From an academic perspective, it is much easier to develop research projects that do not require intensive qualitative information gathering and difficult access issues. For example, it is much easier to do research based on surveys or analyses of governmental Web sites. Likewise, practitioners have virtually no incentive to publish. Most IT managers that I know are overwhelmed with work because they are faced with new technologies and new demands on their time on an almost continuous basis. As a result, few practitioners take the time to write about their experiences. As a result, up until now, there exist few good case studies of public sector information management. Consequently, I owe a debt of gratitude to the practitioners and academics who contributed the case studies in this volume. For many of the practitioner contributors, this is their first formal publication, and I know that you will appreciate their efforts.

Focus on Processes and Issues Makes Cases of Enduring Value

The cases cover a broad variety of specific issues such as the digital divide, the development of Web portals and internal systems such as enterprise resource planning (ERP) systems, inventory control applications, online payment systems, and many other specific applications and issues. Thus the book provides a good sampling of emerging technologies for students. As is common knowledge, the specific information technologies described in this book will become "old hat" in not too long a time. However, these cases provide rich details on how managers and staff handled processes and issues that will reoccur regardless of the specific technologies involved and thus these case studies will remain valuable to students for their study long after the specific technologies have become antiquated. In particular, although these cases cover a wide variety of technologies, most deal with certain key processes such as how to organize and govern IT, the purchasing process and relationships with vendors, training and other human resource issues related to technology, business process re-engineering and the organizational obstacles to it, among others.

Capsule Descriptions of Cases

Most of these cases discuss a wide variety of issues and processes so the following summaries just give a glimpse of what is in each case study and this preface is aimed at whetting the appetites of readers. Three of the case studies provide detailed examples of what happens when new administrations take over local governments and reform and restructure information management. Matt Miszewski, the CIO of the State of Wisconsin, took over a system that was decentralized. Systems had grown piecemeal over the year and each system had customized support but a 40 million dollar cut in the state's budget forced action to make the system more efficient. Miszewski tackled this problem by constructing an enterprise-wide approach with a single architecture, emphasizing a common infrastructure, an integrated financial and management system, and evaluation metrics system. The case discusses the details of how to construct an enterprise structure. The task of building such a system required great attention to IT governance issues and several committees were formed. These committees were intergovernmental in nature including some of the major local governments. The case discusses how a vendor was hired to help the state develop its own solution and how service delivery coordinator positions were created to enhance horizontal communication. The need to have excellent communication between the technical and IT staff is one of the themes of this case. The state employs a customer evaluation form to obtain feedback on their performance.

Norm Jacknis, the CIO of Westchester County, made dramatic changes in the county's IT system. The previous administration had outsourced the IT system to IBM and Jacknis implemented a reversal of this policy, bringing IT back in-house, and the case discusses how this turnaround was accomplished including reorganization of the IT system toward a functional system. The new county executive had first-hand experience with IT, and the themes of paperless and more efficient government due to effective use of IT played a significant role in his administration. The county executive required that the heads of the departments (commissioners) attend an "IT boot camp". This case emphasizes the importance of planning and use of IT as an economic development tool. Westchester County used their IT resources to promote and develop a strong network of businesses using virtual cooperation and "coopetition".

Glenn Trommels discusses the revamping of the City of Rockford's information technology department. He describes how many of the systems were broken and the steps that he took to deal with the problems. Basic security issues needed to be fixed, and the department needed to reorganize in order to get away from a stovepipe mentality and move to a more integrated system. Despite the importance of the technical issues, he found the most basic need to create a team spirit. Problematic relationships with information technology's customer departments were addressed by the adoption of a request tracking system in which regular feedback on the progress of projects was provided as well as assessment of customer satisfaction with project outcomes. Communication and marketing play a significant role in this and other case studies, and the cases emphasize the importance of soft, non-technical skills in IT management.

All three of the previously-mentioned case studies emphasize the importance of leadership by political executives and generalist managers in providing the impetus and authority to achieve reform and integration. In most cases, technology heads do not have the authority to force change themselves, and consequently, they must depend for support from top executives to implement changes that cut across line departments.

Dave Bloch provides a case study that focuses on one method for integrating technology across departments in the County of Nevada (California): communities of interest. This case shows the importance of planning, stimulated in part by the Year 2000 crisis. The county's leadership searched for examples of other fast-growing counties and studied how they achieved better integration of their IT efforts. Nevada County's approach was to form six different "communities of interest" in which departments with related needs were grouped together into a community (of related departments) that had the authority to approve or reject major IT infrastructure projects. Leadership by the Chief Administrative Office, Ted Gaebler, was important to the success of the project. Also, important was the fact that the new structure had teeth and a substantial pot of funds associated with it. Bloch describes the application of the new approach to several different projects in order to provide lessons in how to manage with this new IT governance model.

Don Carlsen provides a tool kit to do IT governance. Carlsen identifies governance issues that most organizations share such as the lack of a process for linking individual projects with organizational strategy, the lack of capacity analysis to determine the capability of the organization to deal with new technologies, and the lack of adequate project management skills among staff. One tool is a good strategic technology plan. The process of developing Naperville's initial plan led to the discovery of a solution of a problem that end users had experienced with the organization's financial system. The organization's HR department developed a training program to enhance project management skills since so much of the staff's time was engaged in managing projects. Carlsen describes how the organization developed a more realistic assessment of capability. He then proceeds to discuss how employee teams were used in the budgeting and capital improvement plan processes to provide an in-depth assessment of proposed technology projects. Carlsen also discusses their usage of the balanced scorecard system which is an increasingly popular tool for ensuring that information technology projects are aligned with the organization's strategic objectives.

Louis Boglioli shows how even a small community can achieve innovative technologies. He also demonstrates that major productivity improvements can be achieved by more efficiently using the existing system rather than purchasing a new one. He estimates that Stuart (Florida) was only making use of about 10% of the capability of their financial system prior to his reforms. His case study demonstrates that small communities, even if they are wealthy, often have to subsist on limited funding for IT projects so making more effective use of an existing system is a necessity. He discusses how they conducted an analysis of business processes in order to show that the existing IT system could accommodate the organization's procedures. Training was essential to improve usage of the existing system, but Boglioli shows the limitations of one commonly used method, the "train the trainer" approach.

Larry Gunderson provides an in-depth discussion of the project management complexities of developing an application (computerized maintenance management system) that attempts to employ data from Naperville's GIS system for use in other application systems. As with many major applications, the system required work by several departments (public works, water, transportation-engineering, and information technology, in this case) to be successful and the degree of support varied among the departments. Also, the existing workflows of the departments conflicted with those required by the new system. His case shows the risks associated with being one of the first governments to implement a system—the project advanced as the vendors acquired more experience. Eventually, the implementation was assisted by a consultant who carefully mapped business processes of the work order flow using a business mapping software package. The case also illustrates the importance of project management (e.g., Gantt and work breakdown structure techniques were employed), leadership, and champions.

A majority of case studies concern successes, but we often learn more from case studies of failures about what not to do. Kimberly Furumo provides a detailed case study of the failed implementation of an ERP system in a university. Her case emphasizes the importance of sectors and how the differences between public and private sectors contributed to the ERP failure. Furumo's case points out that the CIO position in public organizations is usually at a much lower level of hierarchy than in private businesses and that public unions and longevity of civil service employees make the implementation of business process changes necessary for ERP systems much more difficult in the public sector. Furumo describes how the IT department refused to provide support requested by the implementing line agencies, and the project management also suffered from the fact that team members had to continue to perform their current jobs while at the same time devoting large amounts of time to the new system. The ineffective relationship between IT and end-user departments was the key element that led to the failure of the new system.

By way of contrast, Paul Taylor portrays a very successful implementation of an inventory control system in Los Angeles. Taylor shows how vendor relationships are numerous and complex in large cities—the city had over 2,000 contracts with vendors. Spending on inventories was often a method adopted to hide end of the year balances with wasteful spending. Payment was slow and thus vendors were frustrated with the city. One of the pre-requisites that the city established for the new system was that no additional funds were to be allocated for it—that the new system must fund itself. Taylor argues that this requirement actually assisted implementation by enforcing discipline on the effort. Taylor describes how the project team had to build internal and external support for the new system. Women and minority firms feared that the new system would undercut their gains in obtaining contracts. Vendors played a key role in implementing the Peoplesoft system with one contractor performing the implementation function and another to do quality assurance. As with most purchases these days, their goal was for a "vanilla implementation" and, in this case, the project was successful resulting in large savings due to slashed city inventories and winning discounts from contractors due to early payments.

Milton Petersen draws upon a wealth of experiences with software purchases to provide insights into legal aspects of purchases. Petersen emphasizes sector differences due to public organizations' risk aversion, the fishbowl openness of public purchases, and the complexity of governmental goals. Still many of the steps to a successful purchase revolve around sensible actions similar to those of the private sector such as gathering the requirements for the new system, but Petersen emphasizes the need for political will and organizational champions for implementing complex new systems.

Much has been made in the past of the importance of writing a good "scope of work" in developing RFPs, but Petersen points out that there are actually three scopes that organizations must pay heed to: functional, process, and data scopes. Petersen argues that it is crucial to pay attention to the initial staff recruited for a project because those in it from the beginning tend to take ownership of it and be more committed to its successful completion. He describes how parts of an RFP can be written as a series of questions for vendors that make it easier to make valid comparisons among the vendor submissions. Governments need to pay attention to the management of RFPs, using this as the opportunity to take charge of the process or vendors may take over. Relationships with vendors are crucial, and Petersen points out that the contract should be mutually beneficial and that "squeezing too hard" can harm the long-term relationship. Part of the project management process is to record and report to the vendor any and all problems encountered during the project. Managing RFPs and subsequent contracts is a major part of the jobs of governmental staff, and Petersen's case provides several good practices to be followed.

Several of the chapters detail innovative uses of Web portals and related Internet applications. Curtis Turner of the Department of Labor provides a detailed case study of the conception, implementation, and operation of the department's GovBenefits.gov Web portal. This portal serves as the major gateway for citizens to search for governmental benefits. The Department of Labor is the leading partner in this effort that has 16 federal partners, making this an excellent example of how to go about constructing an interagency e-government project. As might be expected, IT governance issues were major for this project, and six different project teams were established: project management/controls that focused on procurement, scheduling, budgetary, and reporting; product management focusing on site content; Web site update to manage workflow to update the Web site; technical development for software and hardware technical issues; change management for managing relationships with partners, marketing, and outreach; and verification and validation that focused on security and operational issues. A key issue in these intergovernmental benefits is to obtain buy-in from partners. However, in order to do this, you have to be able to answer the question, "What's in it for me?" The partners have to agree on a funding formula that is satisfactory to all—in this case, they used a formula based on the number of programs represented on the site and the dollar value of those programs on the GovBenefits.gov Web site. Labor's plan tried to establish as many strategies as possible to get buy-in, trying to institutionalize the interagency nature of the system. There was relatively little money available for marketing, and the case describes how they made good use of these limited funds, detailing which marketing strategies were most successful.

Steve Cantler describes how the City of Tampa created an online customer service center using organizational sources without the assistance of a vendor. Customer service systems are crucial because they affect how citizens view the efficiency and effectiveness of the government. Cantler describes the three prime requisites of customer service systems: (1) They must not assume that citizens know which agency is most appropriate for dealing with the citizen's question; (2) Access must be on a 24/7 basis; and (3) Citizens must be informed of what is happening to their request. Although the system was aimed at making government more responsive, it also assisted government's employees in managing their jobs by allowing them to search through and manage their service requests in a flexible manner. The project had an interdepartmental advisory committee set up to monitor the project. The agency still maintains traditional service request mechanisms such as the telephone but even if the citizen submits requests through these traditional methods, they can still search for the status on the computerized system. Although the system was developed by the City of Tampa, it requires intergovernmental cooperation and coordination in order to deal with the fact that citizens do not know and should not need to know which actions are in the province of the city versus other governmental organizations. In short, citizen-oriented e-government requirements force organizations to be intergovernmental in the design of their systems.

Reinke and Johnson's case study reveals a county's considerations in deciding whether to continue or drop convenience fees in order to increase use of their online tax payment system. The case illustrates the complex calculations involved in some e-government applications. Convenience fees also have ethical implications because those most likely to use it may be wealthier people. Many small and large jurisdictions do not have the IT resources to implement the systems themselves so IT vendors are involved. Governments may have to risk eating costs during the short term by eliminating convenience fees in order to spur increased use and thus obtain longer-term benefits when a sizeable portion of the community switches to online payments.

Bogdan Hoanca provides a case study of the use of telemedicine to improve medical care in Alaska. It is difficult, costly, and often impossible for residents in outlying areas to be transported to the few regional medical centers in Alaska. The Alaska Federal Health Care Access Network (AFHCAN) represents another example of complex interorganizational project resulting from the collaborative efforts of the Department of Veteran's Affairs, Department of Defense, the U.S. Coast Guard, the Indian Health Service, and the Alaska Native Tribal Health Consortium. As with all complex systems, the IT governance system was complex including a steering committee and six different committees to handle business, legal, informatics, technology, and training issues. The system allows health providers in local village clinics to gather patient information into an electronic case and to transmit the case to a medical specialist at a remote location via a secure network. Ease of use is a necessity for such a system because the system tends to be used on a sporadic basis and many of the users have less than a high school education. The system has been judged a success on the basis of usage figures, costs saved due to the avoidance of flights, and anecdotes of successes. Hoanca points out that this is a system that could only be developed and supported by the public sector and that AFHCAN is now looking to cut their costs by selling the system to other organizations.

Mete Yildiz describes how Turkey implemented a Web portal-based communication system with the goal of providing citizens with information so they could participate more adequately in the political process. The system also provided job training to elected and appointed government officials. This case shows that Web applications in other countries face many of the same challenges as in the U.S. and that many similar strategies are adopted. Their approach to project management was to integrate the vendor into the management team. They also chose to use open source software in order to contain the costs of the project. Another cost-saving measure was to adopt a distributed system in which local officials entered their own data into the system. Yildiz outlines the serious challenges facing the system including "fights" that developed from online forums and sometimes threatened to escalate.

J. Ramon Gil-Garcia and Sharon Dawes provide in-depth analysis of how New York State developed a coordinated Web portal in the context of a decentralized IT system involving some 60 state agencies. They detail some of the forces that encouraged a movement toward coordination including the Y2K threat, the election of an administration concerned with efficiency and business-like methods, and laws that forced policies such as accessibility standards and privacy policies. Faced with competing demands for integration and decentralization, the solution adopted was to employ categories and common headers and footers on all Web sites but to allow agencies to employ their own designs for other aspects of their Web sites. This mixed approach allowed them to build the Web portal with limited central staff and funding and no single leadership authority. Communication issues proved to be important due to difficulties of exchanging information among program people, Web staff, and IT people. There are several ongoing challenges associated with this decentralized approach. One concerns content ownership and another concerns training and related human resource issues. There are differences in the Web skills present among the agencies, and civil service laws make it difficult to attract and retain qualified staff. One of the points that this case brings out is the tremendous impact that national rankings have on Web sites. It is clear that leadership of organizations pay close attention to these rankings and thus the criteria used to judge Web sites by these national ranking systems are likely to get wide dissemination and influence the structures of Web portals as states and local governments voluntarily seek to improve their results.

Intergovernmental and interorganizational issues are discussed in many of these cases. The Bureau of Housing Services case study by Luna-Reyes, Pardo, Ochoátegui, and Sanabria depicts an especially challenging case. Several governmental organizations had to work together to construct a new information system to improve services for the homeless funded by these governmental agencies and the private sector organizations that delivered most of the direct services. This case illustrates that in the human services sector, the end users of many "governmental systems" are actually employees of private sector organizations. The Bureau of Housing Services had previously tried to mandate a new system, but this effort failed due mostly to resistance on the part of the private service providers. The case shows how the governments and private providers went about constructing a solution to a difficult dilemma. The system needed to meet different needs of the partners and also integrate different databases in order to be effective. The governmental organizations were especially interested in obtaining valid and reliable accountability information. The private providers were concerned with obtaining information that would help them provide better services. Especially sensitive issues concerned the definition and measurement of outcomes that affected the evaluation and reimbursement for services provided by the private agencies. The solution was to develop system prototypes that organizations could check out prior to making final decisions about adoption.

Schulz and Tuma's case study demonstrates how county and municipal governments successfully coordinated to construct a collaborative communications center. The case shows how Waukesha County became the lead agency in the cooperative effort. It requires a complex

IT governance system with five different committees set up to handle the effort including a "Partners Committee". As with other interorganizational efforts, the lead organization (Waukesha County) had to deal with the concerns of their partners including fears about greater costs to municipalities, concerns that the system might give preference to county police operations, and worries about what would happen to existing municipal employees under an integrated system. A funding formula agreeable to all was developed. The case also illustrates the tensions between having a "best of breed" versus a single integrated system. The collaboration presented significant human resources issues. One issue concerned how to transfer employees from other municipalities into the new department. A second concerned the fact that extensive training was required to operate the system. Evaluation of such systems is also complex. Response time is one of the major measures used, but the case discusses why response time is not a very good, stand-alone outcome measure. Inevitably, the system's role in dealing with major criminal justice incidents becomes part of the public's perception of system efficacy.

Thurmaier and Chen's case study illustrates another interorganzational effort. This one concerns the attempt to build a knowledge management system through the collaboration of Iowa's CIO, the Iowa Department of Management, and a local government association. The case shows how cultural differences among the three major organizations involved heavily-affected crucial issues such as the form of payments employed. Issues of control over the Web site also needed to be worked out. The Iowa Secretary of State preferred to have an independent system which they controlled while the (Iowa) Information Technology Enterprise in the Department of Administrative Services preferred an enterprise-wide approach that emphasized shared resources and services. The case also emphasizes the crucial element of information stewardship and how difficult it is to achieve and ensure the integrity of data.

Jim Landers presents a detailed account of the development of a GIS application aimed at helping Indiana develop policies for their enterprise zones. The effort leads to the creation of maps useful for analyzing alternative policies for the zones but also shows how difficult it can be to gather certain critical data and that some key variables must be based on estimates. Also, the case study emphasizes that making better data and GIS applications available does not necessarily lead directly to policy changes because general budgetary issues and pressures overwhelm other factors.

Many of the case studies touch on the importance of accessibility of digital government systems. Alex Pettit and Anthony Caranna's case study depicts what they call the "Techonomic Divide". Their point is that it is not just computers that separate users from non-users of a digital system but non-users lack other pre-requisites to participate in the digital economy such as credit cards, checking accounts, and cell phones. They detail the efforts of Denton County (Texas) to develop kiosks that would alleviate this techonomic divide. They employed a kiosk that would accept money as well as credit cards. Still, many did not use the electronic system until faced with the threat of disconnection. Pettit and Caranna's case illustrates the challenge of online payment systems such as whether the government wants to emphasize cost savings or better service as their primary goal.

Cross-Cutting Themes of the Case Studies

Taken together, these 21 case studies provide deep insights into the challenges and successes of digital government. Although the cases cover a multitude of specific technologies and some idiosyncratic aspects, readers will find many common themes in the case studies. In particular, you will discover that the same processes and issues are discussed in several different case studies. These processes and issues will remain important even while the specific technologies change. In Figure 1 (adapted from Rocheleau, 2006), I outline key forces and actors that are important to public management information systems that I employed in my recent book, *Public Management Information Systems*.

Next, I outline the most important common processes and issues that appear in the cases but readers will find many other themes in the cases.

IT Governance

Virtually all of the cases discuss IT governance issues. This is not surprising given the fact that one of the major goals of digital government is to serve citizens and other customers in an integrated manner. Consequently, most major projects cut across departmental and organizational boundaries necessitating often complex forms of IT governance. For example, Cantler's study of Tampa's customer service center and Turner's account of the development of the Federal Department of Labor's GovBenefits.gov Web site both required that these applications be constructed so that citizens could use them without any specific knowledge of the particular agencies that were actually responsible for dealing with their problems. IT governance issues are especially complex when they involve independent agencies and

Figure 1. A framework for understanding governmental information management

External Environment	Organizational Environment	Services	Outcomes

Underlying Forces:
Governmental Control
Technological Changes

Underlying Forces:
Organizational Resources
The Informal System

Critical IT Processes:
Planning
Purchasing

Critical Managerial Skills:

Key Actors:
Vendors & Consultants
Citizens & Legislative bodies
Business and Other Private Organizations
Other Governments

Key Actors:
Top Management
IT Management
Departmental Managers
End Users

Implementation & Project Management
Sharing Data & Systems
Training & Knowledge Management

Communication & Marketing
IT Governance
Political Leadership
Ethical Evaluation

Nature, Quality, and Accessibility of IT Services

Degree of Responsiveness to goals of political system

they must be solved in order for the application to have any chance of success. There are several different skills required to solve governance dilemmas as Carlsen points out in his discussion of tools that can be used to achieve IT governance. These skills are not generally taught in computer science-oriented programs. Even if the system is developed and run by a single unit of government such as Tampa's customer service request application, IT governance issues are important in regulating interdepartmental issues, and the Web site had to integrate with other agencies in order to meet citizen needs in a comprehensive manner so interorganizational coordination was required too. In short, skills concerning IT governance are essential to managing information technology in government.

Sharing

Formal sharing of IT sources among governments is not as common as it should be, but it does take place and the case study by Schulz shows the steps that are likely to be needed in order to achieve such sharing. Most governments tend to want to go it alone in major IT projects, but there are significant cases of sharing, especially concerning smaller organizations with limited resources who band together to share potentially-expensive applications such as GIS (Rocheleau, 2005), ERP (Hall, 2001), and other systems. It is my belief that there exist tremendous unexplored possibilities for the development of shared applications among governments.

Leadership and the Role of Political and Generalist Managers

Many of the practitioner case studies in this volume have been written by IT leaders and experts in their respective organizations, but as one reads through this volume, you find that there is a great need for leadership that can only be provided by political and generalist managers, not the heads of IT. Since most major new systems cut across departmental if not organizational boundaries, it is impossible for the IT department and its staff to force change. As is described in many case studies, attempts to change IT systems often result in resistance and, as Furumo documents in her case study, failure. As Petersen says, there has to be a political will to persist in difficult major system purchases and success stories such as the Westchester County (Jacknis & Fernqvist) where the chief executive officer took a personal interest in IT projects and spurred commissioners to learn more about IT. In the Wisconsin (Miszewski) case study, the CIO emphasized the need to emphasize horizontal communication and coordination more which was achieved by employing service delivery coordinators to perform these functions. However, it is possible to achieve change without strong central leadership as Gil-Garcia and Dawes show in the New York State Web portal case.

Politics and IT

A related lesson is that politics plays an integral role in stimulating change in digital government. Information technology used to be a back office issue. The invisibility of IT was symbolized by the fact that IT departments were often located in the basements of buildings. Now IT has become a front office concern and is viewed by many executives as an essential tool to achieve positive results so their administration will be viewed as successful. The politics of information technology are not always easy—for example, should governments eat convenience fees in order to spur usage of online systems? This is an issue posed by Reinke and Johnson in their case study of an online payment system. Most IT professionals I know prefer to avoid politics and look to their political or generalist leadership to handle political issues but that is not always possible.

Planning

Although planning is not the central focus of any of the individual case study, it is clear that many of these case studies required extensive planning, especially those that are intergovernmental and interorganizational in nature. Carlsen includes planning as one of the key IT governance tools, and he illustrates how the communication evolving out of their development of a comprehensive IT plan led the solution of a problem with their finance application. Jacknis and Westchester County integrated economic development efforts into their IT planning.

Ethical and Legal Issues

Legal issues play a huge role in any purchase of a complex system. Petersen's chapter details a myriad of possible legal problems that can occur and provides suggestions on how to avoid these problems. Ethical concerns play a significant role in the Bureau of Housing case where privacy issues such as for abused women conflicted to some extent with the desire for accountability to measure outcomes of the service. Taylor's study of the reform of the purchasing system for Los Angeles led to concerns on the part of minority and female firms. Pettit and Caranna's study suggests that the move to digital government may be ignoring the most vulnerable part of the population who have no capacity to take advantage of digital government. Gil-Garcia and Dawson's study relates how states adopt federal (Section 508) standards for accessibility of their Web sites.

Evaluation, Accountability, and Data Stewardship

In a majority of cases, there are data and other sources of information used to assess the success of the IT applications and innovations. The difficulties of evaluation are discussed in several cases. Carlsen discusses their application of the balanced scorecard system which has become a popular method used by governments to ensure alignment as well as accountability though he notes that such systems consume quite a bit of staff time. For some new applications such as the inventory control system described by Taylor, there are some obvious and easy to measure outcomes such as reduced inventory levels and cuts in purchasing costs. But Jacknis points out that for some applications, even if money is saved on a per unit basis, success engenders higher usage and thus total costs may be higher so there is a potential conflict between cost-cutting and service goals. An essential aspect of any evaluation system is that the data must be valid and reliable. Gunderson's study of Naperville's computerized maintenance management system and Chen and Thurmaier's account of the development of a knowledge management system both document the difficulties of achieving data integrity.

Project Management, Business Process Re-Engineering, and Human Resource Issues

The cases are replete with project management issues and business process re-engineering issues. It is now customary for organizations and vendors to encourage a "vanilla" implementation of systems but even if the organization is able to achieve such an approach, complex problems remain. As Gunderson's case shows, many line departments may be unwilling to devote the staff and other resources to implement the project, and he discusses how project management techniques such as Gantt charts can be used to delay the most difficult tasks until the end. Several of the cases discuss problems with trying to get the new system to mesh with existing processes and the problems that occur when re-engineering of processes is required. The Chen and Thurmaier and Gunderson cases reveal that turnover in key staff can hurt or help projects. Carlsen describes how Naperville sponsored training in project management. The complexity of interorganizational and interdepartmental projects makes project management all the more difficult.

Human resource issues such as training are closely related to project management concerns. In virtually every case, the importance of training is emphasized. Other human resource issues concerning lack of flexibility in civil service rules and dealings with unions also play a significant role in some cases. The inclusion of IT skills in position descriptions can be important. In order to deal with these dilemmas, the IT and human resource staff will have to cooperate.

Vendors and the Procurement Process

Except for a few projects such as Tampa's, vendors play a key role in the case studies. Most applications are purchased rather than developed in-house, though the IT staff often has to adapt and tweak the systems to meet organizational needs. The Westchester County study (Jacknis & Fernqvist) tells how the county implemented an anti-outsourcing initiative to bring IT back into the governmental fold. Nevertheless, in most cases, successful projects result from good working relationships between governments and vendors. Thus the development of an effective relationship is a necessary and challenging task. As Petersen relates, it is good to have competition for RFPs continue on as late as possible in the purchasing process so that governments can achieve the best value for their expenditures. On the other hand, for the relationship to work for the long haul, the vendor must feel that the contract is favorable to them too and, if the government pushes too hard, this relationship can be harmed resulting in problems and possible vendor turnover. Vendors can play different roles in organizations. In many cases, governments hire them to do jobs they lack the skills for, and this task may be performed on an ongoing basis. In other cases, organizations hire vendors to teach them how to do the jobs themselves. Thus managing contracts and vendors is a key part of the job of IT staff, though in some complex projects such as the GovBenefits.gov case, vendors are hired to implement the program and another vendor is hired to monitor these other contractors.

Communication and Marketing

One point that is common throughout all of these case studies is that non-technical issues are the cause of the most frequent problems. Successes are most common when communication is good. Several of the cases emphasize that need to take actions to improve communication between technical IT staff and others. For example, in Wisconsin, an IT catalog was developed to make line agencies aware of their services. Gil-Garcia and Dawes cite communication between technical and program staff as an obstacle to the development of the New York State Web portal. Likewise, communicating with citizens can be important and difficult as Pettit and Caranna show in their analysis of what they refer to as the "techonomic divide". Marketing has become an essential aspect of IT management, especially for those aimed at external constituencies. The Federal Department of Labor GovBenefits.gov Web site got a major boost in usage after it was mentioned in a Dear Abby column so unconventional marketing can be most effective.

Implications for IT and Generalist Managers

As information management has become more strategic and interorganizational, the jobs of IT managers have become more complex. Soft knowledge and skills such as politics, communication, project management, and knowledge of ethical and legal issues have become much more important. Most IT managers did not receive training in these issues during their formal education and training in information technology. They must learn these if they are to succeed. Most learn them quickly on the job if they are successful, but reading these case studies will provide insights on how to deal with many of these challenges.

Generalist managers cannot afford to ignore the importance of information and communication technologies. IT issues such as municipal broadband and wireless systems can become key issues of public debate that generalist managers cannot avoid. Likewise, the employment of more effective uses of information technologies is a way to deal with cutbacks in budgets and to communicate with citizens. The case studies reveal that leadership from these generalist managers is a critical success factor. This book provides a roadmap to such leaders on the important processes and forces that they need to deal with.

References

Hall, K. A. (2001). Intergovernmental cooperation on ERP systems. *Government Finance Review, 17*(December), 6-13.

Rocheleau, B. (2005). Interorganizational and interdepartmental information systems: Sharing among governments. In G. David Garson (Ed.), *Handbook of public information systems* (2nd ed., pp. 61-84). Boca Raton, FL: CRC Press.

Rocheleau, B. (2006). *Public management information systems.* Hershey, PA: Idea Group Inc.

Acknowledgments

Many of these cases are written by practitioners who had to do these cases on their own time with no expectation of rewards other than the satisfaction of sharing their experiences with readers. I very much appreciate their willingness to contribute to this effort. Likewise, the academics who contributed to the book also deserve praise for their willingness to employ time-consuming qualitative methods necessary to construct their case studies.

Each of the cases in this book received anonymous reviews. In many cases, the authors of the cases studied acted as reviewers for each others' studies. But I also want to thank other reviewers who contributed their time and expertise to the reviewing effort: Victor Ambroziak, Drew Awsumb, Doug Bingenheimer, Susan Cable, Julia Cedillo, Pete Collins, David Connelly, Dina Desiderio, Sam Ferguson, David Haradon, John Nitz, Jane Norris, Molly Norton, Lee Plate, Jeffrey Roy, Genie Stowers, Chris Westgor, and Liangfu Wu. Thanks also to all of my students in my Spring 2006 Information Management and Government course at NIU who provided valuable feedback on the cases: John Anderson, Eric Deloy, Brandon Dieter, Samantha Fisher, Michael Garrity, Michael Marzal, Janel Oelstrom, Michelle Pankow, Nyoka Polyak, James Richter, Patrick Rigg, Jason Slowinski, Gwendolyn Veasey, Matt Supert, and Ben Wehmeier. I would also like to thank certain organizations and listservs that were kind enough to allow me to recruit participants for the book including the Government Information Management Science Association, the Innovations Group Organization, and the Citywebmaster listserv.

I would not have been able to successfully complete the project without outstanding help from Kristin Roth, the Development Editor at Idea Group Inc. (IGI). She answered countless questions throughout the project, quickly, with expertise and good humor, and I appreciate her assistance very much. Jan Travers of IGI also provided important help on the project. Ellen Cabrera of the Division of Public Administration has shared generously of her time and expertise in preparing the manuscript. I would like to thank my wife, Georgette, for her love, support, and assistance, not only with this project but throughout my career.

Bruce Rocheleau
Northern Illinois University, USA

Chapter I

State of Wisconsin IT:
Destroying the Barriers to Borderless Government

Matt Miszewski, State of Wisconsin, USA

Executive Summary

Wisconsin Governor Jim Doyle inherited a $3.2 billion deficit when he took office in January 2003. His plans to institute a meaningful, long-term fix to the state's budget problems included using technology to streamline state government and build the foundation for ongoing cost savings. State CIO Matt Miszewski assumed he would have to carry out the governor's directive without any additional funds for information technology (IT), but then the legislature pushed through an additional $40 million cut to IT funding across state agencies. This case study describes the strategies Miszewski and his colleagues in the state's Division of Enterprise Technology devised, and are in the process of implementing, to deal with having to do much more with considerably less.

Background

When Governor Jim Doyle came into office in January 2003, he inherited a $3.2 billion biennial deficit in the state's general fund, based on projected revenue vs. required spending obligations. No Wisconsin governor had ever faced that much of a shortfall—not even close. State government had been operating amid structural deficits (the amount of money needed to maintain current services exceeding the revenue generated by the state's current tax system) at least since the mid-1990s (Reschovsky, 2002), and it was up to the new governor to make the difficult choices needed to produce a balanced budget—not just on paper, but in practice.

Governor Doyle also resolved to fix the state's budget without raising taxes, despite assertions on both sides of the aisle that it could never be done. But his 12 years as Wisconsin attorney general and his analysis of the state's financial mechanisms convinced him the problem was not that Wisconsin residents and businesses were paying too little—the problem was how the state's elected officials and public-sector organizations were using the money. Wisconsin government needed fundamental change in its approach to both budgeting and spending, and government units, both at the state and local levels, had to thoroughly reassess how they did business together. That was the only way to protect Wisconsin taxpayers and preserve the state's traditional priorities of excellence in education, affordable health care, quality local services, and a clean environment.

Governor Doyle's work to produce a more efficient and effective government for Wisconsin residents is by no means finished, especially considering the continuing financial pressures at all public-sector levels. But he has produced two consecutive biennial budgets that balanced the books while maintaining Wisconsin's commitment to first-rate schools and public services. He also has made streamlining state government and building the groundwork for ongoing cost savings a top priority. His ACE (Accountability, Consolidation and Efficiency) Initiative is accomplishing this by focusing on efficiencies in four key areas: information technology (IT), procurement, state facilities and human resources. The governor's approach to IT is one that most citizens can identify with, even if it has made my life as State CIO considerably more complicated. He correctly points out that citizens do not care about the supposedly unique needs of individual government agencies, or branches of government, or levels of government. Citizens believe that, through information technology, governments have what they need to work together, to communicate in common formats, to streamline services, to make government less expensive, and to make citizen interactions with government quick and easy. In contrast, I could point out the complex way in which government IT has evolved, and the fact that the public-sector IT environment is still characterized primarily by organizational silos and legacy systems. I could point out that traditional budgeting and funding procedures—that is, agency-by-agency, often with jurisdictional blinders on, an approach that, try though we might, we can't change overnight—actually discourage collaboration.

But it would not matter. Governor Doyle agrees with his constituents. Government IT professionals have the tools we need. We already have the technologies necessary to make government more citizen-centered, share information, integrate systems, save money, and make those savings available for our schools, our infrastructure, and the health and prosperity of our families. The governor insists that what we have been missing is the organizational component—namely, the political and administrative resolve to collaborate across agencies and jurisdictions, and the determination to achieve integrated government services without additional funding and without waiting for budget processes to catch up. So, regardless of any protests I could come up with (which, quite honestly, I'm not inclined to come up with—I agree with citizens and the governor on this one, too), the governor has told me: Make it happen. Get it done. Use state government IT to transform how governments work in Wisconsin, both internally and externally, and achieve the service levels and generate the savings that will make a real difference to our residents. (And, the governor could have added, do not bother him in the meantime, because he has his hands full with all our other public-policy priorities.)

This case study examines the overall goal, strategies, and initiatives developed and implemented by me and my colleagues in the state's Division of Enterprise Technology (DET) in order to meet Governor Doyle's challenge. We decided that his directive to us does not involve incremental changes—it requires a revolution. Here is how we are conducting that revolution.

Setting the Stage

When Governor Doyle appointed me State CIO in March 2003, I arrived to find the state agency IT environment a combination of centralized and distributed systems, with a heavy emphasis on the latter. Mainframe computers and their associated services were centralized within the Department of Administration (DOA) as of 1992, while most agencies maintained separate information technology (IT) work units, complete with server support, network support, and application development and support. This evolution is typical of many large organizations and enterprises. The IT infrastructure was built piecemeal to serve specific needs for particular agencies or even individual applications. Separate support organizations were built within each agency as well. Wisconsin's CIO has statutory authority to manage the state's approximately $400 million annual investment in IT, and enforce IT-related policy decisions across the executive branch, but that position and those powers were not created until the 2001-03 biennial budget. Prior to that, agencies were essentially on their own, and the enterprise IT environment I found reflected that.

This decentralized approach was not without its success stories; individual agencies had produced some popular e-government services, for instance, and Wisconsin generally fared well in assessments done by organizations such as the Center for Digital Government. But as the number of applications and servers on which they run grew over the years, this environment became increasingly labor intensive, expensive, and difficult to manage from an enterprise standpoint. One former DOA deputy secretary used to cite the example of an application DOA had procured for a common business need and was attempting to get into wider enterprise use; one particular agency declined, with the explanation—apparently provided in all seriousness and with no hint of irony—that the DOA-offered solution met only 22 of that agency's 25 listed requirements. That is not the approach that will promote integrated services between agencies and cost savings across the enterprise.

In early 2003, enterprise management essentially consisted of DOA providing and billing for mainframe services, a multi-protocol data network for state agencies, and voice/long-distance networks (via vendor service contracts) for state, university, and some local government customers. And while those services were (and are) by no means insignificant, virtually no one at any agency was making the argument that this was the optimal IT environment for maximizing taxpayer value. The question was what should we be striving for instead, and how should we be trying to get there. And when those basic questions were raised, I saw discussions among even the best-intentioned and most-conscientious agency professionals devolve into mind-numbing exercises in bureaucratic paralysis. There seemed to be countless compelling reasons why we could not get better, when it likewise seemed obvious that we absolutely had to be better.

And then our friends in the state legislature gave us $40 million reasons to keep trying. One of my first introductions to the legislature as the state's new CIO was a meeting with Joint Finance Committee member Senator Ted Kanavas, in which he told me that state agency IT budgets would be slashed by $40 million for the 2003-05 biennium. He suggested I recognize this "opportunity" to reorganize the state's use of IT, or resist, and allow him and other Republicans to make life miserable for me and our Democratic governor (McKay, 2004). I decided I liked that first option a whole lot better, but really, using an enterprise IT approach to help reduce the state's budget deficit is how Governor Doyle and I had been operating all along. Again, the question was how to overcome institutional inertia, and, for the long run, eliminate the basic assumption that, because we were the public sector, this inertia was somehow inevitable.

Interestingly, and contrary to common perceptions of the public sector's ability to adapt, it was my own DET senior leadership team—longtime civil servants—who truly got us on our way toward operating as an enterprise with a genuine enterprise mission. I called these seven individuals together in mid-2003 to let them tell me what our vision for enterprise technology should be, and have them chart a path to achieve that vision. My short time in state government had already convinced me that public-sector IT professionals were by no means inherently resistant to change, or afraid to take chances. On the contrary, they were some of the most talented and visionary people I had ever worked with. They just were not used to being asked the kinds of questions I was asking them. I wanted to pull them out of thinking operationally (what are we doing now and what will the near-term logical results be) and, rather, get them to envision the future they wanted (what do I want to see if I return to these halls 30 years from now), and think about how we could build that future.

In response, the team re-examined and re-validated much of the work done through earlier strategic planning initiatives. In other words, they did not feel it necessary to start from scratch where the organization already had identified visionary goals that were still valid. But, without my prodding and to my definite surprise, they went an important step further. In various ways they proposed, and then we worked together to articulate specifically, what we ended up calling our BHAG. So, what in the world is a BHAG? The letters stand for Big, Hairy, Audacious Goal, and it is the guiding principle, the raison d'être, the one statement that captures the essence of why DET exists. The senior leadership team agreed that everything we do in this organization should relate directly to our BHAG. It should accurately describe what we are appropriately doing now and, most importantly, create a vision of what we should find, and what we should be doing, if we came back to DET 30 years from now. The DET BHAG is: We will revolutionize the delivery of services by destroying the barriers to borderless government.

The idea of using IT to enhance service delivery was not new in Wisconsin state government—most agency business leaders and technology professionals believed in the power of IT and are by nature forward-thinking individuals. Institutionalizing a revolution is what is new. We determined we need to look at every avenue of service delivery and analyze whether we are delivering that service in the best way possible from the point of view of our ultimate customer: the taxpayer. Taxpayers are not impressed by the fact that they have to be licensed in separate departments for their boat and the trailer that carries it. They just want to be able to easily apply for and renew needed licenses in the quickest and most efficient manner.

Destroying the barriers to borderless government is a principle that applies almost universally across what we do in DET and what we feel we should be doing in the future. Eliminating the silo mentalities, both within state government and also throughout all levels of government, has never been more vital. Security, for instance, is an excellent example of how our old paradigm leaves our nation at risk within our interconnected world. If we do not share information on vulnerabilities, patterns, and attacks, we no longer risk the subversion of one or two systems—we put all our citizens in jeopardy. And when we destroy the barriers to effective information sharing, we help to defend everyone, as exemplified by the Wisconsin Justice Information Sharing (WIJIS) System (http://oja.wi.gov/WIJIS/). If a system such as that one, designed to destroy intergovernmental barriers, were in place in Florida before 9-11, Mohamed Atta, when he was pulled over by a Florida police officer, would have been detained, as he was already on a federal watch-and-detain list. Instead, that list was on a federal system not accessible by local police. We no longer have the luxury of building up or fortifying the walls that divide us.

Once we had our BHAG, we had to use it to shape and add specificity to our enterprise IT vision, our business plans, and our initiatives and projects. And so the stage was set for putting our BHAG into action.

Case Description: Establishing a Foundation for Enterprise Agility

We believe our BHAG gives us a clear goal and a standard through which to evaluate all our efforts. But we needed a framework to organize, and to understand the interconnections between, our initiatives and projects. Since the 2001-03 biennial budget, DET is required to submit to the legislature, during the fall of even-numbered years, an enterprise strategic plan for the use and application of information technology (what we commonly refer to as our "enterprise IT plan"). This was our opportunity to use the BHAG to design an understandable, achievable plan for state agencies and our intergovernmental partners.

The last thing we wanted to do was repeat what we thought to be a basic mistake of past cross-agency IT plans: namely, they become a laundry list of progress reports on current projects. Those are just fine as far as they go, but such "plans" usually lack a coherent and unifying strategic vision (or, even worse, one is superimposed after the fact). We wanted to produce a plan that built a lasting foundation for true agility, efficiency, and cost-effectiveness in an interconnected and complex environment. More than just listing what we're doing and how it's all going, we wanted readers to understand why we're doing what we're doing, and how the activities fit together.

With the BHAG as our guiding principle, we used the enterprise IT plan to outline for our business partners three fundamental strategies: First, we will build an enterprise ecosystem that clearly defines the interconnections between the many technology infrastructures across all government levels. Second, we will build and balance the enterprise portfolio by making better-informed and strategic decisions about investing in our infrastructure. Finally, we will build a widely understood standard of enterprise accountability to establish an environment where we measure performance based on real data.

Build an Enterprise Ecosystem

Technological agility requires recognizing the degree to which infrastructures do, or should, interconnect. Unfortunately, the ways that changes in one agency or one system can impact other agencies and systems throughout multiple jurisdictions were often unanticipated until service delivery was negatively affected. We are extending our enterprise view so that technology solutions take into account the business issues not only of state agencies but all other levels of government that affect citizens. We are seeking horizontal and vertical integration of IT functions to be truly efficient and cost-effective, and the potential ripple effects of system changes have to be comprehensively evaluated and understood on the front end. When those mechanisms and that collaborative mindset are completely in place, we will have built an "enterprise ecosystem", where IT can be both agile and responsive, yet sensitive to the complex relationships between systems, agencies, and governments.

Build and Balance the Enterprise Portfolio

We face significant challenges across the enterprise with inconsistencies in, or the lack of, information about IT assets. While major initiatives such as the consolidation of servers contribute to a more thorough understanding of our environment, we are continuing to build a knowledge base to extend our enterprise view. We are also implementing a framework to support alignment of technology investments with articulated business strategies. That requires a structured approach of continuous, repeatable, and easily sustainable processes for mapping technology decisions to business requirements. While several agencies had been exemplary in their use of IT portfolio management or IT investment management approaches, we must establish a consistent approach for aligning and balancing IT investments across agencies.

Institute Enterprise Accountability

Convincing business leaders to invest strategically in IT during a time of severe budget constraints requires evidence of fiscal responsibility from us, the IT community. We must measure this evidence, again and again, to continue to prove the worth of enterprise IT, which ultimately must directly contribute to the efficient use of taxpayer dollars.

Evidence of Fiscal Responsibility with IT Investments can be Demonstrated by:

- Specifying how an investment alternative directly or indirectly supports articulated business strategies;

- Identifying the degree to which available infrastructure components were reused;

- Evaluating the costs and benefits of a technology solution and alternatives;

- Re-engineering business processes when appropriate to take advantage of best practices and technology opportunities; and

- Exploring alternative approaches to delivering enterprise services, such as franchising or creating centers of excellence, where collaboration and resource sharing are the norm.

Foundation-Building Initiatives

With those three fundamental strategies (build an enterprise ecosystem; build and balance the enterprise portfolio; and institute enterprise accountability) in place, we wanted to articulate foundation-building initiatives, that is, make it clear and specific what higher-level outcomes our individual projects and initiatives were working toward.

To achieve agility and balance within the enterprise, we need to establish a firm foundation for delivering cost-effective and high-quality services. To do that, we are establishing one enterprise architecture, one shared infrastructure, and one application base. Those initiatives form the underpinnings of an integrated environment that supports timely and efficient delivery of critical services. To effectively manage an integrated environment, we must institute a consistent and disciplined framework that guides decision making about the selection and funding of IT investments. To that end, we are establishing one enterprise IT finance system and one management and measurement system.

The remainder of this case study focuses on specific projects and efforts we believe particularly exemplify how we are pursuing our BHAG via our enterprise IT plan. But it's important to recognize that these projects all fit within our five foundation-building initiatives (and some clearly overlap between multiple foundation-building initiatives). No particular project's justification is taken for granted: The project has to contribute toward the foundation-building initiatives, which are in service to our fundamental strategies for achieving our enterprise IT vision, which promote our BHAG, as shown in Figure 1.

Figure 1. Enterprise IT plan

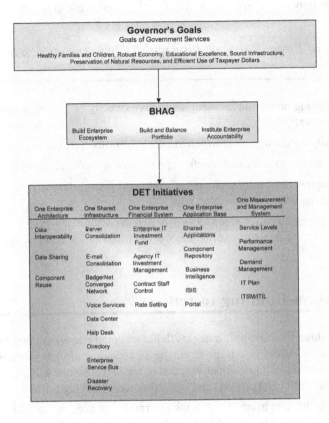

Key Projects and Activities

We consider the following projects and activities to be essential—and emblematic—as we work to achieve our foundation-building initiatives and, ultimately, our BHAG.

Input from the Extended Enterprise (Drives All the Foundation-Building Initiatives)

Governor Doyle has directed that we manage enterprise IT for our extended enterprise, that is, not just state agencies but all the levels of government that affect Wisconsin residents. Wisconsin has a long (and I would argue proud) tradition of decentralized government: We want our neighbors making the key decisions about how our municipalities and schools operate. That means that using an extended-enterprise approach to IT management has to involve addressing the challenges and concerns of local governments. This all sounded great to me, until I was reminded that Wisconsin has more than 1,900 general units of government, including 72 counties, 190 cities, 400 villages, and 1,265 towns. In addition, Wisconsin has 11 federally-recognized tribal governments and 440 school districts. I had to find some practical manner of incorporating local-government and tribal feedback in pursuing our BHAG.

Fortunately, a vehicle already was in place to accomplish that, with only a few modifications on our part. The Technology Leadership Council (TLC), formed in October 2002, assists the State CIO by helping to provide policies, directions, and strategies in managing enterprise IT. Currently, the TLC comprises 25 members, including the CIOs or IT directors from 20 state agencies, the heads of the IT departments of three of the state's most populous counties (Milwaukee, Dane, and Waukesha), a representative of a professional organization of local-government IT employees (Governmental Information Processing Association of Wisconsin), and the IT director of the Great Lakes Intertribal Council. Among the changes to membership I made was expanding the state agency representation to its current level (especially to include our state Department of Public Instruction, which oversees PK-16 instruction) and adding the tribal representation.

The CIO serves as permanent TLC co-chair. Members select a rotating co-chair from among themselves on an annual basis. That co-chair serves for one calendar year and may not serve more than two consecutive terms. The TLC meets monthly, and during the course of the past three years, has chartered a number of sub-committees to address enterprise IT issues. While the number of active sub-committees has expanded and contracted as needed, they are organized around seven domains (i.e., topical areas): networks, servers, desktops, applications, information (e.g., records and forms management), IT management (e.g., budgeting and workforce planning), and information security and privacy. Sub-committees are chaired by a TLC member and a technical expert from DET, and staffed by subject experts from the IT departments of state and local-government agencies.

The TLC's activities could form an extensive case study in itself. But all of the initiatives cited next have been significantly influenced by TLC-generated feedback, and some were direct products of TLC sub-committees (e.g., e-mail consolidation and the consolidated desktop buy). Quite honestly, my day-to-day work would be a lot less complicated if I had not allowed mechanisms for continuous interagency and intergovernmental feedback, and there are TLC meetings where it seems the sole purpose was for members to tell me what a lousy job I'm doing. But the insights provided from a diverse forum like the TLC are invaluable for building an enterprise ecosystem, and in general, if you're thin-skinned, you probably do not want to work in enterprise IT management.

Wisconsin Enterprise Architecture Team (One Enterprise Architecture)

In order to build an extended-enterprise ecosystem as described earlier—which is necessary for us to achieve our BHAG—I knew we needed a framework for developing technology solutions that meet the business needs of the extended enterprise in the most cost-effective and efficient means possible. At the outset of this process, Wisconsin, like most states, had a highly complex IT infrastructure made up of a large and diverse set of hardware and software configurations. Maintaining this highly complex web of IT systems across the enterprise required significant support costs and created barriers to the effective information sharing needed for critical business functions.

By establishing a consistent and standardized technology direction, we will simplify the environment and save money in the process. Enterprise architectures offer a framework around which the state of Wisconsin can build a technological infrastructure to facilitate the responsible and efficient deployment of information assets. The state's enterprise architecture will provide high-level guidance for aligning business drivers and architectural requirements with underlying technological components.

In general, the overarching decision criteria of our enterprise architecture will be:

Does the proposal/project/activity promote interoperability? How does it play with the rest of the infrastructure—what are the impacts?

Does it lower the total cost of ownership or increase the benefits of performing the related business functions via this technology?

How does it affect enterprise agility? If implemented, would it require significant effort to undo/rollback or migrate from in the future? What is the depth of commitment required?

We have taken important steps toward establishing an enterprise architecture, starting with assembling the Wisconsin Enterprise Architecture Team (WEAT), to develop and help implement an enterprise architecture for the state. As a reflection of our extended enterprise, WEAT includes not only representatives from state agencies but also from the University of Wisconsin and local governments (Milwaukee and Rock counties). The team has produced a strategy and business plan.

In parallel, WEAT is providing invaluable consultation on a variety of enterprise issues, including reviewing all the standards and policies to be utilized for the consolidation of nearly 2,200 servers from individual agencies into a single data center supported by DET (see the Shared Information Services (SIS) Initiative described next). As part of its immediate target architecture work, WEAT also is taking on the development of an integration reference model, in order to break down the technology barriers to effective data sharing and interoperability. The expected result from this work will be a simplified technology infrastructure developed and deployed using open standards. Ultimately, this will result in streamlined intergovernmental services, as common application components are reused across the enterprise.

Procurement for an Extended Enterprise (One Enterprise Architecture and One Shared Infrastructure)

An enterprise architecture also facilitates the leveraging of technology investments to provide cost-effective services to local governments. For example, a recent interagency, extended-enterprise approach to desktop purchasing resulted in a strategy to target a single provider and a single base desktop model for the majority of staff. This effort resulted in a contract for buying desktops and laptops that's expected to save more than $3 million per year across state agencies, with local governments able to take advantage of the contract's purchase terms as well. Milwaukee County has already reaped the benefits, having saved nearly $84,000 on desktop purchases during 2004.

This is not an isolated example—DET has been explicitly conducting procurement negotiations with the extended enterprise (i.e., local governments in addition to state agencies) in mind. In late 2003, DET negotiated terms with Microsoft on an enterprise agreement that were as good or better than those for all other states except California and New York—not bad, considering Wisconsin's size compared to theirs. The savings on licensing per desktop is between $500 and $700, which adds up quickly, considering we have 62,000 desktops in the state executive branch alone. We saved nearly $3 million on licensing during fiscal year 2005 just on the state agency level, and because local governments can also take advantage of the licensing terms, we expect multi-million-dollar savings for the extended enterprise per year.

Meanwhile, a contract we negotiated with a major cell-phone vendor offers local governments the same low pay-as-you-go rate plan the state has. Wisconsin taxpayers can expect more than $2 million in savings for local governments during the three-year contract term. Our enterprise service bus (see the following) also was procured by the state so that it would be available to counties.

Shared Information Services (SIS) Initiative (One Shared Infrastructure)

This initiative is also commonly known as "server consolidation", but it includes consolidating both server and local area network (LAN) services throughout executive-branch state agencies. It's not an exaggeration to say that this is easily the most comprehensive, complicated and significant cross-agency IT initiative since mainframe services were consolidated in 1992, and it drove much of the customer service-oriented reorganization of DET in late 2005. The server portion of SIS also includes consolidating e-mail services and migrating to a new, enterprise-wide e-mail system.

The bottom line is that we are consolidating within DET the operation of nearly 2,200 servers currently spread throughout state agencies, and, in doing so, reducing that server total to approximately 1,700. The number of e-mail servers in state agencies will go from 220 to about 30, resulting in a major cost reduction on a per e-mail account basis—from as high as $15 per mailbox to about $5.

Servers will be migrating to the DET data center beginning in mid-2006 and most likely through the calendar year 2008 (we opened a new, Tier 3 data center in April 2006, with some characteristics of a Tier 4 facility, based on the Uptime Institute's definitions of tiered data centers—the previous DET data center was Tier 1). With these services centered in DET and billed to agencies, we expect to maintain or improve service levels, reduce capital acquisition costs, reduce ongoing operational costs, and more effectively deploy information services. A cost-benefit analysis done in the fall of 2004 indicated that during the first five years, SIS will generate cumulative net savings of more than $13 million, and by year 5, the ongoing savings should exceed $8 million annually.

SIS implementation has required extensive interactions and synchronization between teams dedicated to technical foundations, organizational development, service development, and agency rollout, as shown in Figure 2. Moreover, the project teams were composed of staff from many agencies. Considering agency resource constraints and the time investment required from staff already eminently busy, these teams were not easy to assemble nor maintain, but we believe multi-agency participation is absolutely necessary. State staff must be prepared to take over and effectively manage the new shared-services environment when implementation is complete. That cannot happen unless state personnel play a critical role in developing that environment, with the buy-in and understanding that come from such participation. One of the major payoffs of SIS so far, with all the inventory assessments and interagency collaboration it has entailed, is that now the enterprise can manage IT using actual data generated from agencies, instead of vague estimates.

Having a consulting firm come in and essentially give state agencies their marching orders is another way to take on an endeavor like SIS. And, undoubtedly, there are plenty of firms more than willing to do it that way. We concluded that that's not the best strategy for maximizing the long-term benefits of SIS, and chose a consulting firm that agreed its role was not just to give us "the answers", but help the multi-agency project teams develop their own solutions. First of all, unless you're a true believer in one-size-fits-all enterprise IT—and

Figure 2. Shared information services

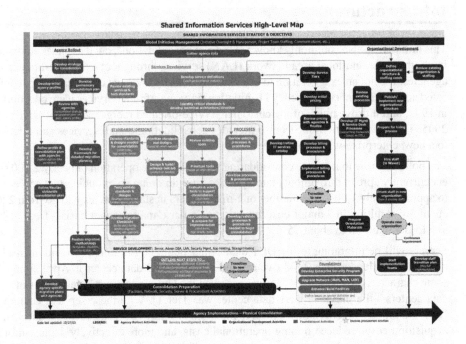

we're not—there probably are no obvious answers going into an effort of this magnitude. Secondly, SIS constitutes as much (if not more) a cultural change for enterprise IT as it does a technological change, and that kind of cultural shift must be generated within state government.

BadgerNet Converged Network (One Shared Infrastructure)

Based on Governor Doyle's directions, the state is installing the BadgerNet Converged Network (BCN), a single and more powerful data/video network that will be shared by state agencies; local governments; tribal nations located in Wisconsin; public and private K-12 schools; the University of Wisconsin System; the Wisconsin Technical College System; private colleges and universities; libraries; and museums. The previous network configuration—known simply as BadgerNet—carried voice, data, and video independently on three separate networks. (BCN is designed to allow state government's voice services to be added at a later date if this option is determined to be desirable and financially feasible.)

Our vision was to create a seamless, flexible, high-quality network to serve the needs of all eligible customers through 2010 and beyond, and to ensure the highest levels of operability among customers. BCN was purposefully designed as a standards-based network to give it the flexibility to grow and be used by applications not yet developed. By standards-based, we mean that the network does not rely on a single proprietary protocol (i.e., the rules that govern the exchange of information on the network). In fact, BCN handles multiple protocols, and because we have created a standards-based network, we will not have to start all over if a particular protocol becomes obsolete.

BCN provides the foundation for another important activity now underway: the Shared Information Services (SIS) Initiative described previously. BCN is the highway upon which traffic will flow between the state's new data center, state agency locations, and external customers.

BCN also is an integral part of Grow Wisconsin, Governor Doyle's economic-development plan. In the model we've designed, state government is the anchor tenant, and the prime contractor must allow sharing of the installed infrastructure with commercial business and residential customers throughout the state, in addition to providing service to political subdivisions and other public entities. This will help spur the delivery of broadband Internet service to parts of the state where it was previously unavailable due to geographic and economic barriers. In the educational arena, BCN positions our schools and colleges to be at the forefront of e-learning.

Because this project is so fundamental to our BHAG, and the stakes were so high, a conscious decision was made from the beginning to involve people with many different backgrounds and skill areas throughout the design process. The business case for BCN was formulated by DOA and a customer advisory group that included representatives from all the user groups mentioned earlier, after meetings were held throughout the state where stakeholders and residents could offer input. There was no room for territorial experts or intractable positions—we wanted to hear all the ideas, whether they came from one of the network engineers or a third-grade teacher at a focus group meeting in northern Wisconsin. If we had not established those collaborative approaches from the start, the likely result would have been the emergence of several smaller—and probably more expensive and less connected—networks throughout the state.

Geographic Information System Services (One Shared Infrastructure)

By the end of 2005, I had successfully managed to create within DET an Office of Geographic Information and hire a Chief Geographic Information Officer to lead it. The Office of the GIO will be the statewide coordinating body for enterprise geographic information system (GIS) services.

Our vision for the Office of the GIO is that it will provide effective geospatial resources to state agencies and stakeholders to benefit and serve the public, the environment, and the economy. Delivering GIS in an enterprise fashion will improve critical services to state agencies and citizens and decrease their overall cost. The state will benefit from an enterprise GIS through sharing infrastructure (hardware and software), resources (people), and processes across agencies. In establishing the Office of the GIO, it was important for me to make the case for enterprise GIS as an important asset for the public—not just bureaucrats—and the need for integration of spatial data with tabular data for better decision making.

It seems fitting that while our IT environment is undergoing a transformation to an extended-enterprise approach, GIS is doing so at the same time. The state Department of Resources and Department of Transportation have built significant GIS infrastructure for program use during the last 10 years, and recently there are a number of state agencies—namely Military Affairs; Workforce Development; Agriculture, Trade and Consumer Protection; Justice; and Health and Family Services—which are quickly building their GIS capabilities. Beyond that, agencies such as DOA, Corrections, Public Instruction, and Revenue have an interest in using GIS to support their business objectives. Instead of repeating the mistakes of the past (i.e., independent development with little or no enterprise collaboration), we decided to bring these agencies together to share resources, infrastructure, and data administration. Additionally, it will benefit all agencies to build common GIS service offerings, develop data distribution and management policies and standards, and collaboratively work with local and federal entities to more effectively manage GIS information within the state.

Most importantly, implementing an enterprise GIS program provides a model for extended-enterprise sharing. The Office of the GIO will facilitate the coordination of previously disconnected efforts at the state and local levels to provide data sharing, standardization, and collaboration to improve the state's overall GIS landscape. That sounds like a formula we'd like to repeat in a number of areas.

Our current GIS activities include developing and implementing:

1. GIS communications program;
2. Wisconsin Enterprise GIS (WEGIS) strategic plan;

3.   Enterprise GIS data repository;

4.   WEGIS Web mapping infrastructure and services; and

5.   Enterprise addressing tool.

Enterprise Resource Planning: Integrated Business Information System Project (One Enterprise Application Base)

One of the primary challenges we face in achieving our BHAG is being able to communicate across organizational boundaries, both horizontally and vertically. It is impossible to manage any operation effectively without being able to see what is happening.

Government in Wisconsin has been hampered in its effort to manage scarce resources by the fragmented nature of its administrative systems and processes. Fragmented processes and applications reflect fragmentation in the underlying data, making it difficult or impossible to answer simple operational business questions across the enterprise. Instead, each individual repository must be found and the data understood and transformed, and then all the individual pools of transformed data must be pasted together to try to make a single picture. Too often, even this Byzantine approach to generating information is thwarted by inconsistent data identification. For instance, there is no common use of commodity codes across state government, so there is no way to determine our total spending for any commodity without examining each individual purchase order by hand and recoding it. That leaves us unable to make the best possible bargains with vendors.

If we are to revolutionize service delivery, we have to completely rewrite our basic administrative paradigms. The integrated business information system (IBIS) project is designed to pull all administrative systems of one kind together, and then take those consolidated systems and make them seamless by giving them common access to uniformly defined data. We plan to do this by standardizing administrative processes and replacing the many legacy systems that support those processes with a single enterprise resource planning (ERP) system. This will give us the consolidated functionality we need ready-made, rather than having to design and build it from the ground up.

Table 1 describes current scenarios compared to post-IBIS scenarios.

The IBIS project fundamentally involves examining existing business processes and standardizing them across state agencies. With new processes defined, we have documented requirements, and using those requirements as our guide, we are selecting the "closest fit" vendor package that has been used successfully by at least one state government. We intend to implement the package without customization but with supporting interfaces and "bolt-on" modules, where necessary.

When we complete the IBIS project, we will be able to manage state government more effectively and relate state government operations more clearly to the efforts of local governments. As an example, when we offer local governments the ability to "piggyback" on state contracts—which we intend to do to the full extent possible—it will be a meaningful offer for the best pricing we can get, with full information on the state of Wisconsin's total spending on individual commodities.

Table 1. Before and after the IBIS project

As Is	To Be
No enterprise procurement or purchasing system. Unable to report statewide expenditures on commodities or across business areas.	An enterprise procurement system to facilitate strategic sourcing and provide a vendor service portal.
More than 59 systems maintained and supported to meet the state's needs for financial management.	One integrated financial system to maintain and support.
More than 38 systems support human resources and payroll.	One integrated human resource and payroll system.
Lack of data integration necessary to produce enterprise-wide reports.	Ability to produce timely, accurate, and decision-useful enterprise-wide reports.
Growing costs to support legacy systems.	A significant return on investment from replacing fragmented systems with a single, seamless package.
Business interfaces supported by manual re-entry of data with attendant costs and error rate.	Single entry for all transaction data into a central database with attendant improvements in reporting capability and reduction in costs.
Elevated risk of legacy payroll and budget systems failing.	Reduced risk of system collapse, both currently and in the future, as package upgrades take the place of repeatedly modified code.
Opaque systems unavailable externally.	Web-based services providing citizen and vendor self-service functionality.
Paper-driven human resources processes.	Employee self-service capability.

A Customer Service-Driven IT Organization (Enhances All the Foundation-Building Initiatives)

As described previously, many of our enterprise efforts involve some form of consolidation or centralization of like services. One of the most complex is SIS, which involves the centralization of all distributed server and network services. Central to the success of SIS is the effective and efficient delivery of enterprise IT services—simply put, if DET cannot deliver for its customers after taking ownership of all the server and network services, we will have jeopardized all our efforts toward achieving our BHAG. To reach our goal, the enterprise needs to be responsive, flexible, and agile in IT service delivery, and improving the way we do business begins at home, with us, DET.

Organizational structures of the past were based on the mainframe model, where all services stemmed from one large server. Staffs were divided into components of the mainframe environment, creating a siloed approach to support. While this structure worked for the mainframe, it was lacking in flexibility and cross-communication when transposed on the distributed server environment, where diverse server platforms were integrated into single application systems. We needed a new organizational structure to provide cross-communication between technical groups and to focus on service delivery, rather than support of specific individual technologies.

Our new organizational design (see Figure 3) brought all technology areas into one bureau (Infrastructure Support). This facilitated standardizing support processes and procedures across technology sections. A Bureau of Customer Relations was eliminated and a new role of service delivery manager was created, which reports directly to the State CIO, giving the position delegated authority of the CIO for service delivery.

Positions were created for service delivery coordinators (SDCs). The SDCs have delegated authority to work directly with technical staff horizontally across the organization. Their focus is on service delivery across technology support areas. They have the ability to dynamically create SWAT teams to address service outages, the development of new services, and additional support that may be required by a specific agency. The horizontal approach to providing support eliminates the silos that existed in the old organizational models.

The SDCs are directly responsible for IT service delivery, deployment, management planning, design and development. They directly manage the complete life cycle of a specific service or group of services within our enterprise IT services catalog (see next). They must have a broad understanding of both technology and its potential to address the business needs of a specific customer constituency.

Figure 3. Organizational chart

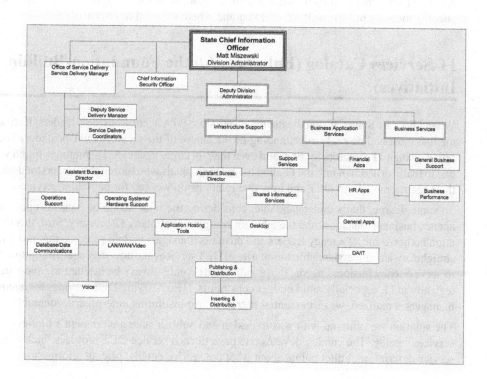

We then established a second support role for outreach into the state agencies—the customer service manager (CSM). CSMs are designated as the liaisons between agency business needs and enterprise IT service offerings. In other words, they are enterprise staff who understand the business of the agency and provide support for enterprise services to that agency. They provide outreach, information, support, business services, and technical assistance to executive management, IT managers, and staff within state agencies and other governmental units.

Agencies also have the opportunity to assign an agency staff person to function either part- or full-time as their internal CSM. The agency-based CSM participates in all enterprise CSM meetings, facilitates resolving enterprise issues, and works with DET SDCs in developing new or enhanced services. They also work closely with their agency business units in IT planning and support. The agency CSM is paired with one of the enterprise (i.e., DET-employed) CSMs to facilitate DET coordination efforts, and spends a portion of their time on-site at DET—as much as their enterprise counterparts.

By opening the door to agency staff participation in customer service delivery, DET is beginning to establish a true partnership with agencies, acknowledging the complexities of their business needs, and demonstrating the commitment to a trust relationship.

It's one thing to have an organizational design and roles that we believe directly enhance our customer service. It's another thing to try to measure—again and again—the quality of our customer service. We decided we would let our customers tell us if we were delivering quality customer service or not. Our goal is to earn and maintain a rating of 4 or 5 (on a scale of 1 to 5) from at least 90% of DET customers. Once our shared information services initiative (see earlier) is fully implemented, those grades from our customers will be a crucial, ongoing measure of how well we're doing and where we need to improve.

IT Services Catalog (Enhances All the Foundation-Building Initiatives)

When I became State CIO and began my discussions with agency business leaders, it struck me that most had no real understanding of the nature of the services DET provides. They relied on their IT directors for that, and even then, in larger agencies, I sometimes found you had to really drill down into the IT shop to find individuals who thoroughly understood what their agency buys from DET and how that relationship worked for particular services.

To some degree, that's understandable, considering the wide scope of issues dropped on agency business managers and the inherent complexity of many IT services. Still, this situation bothered me. If agency leaders and business managers had no resource that provided straightforward, understandable summaries of DET services and how they could be optimized to serve agency business needs, those individuals would always be hesitant to invest strategically in IT, especially amid budget constraints. Demystifying DET services for agency managers, I realized, was an essential ingredient for instituting enterprise accountability.

The solution we came up with was to design and publish state government's first-ever IT services catalog. The catalog devotes one page to each service DET provides, including a service description; bullet points about what the service entails; pricing information; cost-saving tips for agencies; and consumption trends. The text and graphics are specifically constructed to be understandable by non-technical staff.

We published the first catalog in January 2005. Because the SIS Initiative resulted in the transformation of several services and the formation of new ones, we published a second edition in January 2006, which grew from 22 to 28 services, all of which were updated. Meanwhile, we have published an accompanying Web site, which expands the description of each service and provides a pricing tool that clarifies the available choices. To the best of our knowledge, no other public-sector IT service organization has published a service catalog comparable to ours.

With both editions, I've stressed to our customers that the IT services catalog will never be considered a "finished product". We always want to make it more useful and accessible. We've asked customers how we can improve it, and are using their feedback to update the Web site on an ongoing basis and the printed edition on at least an annual basis.

Service-Oriented Architecture (Contributes Toward All the Foundation-Building Initiatives, Especially One Shared Infrastructure)

Like many large enterprises, the state of Wisconsin faces the challenge of optimizing a vast, fragmented IT landscape that has grown through the course of several decades and billions of dollars. Uncoordinated technical investment in short-term service improvements has led to increasing long-term technical deficits that have progressively burdened our funding base. Recognizing, as Albert Einstein once said, "We cannot solve our problems with the same thinking we used when we created them", Governor Doyle and DET have created a vision in which IT transcends the boundaries of government rather than reinforcing them, and provides citizens with transparent access to government services regardless of underlying jurisdictions.

Historically, IT initiatives tasked with overcoming government boundaries have been ad hoc affairs facing a governance void, bridged only by situational cooperation between agencies with little incentive to work together in the first place. The legacy of that includes innumerable point-to-point system communications and islands of duplicative and poorly synchronized data.

In response, we've pushed the concerns of system integration and information sharing to an extended-enterprise level, and embarked on the pursuit of a service-oriented architecture (SOA). An SOA will provide a foundation for extended-enterprise IT collaboration through a shared set of investments, patterns, standards, and practices. The effort began in late 2003 with the acquisition of an enterprise service bus (ESB) solution to serve as a backbone and catalyst for the state's emerging SOA.

ESB technology uses XML and Web services to simplify the task of exchanging information among incompatible applications and hardware platforms. Our ESB product selection was guided by support for open standards, flexible options for enabling existing resources, and a low cost of entry relative to past enterprise application integration solutions. Ultimately, the ESB is seen not as a product, but as a component role within a wider SOA context, and the state's return on its early investment will depend largely upon its ability to sustain this distinction.

While the fundamental concepts behind SOA are not new, the wide and rapid adoption of integration-enabling Internet, XML, messaging, and Web service standards is unprecedented. We can take advantage of that trend to energize a shift in the nature of enterprise IT from a large collection of internally coupled, complex and fragilely-connected silos to a community of peers, who orient themselves as service providers and consumers working together under a cooperative architecture. This definition of SOA will take time to evolve, but at stake is the fundamental mission of IT to serve the purposes of government rather than constrain them.

Fortunately, this has been recognized by a number of local, state, and federal government entities for some time. With converging agency momentum supported by a developing SOA infrastructure—and open standards available to guide interoperability, procurement, and development decisions—Wisconsin's enterprise IT is positioning itself to effectively meet the increasing number of information sharing needs arising from all government levels.

In the fall of 2005, University of Wisconsin-Madison CIO Annie Stunden and I held the state's first enterprise-wide SOA summit (documented at http://soa.wisconsin.gov/), which brought our organizations together with partners from across state and local government to share and discuss the extended enterprise vision and how SOA initiatives will support it. Through this summit and its follow-up activities, agency relationships are being reinvented through collaborative partnerships focusing on shared services, interoperability, and economies of scale. We are re-examining government service delivery through a citizen-oriented perspective so that the boundaries of government do not interfere with its mission.

Since the summit, DET staff are working with staff from state agencies, UW-Madison and local governments to: Schedule ongoing topical SOA events, including SOA as it relates to the mainframe, Java, Microsoft and open-source platforms, security and information management; Develop implementation guides to establish a common set of repeatable SOA-related architectural patterns for information and process sharing; Define SOA implementation and support process modules to bring consistent activities, roles, responsibilities, and project management practices across agency boundaries; Form enterprise integration and interoperability groups along lines of government business to establish interoperability standards, identify shared services, and collaborate on shared infrastructure; Identify and define requirements for shared investment in SOA-related product licensing; and Integrate our SOA architecture with other enterprise-wide initiatives, including identity and access management, portal implementations, collaboration services, and ERP procurement (our IBIS project described previously).

The future of IT in Wisconsin is not about better technology—it's about better government. Governor Doyle has made it clear that from now on, the problems of any agency or jurisdiction are the problems of all agencies and jurisdictions, and that the successes achieved within any agency or jurisdiction must be extended to all agencies and jurisdictions. That is the principle that drives our pursuit of an SOA, and, for that matter, all our efforts to achieve our BHAG. Ultimately, our success will not be measured by the elegance of our IT infrastructure. Our success will be measured by the quality of the lives of our residents, their families, and their communities, in whose interests our government was created.

Conclusion

I recognize that most of this case study focuses on what we are in the process of doing, not what we have already fully accomplished. That simply reflects the scope of the revolution we're instituting in state government IT.

I do not believe in incremental change, at least not when it comes to the enterprise IT environment (or lack thereof) that I inherited when I became State CIO. We needed to rebuild, from the ground up, how we thought about and managed enterprise IT, and more basically, how we even defined our enterprise. We had to—for what was really the first time—focus our efforts on activities that clearly supported business outcomes. We had to become accountable for the decisions we made and the outcomes we produced.

The projects and activities described in this case do not represent magic bullets—even if another state adopted a BHAG and an enterprise IT plan very similar to ours, it could understandably generate different kinds of projects, depending on that state's particular circumstances. But I do believe that all our activities are now oriented toward generating sustained change across our extended enterprise, destroying the barriers to borderless government, and fundamentally improving service delivery for Wisconsin residents. I believe we now have a readily identifiable goal and framework for our enterprise IT efforts.

When I submitted our enterprise IT plan to the legislature in the fall of 2004, I made it clear that the strategic direction laid out represented a multi-year effort demanding rigorous alignment and realignment of priorities to be successful. IBM's initiative to simplify its technology environment and create a shared infrastructure spanned 10-plus years from initiation to realization of results (Working Council for Chief Information Officers, 2003). Similar efforts to streamline and simplify corporate enterprise technology at Cisco Systems (Working Council for Chief Information Officers, 2001) and Allstate have been multi-year efforts with significant measurable results (Working Council for Chief Information Officers, 2002). So we understood the reality of what we were taking on. We will not attain enterprise agility overnight. But we will focus our enterprise work on establishing a firm foundation for enabling agility and, ultimately, achieving our BHAG.

References

McKay, J. (2004). The odd couple. *Government Technology*, January 6. Retrieved January 4, 2006, from http://www.govtech.net/magazine/story.php?id=83610&issue=1:2004

Reschovsky, A. (2002, May). *Wisconsin's structural deficit: Our fiscal future at the crossroads.* Article published by the Robert M. La Follette School of Public Affairs, University of Wisconsin-Madison. Retrieved January 4, 2006, from http://www.lafollette.wisc.edu/publications/otherpublications/wisconsinprimer/2002/StructuralDeficit2002.pdf.

Working Council for Chief Information Officers. (2001). *Visualizing IT value creation: Tactics for communicating IT contributions to corporate strategy.* Corporate Executive Board, Washington, D.C.

Working Council for Chief Information Officers. (2002). *Enabling enterprise data visibility: Case studies in alignment of data architecture and business strategy.* Corporate Executive Board, Washington, D.C.

Working Council for Chief Information Officers. (2003). *Institutionalizing IT cost efficiency: Disciplines for embedding ROI transparency and accountability.* IT Cost Savings Series, Corporate Executive Board, Washington, D.C.

Author's Biography

Matt Miszewski was appointed Wisconsin State CIO by Governor Jim Doyle in March 2003. He oversees the state's approximately $400 million annual IT investment. Prior to his appointment, Miszewski worked in the private sector. He started his own company, Topical Networks, which provided IT consulting and enterprise resources systems to national clients. He also was a founding partner of the firm people.political, which supplied political data-management tools to candidates and labor organizations. As an attorney in private practice, he focused on labor law and advised high-tech firms. Miszewski became president of the National Association of State Chief Information Officers (NASCIO) in October 2005. Government Technology magazine named him one of the Top 25 Doers, Dreamers and Drivers for 2004.

Chapter II

Westchester County Case Study

Norman Jacknis, Westchester County, New York, USA

Scott Erik Fernqvist, Westchester County, New York, USA

Executive Summary

Prior to 1998, Westchester County (New York) outsourced vital IT functions, lacked a significant Web presence, and relied on outdated and inconsistent technology which played a peripheral role in government operations. Its economic growth was stagnating in a changing economy. This changed with the arrival of a new County Executive, Andrew J. Spano, and the county's first Chief Information Officer, Norman Jacknis. Now, the new Department of Information Technology, with a more modern technology foundation and approach, plays a central role in both government operations and the county government's vision of how it can serve Westchester's residents.

Background

Westchester County, with a population nearing one million residents, is the 500 square mile region just north of New York City. Its geographical setting is a favorable one, with the

Long Island Sound on the southeast and the Hudson River on the west. Within its borders, the terrain is largely rolling hills, intersected by the Croton, Bronx, and Saw Mill rivers. To this day, the county remains one of the most heavily forested in New York State and has retained much of its rural character, while adopting the urban and suburban lifestyles dictated by its proximity to New York and a well-developed regional transportation network (Cochran & Green, 1982).

Although historically known for its wealth and highly-educated, white-collar population, Westchester has evolved in recent years into a much more diverse county, with a larger portion of immigrants and pockets of poverty, especially near its border with New York City. As a result, the county government spends a greater portion of its budget than it ever did on affordable housing initiatives, child care, public transportation, and various social services. Since September 11th, however, the county government has increasingly emphasized protecting and keeping its residents safe. As just one example, where one police officer used to man the main county office building in White Plains over an eight-hour shift, five officers now guard the building and its employees around the clock.

Under New York State law, the county is a creature of the state. It thus has to operate within some of the most restrictive civil service and government procurement rules anywhere in the country, perhaps the world. It also has been subject to numerous unfunded mandates by the state, which must be paid from county property and sales taxes. One particularly burdensome mandate is Medicaid, in which the state requires the county to fund half of the non-federal portion of the program, although the county has no legislative authority to limit the extent of what is now the nation's most generous set of benefits.

Nevertheless, within these constraints, the 4,655 full-time, year-round Westchester County employees have long enjoyed a reputation for professionalism and efficiency. Like other large, affluent counties outside of major cities, the public has generally demanded high-quality service delivery and have not been tolerant of administrations which failed to meet those standards. Similarly, Westchester is considered to be among the country's most financially well-managed counties, as reflected in its AAA bond rating—the only one in New York State and one of the few around the country. (It has an annual budget of about $2 billion.)

Going back to colonial times, there has been a very strong tradition of home rule at the local government (not county) level. So, in Westchester County, there are 43 full-time, independent city, town, and village governments. There are dozens of school districts, dozens of fire departments, dozens of libraries, dozens of police departments, and numerous water districts. The county even has four dozen answering points in its 911 system—perhaps the most complex 911 system in the world. In many ways, this tradition constrains the power of the county government. It has also made county government the least visible level of government. County officials sometimes joke that the government is Westchester's "two billion dollar secret". Despite this tradition, the county government has grown in size and responsibility over the years. In part, this reflects a nationwide trend for cities, towns, and other local public entities to transfer functions to the county level. During the 1960s, for example, 40% of all counties responding to a federal survey reported that they had assumed responsibility for police protection previously provided by a local municipality. Only 3% had shifted this duty in the other direction. Similarly, 27% had taken over responsibility for jails and corrections, 37% had assumed the library management function, 45% had become responsible for planning previously done at a more local level, and more than 20% of all counties now said they were responsible for roads, highways, sewage, refuse collection, and public welfare. In each case, a dramatically smaller percentage of reporting counties had conveyed these responsibilities to local municipalities or other "sub-county" agencies (National Association of Counties, 2006). In part, the county government has grown because it was the only government large enough to address many of the problems facing residents or big enough to provide services that were uneconomical at a lower scale, such as the bomb squad. County leaders also took on the responsibility for some unusual activities.

In addition to the more traditional responsibilities, such as providing public health, safety, and social services, the county also operates a regional airport that services over one million passengers each year and has the largest corporate jet fleet in the country. Westchester is the only county in the nation to own and operate an amusement park—historic Playland—which was established more than 75 years ago as one of the terminal points for an extensive county parkway system that still exists.

Originally, county government was dominated by a Board of Supervisors, that is, those who led the various cities and towns. The position of an elected county executive is a relatively recent innovation, going back only a few decades. As a result of the one-man, one-vote rule mandated by the U.S. Supreme Court, the Board of Supervisors was replaced by a Board of Legislators. Thus the last direct tie to local government was cut. This too has helped officials in the county government to set an independent course of growth in the functions that they are willing to take on.

Setting the Stage

Traditional IT Results In Outsourcing

Information technology was introduced into Westchester County Government in the 1930's when Remington Rand 90-column punch-card machines were installed by the Department of Welfare (Social Services). The years that followed, particularly the late 80's to early 90's, featured gradual growth and a continuation of a tradition of generally centralized delivery of IT service.

But significant upheaval was looming. Partly this was a result of deficiencies in delivering IT services. For example, as PCs became more popular in homes, many non-IT employees wondered why the PCs in county government were set up to hide Windows and only provide a terminal-like interface to an antiquated e-mail system. Partly the upheaval was a result of ideological changes in government. By the late 1980s, the interest of the private sector in the concept of "outsourcing" had also taken hold in federal, state, and local governments across the United States. Even recently, a study found that 74% of municipalities expected to save money with privatization, while only about a third expected higher quality or services not otherwise available (Fruth, 2000).

Having only closely been re-elected in the 1993 elections, Republican County Executive Andrew O'Rourke was searching for ways to overcome the public's dissatisfaction with his county government. Given the build-up of interest in outsourcing, in 1995, he commissioned a study by Bennett Kielson Storch & Company LLP, a local accounting firm that had long been the county's outside auditors and close to those who ran the government. Their June 1995 review of the information systems division focused on operations, service delivery, and satisfaction/dissatisfaction.

The results from users were mixed, but mostly negative. Only a few departments seemed to be satisfied, and almost all departments expressed concern about the high cost of IT services. Among the departments that made extensive use of IT services and seemed satisfied was the independently elected County Clerk (then Andrew J. Spano). Most common areas of dissatisfaction were hardware/software support and application development. The Medical Center provided a list of 20 outstanding hardware installs/upgrades/relocations which were over six months old at the time of interviews. There were many recorded complaints about missed deadlines and undelivered projects.

The final report recommended eliminating "non-critical" or "non-essential" information systems operating expenditures or capital purchases. It also recommended that the county issue a request for proposals (RFP) to outsource county information systems, based upon an estimate of $3 to $5 million in annual savings. Officially, for these reasons, County Executive O'Rourke moved ahead with a plan to outsource almost all of the staff and operations of the information systems division. The Charter of Westchester County grants the County Board of Legislators power to "create, organize, alter or abolish departments, commissions, boards, bureau, offices and employments and/or transfer their functions and duties" and to "fix the number of deputies, assistants, clerks and other persons to be employed in the several departments, offices and commissions of the County" (Westchester County Board of Legislators, 2006). It also has the power to approve or disapprove the granting of county property and involvement with leases.

A majority of the legislators were not convinced by the county executive's arguments and suspected that there were political reasons and relationships that led to the decision to outsource. For their part, the employees of the information systems division undertook an extensive lobbying campaign, which seemed to resonate with the legislators. So there was a coalition of three Republicans, one Conservative, and six Democrats against outsourcing and seven other Republicans supporting the administration's plan to outsource.

But this legislative majority failed to dissuade County Executive O'Rourke from moving forward with his plans. When he signed a 10-year outsourcing contract with IBM for $102 million on January 1, 1997, to manage the county's information systems, opponents were quick to spring into action. Although, in principle, all employees had been offered jobs with IBM, their union (the Civil Service Employees Association) obtained a preliminary injunction restraining the implementation of the outsourcing contract. Thereafter, on January 6, 1997, the Board of Legislators passed resolutions in an attempt to have the county hire back all outsourced information systems workers. The ensuing litigation focused in part on whether the contract with IBM was legal, given that it was not endorsed by the Board of Legislators.

The administration's hopes for cost savings, increased efficiency, and improved service delivery failed to materialize during the 18-month period during which outsourcing was in effect. There were numerous user complaints of even worse service than had existed before and a "taxi meter" mentality in which even the discussion of possible new systems ran up the bill with IBM.

According to a 1997 article from *Computerworld*, "Snafus plague IBM/county deal" (4/21/97), a three-day computer outage at Westchester Community College signaled things were only growing worse with the county's outsourced services. As Darrell A. Fruth points out in *Economic and Institutional Constraints on the Privatization of Government Information Technology Services*: "The experience of Westchester County demonstrates the potential pitfalls of outsourcing public information systems without clear authority (p. 3).

The outsourcing's major disruption of past patterns of carrying out IT services in the county led to an epiphany of sorts for the Board of Legislators and the outsourced employees. The board decided that the county needed to have a chief information officer—someone to provide strategic leadership and professional direction for IT activities in the county's operations and to provide both the county executive and the board with advice on how best to use technology to achieve their goals. The board created such a position in the 1998 budget, at a salary high enough to attract the talent they wanted. For their part, most of the former employees did learn that the traditional IS way of doing things would have to change.

When a judge threw out the contract as illegally executed, IBM also was anxious to end this unhappy chapter—although they did press for a significant financial settlement, which they never did receive and eventually abandoned.

Case Description

An About-Face For Westchester IT

In response to these events, the county was set to have its first CIO in January 1998 and the returned employees at the beginning of March 1998.

It would also have a new County Executive, Andrew J. Spano, who was elected by a large majority in November 1997, against the Republican candidate, the Rye City Mayor Ted Dunn. (Andrew O'Rourke decided not to chance running for re-election yet again, in face of a likely loss.) As only the second Democrat to be elected county executive (or to any county-wide office) in the county's history, this election was taken as a signal for change.

As county clerk from 1982 through 1993, Mr. Spano has used technology extensively to modernize the operations of his office and had won national and state recognition for these efforts. He was so convinced of the value of technology that, in the eighties, he was sometimes referred to by less sympathetic observers as "George Jetson". Following his decision not to run for re-election as clerk in 1993, he started an e-commerce company, which was one of IBM's first e-commerce business partners.

In his last term as county clerk, he also helped co-found a citizens-based, grass roots, non-profit group, which effectively functioned as Westchester's local Internet Society. (Since it was in the days before most people understood or even had heard of the Internet, its name was the Westchester Alliance for Telecommunications and Public Access—WATPA.)

One resulting project he undertook was to create a video showing the positive and negative impact of railroad development and drawing the parallel with the Internet and telecommunications infrastructure. His explicit warning was that Westchester would suffer in the future if it did not substantially improve its technology infrastructure and take advantage of the Internet.

So it was no surprise that in his first speech as county executive, Spano offered an axiomatic belief in technology that was diametrically opposed to the belief of his predecessor—"paperless government" and "e-government" were recurring themes in many of his major addresses upon taking office (Berger, 1997). O'Rourke thought of technology as a back office, subsidiary function, and a cost center to be kept in check. Spano promised early on to make government more accessible and cost-effective through technology, not in spite of it. Spano needed to have IT operations within the county government as an essential part of his vision and what he hoped to achieve.

One of the other co-founders of WATPA was Dr. Norman Jacknis, whom Spano knew from his community volunteer activities. In the early '90s, Jacknis was still an executive in the software industry. At the time WATPA was founded, he was director of Internet/Web product development at the American R&D lab of the big British computer company (ICL). As chair of WATPA in the mid '90s, Jacknis led an effort to provide free Web site design and hosting for non-profit groups around the county. As it turned out, one such group that needed a Web presence was the County Board of Legislators, for even the minimal Web site that the administration provided did not acknowledge the existence of the board. The volunteer effort by WATPA turned out to be a great success from the board's viewpoint, as they became one of the earliest county legislative bodies on the Internet and had searchable minutes going back to 1996.

The new county executive appointed Jacknis as the county's first CIO to start serving on January 1, when the new administration started. As a technology leader known to the board and the new county executive, Jacknis came to the position with the credibility needed to initiate major changes.

County Executive Spano then proposed the creation of a new Department of Information Technology (DoIT) for the budget year 1999, as part of a re-organization that disbanded General Services. But this would be a new, more essential department and would include all aspects of information and technology, including the County Archives and Records Center (which Spano had established as clerk) and Geographic Information Systems (which had been in the Planning Department). It would centralize IT services that had sprung up in many departments as a result of dissatisfaction with the outsourcing. It also included video production and graphics design activities that gave it the full range of creative resources necessary for a successful Internet presence.

To this day, the department's mission reflects the role of technology envisioned by Spano upon taking office: to help county government operate more effectively and efficiently; make government services and information more accessible to the public; and to help protect our residents' safety. County Executive Spano took a variety of other substantive and symbolic measures to get the rest of the county's senior management and employees to understand how important technology would be in his administration. By allocating a record amount of money to DoIT—today the department spends roughly $40 million per year—Spano provided the raw material with which he and Jacknis could effect their desired transformation. He banned paper-based internal communications by the end of his first year in office. He sent all commissioners and deputies to a one-week "boot camp" on computers. He joked that he would send an e-mail over a weekend announcing a budget cut for any department whose commissioner did not respond by Monday morning. He held reviews of each department's Web site once or twice a year with the commissioners and their staffs.

He provided the funds for every employee to have access to a PC, the Internet, and so forth. More than 2,000 employees were trained on the use of Microsoft Office and the Internet. Spano also placed the office of the new CIO right next to his in the county's executive office suite. He included the CIO in very small, weekly "inner circle" meetings on issues that covered policy and administration, not merely technology. For some county employees earlier than others, but for all within a relatively short time period, the perception of technology's role in the county began to change as well.

There would be a change in the model of IT service delivery, a new foundation for network-based services, a new and expanded use of the Internet, and a new critical role for IT in economic development. What follows is a description of these intertwined efforts.

The Anti-Outsourcing Model of IT Service Delivery

While the return of the former county IS employees meant that he would need to create a new organizational structure, Jacknis' first and longest running organizational priority was to change the culture that had existed. The new CIO developed an approach to service delivery that was also perhaps the opposite of the way the outsourcing model had worked in Westchester. This was somewhat unusual in that many senior IT people in other public organizations were doing their best to emulate the business model of private outsourcing companies. Having spent most of his career in the private sector, Jacknis thought that a different model was needed when operating inside the government—especially in an environment of the kind that Spano had begun to create.

This approach had a number of features:

1. It was an inherently enterprise, rather than departmental, orientation. In that respect, it supported the goal of the county executive to present the government to its residents as a unified, service-oriented organization. As the saying went, "you shouldn't have to pass a civics examination in order to get the county to help you—you needn't have to know which department handles which functions". Thus, there was a shift away from single department systems. Instead, the initial assumption now would be that any problem appearing in one department was likely to share underlying characteristics with problems appearing in other departments—and that the county could invest once in a system that would solve those problems across departments.

2. In general, the new approach also meant an increase in internal development of software and systems, especially for critical and strategic operations. In the face of the Y2K problem (which neither the old IS division nor IBM had made much preparation), DoIT was forced to buy off-the-shelf software packages. Since then, however, except for small, non-strategic areas, systems are mostly developed in-house. With the adoption of a three-tier, services-oriented (J2EE) architecture, the acquisition of third-party software now focuses on components, rather than monolithic, silo packages.

3. To support this architecture, Jacknis created an Architecture Committee and a Software Infrastructure team. The Architecture Committee, including representatives of different teams and skill sets within DoIT who meet once a week, is charged with developing technology standards that apply across all systems and also reviews applications for compliance. The small Software Infrastructure team maintains and manages the software components—the "enterprise bus"—that form the foundation of DoIT's county-wide software solutions. In that sense, it is the equivalent of the small team that is responsible for maintaining the hardware on which all the software operates.

4. It encouraged all county employees, especially DoIT employees, to abandon the idea that DoIT was merely a vendor or "service bureau" to county government departments. Instead, they were to think about technology services from the perspective of the residents of the county.

5. In turn, this meant that DoIT would work closely with departments, well beyond traditional IT limitations. This would include taking the lead in business process re-engineering, statistical analysis of operations, and generally acting as strategic advisors to the departments. The CIO set up periodic (often monthly) meetings with commissioners of major departments to go over technology issues—not who would get what new PCs, but both technology and non-technology suggestions on how the commissioner could achieve his/her mission and goals.

6. A process of continuous prioritization, along with generally fixed allocation of resources and short-term deliverables, was introduced. As a practical matter, this meant that, as part of the annual budget process, the CIO would allocate staff resources to department projects based upon the priorities of the county executive and the business plans of each commissioner. Once the budget was passed, DoIT would generally operate within those resource constraints, but would encourage department commissioners to adjust their priorities as necessary. Thus, if a new problem arose, for which DoIT could help find a solution, then other projects for that department would be pushed down the priority list.

7. This process was made more palatable by an emphasis on frequent, short-term deliverables. In that way, departments would see something of value that they could use.

8. This approach also forced DoIT staff to adopt a more agile, flexible methodology to software development. The classic "waterfall" approach to software development was replaced. This was especially significant for its elimination of the "written in blood", large requirements documents that had been part of traditional IS in the county and also IBM's outsourcing period. Jacknis pointed out that most users, let alone most software developers, have difficulty envisioning what a system will be like based upon the traditional requirements documentation. If, as they were instructed to do, the DoIT staff lived with the departments they helped and understood both the policy and operations of those departments, then there should not have to be an extensive discovery of requirements. Instead, the focus was shifted to the design of a solution, followed by the delivery of usable, frequent "software packages" to users and encouragement of user feedback based upon something that was real and tangible.

9. The efficient delivery of solutions is made possible, in part, by a conscious emphasis on reuse of previously-built components and network-based services. As an example, DoIT's case management framework provides a generic, common perspective on

case management across county departments and affiliated non-profit agencies. The county's software staff—called "software architects" in order to emphasize the new approach—have used this framework to build systems which are used for several different programs, including juvenile delinquency, homeless management, child care services, and general social services. At the presentation layer, the users see screens with language and rules appropriate to their program interests and functions. Underneath, they share a common set of software components and database structure. This enables us to build one richly-featured solution for case management for less money rather than purchasing outside of government, thus allowing them to have technology for the first time, while making it easier to share data with other agencies.

10.   Also, as a part of this approach, Jacknis moved DoIT staff to focus on delivery of new services and systems to help the county achieve its goals. To the extent possible, this would minimize staff time spent on maintenance and traditional internal operations.

11.   In order to make this shift possible, DoIT also purchased a variety of tools to automate and increase their productivity in handling the traditional tasks that had so consumed them in the past. This included early use of remote control of desktops, automated job scheduling, and quicker, less staff-intensive solutions to tasks such as database optimization. It also included the replacement of two mainframe data centers (one for IBM, one for Unisys) with a data center based upon dozens of generally Intel-based servers running UNIX/Linux or Windows. This saved the county several millions a year in hardware and staff costs. It also made service delivery more reliable from the users' point of view, since the impact of any problems would be isolated to particular applications. In the past, if there was a problem with a mainframe, the whole county government was "down".

12.   This meant as well reduction in excessive specialization among DoIT staff. In the past, there were separate staffs responsible for requirements, development, testing, operation, and so forth. In 1998, teams were set up to cover major functional areas of county government, such as health/human services, criminal justice/public safety, physical facilities, and so forth. Under the new approach, with the exception of ensuring that the servers' operating system was functioning, each DoIT team would be held responsible for the full life cycle of the products they delivered. If a mistake was made in the design or development, the originators of those mistakes would have to deal with the consequences.

Westchester Telecom

Going back to their days in WATPA, Spano and Jacknis were acutely aware that Westchester's future would be limited by its inadequate telecommunications infrastructure. With the exception of the "Platinum Mile" (an area of corporate headquarters parks along Interstate 287 near White Plains), telecommunications and data services in the rest of the county were behind those of most areas of the country that Westchester competed with.

In meetings with the major telephone company, it was clear that Westchester would continue to be at the bottom of the priority list. The company's executives were focused on winning a competitive war in Manhattan's downtown and midtown area, which sucked investment from other areas. That the company had been able to do so without public comment from most Westchester officials was another reflection of the lack of understanding of the importance of technology on the part of those officials.

That attitude was to change with Spano and Jacknis. One of their earliest initiatives was to create what they called "Westchester Telecom". With its focus on economic development, this network would go into every corner of the county, not just the "Platinum Mile". To ensure this coverage, they identify more than 500 sites from every part of the county that was the result of the pooling of the telephone and data communications budgets of the county government, the independent 38-library cooperative system, local governments, the major hospital center, and the cooperative technology service center for the local school districts—worth approximately $50 million over a five-year period.

Their approach looked for a strategic advantage for the buyer in the changing structure of the telecommunications industry. In what was then a first such attempt in the country, they sought to convince competitive telecommunications companies that this would serve much as an anchor store in a new shopping mall. It would be big enough to justify a company's investment necessary to build out significant fiber capacity throughout the county, although clearly not enough to make profits. The profits would come from the commercial customers who would take advantage of the high-speed telecommunications network that would now be at their door. In turn, that would help them become more competitive and grow more, thereby achieving the economic development goals.

With the county's contract alone set at $25 million, this was one of the largest public works projects in its history, and thus it was especially important that a rigorous procurement process be followed. After both an RFI and then an elaborate RFP, the county selected the proposal with the lowest prices, greatest bandwidth, and best service record. (It was fortunate that they had achieved the best marks on all of these dimensions, as the attempts to exercise political pressure on the process was understandably great.)

The Westchester Telecom Network was built by Lightpath (the telecommunications subsidiary of Cablevision, one of the two dominant cable companies in the New York metropolitan region) over the course of three years from 1999 to 2001. There is now a fiber backbone (operating at OC-192 capacity) which is over 700 miles long and links county offices, town halls, schools, libraries, hospitals, police, fire departments, and even sewer pump stations throughout Westchester County with voice, video, high-speed data, and Internet services.

The economic development purposes were also achieved. This network has provided dozens of office buildings (and their resident companies) with the same capabilities. It has helped to trigger a revival in the historic, formerly industrial city of Peekskill in the northwest corner of the county. With almost every part of that city within a short distance of the backbone, new economic growth and even an artists' colony has arisen. Elsewhere, the network has made it possible for the county to convince companies that had previously ignored it to locate major facilities in Westchester. These include the world headquarters of Lenovo (now the world's third largest PC maker), New York Life, Morgan Stanley, and Nokia. More on this next, when we discuss technology's role in economic development more generally.

The Westchester Telecom project was also a budgetary success. The cost per phone went down dramatically by 40%. More important, the average monthly cost for data in 1999 was $646.24 per megabyte (MB), whereas today the average cost is $15.57 per MB, or 3% of the original price. With the decreased cost, the county government ended up with much more data communications capacity than it had before. It now had a real metropolitan area network. Savings were generated in other, less obvious, areas as well. For example, new videoconferencing capabilities have greatly reduced county travel time and expense between the widely dispersed county offices.

Public sector organizations, including school districts, hospitals, libraries, fire and police departments, and a majority of the county's municipalities, have been equally motivated by competitive pricing and service delivery to participate in Westchester's end-to-end fiber-based network. Since the contract had volume discounts, the county's unit costs have gone down as additional public entities have tapped into the network.

While the cost per unit has gone dramatically, the increased use of technology has been reflected in somewhat higher total costs now for the network. The amount of data being transferred via the county's network has reached unprecedented levels and will only continue to grow as additional users tap into the network and bandwidth increases. This example highlights the curious way in which cost savings resulting from improved technology can be offset by new demand and increased use.

The network has also made possible better coordination and data sharing between local municipalities and the county. It has also encouraged distance learning and progressive teaching methods, since the county now offers schools and libraries across Westchester free county-wide (actually world-wide) videoconferencing services over the network. Going out to the public, the network has enabled Internet-based services that require the high bandwidth it supports. The tie-in with the cable television infrastructure has also made possible future connections, such as videoconferencing between county offices and the homes of our residents.

Commenting on the project, County Executive Spano said: "Westchester Telecom puts us on the map in the areas of technology, education, and economic development—light years ahead of most other communities. It is a true information superhighway that will exponentially improve the quality of life for Westchester residents, providing better and more accessible education, healthcare, and government service. It will bring universal access to services and bridge the digital divide. It will also lay the groundwork for future economic growth, much the same as the post roads did in the eighteenth century and the railroads did in the nineteenth century" (Optimum Lightpath, 2006). In 1999, then Vice President Al Gore cited Westchester as the nation's first "Access America Community" for its pioneering work in developing this electronic network.

Critical Role of the Internet

With the telecommunications foundation—the Westchester Telecom Network—in place and the concomitant increase in the speed of Internet connections that became available in residents' homes, the next critical step was to leverage the Internet.

One of the reasons that the county government had been a "best kept secret" was that there had been no effective way to communicate with the majority of its residents. While the county is big, from a media viewpoint is only one small part of a 25 million person media market. The newspaper with the largest circulation is the *New York Times*, which provides little coverage of county government. The major news radio stations are Manhattan-based.

The major broadcast television news also comes out of Manhattan. While these outlets have Westchester bureaus, very little of their coverage is devoted to Westchester County Government. Thus, the Internet had to become the major way for the county executive and government to communicate with Westchester residents.

Since there were only a few Web pages before 1998, a major design and content infusion was necessary. The Web site itself was designed in-house by a small team of graphic design and software professionals. This effort also started a long standing cooperative effort between the Department of Information Technology and the Public Communications (i.e., press) Office of the County Executive. Spano and Jacknis were frequently and intimately involved in the Web design process. However, they both knew that just redesigning the site and increasing its value would be to no avail if no one went there.

So, in 1998, the county began a year-long county-wide campaign promoting the Web site. The county logo was changed to a stylized version of the domain name—Westchestergov. com. The background wall paper for the county executive's press conferences was layered with the new logo. Each county bus and other vehicle was painted with the new logo. Signs on entrances to the county and its facilities had the logo. Business cards were replaced to include the logo. Every press release had a link to the Web site. Any and every way that the county could think of marketing the Web site was used. Within the first year, the number of visitors to the site tripled. By this point, a majority of adults in the county use the Web site at least once per year. And more adults use the county's Web site than subscribe to either of the major newspapers in the county.

The use of the Web as a foundation for applications has extended to not just public facing Web pages, but those that are used by county employees to provide public services and those that are used by other government or non-profit agencies to provide service.

The Web thus has evolved into being used for a variety of purposes:

1. **The Web allows the county to *educate people*.** In addition to the local news and the normal business of government, there are now specialized sites devoted to helping people understand what they can do about water quality. Another site provides focused information about health for women of various ages. The County Archives has found that its Virtual Archives enables the public to see and read some of the most important historical documents, without having to handle and thus possibly destroy the originals. There is a library of video Web casts on various subjects.

2. **The Web can *involve and empower people in decision making*.** The county's Web site enables residents to write to the county executive and other officials. A visitor can ask the county to send an electronic message (both e-mail and fax) to relevant public officials. This has been used in attempting to bring down the cost of Medicaid, bring the Empire Games to Westchester, and to reduce the application of the Alternative Minimum Tax on the middle class here. The county executive's presentation of the annual budget and the subsequent press conference is Web cast live, with encouragement of subsequent comments on the proposal.

3. **The Web can be used to *communicate quickly and efficiently with many people*.** The county uses the Web site to encourage people to sign up for emergency notifications via a variety of media, but it also replaces the home page with an emergency

information page whenever the County Emergency Operations Center is activated for a major event. This is much more efficient than other means, such as outbound telephone calls or even e-mail.

4.   **The Web can *create efficient and fair markets*.** Although apparently forgotten in recent times, one of the long standing functions of government has been the role of umpire in the free marketplace. It can help to ensure that all players in markets operate with the maximum information that traditional economic theory presupposes. For example, Westchester's Web site has long offered comparisons of gasoline prices and home heating oil prices. Similarly, in an attempt to break open a stranglehold by a small number of waste haulers (some associated with organized crime), the Web site offers an application that encourages more waste haulers into the market and shows evaluations of the reliability of the haulers.

5.   **The Web can *spur economic development*.** Indeed, the Web brings a new dimension to local economic development and wealth creation. In addition to the role that technology has played in spurring economic growth (described elsewhere in this study), there are a number of Web applications that are intended to help. These include an extensive Web site for our office for economic development, a joint effort with a real estate information service that allows prospective commercial tenants to search a data base of available office space, and a site devoted to providing all the information that potential film producers want.

The Web site has even featured the county's global trade initiatives. For example, during trade missions to China, we would daily post a summary (including pictures and sound) of the activities during the day. The report on the Web of our first mission to China in 1998 won a National Association of Counties (NACo) award.

6.   **The Web can help *protect people*.** In addition to notification during emergencies, the county Web site has featured information on such subjects as how to protect children from Internet predators and how to evacuate if an incident occurred at the nuclear power plants in the county.

Internally, Web-based applications have been used in many ways to improve the management of public safety resources. The county has developed a Web-based application to automate the Emergency Operations Center. This can be used both within the EOC room itself as well as by outside agencies. In conjunction with this application, there is an expert system to help ensure that all relevant factors are addressed in an emergency, suggest actions, and explain why certain actions are being recommended. (September 11th taught us that experts can become unavailable and a crisis makes anyone forget things.) To coordinate field care by tracking individuals in a chemical, biological, or nuclear incident, there is a Web-based reception center and tracking system that can be accessed securely over the Internet.

7.   **More generally, the Web helps us *run a more efficient government*.** The paperwork, that the county executive demanded be eliminated, has been replaced by intranet-based applications.

Externally, the county has "Web-enabled" government processes for residents and businesses. This includes filing complaints about consumer "rip-offs" or reporting standing water or reporting an odor from the sewer system. These are usually Web applications, in which the public submits its information to a database, which is immediately presented to staff to handle—a two-sided application. In the case of the odor complaints, this also is integrated with the GIS system.

8.   **The Web can be used to *coordinate public and non-profit agencies.*** With its many such agencies, Westchester is an ideal location to use the Web to provide the integration that is necessary in face of the official separation. In this way, the Web enables the county government to be a virtual back office for the many municipal and other agencies, while they still retain local control over policy.

This has been used in the creation of a criminal justice data warehouse that combines information from several county government databases as well as a Westchester Telecom-based federated database of arrests (including mug shots and fingerprints) by the many local police departments. Because of the breadth and depth of information, its search capabilities and its availability over a secure Web site, it has become the information source of choice by investigators from the state police down to small village police forces.

Similarly, a secure Web site is used by dozens of regional hospital emergency rooms to communicate any special situations or the diversion of certain types of cases because they have run out of capacity. This is automatically linked into the system used by the county's Fire/EMS Dispatch Center, so they know what to tell ambulances. This is also used in conjunction with the county-developed Community Health Electronic Surveillance System (CHESS), a highly-sophisticated computerized early warning surveillance system that reveals unusual levels or patterns of disease. CHESS is used daily in 100% of county hospitals to collect, track, statistically analyze, and share data with the New York State Department of Health.

The county GIS, offered over the Web site, has become a shared planning tool by the many municipal planning agencies around the county and even at the state and federal level. Westchester was the first county in the country to be part of the Federal Geospatial-One Stop Web portal.

The county developed a Web-based case management framework for use in social and related services that supports workflow, image capture and organization, and multiple cooperative users. This one software foundation has applications in many areas and is used by internal employees, but is also used by non-profit agencies supplying many of the services. In that sense, these Web applications have provided technology to these agencies that they would not otherwise be able to have, while ensuring the proper sharing of information between them and the county.

The Web site even enables residents to coordinate among themselves. There is a "Treasure Hunt" page that encourages the exchange of reusable items, instead of filling up landfills. The "Westchester Access" Web site is specifically devoted to encouraging local businesses (and the county) to supply surplus personal computers to needy community groups, thus helping to overcome the digital divide.

The county has also experimented with providing intelligent and individualized Web services through the application of expert system technology. In 2001, the county began an effort to build an online "community help desk" which codified the county's knowledge on the topics of "elder abuse" and "youth at risk". This site conducted a conversation with the user, branching as appropriate and ending up making recommendations and references for additional services (if the user wished to provide a name and other contact information). The initiative was nominated for a national e-government award for its innovative combination of the Web, expert system technology, and integrated back-end systems to deliver personalized services. The anonymity of the Internet encouraged more people to use the community help desk to help others—in six months, the site received over 11,000 visits.

User needs are regularly considered due to the online comments/questions form created by IT staff. Visitors who submit comments or inquiries subsequently receive replies from either the county-wide or department Webmaster. Webmasters are receptive to user feedback and often make changes to the site based on the e-mails received. In a conscious effort to overcome linguistic barriers to delivering information, the county translates its most important pages into Spanish for the growing local Hispanic population. A smaller number of pages have also been translated into Chinese.

Jacknis has also noted that, "we've gone beyond the Web. [For example,] We have voice recognition, so you can get on your telephone, call up our computers and talk to a computer to find out where the cheapest gasoline price is in your neighborhood" (Jones, 2005).

Although commonly referred to as e-government, Jacknis refers to Westchester's i-government approach. The four I's are:

- **Integrated:** Enterprise-wide view, rather than department view, offered to the public.
- **Interactive:** See it on the Web; do it on the Web; make it interesting and fun.
- **Intelligent:** Make it smart, especially by codifying and using expert knowledge (and expert systems software).
- **Individualized:** Replace "too much information" with, mostly, what you want to see, like a conversation with a computerized concierge.

Technology's Role in Economic Development

Given County Executive Spano's recent background in e-commerce and Jacknis's years of international experience in the software industry, they were especially aware of the global forces changing and more closely interconnecting the economy—even the Westchester economy. As a result, from his first day on the job, the CIO's responsibility has included nurturing the county's economy and especially the prospects of its IT companies. This has meant that, in Westchester, technology has played a new and critical role in economic development. We have already noted the impact of the Westchester Telecom Network and the use of the Web in economic development activities. But the role of technology and the CIO goes beyond that.

As Jeremy Rifkin (2004) points out in his exploration of network commerce in a global economy (*The European Dream*),

"Software computers, the digitalization of media, the Internet, and mobile and wireless communications have, in less than two decades, connected the central nervous system of nearly 20 percent of the human race, at the speed of light, twenty-four hours a day, seven days a week. Today, one is instantaneously connected, via the World Wide Web, to literally a billion or more people, and able to communicate directly with any one of them." (p. 182)

The new CIO wanted to take full advantage of the speed and productive potential made possible by the software, communications, and telecom revolutions. Jacknis understood that if he did not adapt the county's technology to a new global economic system where competition is stiff and failure often hinges on subtle variations in the quality of goods and services, the economic base of the county would quickly become outmoded.

Networks operate on the principle that by optimizing the benefits of the other parties and the group as a whole, one's own self interest will be maximized in the process. This has played a role in the concept of "co-opetition" (cooperation among competing companies) that were developed and applied in Silicon Valley. In a network, parties effectively become a single entity engaged in a common task for a period of time. This is especially important to smaller and mid-sized companies who are without the global resources of such other Westchester corporations as IBM, Pepsi, and MasterCard.

An initial implementation of this idea by Spano and Jacknis in 2000 was the formation of a Westchester Information Technology Cluster (WITC). It was intended to showcase and harness the collective expertise of small to mid-size technology companies in the county. To bolster its marketing clout and presence, this alliance of about 150 high-tech companies was intended to offer itself as a "virtual corporation". Clearly the Westchester Telecom Network would make possible the virtual work groups that this implied.

Jacknis often likened the WITC to an agricultural marketing cooperative in which a number of companies operate independently, are financially independent, but present themselves as a unified company in terms of marketing and other ways.

Unfortunately, the WITC as a group eventually dissolved as a split occurred between those companies who were product and growth oriented on the one hand and those who were content to provide local basic technology consulting services. The county has nonetheless continued to provide support to the former group.

More generally, Spano and Jacknis understood that many small to mid-sized local companies were filled with people who had excellent technical skills and were doing creative work, but who did not have the expertise or heft to market themselves globally. Thus, the county government took on the role of promoting these companies through the use of technology. Using the Internet and the Westchester Telecom Network's global communications capabilities, the county would promote the "Westchester brand" and help open doors for these companies.

Given the fact that global economy is now so tightly integrated, Westchester has placed particular emphasis on helping local companies with global trade. The county government wants to help ensure that these companies get their fair share of the increase in that trade. This has led to trade missions to China and to various locations in Europe. All such efforts have significantly depended upon the use of technology, including hosting many international videoconferences intended to find suitable business partners for local companies. These videoconferences have been held with companies in Chinese cities, in Chile, in Germany, in Italy, and elsewhere. The county has also made a standing offer to any small to mid-size business to use its international videoconferencing capabilities for free. (It has also set up Internet-based communications so that foreign and local companies can work together.)

Current Challenges Facing the Organization

Westchester County is proud of its turnaround in IT and its accomplishments. But it is not without challenges. Some of these challenges arise from its successes, which introduce new problems and opportunities, and others arise from the nature of government and the inherent difficulty of sustaining innovation.

Untangling Government Complexity

As noted, the county's use of its Web site has been extensive and successful. However, despite past attempts to provide users with an individualized and integrated view of the county government—the goals of i-government—the very success of the Web site has perhaps made it more likely that residents will feel overwhelmed. Whereas once they knew too little about the county government, perhaps now they are presented with too much.

Too much of government is still organized along department lines, even when an individual's problems cut across those departments. Thus one continuing challenge is to achieve integration, both technically and organizationally, so that the government really looks and operates like a seamless entity to the residents of the county.

Partly, this will occur as the approach to IT service delivery continues to mature, especially the network-based services architecture. Partly, this will occur as a result of a redesign of the county's public Web site. The site's new information architecture reflects a deeper county-wide layer of services and information, perhaps making it unnecessary to ever see a departmental Web site. The Web site also faces the challenge of continuing to be an interesting place to visit. Thus, a revised Web site will take advantage of the pervasiveness of high-speed Internet connections among residents by delivering richer content, both graphics and video.

The county also needs to go beyond its success with the Web by offering services in different media. We have started with offering the gas and oil price application over telephones, through the use of Voice XML and speech recognition. We will continue to expand this capability to such areas as the GIS—tell us an address and the system will tell you where to find what you want within whatever distance you want.

Increased Security

The importance of the Web and the Internet in general has not gone unnoticed by those who would attempt to harm the county's systems for "fun or profit". Thus a continuing challenge is to find better ways to ensure the security of these systems. To significantly upgrade the county's defenses in the face of continued threats to its technology infrastructure (and that of its related agencies in the state and federal government), there will need to be defense in depth against external attacks. This means essentially that every computer must have its own form of firewall. It also requires of automated reviews of any computer on the network to ensure compliance with anti-virus updates, operating system upgrades, and so forth—and automatic quarantine if that review fails or if the computer acts in an unfriendly way.

In addition, with identity fraud and theft, the county will need to institute a new means of authenticating and determining access by users to county systems that goes beyond the time-worn user ID and password approach. This will have to include investments in biometrics and other software.

Going Beyond Databases and "Applications"

Another success leads to new opportunities. In particular, DoIT has now "automated" al-most every operation of county government. In so doing, every day, the county builds up an enormous amount of data. Although this has clearly helped county employees to be more productive and deliver services more effectively, they are still operating in an "in basket, out basket" mode. In other words, once they complete a transaction, it is forgotten.

The challenge now is to use all of this data that has and is continuing to be collected—to use it to determine how to improve. In particular, DoIT is leading an initiative to analyze the data, with advanced statistical techniques, so that departments will learn which programs are most effective for which individuals or problems.

This will necessarily lead to changes in the way they do some things and even abandoning some past patterns. The results of these analyses will need to be incorporated, frequently using expert systems technology, into the application software that is used in day-to-day operations.

This effort also will be tied into the budgeting and financial system so that monetary invest-ments are better related to outcomes that mean something to our citizens.

Sustaining Innovation

Perhaps the most difficult challenge is sustaining an environment of innovation. Government, in general, is risk averse. Public officials can be criticized for almost any event happening on their "watch" and usually are. They are even criticized for their successes. County Execu-tive Spano has always had a willingness to support many innovations (within his strategic vision), rather than the traditional approach of focusing on a couple of carefully controlled signature "initiatives". For many years, this was a rather clever way around the standard game of criticism. There were so many things going on and so many small (but related) successes, that criticism of the many fewer failures was not an effective strategy for opponents.

However, this strategy is hard to sustain for many terms. Even though he was re-elected to a third term in November 2005 with an 18-point margin, carrying along other winners of his party, including a majority on the Board of Legislators, the opposition has built one decision at a time. Any administration faces the equivalent of the barnacles which slow down a ship that has spent many years in the water. In politics, you just naturally pick up more enemies or at least more people who will question and attempt to hinder your decisions and programs.

Within DoIT, sustaining innovation is also a problem. Whereas once the technology staff was so reviled it was outsourced, it is now so successful that the workload can be overwhelming—even with increases in IT staff that the county has budgeted. In a successful IT organization, demand always outstrips available resources. In a very successful IT organization, demand vastly outstrips available resources, but the staff always tries to meet the demand. The resulting exhaustion can lead to reduced creativity and sometimes forgetting the principles and approach that led to success. With all that said, Westchester's technology is positively in a better place than it was in 1997, as are its technologists.

References

Berger, J. (1997, November). The 1997 elections: Westchester; Democrat elected county executive. *The New York Times.*

Cochran, S. S., & Green, F. E. (1982). The history of Westchester: The first 300 years. *History of Westchester.* Retrieved February 13, 2006, from http://www.westchestergov.com/history/

Fruth, D. (2000). Economic and institutional constraints on the privatization of government information technology services. *Harvard Journal of Law & Technology, 13*(3), 1-3. Retrieved February 1, 2006, from http://jolt.law.harvard.edu/articles/pdf/13HarvJLTech521.pdf

Jones, J. (2005, March). Top 25 doers, dreamers and drivers. *Government Technology's Public CIO.* Retrieved February 4, 2006, from http://www.public-cio.com/newsStory.php?id=2005.03.07-93301

National Association of Counties. (2006). *The history of county government* (pp. 9-10). Retrieved February 17, 2006, from http://www.naco.org

Optimum Lightpath. (2006, July 21). *Westchester Telecom Case study.* Retrieved February 2, 2006, from http://www.optimumlightpath.com/

Rifkin, J. (2004). *The European dream.* New York: Tarcher/Penguin.

Westchester County Board of Legislators. (2006). *Westchester county charter.* Retrieved February 18, 2006, from http://www.westchesterlegislators.com/History/countycharter.pdf

Authors' Biographies

Norman J. Jacknis was appointed Westchester County's first Chief Information Officer in January 1998. Dr. Jacknis also plays a key advisory role and works closely with the county executive and the Board of Legislators. As the County's IT Commissioner, he directs all of the county government's technology efforts. In addition, Dr. Jacknis serves as one of the few local government CIO's on the New York State CIO Council, where he is also co-chair of the Technology Committee that sets the standards and architecture for the state. He represents the County Executives of America on technology issues at the federal level and is a member of the national Partnership for Intergovernmental Innovation. He received his Doctorate, Master's and Bachelor's degrees from Princeton University. Before taking this position, Dr. Jacknis held a variety of executive positions in the computer software industry.

Scott Erik Fernqvist is the Special Assistant to the Chief Information Officer of Westchester County, and works on a variety of public policy issues and projects in support of the county's Department of Information Technology. Having lived in Sweden and worked for several years in the field of cross-cultural exchange, Mr. Fernqvist is also able to assist the county on global trade initiatives across much of Europe and Asia. Mr. Fernqvist received his BA in European studies and fine arts from New York University and is currently working toward an MS degree in international management from Manhattanville College.

Chapter III

Repairing the Broken Information Technology Department

Glenn Trommels, City of Rockford, Illinois, USA

Executive Summary

After 13 years of IT experience in private enterprise, taking over the City of Rockford's IT Department proved to be a shocking experience. The state of the city's IT organization, processes, technology, network security practices, customer service practices, and organizational relationships were all examples of industry "worst practices". This case study documents the initial state of the IT Department as the author found it and the steps taken to turn it into a responsive, value-adding organization. The study examines all aspects of the process including:

- *Communication and relationship building with other city departments;*
- *Taking ownership and responsibility for IT strategy and decision making;*
- *Centralizing IT purchases;*
- *Establishing hardware and software standards;*
- *Establishing a centralized help desk;*
- *Technology assessment and improvements; and*
- *IT process improvements.*

Background

Located in northern Illinois, roughly 90 miles west of Chicago, the City of Rockford is Illinois' third largest city with approximately 150,000 residents. Like many industrialized cities, Rockford's industry took a major hit following World War II. Many core industries, including furniture and agricultural equipment manufacturing, were nearly extinct by the 1960s, while others, including machine tool and fastener manufacturing, are a fraction of the size that they once were (2005). By mid-1983, the city's unemployment rate hit record levels of 25%. Today, Rockford suffers from one of the highest crime rates in the state and the local school district's truancy rate is four times the state's average. To say the least, our community has some challenges to contend with.

The municipality has about 1,200 employees and is comprised of 10 departments: Police, Fire, Public Works, Community Development, Human Services, Building Department, Legal Department, Finance, Personnel, and the Mayor's Office. Like many municipalities, the city is funded by property taxes, sales tax, a variety of "use" taxes, along with state and federal funding and grants. Compared to other Illinois municipalities of similar size, Rockford's $202 million dollar annual budget is only 69% of the City of Aurora's (2005) $290 million dollar budget, and is a meager 60% of City of Naperville's (2005) $332 million dollar budget. In short, Rockford does not have a lot of financial resources, and maintaining basic capital equipment and core services has been difficult.

Setting the Stage

The City of Rockford municipality has traditionally not been on the cutting edge of management practices, business process review, or technology adoption. Perhaps this is the result of the "status quo" attitude of previous administrations which seemed to take little interest in wringing any efficiency out of the organization. This attitude seemed pervasive throughout the top levels of the organization.

Not surprisingly, the city's IT leadership and staff suffered from the same lethargic attitude when supposedly providing technical leadership and service to its customers. Coming from 13 years in private industry IT, I was shocked to note the complete dependence on paper-bound process, lack of motivation to become more efficient, total absence of IT standards, and no business process automation efforts in many facets of the city's operation.

Illustrative of the organizations attitude was a comment made to me by one of the city's department heads when I was explaining the need to upgrade the archaic PC hardware for one of the few GIS technicians at the city. "We've never had a discussion related to the efficiency of our employees", the department head declared. I was absolutely dumbfounded and discouraged by this comment. Was employee efficiency something that really needed to be debated? I could certainly understand if new hardware was not a fiscal priority, but that was not the argument. Not surprisingly, our GIS technicians continued to struggle with inadequate tools.

Not uncommon to other public and private organizations, the city's IT manager position reports to the finance director. In the City of Rockford, the Finance Department was the first to use computers to keep track of revenues and expenses. Over the years, however, PCs began to creep into the organization, beyond the scope of the Finance Department. Surprisingly, the city's IT Department was seemingly able to decide what it wanted, and what it did not want to support and maintain. How the other city departments allowed this to happen is still a mystery to me.

To be fair, there are outstanding employees at the city. Many are very dedicated to public service, and they care about the quality of their work. However, the organizational attitude just did not give these hard working employees the support they needed to truly excel at their jobs. Because of the status quo organizational mindset and the lack of accountability of the previous IT manager, I found the IT organization to be in shambles: a case study of many management and technological "worst practices". The following examples illustrate the IT Department crisis I discovered in the first few months after I took the helm of the struggling IT organization.

Are We Supposed To Work All Day?

In terms of work ethic, most IT department members felt it completely appropriate to take multiple breaks, play computer games at length, surf the Web on non-work related sites, and engage in prolonged discussions not related to work. I was getting nowhere near an honest day out of most department staffers. Fortunately, I had several individuals that managed to stay focused on the job and who actually worked hard.

The worst case of this lackadaisical attitude surfaced when our financial system crashed one day. The staffer most knowledgeable about the system made no effort to diagnose or debug the problem. Instead, he placed a call to the software vendor and continued to play his game of FreeCell. Meanwhile, all of the financial system customers were sitting idle. After kindly asking the game-playing staffer to conduct his own investigation, the problem turned out to be a simple service that had stopped running on the server. The problem was fixed in minutes, instead of the hour or two it would have taken had he waited for the vendor to reply.

Obviously, the lack of urgency by IT staffers was, at best, not keeping other city employees productive. And, at worst, it was preventing our customers from being able to work at all.

We Do Not Like Passwords!

I found the desktop security "policy" to be an IT manager's nightmare. Network user names matched passwords, which matched the computer workstation names, which were clearly labeled on the front of each workstation! Further, nobody was given the ability to change their own password. I thought I had heard it all, until I learned that the IT Department actually instructed employees *never* to log off their computers!

Aside from the obvious security flaws of this "policy", some other interesting problems arose. For example, as is common, some employees have a business need to float between several computers. Because user names were, in essence, tied to computers and not people, employees had a unique e-mail address for each workstation they had a need to log on to. Technology had become a barrier to efficiency.

When I queried the so-called network administrator about the unusual security practices in place, I was informed that passwords made his job more difficult. More disturbing is that our third-party financial auditors had uncovered and documented this poor practice many times during the course of their yearly audits. For some unknown reason, the IT manager at the time never saw a need to change this practice.

Do You Have A Home Computer? Great, You're Our IT Guy!

Municipalities are interesting organizations. I have learned through discussions with my peers at other municipalities that we like to act like conglomerates: completely separate organizations under a single holding company we refer to as the municipality. To a certain extent this is true. For example, the Fire Department has a completely different business model than the Community Development Department. However, there are significant problems with this stovepipe mentality, especially in municipalities our size.

The "we do it all" philosophy seems to be especially pervasive in public safety departments. Being new to municipal work, I was surprised to learn that the Police Department (PD) had a completely separate IT Division. How did they staff this division? The criteria seemed to be if an officer had a home computer and had any PC-related knowledge, then he was the right one for the job. No formal IT training. No authority to set and enforce policy. No oversight responsibility. No standards. The result? An IT nightmare.

I discovered that sworn and non-sworn PD personnel installed anything they wanted on city-owned computers. In one example, an officer could not do his job because his computer would not function properly. We discovered that he had installed his personal "Juke Box Maker" on his work PC. I had it uninstalled, and his computer was functional again. Just a week later, we received another loud complaint from the same officer, claiming problems similar to the week before. You guessed it—the "Juke Box Maker" had been reinstalled on the PC.

IT security was a disaster at the PD. I discovered multiple unprotected dial-up connections to the Internet. Worse, I found wireless access points on the network which were happily broadcasting their availability to anyone within range of the PD's downtown location.

Due to lack of IT oversight, multiple copies of the same or similar personal databases abounded at the PD. I discovered nearly 600 databases on the PD's file server. Many, simply copies of the same database propagated from one user to another. To keep all these in sync, multiple users just keyed in the same information into their copy of the database. The duplication of effort was enormous.

I found the relationship between the PD and the IT Department to be extremely strained. The relationship was reduced to nothing more than posturing, with little work being accomplished. Because of this situation, an outside consultant was hired at the PD to act as a pseudo IT staff person. And, because the consultant knew more than the PC-hobbyist officer, he began to take over core IT resources at the PD, rebooting servers, and changing administrative passwords with no notification. Clearly, a situation out of control.

Who's On First?

The classic Abbott and Costello routine came to mind when I found out how the IT Department handled requests for service. There was no process in place, no logging of requests, no tracking, no dispositions, no customer feedback, no metrics, nothing. How, then, did IT customers request service? They just called their favorite IT staffer. No answer? They called the next, then the next, until someone picked up their phone. Failing that "process", customers were forced to walk to the IT Department to find someone who could help them. If the requestor did happen to catch an IT staffer at their desk but forgot to relay some important information in the original request, the customer was forced to repeat the same process. Many times, this would result in a different IT staffer working on the same problem.

Because of the total lack of request tracking, the IT Department had no idea where the bulk of their requests were coming from, what types of problems they responded to most often, or where they were spending their time. From the customer's perspective, their requests just fell into a black hole. Understandably, customer satisfaction was extremely low, and the IT Department was the bane of the city.

Why Rush? It All Pays The Same.

As a municipality, we have multiple locations spread throughout the city. Customers at remote locations were the most poorly served since they did not have the benefit of simply walking over to the IT Department to report a problem. When the IT Department did provide service to remote customers, they hopped in the IT van and made a run to the remote location. The problem may have needed desk-side service, but most times it did not. IT staffers routinely burned 40 minutes of travel time to spend 10 minutes on a resolution. I was informed that there was no way to avoid the travel time.

When it was time to roll out a batch of new PCs or laptops to any department, the inefficiency was unbelievable. The pinnacle of inefficiency was exemplified by a rollout of roughly 60 laptops. A single IT staffer "plugged and chugged" CDs into each and every laptop to manually configure each one. When I asked why they had not implemented an imaging process to replicate the configuration quickly and easily, I was told that it was not possible. All of this wasted time was a disservice to our customers who were forced to wait inordinate amounts of time to have their requests fulfilled.

We Do Not Plan For Anything Going Wrong.

In terms of technology, "don't change anything" seems to have been the mantra by which the IT Department worked. I found critical, back-end hardware, which was 10 years old, had no replacement parts available on the market, and disk redundancy slowly being removed in favor of extra capacity. The most amazing part of this was that neither my predecessor nor the staff in charge of administering this hardware ever considered a replacement. Many "servers" were re-deployed PCs with no disk or power redundancy. Tape backups were being done, but the tapes were simply stacked on top of the servers. Where did I find all the servers and backup tapes? In a community room that was home to various printers, stacks of paper reports, and coffee supplies. There was a keyed lock on the community room door but because of the printers, foot traffic is heavy and the door is mostly left open. Other "attributes" of the server room included an exterior window and a water-based fire suppression system. Our critical servers and server room were not exactly designed for disaster prevention or recovery.

Is The System Down?

Given the decaying infrastructure and lack of disaster prevention, it is not surprising that many services stopped functioning. It seems that the IT Department was comfortable being in fire-fighting, reactive mode rather than avoiding problems by pro-active management. The IT staffers had no idea of pending trouble in the server room, or if a service had stopped completely. It was left up to our customers to call to report a critical services outage. The IT Department was flying blind. Recall the "process" of reporting problems from earlier? When a critical service did fail, the result was usually a mix of customers and IT staffers standing in the "community room" wondering what went wrong.

Case Description

Given all of the "worst practices" implemented at the time, it is difficult to imagine a worse situation. So many problems, such poor customer service, such a crumbling infrastructure. Most disturbing is that most of the IT staff at the time thought that everything was running just fine. Where to start?

Admittedly, I am not the best IT manager. There are many others in my profession whom I look up to. What follows is a simple, common sense approach to repairing a faltering IT organization. There are no "silver bullets" in the IT world, or at least I have not found any in my 17 years of IT experience. The following case study is no exception.

The Starting Point: Building a Team

After observing the IT staff in action for several weeks, I issued all of them a questionnaire regarding their responsibilities: what was good about the department and what they would change if they could. The results were very wide ranging, telling, and somewhat predictable.

For those who had some responsibility for the current business and technological infrastructure, the answers leaned toward "everything is fine" and "nothing needs to be changed". At the other end of the spectrum were those who had some current skill sets and could see the poor service our customers were receiving. "Start from scratch and retool everything" was more their response. Based on what I had already observed, I was much more inclined to do exactly that.

As part of the observation and interview process, I also examined how the department worked as a team. I quickly discovered that the department was simply a collection of individuals, a group, and not a team. There was little communication among the members, and they typically interfered with others in the IT Department unintentionally. A team mentality is critically important to an IT organization. Bob Lewis (1999) observed,

"What's the difference between a group and a team? In a team, we're all smarter than any of us are. In a group, we're all stupider. Groups do dumb things. Groups turn into mobs and do ugly, dangerous things." (p. 306)

Bob Nelson and Peter Economy (1996) also noted, "Teams offer an easy way to tap the knowledge and resources of all employees—not just supervisors and managers—to solve an organization's problems" (p. 189). There had been some personality conflicts in the past within the department so I focused on simple communication strategies to get the department members to at least start talking with one another.

Having bi-monthly department meetings opened up dialog between all members of the department. I put an agenda together that gave everyone an opportunity to speak about tasks and projects they were working on. At first, the meetings were a series of reports. As we continued to meet, I asked prompting questions and encouraged comment. It took a while before others joined in to offer suggestions and guidance. Once the staff started to benefit from the meetings, they actually started to ask each other questions outside of the meetings.

There were, and continue to be, certain personalities that just do not work well together. I do not force the issue but demand that they treat each other with respect and act professionally at all times. To further build on the notion of "team", I initiated a team interview process for new hires in the IT Department. I am not at all interested in the "Lone Star" IT hero. Rather, I look for someone who has solid IT experience, has demonstrated an aptitude to learn, and above all, can work effectively as a team member.

Team interviews have a few key benefits. They allow the current IT staff to be part of the decision making process, greatly enhancing buy-in of the new hire. They have an opportunity to decide if the person will work well as part of the team, further cementing the team spirit. Finally, the team can ask more technical questions of the candidate, further evaluating the person's skill set.

On more than one occasion, I have been convinced to hire the candidate that was not necessarily my top pick. While I have only hired a handful of employees since I have been with the city, I have not yet been disappointed. I was pleasantly surprised after the first team interview when my staff thanked me for the opportunity to be part of the process. Team building is an everyday, continual process. I cannot emphasize this enough. It is a job that is never complete.

Marketing: Is It Really For an IT Shop?

You bet. With the customer neglect that had been allowed to occur over the years, the other departments in the city were extremely dissatisfied with the performance of the IT Department. I had a lot of fence mending and relationship building ahead of me. In the first month at the city, my supervisor set up meetings with every department head and welcomed them to bring any of their staff. I was expecting dissatisfied customers but did not expect the thrashing I received! The organization had clearly been ignored by the IT Department. While some department heads exercised more diplomacy than others at these meetings, the message was consistent and clear: IT needed to be more customer-focused.

I was sympathetic but was careful not to over promise, knowing that doing so would amplify the problem. Instead, I offered to meet with each department head or delegate on a regular basis. I let each department decide the frequency of the meetings. Some were weekly and others were ad hoc. The key was communication on a regular basis. Even if the message is not what the customers wanted to hear, it was far better than just ignoring them and their business needs as was done in the past. Mark D. Lutchen (2004) summarized it best when he simply entitled one of his chapters "IT Management is about Relationship Management" in his book, *Managing IT as a Business* (p. 59).

Like team building, relationship building is a continual, ongoing process that never ends. Managing an IT Department is primarily a "people" job, not a technical job as most would suppose. Once the communication channels were opened to other departments, the IT Department became more engaged in the business process of the various departments. That solved some critical problems related to the procurement and purchase of systems we were expected to support. In the old model, departments made technology purchasing decisions without any input or guidance from IT. When that happens, there is no chance of implementing standards or common technology platforms to drive costs down and efficiency and interoperability up.

Standards: The Cornerstone of IT Efficiency

Hardware, software, and process standards are absolutely critical for an IT shop to control costs and to reap any kind of operating efficiency. Does this mean we should hold by our standards no matter what? No. Hardware and software standards provide a framework for technology purchasing decisions but our real mission is to support the business needs of the organization. If a new piece of hardware or software comes along that greatly enhances the ability of a department to do its job, and there are no other solutions that fit neatly within the framework, then we need to find a way to support it. Having said that, though, most times there are functionally equivalent alternatives in the marketplace, and one of them will fit your framework.

Why is a standard technology platform so important in keeping costs down? One very important reason is skill sets. The more varied the technology is in an organization, the more skills need to be inventoried on staff, and the more training needs to be conducted. And do not forget you need a backup plan for when those staff with unique skills go on vacation or are out sick. Another staff person needs those skills or you need an outsourced method of providing backup. Either way, it can add up dollars fast without adding much value to the organization.

Another way a standard technology platform can drive down costs is by avoiding "glue" technologies. For example, some IT shops base their core network operating system on Novell Netware, some Microsoft Windows, and others a Linux distribution. On their own, any of these can perform the functions needed to provide core file, print, and authentication services. Start to mix them in an IT environment, however, and you have to add and support yet another layer to allow these systems to communicate, or "glue" with each other. It is a non-value added proposition.

When I finally took over IT support responsibilities for the PD, I migrated their core network operating system from Novell to Windows. Not because Windows is a superior product, but because my staff had formal training in supporting Windows and none in supporting Netware. Yes, the decision ruffled some feathers at the PD, but it began the consolidation of platforms and skill sets I needed to inventory.

Remember the poor IT staffer who had to "plug and chug" CDs to configure those 60 laptops? Here is where standards can pay big dividends: the desktop, or laptop, as the case may be. Imaging (a.k.a. ghosting) is a mature technology that can cut hours of configuration time to minutes. Purchasing computers from different manufacturers based on the "deal of the month" may save money on the acquisition cost, but it is more than eaten up by the variability it introduces and the resulting costs associated with set up and configuration. The more variability in hardware, the more images need to be built and maintained and the higher the support cost go. Again, it is a lot of non-value added work.

Standards can be applied to many facets of an IT technology platform: servers, PCs, backup systems, GIS systems, databases, network hardware, network operating systems, reporting tools. The list goes on and on. The critical part of standards is to stick with them unless there is an absolute business need to do something different. There is always a need to stay current with new technology, but those decisions should not be made on a whim. Changing to something new just for the novelty of it is bad because "different" translates directly into dollars.

Process, Measurement, and Metrics

As part of enhancing customer service, we had to get a handle on all of the service requests that were flowing into the IT Department. We obviously had to build or buy a solution to manage and track the requests. Given the surrounding chaos, we chose to quickly purchase a commercial off-the-shelf (COTS) application that we could use for this purpose. As an added bonus, the application we chose could also be used for IT inventory management.

When we implemented this, we set up a help desk phone number and e-mail address. We also created labels with the help desk contact information so we could put this information on each computer. For the first time in the city's history, customers had a single point of contact to request service from the IT Department. No more did our customers have to do the "round robin", calling each IT staffer to get service.

From the IT side, we could track multiple requests for the same issue and manage request for service by priority instead of FIFO (first in first out). After we set up this simple system, my most gratifying moment came when I called back on a service request. The customer was so amazed that someone responded to her request that she stuttered and stammered just to offer her thanks. Another benefit realized from the help desk application was the reporting that could be performed on all requests. We have been able to demonstrate the need to replace certain hardware because we now had the statistics to back up our assertions.

In an effort to reduce our enormous "shoe leather" cost in servicing requests at remote locations, we adopted a remote control application so we could view, diagnose, and resolve problems without having to leave the office. Modern remote control applications are very feature rich, giving IT staffers a range of diagnostic tools. We could now respond to service requests at all locations with the same level of promptness.

Another simple step we took to enhance customer service was to pro-actively monitor our critical hardware and services. We implemented a very cost effective (less than $1,000) software tool to send us e-mail notifications when problems began to arise or when a server crashed. We now could react to problems before our customers began calling, or we could resolve pending problems before they interrupted service—another "first" for the IT Department.

This tool also tracked downtime metrics so we had another metric for helping us steer our technology upgrades and investments.

Simple, inexpensive solutions can make a huge difference. Over the past several years, under tight financial constraints, we have made incremental updates to the core IT infrastructure—putting our dollars where we felt we could either improve customer service, improve our efficiency, or both.

Current Challenges Facing the Organization

I do not want to leave the impression that we are the shining star of municipal IT. Far from it. The City of Rockford's IT Department still faces a number of significant issues. The most significant issue is a lack of funding for IT initiatives. In a city that has one of the highest crime rates in the state, arguing for technology improvements to foster operation efficiency pales in comparison to police officers and squads cars. I do not think this is a unique situation in Rockford. Public safety is much more tangible to Aldermen and constituents than is operational efficiency.

Because of funding issues, replacing aging equipment and applications is taking much longer than it should. We have made some significant changes for the better, and our uptime of systems is far better than what it used to be. Our mid-range goal is to provide "four nines" (99.99%) availability for all of our critical systems. Four-nines availability translates into about 50 minutes of downtime in a year. This is achievable with quality hardware, pro-active monitoring, and defined system administration policies. Five-nines (99.999%) availability is about 5 minutes of downtime a year. This is very difficult to achieve without clustered hardware and "cluster aware" applications. There is emerging technology (Virtual Servers) that may make five-nines availability more cost effective to implement.

IT funding is partially dependant on where the IT Department fits into the organization, and in the City of Rockford, the IT organization has traditionally reported up through the Finance Department. As such, the finance director holds a tight rein on IT spending. Obviously, it is the finance director's mission to watch spending, and he has done a wonderful job of keeping the city on financially sound ground. However, having IT as part of the Finance Department relegates it to a cost center line item, something seen simply as an expense.

Our municipal organization, however, is slowly changing. Our newly-elected mayor views IT as an enabler, not just an expense line item. He sees technology as a tool to be leveraged for better customer service; a tool that can be used to help battle our extremely high crime rate; and a tool to bring greater accountability to the entire municipal organization. Because of this, he has elevated the IT manager position to a director, giving greater visibility and importance to technology as part of our business process.

There have also been some key personnel changes at the department head and city administrator level. The interest in operational efficiency and business process automation is gaining momentum quickly. As a result, IT is being looked at to provide guidance and support for new initiatives. Organizational change is an exciting, challenging process, and the IT Department will need to continue to change and evolve to support the business needs of our organization.

References

City of Aurora, Illinois. (2005). *Annual budget for the fiscal year beginning January 1, 2005*. Retrieved April 29, 2006, from http://www.aurora-il.org/documents/finance/budget_2005.pdf

City of Naperville, Illinois. (2005). *Annual operating budget May 1, 2005 – April 30, 2006*. Retrieved April 29, 2006, from http://www.naperville.il.us/emplibrary/AOB05-06.pdf

City of Rockford, Illinois. (2005). *Rockford history*. Retrieved April 29, 2006, from http://cityofrockford.net/about/index.cfm?id=341

Lewis, B. (1999). *IS survival guide*. Indianapolis, IN: SAMS.

Lutchen, M. D. (2004). *Managing IT as a business: A survival guide for CEOs*. Hoboken, NJ: Wiley & Sons.

Nelson, B., & Economy, P. (1996). *Managing for dummies*. Foster City, CA: IDG Books Worldwide.

Author's Biography

Glenn Trommels *is the Information Technology Director at the City of Rockford, Illinois. He holds both Bachelor's and Master's degrees in technology from Northern Illinois University. He has been managing the Information Technology Department at the City of Rockford since 2002 and oversees the technology needs for all city departments. Mr. Trommels started his career in information technology at the Ingersoll Cutting Tool Company in Rockford, Illinois, where he wrote computer-aided design (CAD) software. He later became the company's Design Automation Manager and eventually became the company's first Information Technology Director, managing both design automation and business systems.*

Chapter IV

Becoming an Enterprise:
Developing an E-Governance Structure in Nevada County, California

Dave Bloch, County of Nevada, California, USA

Executive Summary

This chapter provides a case study of how a rural California county transitioned its tech-nological governance from one centered on the perceived needs of individual departments to one integrating technological needs across the entire enterprise. The chapter details the use of "communities of interest", a way of grouping departments with related missions for broad-based analysis of technology needs and solutions. The chapter describes the process the county used to implement this new strategy. The author hopes that use of this method can help other local governments to avoid obsolescence, unmet needs, or overlapping systems in purchase and implementation of technology systems.

Environment and History

Nevada County, California is comprised of 958 rugged square miles. The county begins at the California/Nevada state line just west of Reno, climbs over the summit of the Sierra Nevada Mountains, and then slowly traverses down to the west ending in the lower Sierra foothills above the Sacramento Valley. The county boasts thousands of acres contained in Tahoe National Forest and other public lands. The population of 97,000 is largely contained in the three small incorporated areas, Grass Valley and Nevada City in the west and Truckee in the east.

Nevada County's modern history really begins with the California Gold Rush. Thousands of miners flocked here in the mid-to-late 1800's. But unlike many other areas of California, some of those miners stayed after the "easy gold" ran out and constructed hard-rock mines running deep underground. One of those mines, the Empire Mine in Grass Valley, retains the record as the most prolific gold mine over its lifetime in the state. Another, the Idaho-Maryland, is currently undergoing preliminary engineering for a hoped-for reopening within the next 10 years.

The engineering innovations developed in Nevada County at that time (including the Pelton Water Wheel, the design of which is still used today) continue into the 21st century. A tiny company called the Grass Valley Group formed in 1958 and grew to become the manufacturer of some of the finest video broadcast production and distribution equipment in the world. Dozens of high-technology companies spun off from GVG in the 1980's, when the company was purchased and moved away (it has since returned).

This legacy of technology has been taken to heart by the government of the County of Nevada. Despite its small population, the county is a recognized leader in technological innovation, with an impressive track record of awards. This reputation would not have been achieved, and its continuation would not be possible, without the user-centric governance structure described in this chapter. The courage it took to attempt and follow through on such radical changes harkens back to those brave Forty-Niners who came here from everywhere to seek their fortune.

The Need

In 1999, the county was facing a technological crisis. Major systems, like general accounting, the telephone system, the computer network, and others were incompatible and obsolete. Original vendors were out of business or no longer supporting the systems, parts were unavailable, trained service providers were non-existent. The highest priority was to head off serious Y2K issues; the lack of vendor support would make that task considerably more difficult.

At that time, Nevada County had used the capital outlay method so common across all levels of government (and, often, in industry as well). Individual departments looked at their needs, contacted vendors, responded to advertising, and made purchasing requests for "System A" or "Server X". The fact that an assessor's office database might be completely incompatible with that of the recorder's office was not a factor in their decision-making process. The county administration saw that a better way of governing technology was needed.

The first step in this process was to move IT out from under the General Services Department (which handled other internal services like buildings, grounds, printing, and the mail room) to full department status. In April 1999, a new County Information Officer with an entrepreneurial IT business background, Stephen T. Monaghan, was hired as department head.

The first major assignment given the new CIO was the creation of a three-year strategic plan. But with Y2K only eight months away, critical needs took priority for the rest of that year. Thanks to diligent work on the part of the staff of the new Information Systems (IS) Department, and to good design of the county's major software systems, Y2K problems were minimized in the county, and Mr. Monaghan began work on the new strategic plan in January 2000. (Note that not having to replace major systems in haste became a factor later on, as the county was able to take the time to develop the new enterprise-based governance described next. Many other government agencies were not so fortunate.)

Coincidentally, the county also hired a new County Administrative Officer (the top administrative official; in other agencies this might be a County Executive Officer) in early 2000. The new CAO was Ted Gaebler, co-author of the well-known book *Reinventing Government.* Mr. Gaebler and other administrative officials saw the need and the opportunity to move IT from its department-by-department focus to one encompassing the entire county government—an enterprise approach.

The Process of Change

The objectives of the new enterprise information technology strategic plan were as follows:

- Define an optimum sequence of events to achieve the enterprise information technology strategic plan.

- Facilitate common understanding and support by customers, staff, and county management of the Information Systems Department future direction and goals.

- Provide a framework to manage and control the county information technology working environment.

- Achieve optimum effectiveness and efficiency of automation technology resources.

With a view towards emphasizing e-government in the coming years, the department did not want to create the plan in a vacuum. In cooperation with the Nevada County Economic Resource Council, citizen advisers were appointed to the new "Nevada County Technology Partnership", a group which would provide an "outside-in" view of the county's technology needs.

CIO Monaghan and his new Administrative Analyst Jim Adams embarked on three months of nation-wide research into innovative IT governance methods being used by other local governments. More than 80 different systems, plans, and methods were looked at until they found a system used in Clark County, Nevada that was based on "communities of interest" (CIO). This process grouped departments with similar needs—for example, the sheriff, courts, and probation—into a single community of interest for the purpose of analyzing their technology requirements and possible solutions. Most departments belonged to more than one COI, so technology discussions were carried across different combinations of departments. The system enabled Clark County to coordinate IT planning across their enterprise.

An important parallel existed between the two jurisdictions. Clark County, home of the City of Las Vegas, was (and is) the fastest growing county in the nation. As such, they were in the process to rapidly upgrade virtually every one of their IT systems and business processes, and had adopted an enterprise model to accomplish this. Nevada County also had the need to replace virtually every major information system, although for reasons of obsolescence rather than growth. After considerable study, correspondence, and conversation with Clark County officials, Nevada County IS elected to use the Clark County model and customize it for its own needs.

The most important issue *not* part of the Clark County model was the funding of major IT infrastructure projects. Tying funding directly to the COI approval process would give the entire governance structure real "teeth". In addition, requiring each major funding request to pass through the structure would be powerful evidence to support the expenditure when the issue came up before the elected County Board of Supervisors for approval. (This has since been proven to be true; *every IT funding request that has passed through this structure has been approved* unanimously *by the Board of Supervisors.*)

One cultural aspect of this model would be critical to its success. It was obvious (in fact, central to the whole plan) that individual departments would no longer have the final say in making major IT purchases; but the Information Systems Department would not control these purchases either. The initial presentation of the proposed new structure to the department heads emphasized, "*You* are responsible for IT from now on." Recommendations and decisions would be made not at the individual department level, nor by IS or the CAO, but by the departments working together through their COIs. Information Systems would be available as a resource and a facilitator, but would not have a major role in selecting systems. That important distinction was put in place at the beginning, and is still a functioning policy at this writing in 2006.

The new model (which will be explained in detail next) was met with some skepticism by the department heads. They were used to the old process of "pitching" their system to what was then the IT division administration, finding the money, and purchasing what they wanted. The new governance plan generated comments like "more bureaucratic process; more committees; it will take longer; big hurdles to overcome". The department heads and their analysts would now have to work in conjunction with their peers.

Two powerful factors contributed to the success in bringing departments into participation in the new program. The first was the collaborative management style of CAO Ted Gaebler. Gaebler emphasized that the new CIO was handing the authority for major IT system decisions from his office back to the departments; something he (the CIO) did not have to do. This message was also carried to departments by IS Administrative Analyst Jim Adams in a pro-active campaign of enthusiastic visioning, marketing, and facilitation.

The second, and perhaps more tangible, factor was money. As this process was happening, the technology-driven California economy was doing well and money for system upgrades was available, but the administration and elected officials correctly believed that the "good times" would not go on forever. The decision had been made to use the available extra money to make one-time, long-term investments in infrastructure, rather than creating new staff positions across the county.

A fund of $700,000 had been created in the budget for the first year's replacements and upgrading of major IT systems. CIO Monaghan requested, and CAO Gaebler approved, making that fund available *only* to purchases which followed the new governance model. Although this meant some badly-needed upgrades might have to wait a little longer, the "kick-start" of the new model (and subsequent improvement in decision making) would be well worth the extra time.

The Nevada County Technology Partnership Model

The new governance model, still functioning the same way at this writing in 2006, is pictured in Figure 1.

Briefly, the center layer of the triangle is the *Communities of Interest* layer, where new or replacement technology needs and solutions are discussed by departments providing related services. When needed, a COI can create a *Business Solutions Team* that draws expertise from throughout the county government for research. When a decision is reached, the COI feeds its recommendations to the *Information Systems Steering Board* for final recommendations to the County Board of Supervisors. This process is described in detail in the following text.

How the Process Works

Major system purchases *must* pass through the following process.

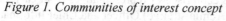

Figure 1. Communities of interest concept

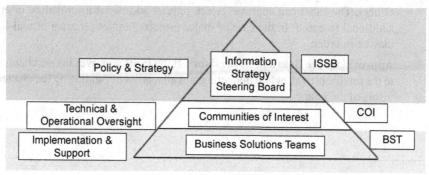

1. **Identify a need.** A department, or occasionally IS itself, decides that some new system or technology is needed. This may be to provide a new service, improve an existing service, replace aging technology, or any other proper purpose.

2. **Research solutions.** Previously, a department administrator would have started contacting vendors or otherwise researching new systems on their own, or would seek assistance from the IS Department. This would put IS management in the position of having to sell the idea to other departments and to the county administration.

    Under the new governance structure, the first step for the requesting department administrator is to bring the need to one of the communities of interest of which their department is a member. The COI members compare their own upcoming technology needs and their current situations, looking for ways to share resources and, as important, avoid purchasing incompatible systems. (Sometimes, another department who was considering a system upgrade several years down the road might be able to join in a project as a partner, speeding up their process considerably. This "fast track" benefit is sometimes another powerful motivator for participation.) The complete list of Nevada County's current (2006-07) COI structure, showing the department and divisional members of each one, is appended at the end of this chapter. Note that an IS staff person, usually a manager, has a seat on every COI to provide ongoing technical assistance.

    In some cases, a COI may create a Business Solutions Team (the bottom layer on the triangle diagram of Figure 1) to look closely into a particular project. The BST may draw from several departments and may include experts from the IS Department. The BST will do research of a more technical nature than the COI members have the time or expertise to undertake. A BST may dissolve after it makes its report, or may continue on throughout the development and implementation of the approved project.

    With continuing guidance and involvement by the COI, the department (with any new partner departments) and IS do research on available technologies and products. IS staff take a resource role in this process, not a driving role. IS has the umbrella view of the entire enterprise as well as knowing the details and limitations of the overall network, but the needs of the departments are always paramount. When research is completed, the research team presents the information and recommendations for purchase to the COI for approval.

3. **Approval by the enterprise.** The COI sends its recommendations to the Information Systems Steering Board. The ISSB is comprised of representatives from each COI, plus the County Executive (formerly Administrative) Officer and Chief Information Officer. The ISSB can approve, reject, request additional information, or engage in additional research. In the case of major projects, a pilot program or real-life demo may be in order.

4. **Approval by the Board of Supervisors.** If the ISSB approves the purchase, it moves to the final approval, actual budgeting and allocation of funding by the elected Supervisors of the county.

Early Examples

As stated, almost every major system in the county was replaced during the five years since adoption of the first enterprise technology strategic plan in 2000, and every one of those using the COI/ISSB process. (Two systems were not replaced, but even those decisions were made using the full process.) Some early examples were the following sub-sections.

County Web Site

Nevada County was late in developing a Web presence. Prior to 2001, a few departments created Web sites on their own. These sites were built using various software packages such as Microsoft FrontPage, Microsoft Publisher, or in raw HTML code. They had totally different appearances and disparate look and feel. A citizen coming to "the county Web site" had no idea when a mouse click took them outside the county site or if they were still viewing official information, since there were no unifying elements.

It took the power of the COI/ISSB structure to pull this together. With a new Webmaster hired in January 2001, IS proposed to build a truly unified county Web site with common graphic elements and consistent navigation. Some departments had difficulty with the idea of giving up ownership of their own site design, but approval through the COI/ISSB structure enabled the county to require every department to become part of the new, integrated "www.mynevadacounty.com" county site. (A single department, headed by an independent elected official, chose to remain separate but obtains outside site hosting from a commercial vendor. That site is linked to the county site as any other external Web site.)

By creating a single Web site for the entire county, IS has since been able to transition to a fully database-driven platform that provides such features as a site-wide search engine, integrated FAQ (frequently-asked questions) list, and easy linking between the content of different departments and offices. The county was able to purchase a single content management system and run the entire site (as well as five others for county and outside agency use) on one server. The total initial hardware and software cost for the system was about $15,000, and primary maintenance of all the sites is handled by a single employee, although departments may choose to have a member of their own staff trained to take care of ongoing content editing.

Financial Applications

Coming into 2000, there was no common financial/accounting system used throughout the county. At the time, five different departments were planning to submit proposals for replacement of their financial systems; all would have been different and incompatible with each other, and each system would have cost upwards of $100,000. The new governance structure brought these disparate departments together to select a single enterprise-level system that would work for all. That financial package is in place and benefiting all county departments (including departments not involved in the original proposals), for less than half the cost of individual replacements and tremendous savings in employee training and system maintenance.

Community Development

The departments most involved in new construction in the county—building, planning, environmental health, and code compliance—were all requesting separate systems for generating, tracking, and archiving permits. Not only was a system purchased that can be used by all, but that system is now integrated with the financial package described previously so that permit fees can be tracked and verified as they move through the financial departments of the county.

Document Imaging

There were three incompatible imaging systems in existence in 2000, and a proposal for a fourth had been submitted. The county now has a single, enterprise-level system in place and available by all departments. The imaging system is integrated with the enterprise document management system, which in turn makes tens of thousands of public documents directly accessible to the public through the county Web site.

Lessons Learned

A few changes have been made to improve the enterprise governance structure since the original adoption in 2000:

1. Originally, COI representatives were only departments heads, and each COI had a chair and vice-chair. COIs are currently transitioning to a membership of department head and a next-level manager from each department. The COI will have two co-chairs, one a department head and the other a manager, and both will also attend the ISSB meetings. The new structure is allowing for more sharing of responsibility and enabling more departmental involvement, especially during periods (for example, annual budget planning time) when department head workload is severely impacted.

2. For the first several years, IS staff or managers were assigned to each COI on an ad hoc basis according to available time and the kinds of projects seen coming into the COI. Recently, the chief information officer has assigned an IS person on a consistent basis to each COI.

3. In 2005, project management by the IS Department was made mandatory for all projects through a resolution by the ISSB. Previously, some projects were managed only by the vendor supplying the system, sometimes requiring IS to step in later when the specific project unexpectedly impacted something else. Information Systems created

a Project Management Division to provide these services, and a project management plan must now be included and budgeted for in every project proposal.

Overall Effects on the Government of Nevada County

The job of the chief information officer has changed dramatically. Instead of being drawn into the politics of having to select one department's favorite system over another, the CIO acts as a peer and consultant to the departments who must sell their solutions to each other, considering the best return on investment for the county as a whole.

Similarly, the CIO is no longer a "money broker", finding money for major systems purchases and negotiating (often back and forth in time-consuming serial meetings with individual managers) which department will pay for what. These decisions are all worked out by the departments within their COIs and the ISSB. The ISSB meets monthly; the frequency of meetings of the COIs varies according to need.

The time to approve a project that worried department heads back in 2000 is almost entirely under the control of those same managers. If a project needs immediate attention, the COI can meet more frequently and move the item through the process more quickly than waiting for information systems staff and administration to have the time to do the research. When the decision is made and approved through the ISSB, approval by the Board of Supervisors happens quickly, since the project has been agreed to by all the players.

The enterprise IT governance model adopted in 2000 has become part of the culture throughout the county. The process is contained in the 2006 Strategic Plan Update recently adopted as policy by the Board of Supervisors in a formal resolution, making it "the law of the land" for major IT decisions. The governance structure is contained in the definition of what the Information Systems Department is and does, in both the County Administrative Code and the annual budget process. In the words of CIO Steve Monaghan, "It is embedded in the working structure—the DNA—of the organization."

Additional Reading

Barrett, K., & Greene, R. (2001). *Powering up: How public managers can take control of information technology.* Washington D.C.: CQ Press.

Bloch, D. C. (2006). *Interview with Nevada county chief information officer Steve Monaghan.* Unpublished. Nevada City, CA.

Fountain, J. E. (2001). *Building the virtual state: Information technology and institutional change.* Washington D.C.: Brookings Institution Press.

Heeks, R. (Ed.) (1999). *Reinventing government in the information age.* New York: Routledge.

Kamarck, E. C., & Nye, Jr., J. S. (Eds.). (2002). *Governance.com: Democracy in the information Age.* Washington D.C.: Brookings Institution Press.

Kavanagh, S. C., & Miranda, R. A. (Eds.). (2005). *Technologies for government transformation: ERP systems and beyond.* Chicago, IL: Government Finance Officers Association www.gfoa.org

Nevada County Information Systems Department. (2001). *2001 Nevada county enterprise information technology strategic plan with supplements.* Nevada City, CA: County of Nevada. Retrieved February 2006, from http://www.mynevadacounty.com/is

Osborne, D., & Gaebler, T. (2001). *Reinventing government: The five strategies for reinventing government.* New York: Penguin Books.

Addendum: The Communities of Interest

The current communities of interest are as follows. Notice how departments (and divisions and commissions) with similar interests are grouped together, and also note that most departments appear in more than one COI.

Community & Social Programs: CEO, Clerk-Recorder, Community Development Agency, Public Health, Housing Division, Library, Public Defender, Schools, Sheriff, Transit Division, Veterans Services.

Development & Environmental Management: CEO, Agricultural Commissioner, Assessor, Board of Supervisors, Building, Community Development Agency, Farm Advisor, Housing Division, Planning, Social Services, Transit, Transportation and Sanitation, Treasurer-Tax Collector.

Enterprise Information Management: CEO, Library, Board of Supervisors, Child Support Services, Clerk-Recorder, Community Development Agency, District Attorney, General Services, Geographic Information Systems Division, Human Resources, Information Systems, Sheriff, Transportation and Sanitation, Treasurer-Tax Collector.

Facilities Management & Maintenance: CEO, Airport, Auditor-Controller, Building, General Services, Sheriff, Transportation and Sanitation.

Internal Services & Administration: CEO, Assessor, Board of Supervisors, Community Development Agency, Public Health, County Counsel, General Services, Housing Division, Human Resources, Information Systems, Social Services, Transportation and Sanitation, Treasurer-Tax Collector.

Justice: CEO, Building, Child Support Services, Public Health, County Counsel, Courts, District Attorney, Probation, Public Defender, Sheriff, Social Services.

Public Safety: CEO, Agricultural Commissioner, Behavioral Health, Child Support Services, District Attorney, Environmental Health, Fire Districts' representatives, Geographic Information Systems Division, General Services, Probation, Public Defender, Sheriff, Social Services.

Author's Biography

Dave Bloch *is currently the Webmaster for the County of Nevada, California. Prior experience included ownership of a Web design and hosting business, executive director of a rural county arts organization, and teacher of radio/television production. Mr. Bloch holds a Master's degree in instructional development and technology from Michigan State University and a BA in speech communication and theatre from the University of Michigan.*

Chapter V

IT Governance at the City of Naperville, Illinois

Donald J. Carlsen, City of Naperville, Illinois, USA

Executive Summary

This case study details the process that the City of Naperville, IL has developed to govern its information technology project selection process. IT governance can be defined as "a structure of relationships and processes to direct and control the enterprise in order to achieve the enterprise's goals by adding value while balancing risk versus return over IT and its processes." While the definition sounds ominous, the reality is that IT needs to connect the needs of the business to process improvements and projects that can enhance operations, create efficiencies, lower costs, and solve problems. The chapter entails the description of the way that business needs and IT projects were connected in the past, why that was a problem for the city and IT, and what was done to try and to correct the problem. The case study includes an overview of a toolkit used by the city as well as a discussion of challenges and the current status of each piece of the toolkit. The toolkit includes:

1. *Strategic technology planning*
2. *Project management*
3. *Capacity analysis*

4.   *Budget/CIP review teams*

5.   *Budget process improvements including project scope and scoresheet*

6.   *Information technology project evaluation team*

7.   *Balanced scorecard*

Introduction

It is my hypothesis that use of the toolkit described in this chapter lowers risk and improves the ability to execute on information technology (IT) projects.

The case study will detail the process that the City of Naperville has developed to govern our information technology project selection process. IT governance can be defined as "a structure of relationships and processes to direct and control the enterprise in order to achieve the enterprise's goals by adding value while balancing risk versus return over IT and its processes." While the definition sounds ominous, the reality is that IT needs to connect the needs of the business to process improvements and projects that can enhance operations, create efficiencies, lower costs, and solve problems.

The basic topic entails the description of the way that business needs and IT were connected in the past, why that was a problem for the city and IT, and what has been done to try and correct the problem. Naperville's IT Department has developed a toolkit that includes the following:

1.   Strategic technology planning

2.   Project management

3.   Capacity analysis

4.   Budget/CIP review teams

5.   Budget process improvements including project scope and scoresheet

6.   Information technology project evaluation team

7.   Balanced scorecard

Because Naperville is a high-growth, dynamic community, I think that readers may find it interesting to see how IT works in an extremely innovative public-sector environment.

Background

The City of Naperville was incorporated in 1831. Over the past 175 years, the city has grown both in population and size to approximately 140,000 residents and a service area of about 38 square miles. Recently, the city is the recipient of the following accolades:

- Best Places to Live—*Money Magazine* 2006 (2nd place nationally)
- Best Places to Retire—*Money Magazine* 2005
- Microsoft Award for Innovations in Government—2003 Public Sector CIO Summit
- Government Finance Officers of America:
    o Distinguished Budget Presentation Award—14 consecutive years
    o Certificate of Achievement for Excellence in Financial Reporting-11 consecutive years
    o Award for Outstanding Achievement in Popular Annual Financial Reporting-2005
- Center for Digital Government Digital Cities Survey Award—Population 125,000-249,000 2005 (8th place)
- National Institute of Government Purchasing—Pareto Award of Excellence in Public Procurement
- Commission on Accreditation for Law Enforcement Agencies (CALEA) for the Police Department and Communications Division
- Commission on Fire Accreditation International, Inc. (CFAI) for the Fire Department
- Special Achievement in GIS award for Outstanding use of Geographic Information System (GIS) technology by ESRI-2005

Organization

The city is comprised of the following departments:

- City Manager's Office (including City Clerk, Community Relations, and Social Services)
- Finance Department
- Fire Department
- Human Resources/Organizational Resources Effectiveness Department
- Information Technology Department
- Legal Department
- Police Department
- Department of Public Utilities
    o Electric
    o Water and Wastewater
- Department of Public Works
- Transportation Engineering and Development Business Group

Each of the departments listed is managed by an appointed, professional department director, who reports to the city manager. The city operates under a council-manager form of government with a city manager who is hired by, and reports to, a nine-member City Council, consisting of a mayor and eight councilmen.

IT Department

The city's IT Department is comprised of three divisions lead by the IT Director. There are about 20 FTEs in the IT Department. The divisions are as follows:

- **Business Applications:** Management of the city's enterprise resource planning (ERP) systems.
- **Network Systems:** Management of the city's wide area networks, local area networks, server, PCs, and enterprise network applications.
- **Geographic Information Systems (GIS):** Management of the city's GIS mapping systems and associated databases.

The city's technology infrastructure consists of the following:

- 940 PCs and laptops for general use;
- 100 mobile laptops used in Police, Fire, Public Works, the Electric and Water utilities, and Transportation Engineering and Development;
- 80 servers;
- 15 sites connected by fiber owned by the city's electric utility using one gigabit per second Ethernet topology.

Budget

The city's total operating budget is approximately $355,000,000. The five-year Capital Improvements Program (CIP) is approximately $400,000,000. The IT Department Operating Budget is approximately $5,000,000 and the IT CIP fluctuates between $1,000,000 and $5,000,000 annually, depending on the costs of the projects included. The major sources of revenue are as follows:

- General Fund-Sales Taxes, Utility Taxes, Property Taxes;
- Electric Utility—Electricity Sales
- Water and Wastewater Utility—Water and Wastewater Sales.

Naperville is somewhat unique in Illinois in that the city owns and operates both the electric and water and wastewater utilities. This means that the city has ultimate control over utility service delivery, and much lower costs than comparable private or investor owned utilities in the area. Also, because the utilities are run much more like a business than traditional municipal government service departments, there are some difficult support scenarios that have to be dealt with, one of them being supporting technology for these departments.

City Plans and Processes

The city has developed a comprehensive set of management processes and plans to guide the business. The processes and plans include:

- **High-Level Strategic Planning:** Mission, vision, strategies, and goals reviewed annually by the city council and directors.
- **Performance Management:** City staff uses the balanced scorecard to link strategic objectives to projects and process improvements.
- **City-Wide and Departmental Risk Assessments:** Prepared by the city's internal auditor and directors.
- **Department Strategic Plans:** For example, the IT Department's strategic technology plan (STP).
- **Operating and Capital Budgeting Processes:** Including the IT Department's information technology project evaluation team (IPET) technology project review.

Setting the Stage

Naperville has always been viewed as a "progressive" municipal government. The city has embraced a philosophy of keeping pace with the rapid population growth and expectations of an affluent, highly-educated population using newer technologies as opposed to adding staff.

Also, many of the city councilmen are current or former management or executive employees from large private-sector companies such as AT&T, Lucent, Amoco, BP, and Uniroyal, and are familiar with newer management techniques and technology.

The utilization of technology in Naperville has always been high. The ratio of city staff to workstations is 1.1 to 1, which is extremely high considering that about 300 employees work in the field as opposed to offices. The ratio is a direct result of the city pushing technology out to front-line workers so that they can have access to data and applications in the field. This allows field staff to enter data directly, and provide information to customers in the moment that services are occurring.

Technology Projects

Some of the technology-related projects that Naperville had among the first of local governments to implement includes:

- Local area networks connecting all PCs in 1989;
- A fully-integrated enterprise resource planning (ERP) system linking financials, community development, and public safety applications for greater efficiency in 1990;
- Mobile data computers (laptops) in police, fire, and other city vehicles in 1993;
- An enterprise geographic information system (GIS) began in 1994; and
- An enterprise electronic document management system (EDMS) in 2003.

Sounds great, so what's the problem? During Naperville's high growth period in the 1980's and 1990's, adding staff was relatively easy. Each year staff went through an annual operating budget and CIP (projects over $25,000 with a lifespan of over five years) preparation process. The process served as the major strategic planning exercise for the year. The process began with a kick-off meeting hosted by the Finance Department. Because the local economy was always strong, and because of our own budget philosophies, there were no spending guidelines set for budget and CIP items and projects. The lack of spending guidelines was intended to encourage innovation and creativity during the preparation process and anticipated that the executive review process would bring budgets in line with finances.

The budget process led to several problems with regard to technology planning.

- There was no formal process for connecting projects to strategies—some attempts were made at integrating some of the many planning processes and at strategic planning, but none had gained any real traction.
- There were no official financial guidelines.
- There was no capacity analysis, so there was no way of knowing if there was enough staff to implement requested or approved projects.
- There was no formal project management discipline.
- Because the process was very condensed, there was little chance for interaction between departments requesting items or projects and the IT Department.

The end result was that the city was working on projects that may have little or no strategic or even tactical value. Also, even more alarming, Naperville had the money to do many projects, but was there enough internal capacity to implement the projects? The IT Department was charting completion percentages for CIP projects, but this was done after the fact.

In 1997, a new City Manager, Peter Burchard, was hired. During one of our first meetings, Peter asked, "so, what keeps you up at night?" The IT Director responded that he was very concerned about the city's technology project selection process. Specifically, was the city doing projects that were strategic and made a difference, solving business problems, and could the city complete approved projects in a timely fashion? Thereafter, the IT Department developed and implemented a new strategic technology process to connect business needs to technology.

Case Description

In order to provide a solution to our problems, the IT Department developed and implemented a set of tools to handle the issues. The tools include:

1. Strategic technology planning
2. Project management
3. Capacity analysis
4. Budget/CIP review teams
5. Budget process improvements including project scope and scoresheet
6. Information technology project evaluation team
7. Balanced scorecard

Strategic Technology Planning

In 2001, the IT Department retained a consultant to develop a strategic technology plan (STP). The purpose of the plan was two-fold. First, to interview all departments and determine their business strategies, then connect technology solutions to the strategies, where appropriate. Second, some departments had stated that there were issues with the city's current ERP vendor (Sungard/HTE), and there was talk about replacing them. Because the city used HTE for financials, community development, billing, computer-aided-dispatch, and public-safety records management, the estimated cost to replace the system was approximately $9M. The arguments for replacement seemed to be based on emotion, and employees were bringing up issues had not been formally presented to Sungard/HTE as a problem. In order to make an informed decision, the STP consultant was asked to verify and document the need to replace the current ERP system as part of the STP process.

The consultant did a good job of determining strategies and assigning appropriate technology solutions. In fact, this was the first time that departments could visualize the connection between what they did, the problems that they were encountering, and how technology could help solve their problems. A short-coming was that the document was voluminous (over 200 pages) and contained no financial or capacity analysis to ensure that the city could pay for, implement, and support the projects. In 2003, the plan was updated internally by IT Department staff. The update was a more streamlined version of the original document designed to aid departments to better understand the connection between their business needs and possible technology solutions.

It was also decided that the capacity and financial analysis processes would be handled through the budget and CIP process and not the STP process.

One example of an improvement to the original plan is that the STP clearly spells out what has to be done and by whom in order to initiate the project. In the past, there was an assumption that the IT Department would magically start working on a project just because a department mentioned it in a strategic technology planning meeting. As a result of the process, departments have a plan for technology projects that they can use for planning and budgeting purposes that is connected to their business needs.

Project Management

Beginning in 2004, in order to get a handle on the number of projects that departments were requesting and necessary resources including implementation hours, hardware, software, and annual support costs and hours needed, the IT Department generated basic Gantt charts for all IT projects. The charts were a first step in getting a handle on exactly what we were facing. After doing research on the subject with the Project Management Institute (PMI—www.pmi.org), the IT Director approached the HR Department to see if there was city-wide interest in providing a basic course on project management. We have a very progressive learning and performance function in our HR Department and they readily accepted a challenge to put a course together. The original plan was to bring in an outside PMI certified project management training firm and run a pilot training program to test the concept. There are many PMI certified courses, and we selected a basic three-day Principles and Techniques of Project Management course. Even though the training plan came up in the middle of the year and was unfunded, after discussing with the city's department leadership team, the plan was funded.

The pilot was a success, and we ended up holding two more classes training 60 employees. Several employees have continued on for more training, and one is a certified project management professional (PMP) with plans for others to receive the same certification. Also, the HR Department is now offering two-hour project management modules to help employees in writing project charters, scope statements, and plans.

Capacity Analysis

After the city's initial experiences with project management were completed, including project scoping, planning, and Gantt charting, the IT Department decided to add a capacity analysis component to our toolkit. Initially, we ran through an exercise where we calculated the total hours available and subtracted holidays and vacations. Next, applying a principle learned in our project management courses, it was known that one could expect a person to be productive for only six of every eight hours per day. This calculation is often not done and very important in capacity planning. Finally, time required to support existing systems was subtracted out of the total. The remaining time could then be used to implement new applications.

The result was surprising. Going into the experiment, there was a general assumption that there was about 4,000 hours to implement new projects. In the end, there was about one-half of that time, or about 2,000 hours available. In order to get even more accurate with the calculation, a PC-based time tracking application was implemented to track time in greater detail. The result of using the application is that the IT Department knows that there is even less time to implement projects than the initial assumptions.

Budget and CIP Review Teams

In the past, technology projects since 2000 submitted for the upcoming budget/CIP year were submitted to the Finance Department and then sent to IT for review. Many times, it was nearly impossible to tell what the departments were looking to accomplish with their projects because the format did not require them to do so, and because the entire budget/CIP process was so compressed there was very little time to ask questions, get answers back, and make a decision. In 2000, the city manager thought it would be a good idea to have employee teams review technology projects and items, as well as other categories of expenditures.

In the case of technology projects, a team of technology-savvy employees receives copies of all technology project and item requests to review. The team meets several times to discuss the project and items and because many of the team members are also the employees responsible for submitting the projects and items, they were able to explain the need, and answer questions. The IT Director is the chair of the team and is responsible for the review of the projects and items and presenting the approved projects and items to the city manager and city council.

Information Technology Project Evaluation Team

In order to make the budget/CIP review teams even more effective, the IT Department instituted a permanent group of employees to review the current process, make improvements to the process, and review technology projects during the budget and CIP review periods and during the year, as needs arise.

Based on discussions amongst the team members, and people that submit projects and by doing some best-practice research with comparable communities, the team incorporated the following steps into the process.

- The process was lengthened by one month to allow for more complete submissions and more time for greater analysis.
- The team offered to consult with submitters before the deadline in order to build a better project.
- The team incorporated a PMI-based project scope statement into the process—the scope statement is required for all CIP projects and budget projects over $5,000.
- The team developed a criteria-based scoresheet that is used to assign points to each project to be used to rank or prioritize projects.

Balanced Scorecard

All of the aforementioned tools can be used individually or in concert. To really make them effective, an organization needs a system to manage and monitor outcomes. Fueled by the Naperville's hunger for innovation and best practices, the city has implemented the balanced scorecard. It's the "frosting on the cake" and pulls everything together. Balanced scorecard is a performance management tool that includes the establishment of strategies, and links projects and processes to the strategies. The balanced scorecard process starts by using tools such as a SWOT (strengths, weaknesses, opportunities, threats) analysis, risk assessments, or other information to determine strategic objectives.

The strategic objectives are organized into one of four perspectives: stakeholders, internal processes, enablers, and financial. The perspectives and strategic objectives that require the most improvement are weighted higher than those that we consider to be doing well. Figure 1 is the IT Department's balanced scorecard strategy map.

Next, departments list all current processes and projects and link them to the strategic objectives. After that, indicators are developed that allow departments to monitor the performance of the strategic objectives and are reported on each month. If the indicator is within the predetermined target range, there is no further discussion. If the indicator is either above or below the indicator, "what?", "so what?", and "now what?" questions are asked to determine what if anything further needs to be done.

Figure 1. IT Department's balanced scorecard strategy map

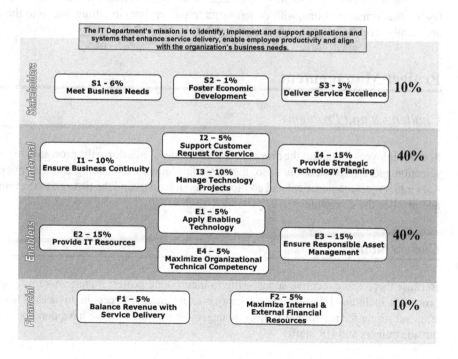

If departments want to look further into the data, the process and projects lists are examined to see if either of those factors are causing problems with the indicator and needs to be addressed.

Current Challenges

Strategic Technology Planning

Challenges and Problems

The main challenge has been to get departments to focus on their business needs as opposed to *wanting* new technologies without regard to strategic objectives and business needs when going through the STP process. Even though the IT Department begins with a format that focuses on business needs, when the IT Department shows up, client departments want to talk about technology without connecting the technology to strategic objectives. Also, some departments follow the STP and others want to reinvent the plan every few months.

Current Status

The plan is currently being updated using IT staff, and it is very time consuming. It is estimated that the city's IT Department spends about 500 man hours developing the format, testing the format, meeting with departments to gather data, inputting data into the plan, and finally meeting with departments to present the plan.

Project Management

Challenges and Problems

Some employees think that the process is overused and slows down the processes of project selection and implementation. Also, there is a fair amount of training and discipline that goes into project management and employees find it hard to find the tie to go to the training, and practice the discipline.

Current Status

Because there was executive sponsorship to incorporate project management into several processes, including IT governance, the city is experiencing success in this area. Also, there is no substitute for the formal project management training that we have done both using outside trainers and HR staff.

Capacity Analysis

Challenges and Problems

The IT Department continues to work on getting more accurate data to use in this area. The challenge is to track time without spending too much time tracking time. Also, the city has approved fewer projects based on knowing that there is less time for implementation and support of new projects, which has caused problems for departments whose projects are not selected.

Current Status

The IT Department has leveraged their experience by helping the HR Department to determine their capacity for projects as well. IT will continue to use this tool to determine our capacity for implanting projects in the future.

Budget/CIP Review Teams

Challenges and Problems

The concept of using review teams has been used by the city for the past five years. Last year, the process for IT projects was changed, and there have been some issues with people not understanding the new process. Some people did not take advantage of the IT Department's offer to consult with them to "build a better project", and their submission did not contain all of the information that was required.

Current Status

Although the changes resulted in a good experience by involving others in the process, the IT Department needs to step up their efforts to market the changes in the process so that people understand the new process better.

Budget/CIP Process Improvements Including Project Scope and Scoresheet

Challenges and Problems

Again, as with the budget/CIP teams, communicating and understanding the process changes was the most difficult challenge. One interesting issue is that the scoresheets tended to over-inflate the value of the project and the IT Department had to spend some time going over the scoresheets and making the values more realistic. Also, some people found it too time-consuming to prepare the project scope and scoresheet, and in some cases opted to not submit a project because of that. Obviously, that presents a problem in that the process may be stifling innovation; however, the caveat is that the process may be working to screen projects that do not have proper justification.

Current Status

The IT Department is working on ways to better communicate, market, and simplify the process. The IT Project Evaluation Team will be used as a focus group to help determine the future direction.

Information Technology Project Evaluation Team

Challenges and Problems

The process is time-consuming and some departments mentioned that they had a hard time giving up staff for this purpose.

More interesting was that some departments did not like that a loophole in the old process was closed that allowed them to move money and do technology projects or buy items during the year as opposed to justifying the purchase and budgeting for it up front. Conversely, departments complained that this process stifles or slows innovation for things that come up during the year.

Current Status

There has not been a meeting for a project that has come up during the year because the first budget/CIP process using the team was just finished. As mentioned previously, the team will be used as a focus group for the budget/CIP process improvements.

Balanced Scorecard

Challenges and Problems

Using balanced scorecard in business, let alone government, is fairly new. The biggest problem is to understand the process, and how it works. It is very time consuming to gather the data, review indicators each month and make decisions about how to keep processes and projects on track. Also, it is a daunting task to link city-wide goals to department goals, to division goals, and finally to individual goals, which is part of the balanced scorecard process.

Current Status

The process has been very rewarding for IT because the system provides a framework for all departments link technology projects to strategies. The city now has solid strategies based on solid data, with projects and process improvements tied to them. The IT Department Management Team reviews indicators every month and strategies periodically. Data that is important to the health of our business is in front of us each month in an easy to read and interpret format.

Experiences and Examples

Overall, because of the tools mentioned, and data that we are now able to gather and measure, we are much better equipped to manage our operation. Specifically, we have had the following experiences:

- We have added two new positions, a Network Systems Manager and an IT Project Manager, to fill needs that we thought we had, but could not easily demonstrate—as mentioned earlier in this case study that has been a difficult task in recent years.
- The city council is more apt to approve projects that are fully justified and connected to strategy.
- Prior to implementing the tool set, the IT Department project completion rate was below 90% annually—over the past three years, the rate has been between 92% and 95%.
- According to bi-annual surveys, our customer satisfaction is up due to better expectation setting and higher project completion rates.
- Overall project submissions are much better.
- Overall financial management is much better.
- Overall, we have a common language of terminology around strategy, projects, and processes.
- Overall stakeholder buy-in has been enhanced—the process has become "demystified".
- Overall, city council buy-in has been enhanced due to IT providing solid justification and performance management data.

Author's Biography

Donald J. Carlsen *is the Information Technology Director for the City of Naperville, Illinois. Naperville is a city of approximately 140,000 residents located about 30 miles west of Chicago, and has been the recipient of many national awards and recognition. Mr. Carlsen has held several positions with the city before being appointed to his current position and holds a Master of Arts' degree in public administration from Northern Illinois University in DeKalb, IL.*

Chapter VI

Cutting the Red Tape to Go Paperless

J. Louis Boglioli, III, City of Stuart, Florida, USA

Executive Summary

A small team of skilled, motivated employees made a sweeping change in their organization for the betterment of all. Management empowered them by enabling their talents and reliable decision making to have a "free hand" in the process. The task at hand was not one that could favor some department or function over others, so the process was not hindered by internal strife, but only ignorance. As we have learned to say there was a classic PEBCAK to blame: Problem Exists Between Chair And Keyboard. By eliminating the barriers and pushing positive innovation on traditional entrenched processes, the organization eliminated its own bottlenecks without the assistance of any outside efficiency experts or consultants. The little City of Stuart has what larger cities can only try and buy because the investment is made at the employee level. When you have the tools and the talent, all goals can be achieved.

Background

The City of Stuart is located on the east coast of Florida parallel with the northern tip of Lake Okeechobee—the big lake in the middle of Florida you can see from space. That puts the city about 120 miles north of Miami. The city was incorporated in 1914, and is currently the county seat of Martin County. Stuart was at one time located in Palm Beach County, but rumor has it, there were so many outlaws in Stuart, they let the city go to another county. In fact, one of Stuart's most notable facts of history is being the hideout location of an infamous bank robbing gang in the early 1900's. On a lighter note, Stuart is known as the Sailfish Capital of the World also, for the many record size sailfish and marlins caught just off the zipcode here in the Atlantic.

Stuart maintains a full-time population of approximately 16,000, but that increases to over-stuffed proportions in the winter time with an influx of "snow-birds", always signaled by an increase in the traffic accidents, and wait lines at local delis for lunch. This is spread out over a jurisdiction of 6.4 square miles. That area is a mix of new Florida modern construction, and old Florida "quaintness". Employees can still be stuck everyday coming and going from work by the original Florida East Coast Rail Road tracks outside of City Hall's front parking lot, as the trains hauling supplies traverse the state.

The city has been considered an affluent community with upper-scale living for predominantly older, retired persons. Nestled on the water of the Saint Lucie River, attached to the Atlantic Ocean inter-coastal waterway, Stuart is a mere two-minute drive from the ocean and beaches. Several smaller exclusive communities border Stuart, where movie stars and various artists maintain residences. So, as in most communities of this nature, the demand for service is high, but the willingness to pay wages is low. The tax base is still primarily commercial however, since few of the residents actually live in the city limits. The most recent taxable value was $1.5 billion.

From that value, the city maintains a general fund budget of $17 million dollars and $36 million all funds. The annual fiscal budget is adopted by a five-member council from October to September, with totals by fund, and budgetary controls at the department level, though still reporting all activity by categories within the departments. This is overseen by a city manager, or weak mayor-form of government. The primary sources of revenue for Stuart are, of course, Ad Valorem revenues, or property taxes, franchise fees assessed on certain utility and service providers, utility taxes charged on the sale of services in the city limits, building permits, occupational licenses, ambulance service fees, and utility charges assessed for the public utilities provided by the city.

Stuart provides potable water, sanitary sewer, wastewater treatment, residential and commercial garbage pickup, stormwater management, fire service, ambulance rescue service, and police force services. Stuart also maintains parks and recreation facilities in conjunction with several water-related amenities. These services are provided throughout the city from various locations such as the water treatment plant, public works facilities, and the public safety complexes. These responsibilities, all reporting to the city manager, are parsed up among 27 departments and divisions. Encapsulated in those is an outstanding group of about 250 full-time employees, varying in ages, skill level, and personalities. And, out of the 250 employees, they have divided themselves up into no less than three unions, one pseudo-union group, and then finally the union of non-union employees. Now all that said, Martin County is still considered to be a "back-water" county and Stuart for years was seen as a "good-ole-boy" network. Great strives have been made to escape that image and reputation, quite successfully under the current administration.

Setting the Stage

That is what brings us to the case study at hand. I have been with the city for 11 years and the current city manager has been with the city for 14 years. So I have been around for the transformation of the government since the beginning almost. And what a transformation it has been. When I arrived at the city, hired as the Accounting Supervisor in Administrative Services, we incorporated accounting, budgeting, investments, debt management, risk management, purchasing, payroll, human resources, utility billing, customer service, cashier, and information services as well. They all knew I had grown up with a computer in my hand, and the director of Administrative Services at that time charged me with getting the organization into at least the 20th century.

I was at that time the youngest full-time employee at City Hall, and of the employees I was now hired to supervise, the least senior one had three years with the city, and the most senior had 26. My introduction into the workforce was not happily received as I was assured to be the "college kid" coming in to tell them how to do their jobs better, they had been doing just fine for the last 20 years.

There was only one PC in the entire city, and my boss had it. Everyone else in Administrative Services had orange colored dumb-terminal screens linked by miles of cabling to an old NCR tower. The police had their own system, and the fire had their own system, and everyone else had nothing. Administrative Services prepared the budgets for all departments. They provided all answers and all reports to everyone, including other departments, concerning the "accounting stuff". To say we were in the dark ages is an understatement.

During my employee orientation, I was offered direct deposit to any 1 of 5 banks in town. I thought this was immediately odd, until my first week at work, supervising payroll. If an employee signed up for direct deposit, we would then keep a list, pull that person's payroll check out of the printed check run, and then stamp it "For Deposit Only" and proceed to drive the check to the employee's bank for them and deposit it. This was the first of many "quaint" practices I ran into during my tenure with the city.

I soon found the root of most of the problems with the users. The city, like many other offices then and today, owned a software package they barely utilized. Not only were many of the employees not using the system, but the ones who were had not received proper or adequate training. Droves of features and abilities existed no one was aware of at all. Employees would spend countless hours producing reports in Excel the system could easily produce if only someone would flip a switch or populate a table. By my estimation, the staff was using less than 10% of the entire system available to them. Surprisingly so, given that long before ERP (enterprise resource planning) was a popular buzz word, the city owned a fully-integrated enterprise resource system, linking their accounting, purchasing, payroll, fixed assets, budgeting, and utility billing systems together. A local reseller of a government system had in fact, used the City of Stuart, as a beta site for a lot of testing and implementation of "linked modules". One upgrade and one piecemeal purchase after another and the city's primary "accounting" programs were integrated. If we bought the system outright today, we could never afford it. Most of the staff was not even aware of some of the modules they owned, and none understood the significance of this linkage, demonstrated directly by the fact staff members were manually posting transactions that could have been effortlessly "interfaced" from one module to the other.

The printer room held in the frequent deafening sound of a printer spitting out three-part paper forms for every purpose from budget adjustments to leave requests. All requests for issuance of checks, payroll timesheets, disciplinary forms, and even requisitions for purchase orders were printed and filled out by hand by the employees and supervisors to be returned to Administrative Services for processing. Each of these processing procedures required several live signatures, reviews, comments, and even then initiated several inter-office envelopes with memoranda to answer various questions and relay comments on each form's content and results.

The first area to address was the acceptance of the state procurement contract for personal computers here in Florida. We began to buy PCs from Gateway Computers for the negoti-ated price set forth by "piggy-backing" the state contract with Gateway. First the users in Administrative Services and then later the trickle-down theory of technology to the other departments, led to a new accessibility of information. We then magically had access to inter-office e-mail practically over night. We were still using the NCR tower box for our core applications processing and using a terminal emulation program to access those UNIX-based applications from our new shiny "cow computers".

After the introduction of the PCs, we began phasing out old processes and phasing in the electronic equivalents of many. A staple of our monthly processes was to print three cop-ies of every department/division expenditure report to date. This gave the supervisors and directors their year-to-date expenses, encumbrance balances, and the remaining portion of their unspent, unallocated budgets. This resulted in about half a box of paper every month, followed by two hours of sorting and distributing to the old "cubby hole" inter-office mail-boxes. There were monthly training sessions on how to "access the system" to lookup the "accounting stuff" previously only accessible to Administrative Services. And, in addition, each summer was a new project to bring a new module on line; of course, I only refer to them as new because we never used them before but already owned them. Management and staff were equally amazed as new features and capabilities crept out of Administrative Service's office about every quarter. The calls for information and requests for reports dwindled from many departments, though some die-hard holdouts remained, destined to never understand what the screen in front of them said, though it was identical to the printed hard copies they were so familiar with and accustomed to during their work life.

As each process was revamped, the scrutiny would turn to the next process that seemed cumbersome or antiquated. If the system already provided for a canned solution, we sim-ply took that portion of the user manual, studied it, and began quietly converting users to the module version. Almost the entire conversion was handled in-house. Our Information Services staff at that time was one full-time employee, one part-time employee, and the frequent meddling of yours truly, mainly in part because Information Services was part of Administrative Services, which was just a fancy name for Finance. I guess having a computer since I was 10 made me qualified to dabble in the technical ring. Today we have a separate department for Information Services with four full-time employees. If a solution was not readily available, we did our best to MacGyverize a solution from some feature set in the module application closest related to the business process in question.

Case Description

Three years ago, in the winter of 2003, a budget amendment request came across my desk asking for additional monies to be appropriated for the consultation, design, and implementation work on a requisition and purchasing system. As I read the description of the scope of services to be provided, and what was being requested by the client, namely the city, I was absolutely beside myself. I began to dig into the issue and found the Public Works Department had already engaged some consulting services to have someone from the outside world come in, interview staff members and employees, and begin to draft a proposal for streamlining the requisition and purchasing procedures.

At the City of Stuart, at that time, we required a three-part paper requisition form to be submitted to Purchasing with all pertinent information related to an encumbered item. To reach that point it had to start as a wish or desire for product or service out in the field somewhere, whether that meant the playground or fire station made no difference. Someone there had to fill out the form and give it to their supervisor. That person had to approve and, in turn, give it to their department head. They had to approve it and, in turn, submit it to their next highest supervisor, or if the chain was shorter, straight to Purchasing, for the first review. From there, it went to the city manager, then back to Purchasing, for them to convert it to a bona fide PO, which would then encumber funds on the accounting system.

A requisition could be delayed in up to five inboxes for days on end in each, let alone if someone is gone on vacation or leaves early and then ultimately could be returned for improper coding and missing paperwork at the top. The users wanted a faster, more efficient, streamlined approach to processing the requisitions with a type of "routing" mechanism built in. Stories of purchase orders taking two weeks to be printed were not uncommon. These requisitions also required different authorizing documentation depending on what was being purchased and for what amounts. Any purchase over $1,000 required three verbal quotes, any purchase over $3,000 required three written quotes, and any purchase over $5,000 required a sealed bid. These "backup" materials had to be attached to requisition the whole process, so it could reach Purchasing however many days later, to be verified if necessary, and/or bid openings scheduled.

The city had come a long way already, but the ability to do "paperless" requisitions had existed in the system since about 1996, but, as with most features, it never had been turned on. Originally the idea was never used because it required user intervention into a "passive" system; in other words, employees had to go look and see if any requisitions existed requiring their input. But unbeknownst to what appeared to be every other employee, our 2001 upgrade had provided us with approval hierarchies and dollar amount threshold limits. Likewise, a very simple but useful HTML interface for approvals was integrated into the module. This same HTML interface provided an active notification system to the members of the predefined approval table as well.

I got involved and notified everyone, including the city manager, it was not necessary to research any outside products or resources, and that Administrative Services would be introducing a new "paperless" online requisition process. The announcement was met with less than favorable response. The city manager has been a proponent of technology and implementing new technologies most of his career. He was the driving force behind many of the advances we and the citizens enjoy today. That was the most paramount support issue available to staff, and if the management had not been sold on the idea, or pushing it themselves, many of the projects would have fallen by the wayside. The city manager directed "us" to implement the features of the system necessary to address the requisition system. At that time, the project team as it may have been called was made up of the finance administrator and the chief information officer. That meant me and the one full-time IT guy had to get all of it done. There was no big project team, or steering committee, or focus group with internal auditing. There were two employees motivated and skilled enough to populate vacant tables in the software system, and turn on the bells and whistles. We two had basically overseen all the other system advances since our employment together. A team existed out of pure necessity and luckily we had come to work in the same office within a month of each other, and we had learned each other's strengths and weaknesses. His were hardware and networking, and mine were decision strategies, numbering scheme designs, and software. Additionally, we assured all the parties involved at first, department heads, and the other employees this new feature was fully-integrated into the existing system, or the ERP no one knew they already owned.

We did not really need the support of the departments since the decision had already been made to replace the paper system completely, and the technical expertise existed nowhere else in the organization with the exception of the Public Safety divisions, who were not fully assimilated into our products at that time. The decision process was quick and somewhat ceremonial at best because we had already demonstrated the robustness of the existing system was lying dormant and the other "modules" we had brought on line had all performed as promised, if not as expected. In other words, the management piece of the organization realized throwing more money at the problem would not solve the issue, and the capital investment in the existing products was there and substantial. Not only was the historical cost of the system still on the books, but also the annual maintenance was being paid to maintain and upgrade the products, many of which had never even been selected from the menu choices.

The initial and immediate reply we received practically from all parties was, "it will never work." Several questions were posed by the users of the system that were supposed to be resolved before any such system could be implemented. How would the numbers for requisitions be determined? How would employees without access to a computer enter online requisitions? How would the required documentation be attached to the requisition? What would happen to a requisition approval should a user along the way be absent? What if a user found an error? How would data entry be validated before reaching the end of the approval process? And, what new problems would this paperless requisition system generate on its own? It seemed to me they simply did not know what to do if they did not need to pickup their customary stack of pre-printed, three-part forms.

First we compared how the software company designed their system to work since we already knew how our traditional business process flowed; could one accommodate the other? The city process involved a department acquiring a stack of pre-printed forms on three-part paper from Administrative Services. Then any employee in a department would fill out the form submit it to their supervisor. They would forward it to the next supervisor if approved, and so on until it reached Purchasing. Then if the coding was correct, go to the city manager, if he approved, would sign it and return to Purchasing, who then entered it into the accounting system, and generated a PO for it.

The software was designed to allow a user to establish named approval groups. These approval groups contained a listing of up to five approvers, designated by their actual login names to the accounting system, and an alternate for each if necessary. Each approver could be required or not, and could have dollar thresholds on approvals.

A requisition is entered in the accounting system and a named approval group may be selected from a drop-down list of available groups. This requisition must be approved by each required member of the approval group in successive order. The approvers may also deny a requisition as well. Each action is logged and date/time stamped, and the approvers may enter comments on the transactions. These comments follow the requisition throughout the process. The existing requisition entry system that had been used by Purchasing for years already, to input the paper forms that came to Administrative Services allowed for text notes and comments entry on them. Should the requisition make it through all required levels, it is then eligible to be converted to a valid PO and encumber funds on the accounting system.

We determined we were only concerned with the first primary level of authorization. In other words, no matter how many police officers there are, and no matter how many sergeants, they all have to have their requisitions approved by the police chief before going any further in the process. So the chief became the first level of approval for the police. Any officer can put in a requisition for a new chair, and that will end up in the chief's approval list.

We then realized to avoid as many coding errors as possible it should go through Purchasing at that point for review. It should logically go to the city manager next, and then back to Purchasing to be converted to a PO. So we built approval group tables for each department/division based on that premise and wound up with most only having four levels of approval.

For example, if an employee wanted to request a new plotter printer for their department, any employee in the city can input a requisition for a new printer to be purchased from their own budget, but approved and installed by Information Services. The user simply puts in vendor information, quote information, and pricing arrangements. They then need to pick the "INFORMATION SERVICES" approval group from the drop-down list and away it goes. The first stop along the way is the Information Services director. If he approves it, it goes to the Purchasing agent to review account information, wording, quote and purchasing compliance, and freight terms. If he approves it, it goes to the city manager for review. If the manager approves the purchase, it returns to the Purchasing agent, who then presses the button and converts the requisition into a purchase order, which then encumbers the funds on the requesting department's budget.

The software allows for automatic number generation, or manual number input. At some point, we would want all auto-number generation, but during the implementation phase, we decided to use up the pre-printed numbers we already had on hand and let the users key them in manually. When a user is entering a requisition that required three verbal quotes, they could include that information in the text notes and comments fields of the requisition. If it required written quotes, the user could also enter that information in the text and comment fields, and just forward the written documentation on to Purchasing through normal inter-office mail procedures.

The next hurdle would be getting everyone access to the system, or so we thought. We actually found that all the requisitions that came from the field in previous years, had already been centralized at the offices of various administrative staff persons with access to computers on the network. This also made the next phase of implementation not as daunting as we had envisioned: training.

We trained one staff person in Purchasing who then went and visited each centralized entry locale for the requisitions, and did a one-on-one training session in the system itself, demonstrating how to lookup vendors, and where to enter text comments and how to populate the fields correctly. At the completion of training, the announcement was made, no further paper requisitions would be accepted from that division except for some unforeseen circumstances, and the department was let lose with the system. When the system was purchased, training had been included in the cost, and more was offered. But the employees who had trained on it originally were no longer involved in the process, no longer worked for the city, or had never retained the knowledge for lack of use and implementation. We could have purchased new training, but the system was easy enough for staff to figure it out and training the trainer methodology usually saves money if the employees have a chance to utilize the system during training, or shortly thereafter.

It took about seven months to finally get at least some electronic entries from every department. It was slower to implement than we expected because, even though we process anywhere from 860 to 1,000 requisitions a year, many are seasonal. Either purchases are loaded up at the beginning of the year, or squeezed in under the wire at the end. Several training sessions needed to be repeated because the length of time between training and actual use was lengthy in many instances.

In conjunction, the HTML interface provided with our 2001 upgrade sends users in the approval group an e-mail notifying them of pending requisitions awaiting their review for approval. This active notification system meant requisitions would not lie dormant waiting for a user to search for work to be done.

Almost immediately though, it became apparent the process was much faster. Processing a requisition could be done in the same day now, sometimes in the same morning. Purchases that are encumbered, but do not require phone quotes, or bids, are the most prevalent transaction in the Purchasing workload, so this greatly reduced the lag time between request and issuance of a delivery document to a vendor in order to provide or secure their services.

Subsequent to that, we have almost entirely eliminated the need for the paper requisition forms. Best estimates rate it at about $4,000 annual savings in printing and paper purchase, as well as the need for storage space for the printed forms—completed and blank. The number of "lost" requisitions misplaced on people's desks is virtually non-existent. And this process has afforded us another rare opportunity—a look into the transformation of an older government system.

It was after the implementation of the paperless requisition had reached about 90%, Stuart fell victim to extensive hurricane damage. I can remember being without power and the same employees, who balked the paperless requisition system would never work for our organization, were the same ones calling in a panic wanting to know how we would ever buy anything ever again without that "nifty" online purchasing "thingy" we gave them.

City works would grind to a halt now that requisitions had to be filled out in paper and sit on people's desk awaiting approval, and the time between getting a quote and issuing a purchase order would be so vast, all our budget estimates would be shot as prices rose faster than we could secure them.

It was quite a gratifying feeling to see a fledgling idea from more than six years before come to fruition in such a single point of commonality. We were all affected by the hurricane damage and power outages and all needed emergency purchases and repairs and were acquiring price quotes that were extremely time sensitive. We managed through it, and the city recovered just fine.

Current Challenges Facing the Organization

Today we are progressing forward with the next phase of the online purchasing system—online receiving as well. Again, this is an existing part of our ERP system, simply never utilized or activated, because the original installers of the base system never envisioned its use. From one upgrade to the next, the feature settings and necessary tables have remained vacant.

The paperless requisition system still has some flaws as it currently exists. The backup documentation still needs to be forwarded to Purchasing separately from the electronic requisition, and only notation of it can be included in the text references of the requisition record. We have looked into digital imaging and "attachments", but access to scanners and the necessary skill set to attach a Microsoft Word document to the ERP system transaction are few and far between. We are considering adding scanners to the network at central locations and increasing the training.

The notifications that come in e-mail to the approvers can only be pre-set to run at certain times of the day, so it is not a "real-time" notification system. Most users have settled on setting up an early-morning notification to catch late entries from the previous day, and one again in the afternoon to notify them of the bulk of entries from the current day. We understand the software provider is working on a real-time notification system for a future upgrade release.

The text and comment fields are limited in length due to basic database design and efficient electronic storage space principles and so many of the notations are not as in-depth as the hand written requisitions would have been. Again, the software company is fielding our comments and working towards expanding the data entry capabilities for end users.

The future is often feared because we value what we have more than what we can imagine.

Author's Biography

J. Louis Boglioli, III, *is currently the Financial Services Assistant Director of the City of Stuart, Florida. Mr. Boglioli received a BBA from Loyola University of the South, is a Florida Certified Government Finance Officer, is MOUS (mouse) certified in Excel and PowerPoint, and has instructed adult learning classes for computers. As a member of the Florida GFOA, he was the chairman of the School of Government Finance, chairman of the Standing Technology Committee, and a member of the Ad Hoc Committee that first created the FGFOA Web site. He currently speaks at different engagements around the State of Florida concerning implementation of technology in government, and was a presenter at the National GFOA Conventions in San Antonio, TX, and Montreal, Canada.*

Chapter VII

Implementation of a Computerized Maintenance Management System (CMMS) for the City of Naperville Department of Public Utilities

Lawrence E. Gunderson, City of Naperville, Illinois, USA

Executive Summary

This case study reviews the process that the City of Naperville Information Technology Department undertook to implement a Computerized Maintenance Management System (CMMS) for the city's Department of Public Utilities–Water. A CMMS is a software system for managing infrastructure with tools for creating and tracking maintenance activities associated with physical assets. Typical requirements for a CMMS include the ability to handle requests for service, process work orders, plan preventive maintenance, provide for tests and inspections, and enable ad hoc searching and reporting. The software that the Naperville Water Utility chose for a CMMS was selected for its tight integration with its Geographic

Information System (GIS), the computerized mapping database that contained a spatial model of the department's water distribution and wastewater collection assets. Many of the challenges that the IT Department had in implementing the CMMS related to issues with the GIS data. In addition, several of the city's financial systems, such as accounting, utility billing, customer information systems, and inventory required integration with the CMMS. The case study will cover the complexities of integration with these disparate data sources that have both a technical and organizational basis. Finally, as with all implementations of software systems, the element of organizational change needed to be addressed. For that reason, business process mapping and re-engineering practices were employed to support the deployment of the software.

Background

The City of Naperville, Illinois was incorporated in 1831. Over the past 175 years, the city has grown both in population and size to approximately 140,000 people and 38 square miles. The city has developed a reputation nationally for its high standard of living, low crime rate, and favorable corporate business climate.

The city operates under a council-manager form of government with a city manager who is hired by, and reports to, a nine-member city council. Reporting to the city manager are the manager's office staff (which includes the City Clerk's Office, Community Relations, and Social Services) and the appointed directors of the following departments:

- Finance Department
- Fire Department
- Human Resources/Organizational Resources Effectiveness Department
- Legal Department
- Police Department
- Department of Public Utilities
  - o Electric
  - o Water and Wastewater
- Department of Public Works
- Information Technology Department

The city's Information Technology (IT) Department supports the technology needs of over 1,000 city employees. The department is comprised of a 21 member staff team that is organized around four functional support areas: business applications, geographic information systems (GIS), telecommunications, and network systems. The IT Department has been the recent recipient of a number of accolades including a Special Achievement in GIS award for Outstanding Use of Geographic Information System (GIS) Technology by ESRI—2005.

The city's total operating budget is approximately $355,000,000. The five-year Capital Improvements Program (CIP) is approximately $400,000,000. The major sources of revenue are as follows:

- General Fund—Sales Taxes, Utility Taxes, Property Taxes
- Electric Utility—Electricity Sales
- Water and Wastewater Utility—Water and Wastewater Sales

Naperville is somewhat unique in Illinois in that the city owns and operates both the electric and water and wastewater utilities. The city maintains ultimate control over service delivery, and is able to provide lower costs than comparable private utilities in the area.

Because the utilities are run much more like a business than traditional municipal government service departments, there are unique issues that the city Information Technology Department has when supporting them.

Setting the Stage

This case study reviews the process that the Information Technology Department undertook to implement a computerized maintenance management system (CMMS) for the city's Department of Public Utilities–Water and Wastewater (DPU–W or simply "the Water Utility").

DPU-W is a division of the Department of Public Utilities, and is led by a director that oversees both the water and wastewater utilities, as well as the electric utility. The department was created in the early 1990s by joining the previously separate water/wastewater and electric utilities into one department. Prior to the creation of the one department, the electric utility had gone through a period of instability. This was due to poor facility planning, prior to a period of high city development and growth, that led to electric outages and general system unreliability. The director, who originally led the water and wastewater utilities and had a reputation for progressive leadership, brought the same approach to the electric utility. This led to an increased focus on capital improvements to replace out-dated equipment and preventive maintenance to extend the useful life of the existing infrastructure.

This progressive mindset led to the Department of Public Utilities' implementation of new technology during the 1990s. SCADA (Supervisory Control and Data Acquisition Systems), automated meter reading, and distribution automation were some of the new systems that were deployed. With SCADA, both the electric and water utilities have the ability to monitor and control critical points of their systems (such as circuit breakers or water pumps) remotely.

During the same time period, the Finance Department (which at that point included the Management Information Systems (MIS) Division, the forerunner to the current Information Technology Department) had also implemented a commercial enterprise resource planning (ERP) system across the city's departments. The ERP system included, among other modules, utility billing/customer information, work orders/facility management, and general ledger.

The Department of Public Utilities embraced many of the software modules in the city's ERP that directly applied to their operations. This was especially true for the Electric Division, which incorporated the work order/facility management module into their workflow for the engineering and design of new electric distribution facilities. The Water Utility, which includes both a Civil Engineering and a Water Distribution and Collection (Water Operations) Division, was less successful in this regard. This was due mainly to the fact that the Civil Engineering Division was not responsible for designing and building systems, like their electrical counterparts, and did not have a need for the software. For the Water Operations Division, which focuses mainly on operations and maintenance activities, staff found the work orders/facility management module to be unsuited to the workflow of their business operations and the orientation of the application to be related more to financial management than their core business.

However, because no other work order/facility management software was available for use, and because of the tight integration of the work orders/facility management module to general ledger and capital asset management that was required by the Finance Department, Water Operations reluctantly used the application.

At about this time, the MIS Division began the process of implementing geographic information systems (GIS) at the city. GIS software has been defined as a "powerful set of tools for collecting, sorting, retrieving at will, transforming and displaying spatial data from the real world for a particular set of purposes" (Huxhold, 1991, p. 25). As with most government bodies, the city's business is primarily location-based, from addresses (calls for emergency services, service requests), to infrastructure (to build and maintain). Recognizing the potential for GIS to greatly enhance the quality and efficiency of city services, Naperville City Council approved a plan for GIS implementation in the fiscal year 1994 Capital Improvement Program.

One the main reasons Naperville implemented GIS was to provide the city's utilities (electric, water, wastewater and stormwater) with a seamless spatially-referenced computer model of each of their systems. Unlike the way assets are modeled in a financial system, in a GIS assets are unique features with geometric shapes (such as points, lines, or polygons) and real-world map coordinates. For example, in a water distribution system GIS database, a valve is a point feature and a water main is a linear feature. The database also stores spatial relationships between features (a fire hydrant is connected to a hydrant line, but not to a water main). This is in addition to the descriptive tabular data that is associated with each feature, which are often called "attributes". Examples of attributes for a water system feature (such as a water main) include pipe diameter, length, and material. The data that is stored in a GIS is essential to the day-to-day operations of a utility as staff at all levels of the organization seek critical information about the infrastructure they support.

The GIS data view of the utility system assets can be contrasted with the financial model typically found in asset management systems. In the financial model, the most important aspect of the data is the type of asset that it is and the date that it was put into service, so that the value of the asset can be determined. While this information is vital from a financial reporting perspective, it does not provide what is needed from a true asset management perspective of the utility. For that reason, GIS is considered to be one of the most important aspects of an asset management information system for a water utility (New England Water Environment Association, 2004).

Another important aspect of an asset management system is a computerized maintenance management system (CMMS). CMMSs provide the capability to schedule, monitor, and track all resource information required for maintenance activities. Most are relational database applications designed for the needs of asset managers, providing the ability to manage work orders, trouble calls, materials inventory, and preventive maintenance schedules. Another key feature of these systems is the ability to enable ad hoc searching and reporting (Kyle, 2001).

In Naperville's case, this was a critical requirement because management and staff often needed to report to city management or Naperville City Council on the progress of important water utility projects that have direct impact on Naperville citizens. These include projects to replace lead-lined water service connections (pipes that connect a business or private residence to the city's water distribution network), or rehabilitate aging sewer mains.

There are many commercial CMMSs available in the software marketplace. In 1997, the city's IT Department and the Water Utility began searching for a CMMS that would best fit the city's needs. Besides the typical software features found in most CMMSs, the main attribute that the city (especially the IT Department) was looking for was tight integration with the city's GIS. After several demonstrations by software vendors and a software evaluation period, the city chose a package called Pipeworks (later renamed Cityworks) from Azteca Systems of Sandy, UT.

Unlike other CMMSs, which required the development of a separate asset database, Cityworks utilized the GIS as its asset database. This allowed for the elimination of redundant data, the ability to use GIS tools (such as geographic searches and data-driven mapping) within the CMMS, and direct linkage of maintenance activities to GIS features.

An important internal political consideration at the time was for the GIS Manager to gain the support of the Water Operations Division Manager for GIS. Since the Water Operations Division was responsible for the Water Utility's implementation of GIS, the GIS Manager believed that the best way to gain the backing of the Water Operations Manager for GIS was to offer IT Department support of a new CMMS software package.

While the selection of Cityworks as the CMMS was an important step for IT and the Water Utility, many other issues needed to be resolved before the software could become operational. These included:

- Creating a new workflow for service requests and work orders using Cityworks software;
- Integrating payroll, inventory, and customer information between the city's ERP system and Cityworks; and
- Developing a GIS-based asset database of the water and wastewater systems to be the basis for Cityworks

Of all of the issues that were critical to the successful use of Cityworks, creating a GIS database evolved into a task that proved to be the biggest single impediment to Cityworks implementation. The following is a summary of the long and arduous path that the city took to developing its water and wastewater GIS.

GIS Data Development

With the completion of the GIS land base (digital data layers of parcels, roads, building outlines, topography, etc.) by the city in 1997, it was possible to create the utility GIS databases that would be spatially referenced to them. Creating utility GIS databases is an inherently complex and time-consuming process that begins with defining a data model for each utility system.

At the time that Naperville embarked on developing water and wastewater system GIS databases, not many examples of utility GIS databases were in existence, and although Azteca Systems had published a data model to be used as a reference, there was no "standard" data model. In addition, no two utility systems are alike, so a custom Naperville-specific data model needed to be created. This was accomplished with the assistance of a consultant that had experience with developing GIS databases for other ESRI software customers. The consultant not only defined the physical data model of the system, but also the specifications for converting the utilities' many disparate data sources, such as paper maps and hard copy reports, into the physical data model. Because no complete set of maps of the water and wastewater systems existed (and those that did were of unknown spatial accuracy) it was determined that a complete field survey, using advanced global position systems (GPS) receivers, would be required. This requirement, in addition to the specifications for data conversion into the utility data model, formed the basis for a request for proposal (RFP) document.

Because of the significant cost of a complete data conversion project, the city project team decided that a pilot project would be a required first step in the process. This would enable the data model and data conversion process to be evaluated and validated on a subset of the entire city utility systems prior to full data conversion. The stormwater system (which was maintained by the Department of Public Works–DPW) was also included in the pilot project and full city-wide data conversion. The reason for this was that it made sense for a data conversion firm to capture all of the similar utility systems (water, wastewater, and stormwater) at the same time from one field survey, instead of separate survey projects for each system. A consultant hired by the city to plan the GIS implementation thought that this approach would save money for the economies of scale it offered and from the fact that it avoided the need to release separate RFPs, and go through additional procurement processes.

While a combined water, wastewater, and stormwater GIS data conversion project may have made sense from an economic standpoint, the city soon found out that it did not work well in practice. Many problems plagued the project right from the outset, some due the fact that the consultant that was selected for the project did not have as much experience with stormwater systems as they did with water and wastewater, others due to the fact that the consultant did not estimate the cost of the project correctly (this problem was also caused by the inability of city staff to properly estimate the number of utility features in each of its systems in the RFP).

Due to the project cost being underestimated, the consultant proposed a change order to the city of over $485,000—over 50% of the original project cost of $837,000—to complete the project. After much internal debate over the pros and cons of completing the project with the original consultant, the change order proposal was rejected by the city manager. This led to the consultant agreeing to only deliver data for approximately two-thirds of the city. After a complete change in the project staff of the consultant, the final deliverable was finally provided to the city in December 2003, nearly two years after the original proposed completion date. This was for a delivery of only two-thirds of the city—the remaining one-third still needed to be completed.

After much internal staff discussion over what would be the best method for completing the final one-third of the city (either with another consulting contract or by in-house staff) the Water Utility's Civil Engineering Division staff proposed that they would complete the project. Additional resources needed to be acquired to accomplish this so the Water Utility hired temporary staff and also purchased GPS survey equipment to enable the field inventory portion of the project. With these resources in place, the Water Utility was finally able to complete both a water and wastewater GIS database in early 2005.

Interim CMMS Implementation

During the intervening years from the original purchase of Cityworks, until the completion of the GIS database, two different initiatives to implement Cityworks were attempted by IT and the Water Utility.

In 1998, it was determined that enough GIS data existed (from an interim Water Operations Division staff field inventory) to enable a limited implementation of Cityworks. Azteca had also created an option in their software allowing "unattached" work orders. This meant that a work order for a task, such as flushing a fire hydrant, did not always have to be linked to an actual GIS feature (if it did not exist in the GIS database). In this scenario, the software would track the work that occurred, including any labor costs, materials, and equipment. This meant the software would function much like other CMMSs: it just would not have the added functionality of being tied to an asset in a GIS database. This appeared to be a workable interim solution to implementing Cityworks, so once it was determined that this approach would be taken, a project plan was created by IT staff.

A target date for Cityworks implementation was set and Azteca Systems was brought on-site for training of Water Operations staff that would use the software. The application, which is built on a standard two-tier client/server architecture, was loaded on the user's desktops. Water Operations was all set for a successful Cityworks roll-out. However, after a couple of weeks with the software in operation, nearly all use of the application stopped.

When asked what the problems were with the software, and why it was not being used, several reasons were provided. The main reason identified was that "double entry" of data was required, that is, labor and equipment costs needed to be tracked in Cityworks, and then re-entered into the ERP system for accounting purposes. When asked why accounting data was being re-entered into the ERP, the answer provided was that Finance Department utility accounting staff would not accept data out of Cityworks: it had to come from the ERP work orders/facility management module.

Another reason cited for the lack of support for Cityworks is that it did not fit well into Water Operations' work order process workflow. Supervisors did not want to change their processes, and most tellingly, the division manager of Water Operations did not feel the effort to implement the software was worth it and did not push his staff to go beyond a cursory effort. The only positive to come out of the abandoned implementation was a list of proposed software enhancements that was forwarded to Azteca.

Fortunately for the city, the investment in Cityworks software was not lost. After the initial development of Cityworks software for work orders, Azteca Systems had added additional functionality to their application. The ability to track service requests, which are a more limited, but common type of task, was added to their software suite. With service requests, almost any activity that did not require capture of capital costs for asset management (which is basically any operations and maintenance activity) could be tracked. The city's Department of Public Works, DPU–Electric, and the City Dispatch Division of the Police Department (who were responsible for taking all non-emergency calls from Naperville residents) became interested in the software. With the Call Center/Service Request module, service requests for activities such as street light repair, electric outage investigations, and pot hole repair could be tracked. City Dispatch would be able to take calls from the public, see geographically through a GIS map interface where the call came from, and forward the request to the appropriate responding department for problem resolution

Seeing the advantage to that approach, especially compared to the process that was being used (an old text-based mainframe application that created a printed request that was forwarded through inter-office mail), the proposed system made much more sense. After a short evaluation period and user training for each of the key departmental staff, in mid-2000 the Call Center/Service Request module was implemented. The implementation was a resounding success and after one year in operation nearly 6,000 service requests were entered. Figure 1 is a snapshot of a Cityworks Call Center screen display showing a service request being created.

Figure 1. Screen display of Cityworks Call Center application

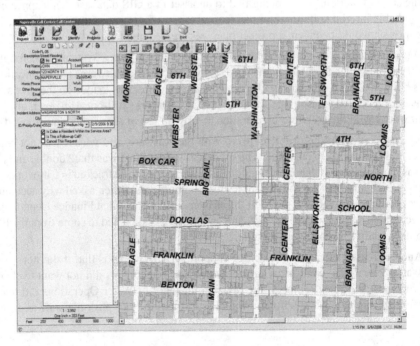

Seeing the success that other city departments had with a service request-only approach to using Cityworks, the IT Department approached the DPU-W Water Operations Division about adopting service requests for their operation. With the GIS data conversion still underway, and the sticky problem of integration of data between Cityworks and the city's ERP system for capital projects still unresolved, the incremental approach to using Cityworks seemed to have the best chance for success.

Water Operations staff gave the IT Department approval to this approach. Recalling the lack of support by Water Operations Division management during the last attempt at implementation, IT went about the planning process in a more inclusive manner. Meetings were held with all project stakeholders prior to the implementation. Potential problems were discussed and an action list of problems to be resolved was generated after each meeting. The software was configured so that Water Operations' unique service request types (for operations such as a water main break, sewer backup, or water shut-off) could be input into the system.

Once all of the outstanding issues were resolved a target date for roll-out was planned. IT Department staff, which had become proficient on the software through its work with other city departments, conducted user training for all of Water Operations' key users (mainly clerical staff that had been responsible for entering work orders into the ERP). The target roll-out date came, and Water Operations began to enter service requests. However, after a few weeks, the amount of service requests entered slowed to a trickle. After another few weeks, no service requests were entered at all, and Water Operations cancelled the monthly implementation review meetings that were held with IT.

Case Description

The city had purchased Cityworks CMMS software originally in 1997. As one of the original users of Cityworks, the city had provided much input to Azteca Systems on the direction of the software. Because the city was an evaluation site for Cityworks, many of the modules and additional software licensing were purchased below normal cost. Originally only designed to be an application to manage the work order process, Azteca had added additional functionality to manage service requests—including those requests generated by Naperville citizens and materials inventory.

After the successful implementation of the Call Center application and service requests for the Department of Public Works, DPU–Electric, and Police Department City Dispatch in 2000, the city was poised to implement the entire suite of Cityworks applications across all of the organization's departments that managed infrastructure. Because of the potential uses for Cityworks, the city negotiated the purchase of a site license of the software that allowed for unlimited use of all of the application's modules across the organization.

From a hardware/software architecture perspective, the Cityworks implementation was designed to take advantage of the city's Metropolitan Area Network (MAN). This allowed for a central database server and application servers to be maintained at the Municipal Center and client desktops to run the software at any city building on the MAN. The city's IT staff chose Citrix Presentation Server software to centrally deploy and manage the Cityworks application suite. Because the software resides and executes on the Citrix application server, the time and costs to install and configure Cityworks for users is greatly reduced (Citrix Systems, Inc., 2006). Application performance is also greatly enhanced because of the Citrix thin client architecture. Because the Cityworks work order application runs within ESRI's ArcGIS software, that application was also installed on the Citrix server.

The Cityworks database can be implemented within any SQL (Structured Query Language) compliant database. The city uses Microsoft SQL Server database, after migrating from its previous implementation of Oracle. A full-time database administrator in IT administers the Cityworks application, as well as the underlying SQL Server database. Because of the projected potential increase in city-wide Cityworks software use, city IT staff purchased a dual processor database server and a site license of SQL Server database user seats. Figure 2 is a diagram of the city's Cityworks hardware and software systems architecture in 2003.

Now that the city's systems architecture was able to support a complete city-wide implementation of Cityworks, IT staff began to refocus on the task that it originally intended to do: implement the Cityworks CMMS in the Department of Public Utilities–Water.

Reflecting on the two failed implementations of Cityworks that occurred in previous years, the GIS Manager in IT (the main proponent of Cityworks at the city) identified what appeared to be the main causes for the lack of success. Some of these reasons included:

- Lack of organizational support for Cityworks in Water Operations at the management level (i.e., division manager, supervisors, etc.). This was in addition to a seeming lack of computer systems innovation within the division, despite strong upper management leadership in the department and an overall progressive, "best practices" approach to water/wastewater system management within Water Operations;

- Concerns with duplication of effort with entering and maintaining of accounting and asset data in two separate systems (i.e., Cityworks and the ERP) by Water Operations staff;

Figure 2. Cityworks' systems architecture

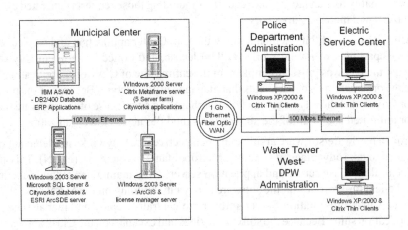

- Lack of support by the city's Finance Department for Cityworks because of a perception that the financial data that Cityworks created was not valid, and that the ERP was the *only* source for these data;

- Feelings of many key Water Operations staff that the effort to implement Cityworks (including learning a new software package) was not worth the value of what the software brought to the organization;

- Concerns with how Cityworks could be incorporated into the Water Operations Division workflow;

- Perceptions by Water Operations staff that the Cityworks implementation was an "IT project" that was being forced on them against their will;

- Lack of experience with a complete Cityworks implementation (including design of new business processes and configuration of the software for work orders) by city IT GIS staff; and

- Lack of a complete water and wastewater GIS asset database due to delays in the GIS data conversion project.

The GIS Manager believed that the many reasons that were holding back Water Operations from implementing Cityworks could be overcome. The development of the water and wastewater GIS was progressing along and an end to the project was in sight. Water Operations was using a patchwork system for managing its service request/work order process that was not meeting its needs, and Water Operations staff were beginning to feel that *anything* was better than what it was using.

Another important factor was that IT staff were aware that there had been a significant investment in hardware and software in the Cityworks systems architecture, and until there was full use of the system, the city would not see a return on investment (ROI) in Cityworks. It appeared that the time may be right to finally get Cityworks implemented at Water Operations. However, this time around a more thorough, systematic methodology would need to be used. The approach would have to address the problems and issues that had been identified in the previous unsuccessful implementations.

Pre-Implementation Process

The GIS Manager began the process of what hopefully was going to be a successful implementation of Cityworks at Water Operations. The first task was to set up a "summit" meeting of all the departments in the city that were responsible for managing business processes (such as service requests and work orders) that were related to utility asset management. This included representatives of the Department of Public Utilities–Electric and Water, and the Department of Public Works. The Finance Department, including the new department director and all staff associated with utility accounting, also attended.

The main goal of the meeting was to foster a common understanding among all of the attendees of the asset management process at the city. Other objectives included providing a forum for the utility departments to explain to Finance staff the problems and limitations of the ERP system for the service request/work order process. In order to help gain an understanding of this process, the attending departments were asked to present their current workflow for others to see.

At the meeting common definitions of what a service request and a work order are were developed by the group. The following are those definitions:

Service Request

- A request for service by an internal or external customer;
- Mainly operations & maintenance (O & M) related;
- Can have costs associated (such as labor and materials); and
- Meant to record the task, and work completion.

Work Order

- Capital or O&M-related (includes new and re-construction);
- Captures costs (labor, material, equipment, overhead, etc.);
- Work is at a specific location and is associated with one or more assets;
- Larger in scope than a service request; and
- May be precipitated by a service request.

In a very forthright presentation, the utility specialist from Water Operations laid out in detail a very cumbersome, antiquated process that involved a lot of data entry into the ERP, but a seeming lack of useful reporting of that same data out of the system. Water Operations also heard how well the Cityworks service request system was working for DPW and DPU-E, especially how it dramatically improved the resolution time for completing tasks.

As a result of the meeting, it was determined that because of the stringent requirements of FERC (Federal Energy Regulatory Commission) accounting it would be best if DPU-E not change its current asset management process using the work orders. Conversely, because for DPW, its main infrastructure (the stormwater system) was currently not being tracked as a capital asset by the city (in the ERP) there was no need to go to the extra effort to track labor, material, and equipment costs for work on the stormwater system at this time. That left the Water Utility, which accept for the need to move some of its capital work costs and assets into the ERP, appeared to be a perfect candidate to use a CMMS-like Cityworks to manage work orders.

Several follow-up discussions to the meeting were held between IT, Finance, and Water Utility staff. The Finance Director, being new to the city, wanted to first understand the issues involved. He also did not want to appear to be inflexible and unresponsive to the needs of the departments that his staff supported. With that, he agreed to a proposal by the IT Department to fund a consultant study to determine the feasibility of implementing service requests and work orders in the Water Utility's Water Operations Division.

Part of what precipitated the request for a consultant study was the opportunity created by the marked increase in the installed base of Cityworks user sites around the U.S. After going from a handful of evaluation sites (such as Naperville) in 1996, to literally dozens of cities, including some large sites like Long Beach, CA, Houston, TX and Salt Lake City, UT, Azteca Systems was becoming a major player in the utility CMMS marketplace. A number of engineering and utility technology consulting firms had become business partners of Azteca's and developed methodologies for implementing the software using a systematic, business process improvement-oriented approach.

The IT Department and Water Operations released an RFP for a Cityworks implementation feasibility study. The project had a limited scope of work due to limitations in funding (the project was not budgeted), but nonetheless included the following tasks:

- Interviewing of key Water Operations staff regarding their current service request/work order flow;
- Developing a process map graphically defining the workflow;
- Identifying and proposing improvements to the process, giving special consideration to how Azteca Cityworks software could be used;
- Defining the new process graphically;
- Identifying of interfaces (at a high level), between Azteca Cityworks and the city's financial/asset management (ERP) software required for the new proposed process;
- Interviewing staff members in both water/wastewater utility divisions (Civil Engineering and Water Operations) that maintain water/wastewater GIS data; and
- Proposing a workflow and suggested personnel for several key GIS data maintenance processes.

The last two tasks needed to be added to the scope because another issue had developed that was having a negative impact on a potential Cityworks implementation. The Water Operations Division, having to meet its business needs for mapping during the delayed GIS data conversion project, had developed its own set of GIS data separate from the Civil Engineering Division. The Engineering Division was responsible for the creation of the "official" department water and wastewater GIS data that was to be used as the asset database for Cityworks. The department now had two conflicting sets of GIS data, and engineering technicians in the Water Operations Division did not recognize the validity of the official department data.

The goal of the IT Department, besides mediating the disagreement between the two Water Utility Divisions, was to use the consultant study to provide a forum for every stakeholder in the GIS data maintenance process to have a say in how the process would be designed. The GIS Manager thought that by having a role in how the data was maintained, Water Operations staff would drop their objections to the data, and accept it as the official department GIS database.

The city selected a respected water utility engineering and information technology consultant for the project, at the limited budget of only $35,600, for what appeared to be a fair amount of work. One of the first tasks that the consultant performed was to define Water Operations' current work order maintenance workflow. This task was accomplished using a workshop format, whereby all of the players in the work order process brainstormed together a list of all of their work activities. The consultant then organized the activities by process and by who performed the task. This was all documented using a business process mapping software package.

Once the current or "as-is" model was created, the consultant re-mapped the process. This time a suggested, or "to-be" workflow, which streamlined the "as-is" workflow and showed how Cityworks could be used to facilitate the process, was created. Figure 3 is an excerpt from the "to-be" business process map.

The consultant then tackled the GIS data maintenance process, using the same "as-is" and "to-be" approach, with data collected from another workshop. A meeting was held with Finance Department accounting staff that identified the data flows and interfaces required between the ERP and the Cityworks database. The final deliverable for the project was a comprehensive report from the consultant that included all of the recommendations for why Water Operations should implement Cityworks, and how they could successfully implement the software.

At the conclusion of the consultant engagement, IT and Water Operations staff met to discuss the report. It was clear from Water Operations that they felt the study was a worthwhile process and there appeared to finally be some enthusiasm from the division manager towards using Cityworks. For the staff in the department, knowing that over 40 spreadsheets and standalone databases that were being maintained on a daily basis could be eliminated by using Cityworks seemed like a huge bonus.

The enthusiasm for the report led to discussions with Water Utility management about funding a project for an Azteca Cityworks implementer to configure the software around Water Operations' work processes and develop tools for integrating Cityworks with the city's ERP. As was for the first consulting engagement, there was not a budget for this project as well. Fortunately another water utility project came in below budget, and this money was earmarked for Cityworks implementation.

Figure 3. Business process map

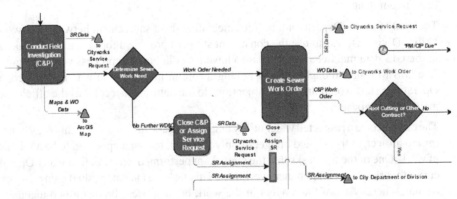

Cityworks Implementation

The two principals that had been leading the project, the GIS Manager from IT and the utility specialist from Water Operations, developed an RFP for the final implementation. The pair went about this task with renewed confidence that their goal of a comprehensive CMMS within Water Operations was finally within reach. The project included the following key tasks:

- Assisting the Water Operations Division with the definition of work order and work types and the priority designation of work activities;

- Configuration of Cityworks software, including: defining codes, setting security and user access, creating inspection and testing templates, and other Cityworks options;

- Defining management and field reporting requirements that Cityworks will support;

- Assisting with the implementation of necessary data integration requirements between the ERP and Cityworks;

- Developing a plan which incorporates the Water Utility's existing and historical work order management data, contained in a number of tables and spreadsheets, into the Cityworks database; and

- Determining an approach for materials management and equipment usage tracking, including coordination with the Department of Public Utilities–Electric (DPU-E) Support Services Division warehouse.

The proposal responses were reviewed by the RFP selection committee, and a consultant was chosen for the project. Although it was not the same consultant used for the first phase of the implementation, the committee was very satisfied with the choice, as the consultant had been involved with several successful implementations of Cityworks in the past. They also had experience with integrating data from the city's ERP software into Cityworks.

When the project began, both the city and consultant agreed to work together to insure that the engagement was going to be a success. The project manager for the consulting firm incorporated the city's RFP specifications into a project charter document that was signed by the key stakeholders. A detailed work breakdown structure was developed that defined all of the project tasks, resources, and deliverables for a Gantt chart that became the project blueprint. When the timeline for the project was developed it was determined that because of the amount of risk and variability associated with data integration, the ERP integration task would be done last.

The consultant project team dove into the project without hesitation, and within the first month of working with Water Operations, maintenance supervisors, and management defined over 50 unique work order templates (forms-based interfaces) for the water system alone. The templates for a water distribution feature (such as a fire hydrant) included all of the following tasks that could be performed on a hydrant, such as: installing, removing, relocating, repairing, replacing, painting, static testing, and flow testing.

The consultant reviewed the completeness of the water and wastewater GIS database to insure that it was ready for a Cityworks implementation. By now Water Utility Civil Engineering staff had been working diligently for almost five years on the effort, and the database was near completion. The consultant did identify a few system features that were missing from the database and a team of IT GIS staff and a Civil Engineering GIS Technician devoted nearly a month of focused effort to complete the task. Figure 4 is a section of a water system GIS map showing water mains, valves, and fire hydrants in downtown Naperville.

With the work order (and service request) templates defined and the GIS database in place, the consultants were able to turn their attention to the ERP integration task. A data integration workshop was held with city Finance Department accounting staff, IT, and Water Operations. At first there was a lot of concern that the accountants would stall the project, making unreasonable demands for two-way data flow between the ERP and Cityworks. But none of these concerns were realized, and the level of integration between the two applications was much less than originally anticipated. In a few instances, the Finance Department only wanted a report from Cityworks that they would manually enter into the ERP.

The remainder of the integration data flow mainly consisted of utility customer information, employee payroll, water meter, and inventory data being loaded from the ERP's DB2/400 database into the Cityworks SQL Server database tables using native SQL Server ETL (extract, transform and load) functionality. The consultant developed an automated Windows Server service that performed this function on a nightly basis.

At this point, the project was right on schedule and the planned roll-out of Cityworks in Water Operations was scheduled for September 2005, only four months after the project kick-off. However, a couple of weeks before the roll-out, the utility specialist asked if the date could be pushed back because Water Operations was not ready. Unfortunately, it was budget season for the city, and the utility specialist was the Water Operations Division's budget manager.

Figure 4. Water system GIS map

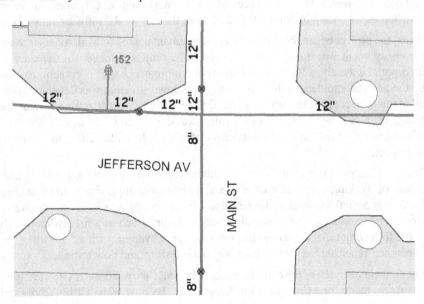

However, after the budget was submitted, Water Operations asked for yet another month extension. The project team, especially the consultant hired by the city, was getting concerned. First of all, the positive energy and momentum that the project had was almost gone, and the consultant's available hours for the project were almost all used up.

It was clear at this point that the main problem that had always vexed the project—a lack of commitment by the Water Operations Division Manager—had not gone away. The Water Operations Utility Specialist was the only staff member assigned full time to the project, and when he could not devote any time to it, no one else was there to step up. The utility specialist was successful in asking another of the division supervisors to assign an engineering technician from his staff to the project. Fortunately, the engineering technician was one of the more outspoken Cityworks proponents in the division, as well as one of the strongest technically. The project immediately began to pick up steam again as the engineering technician began to train key department clerical staff (those that are currently involved in the work order process) on using the somewhat complex GIS-based Cityworks application interface.

A project punch list was developed by the project team. It was comprised of mainly minor technical revisions that needed to be made to the configuration before roll-out and clarification of workflow issues. With that, a new roll-out date was chosen, this time in early March 2006—which was only a few weeks away. However, Water Operations proposed that the roll-out would only be for service requests: the work order implementation was going to have to wait.

The GIS Manager immediately recalled the last time a service request-only roll-out was attempted—and how it failed miserably. No, this time would be different, the utility specialist and engineering technician reassured him, Water Operations would follow with a full work order implementation, as planned.

The GIS Manager was still a little uneasy with this plan. A tremendous amount of effort had gone into the project to this point: a multi-year GIS data conversion project, several consulting contracts, and countless hours of city staff time. The original goal—to implement a computerized maintenance management system using the GIS as its asset database—was within reach, but still not accomplished. Tracking service requests was a great start, and a good springboard to going to work orders, but it was not the project objective.

Current Challenges Facing the Organization

After a few months with a service request-only approach, Water Operations finally implemented work orders. Although it is only on a small scale, it is still very possible that they will expand their deployment in the future. As opposed to past attempts at implementing the software, there is a sense of commitment among division staff towards Cityworks that was lacking in the past. This is most likely due to the excellent work that the consultants did in showing the value of a CMMS to Water Operations, and the extensive configuration work that was done to customize the software around the division's work practices.

Currently, there is some organizational turnover at the management level (the Water Operations Division Manager has left the city) that is causing some disruption to the ongoing roll-out. However, it is anticipated that a more technology-friendly manager will be brought in that will support applications, like CMMS, in the future.

As was in the past, workflow processes and the impact on organizational change among Water Operations staff are an issue. The ability to have access to the Cityworks application out in the field (in utility maintenance vehicles) through wireless connectivity using Citrix thin-client technology is possible. This will allow field staff to be able to report on their activities and close work orders in the field, without adding the additional step of bringing in paperwork to clerical staff. However, the city has decided on a conservative approach to exposing the field-based workforce to technology, as there are indications that many of these personnel are wary of, and often unreceptive to, using computers.

Issues with the GIS data between Water Operations and Civil Engineering staff still come up; however, the process that was defined by the consultant for data maintenance has been successful. The last vestige of the old interim Water Operations GIS data, which is seen in the hard copy maps that are used by field staff, has not been resolved yet. However, a plan is in place for Water Operations to create a whole new series of small scale maps, based on the corporate water and wastewater GIS data, that will go along way towards promoting acceptance of the data by division staff.

Ultimately, what city IT staff have learned from the Cityworks CMMS project, is that having the best technology is not what makes an implementation successful. Far more important is the readiness of the organization to embrace that technology.

References

Citrix Systems, Inc. (2006). *Citrix presentation server*. Retrieved February 10, 2006, from http://www.citrix.com/English/ps2/products/product.asp?contentID=186

Huxhold, W. E. (1991) *An introduction to urban geographic information systems*. New York: Oxford University Press.

Kyle, B. R. (2001). Toward effective decision making for building management. In the *Proceedings of the American Public Works Association, APWA International Public Works Congress*, Philadelphia, September. Retrieved February 8, 2006, from http://irc. nrc-nrc.gc.ca/fulltext/apwa/2001kyle.pdf

New England Water Environment Association. (2006). Asset Management Resource Center. Retrieved February 8, 2006, from http://www.newea.org/AMRC/

Author's Biography

Lawrence E. Gunderson holds a BS degree in industrial education from Western Illinois University and an MS in management information systems from North Central College. He has over 20 years

of experience in the advanced use of computer technology, the last 15 of which have been devoted to GIS, computerized maintenance management systems (CMMS), and enterprise content management (ECM). Mr. Gunderson joined the City of Naperville, Illinois, in 1993 and was appointed to the position of GIS Manager in 1994. As GIS Manager, he was responsible for the implementation of an enterprise GIS for the city. Currently, Mr. Gunderson is the Information Technology Program Manager at the city where he oversees all GIS, ECM, and IT project management activities. Mr. Gunderson has been active in GIS professional organizations such as the Urban and Regional Information Systems Association (URISA) and the Illinois GIS Association (ILGISA).

Chapter VIII

Insuring a Successful ERP Implementation:
Lessons Learned from a Failed Project at a State Public University

Kimberly Furumo, University of Hawaii at Hilo, USA

Executive Summary

This chapter provides a case study of a failed enterprise resource planning (ERP) implementation at a public university. Public universities, like other governmental agencies, may have more difficulty implementing information technology (IT) because of limited resources, increased organizational bureaucracy, and extensive statutory reporting requirements. This chapter begins by identifying what an ERP system is, the difficulties of implementing ERP systems, and the added difficulties related to implementing technology in governmental organizations. In this case study analysis, upper managers, IT staff, and functional department end users were asked to identify why the project failed. Several lessons were learned including the importance of allocating adequate financial resources to IT projects and managing the change process. As organizations move from the centralized legacy system environment which was prevalent in the last half of the 20th century, to the new distributed ERP environment, roles and responsibilities are changing. Readers are provided with practical suggestions that will help improve IT implementation success in governmental agencies.

Background

In the last decade, there has been a move by organizations in both private and public sectors to purchase large-scale, integrated application systems known as enterprise resource planning (ERP) systems. These enterprise systems are large, complex systems that consist of a series of independent modules that can be installed together or one-at-a-time (Hoffer, George, & Valacich, 2005). ERP systems allow organizations to integrate data into a single database, eliminating the need to duplicate information in multiple files, and provide graphical user interfaces (GUI) that allow users to easily extract data and format it for personalized reports.

The potential advantages of purchasing packaged software rather than developing software systems in-house include reduced cost, quicker implementation, and higher system quality (Lucas, Walton, & Ginzberg, 1988). However, since these off-the-shelf software packages are designed for many different users, they tend to be standardized and often require organizations to change their business processes or invest significant resources to customize the software. As a result, many of these ERP implementations do not meet financial, time, and productivity goals (Griffith, Zammuto, & Aiman-Smith, 1999).

Sharma, Palvia, and Salam (2002) identified the significant risks of implementing ERP systems including the degree of fit the package has with the existing business processes and the extent to which the organization's business processes need to be revamped. The changes to business processing that are required, when an ERP system is implemented, lead to user resistance (Joshi, 2005). To deal with this resistance, many organizations have adopted transformation approaches known as business re-engineering processes (BPR) to transform business processes. However, BPR projects are often delivered with less than stellar results (Paper, 1999).

The difficulty of implementing distributed ERP systems may be compounded by the need for organizations to maintain and interface with centralized legacy systems. Many organizations, having invested heavily in legacy systems, are not in a position to scrap those systems but must instead find ways to integrate them with the newer ERP system (Erlikh, 2002).

Research indicates that it may be more difficult to implement information technology systems, such as ERP systems, in public-sector and government-supported organizations such as state universities. This is due to several factors including the greater level of interdependence across organizational boundaries in public-sector organizations. The following passage accurately describes this difficulty:

"The authority of the public organization derives in part from legal and constitutional arrangements. Embedded in those institutions are traditional concerns for checks and balances, often manifested as oversight groups or external organizational control of personnel activity and financial resources. Consequently, public organizations exhibit greater interdependence across organizational boundaries than do private organizations." (Bretschneider, 1990, p. 537)

This greater interdependence leads to greater oversight which leads to more procedural steps and delays. Bretschneider (1990) describes this phenomenon as the higher level of "red tape" experienced by public-sector organizations.

Since public universities are ultimately accountable to the state taxpayers, reporting requirements are extensive. Newcomer and Caudle (1991) suggest that public- and private-sector information systems differ in the variety of users who need to access data from the system. In public universities, state agencies such as the governor's office and the general assembly along with parents, customers, and labor groups require information about students, employees, and productivity measures. The number of administrative staff at most public universities has steadily grown in recent years in order to handle increasing reporting requirements related to taxpayer's expectations of productivity and accountability.

At the same time, funding for many public organizations is diminishing making it difficult to purchase costly technology. To purchase all the modules of an ERP system is often cost prohibitive for public organizations. Instead, expenditures may have to be allocated over several fiscal years budgets leading to phased-system implementations. The centralized legacy computer systems used commonly in the last half of the 20th century are fundamentally different from the modern distributed ERP applications of today. While private-sector corporations are often able to convert from the centralized legacy environment to the distributed ERP environment at a single point in time, public-sector organizations typically have to face the prolonged difficulties and disruption resulting when technology projects are phased.

Another difference between private- and public-sector organizations relates to the location of the information system's chief or chief information system officer (CIO) in the organizational chart. In private-sector organizations, the CIO is at the highest level of the organization. Conversely, in public-sector organizations, the CIO is normally placed at a lower level in the organization to buffer the IS function from the turbulence caused by frequent political changes which result in discontinuities of leadership (Bretschneider, 1990). The lower positioning of the CIO limits its influence and authority in public organizations. Other difficulties that public-sector organizations face when implementing technology relate to the hierarchical organizational structure in these bureaucratic organizations.

In this case study, the failed implementation of a module of an ERP system in a public-sector university will be analyzed. In 2001, the university administration decided to implement the human resource module which was part of a larger ERP system developed by SunGard SCT. After numerous problems, the vice president for business and finance decided to cancel the project in spring 2004. This case study analyzes what went wrong and how the situation could have been improved so that the ERP implementation could have been successful. Problems resulted in large part because upper managers were unaware of the special needs and skills required to manage an information system project in the public-sector environment.

Setting the Stage

South Central University is a public university in a rural Midwestern town with annual funding of approximately $125 million, the majority coming from state revenues. SCU's student population of 10,000 full-time equivalents (FTE) is largely traditional with most students ranging in age from 18 to 23 years. Over 60% of the students come from a major metropolitan area about 180 miles from the campus, and SCU has several residence hall facilities.

SCU provides quality education by offering small-size classes that are taught largely by tenure track faculty. As a selling point to students and parents, SCU administrators often suggest that the university "offers the quality of a private school education at a public university cost". And this opinion is backed up by state leaders and legislators. However, despite this acknowledgement, SCU remains one of the lowest-funded state universities on a dollar per full-time-equivalent (FTE) student basis. This may be due to the fact that despite the lack of adequate state funding, the university continues to offer quality education programs.

SCU is located in a small town where the university is the main employer. While salaries are low when compared to state and national averages, they are adequate given the lower cost of living in this rural geographic area. Many of SCU's employees report taking positions at the university because of the excellent benefits package rather than the salary level. Like many other small rural towns, a significant number of townspeople have been left unemployed because of the closing of several manufacturing plants in the area.

Many of SCU's employees are members of collective bargaining units including the faculty. In addition to the labor unions, the state has a position classification system that public universities and agencies are required to utilize. As a result, the organizational culture supports longevity of employment over merit performance. Individual employees, who attempt to stand out with excellent performance, are often shunned by other employees while supervisors have few tools to reward positive behavior. As a result, employees are often inflexible and resistant to change. There is a commitment to the status quo and to keeping things the same.

SCU, like many other public universities, is struggling to upgrade from the centralized legacy environment to a more modern distributed processing environment. Legacy applications rely on older database structures and programming languages such as COBOL and FORTRAN. These systems are commonly maintained in most government organizations because the cost of replacing a system that still works with a faster and fully-integrated system is often cost prohibitive.

Case Description

In fall of 2001, Bill Hartman, the vice president for business and finance, kicked-off the project by assembling a project team and charging the members with the task of implementing the human resource module of the university's ERP system. Figure 1 provides the planned time-line for the project. In addition to the technical programming staff, the project team consisted of end users in the Human Resources (HR), Budget, Civil Rights/Diversity, and Accounting Departments. The vice president and supervisors from the user departments anticipated a smooth transition to the new system because of the weaknesses of the existing automated human resource system. SCU's Board of Regents had required universities in

Figure 1. Changing time-lines

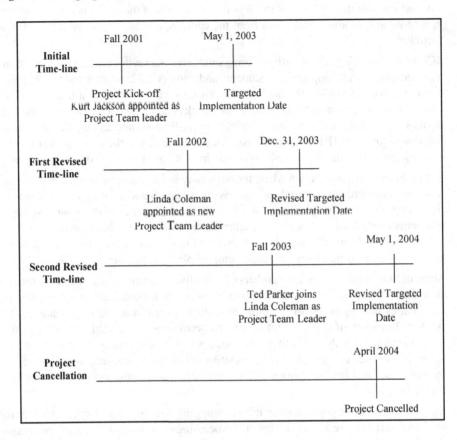

the system to implement a common human resource software system in the mid-1990s that had never really met the needs of the university.

As is common in many projects, an end user from the HR department was chosen as the project team leader. Since the payroll office in the HR department had the most interaction with the existing automated human resource system, it was decided that the Payroll Supervisor, Kurt Jackson, should act as the project manager. Additional members of the project team included three technical IS staff members, two staff from the Budget Department, one employee from the Civil Rights/Diversity Office, two staff from the Accounting Department, and three additional staff from the Human Resources Department. The 12 project team members were instructed to be liaisons for their departments, educate themselves about the new ERP module, collect data for the new system, recommend any system modifications that would be required to meet external reporting requirements, and train staff in their departments once the test system was available.

From the beginning, the project team had difficulty. The ERP module handled business processes differently, and users had difficulty understanding how the various functions of the system (i.e., hiring an employee, paying an employee, tracking employee benefits) came together in the new system. For some team members, who had been through the earlier implementation, it symbolized another forced system implementation. This behavior surprised the supervisors of the various units who believed the implementation would be met with enthusiasm because of the general dissatisfaction with the current human resource software system. However bad the current system was, many of the employees favored it because they had come to understand how it worked and had created procedures to make it more efficient.

The complexity of the new system overwhelmed team members from the user areas, and they unrealistically expected the IT staff to learn how the new system worked and then educate them. On the other hand, The IT staff refused to "hold the hands" of team members and unrealistically insisted that they become the experts for their portion of the new system. To make matters worse, adequate resources were not available to support the project team members. The vice president expected team members to continue to complete their current jobs while trying to squeeze in the work of the project team.

By fall of 2002, a full year after the start of the project, the team leader was concerned that the team would not meet the targeted implementation date of May 1, 2003. Since the university operates on a July 1–June 30 fiscal year, the final test system had to be implemented by May 1 so that it could run in tandem with the existing system until July 1st when the new system would go live. Realizing there was a problem, Kurt, the project team leader, met with Bill, the vice president of business and finance, to get permission to extend the time-line. Bill was not happy with the request and decided to replace Kurt as the team leader with a technical person from the IT staff. Linda Coleman, an analyst programmer, was chosen to succeed Kurt.

Linda was no more successful in getting the project team to complete its task. By late spring of 2003, it was clear that the new system would not be ready for implementation prior to the start of the fiscal year. While frustrated, Bill decided to postpone system implementation until December 31, 2003, the end of the calendar year. Despite Linda's best efforts, it became evident that this date could not be reached either. In frustration, Bill called the project team and their supervisors together to discuss the problem.

Clear goals and an implementation date of May 1, 2004 were established and the director of the Human Resource Department, Ted Parker, agreed to step in and co-lead the project team with Linda from the IT Department. Linda had voiced her concern that the team members were late in completing tasks, and she did not have the proper authority to enforce the time-line. Team members expressed frustration that their everyday work tasks left them little time to complete the team's work.

At the end of April 2004, on the advice of Ted Parker, Bill cancelled the project indefinitely. In the end, the university had invested significant resources in the project for almost three years before coming to the conclusion that it was an impossible task. To understand what went wrong, the vice president directed his special assistant to do a follow-up study and prepare a report of what went wrong.

Interviews with the project team members and the supervisors in the user departments identified several problems. There was dissatisfaction with the ERP product, criticism of the project team leaders, a perceived lack of support by upper management, and severe resistance to change. Tables 1 through 3 provide summaries of the perceived problems from the perspective of IT staff, managers, and end users.

Table 1. Problems reported by IT staff in the ERP implementation

Team Members from the IT Department	• These team members wanted to limit the number of program modifications because they reported programming staff time to be limited. • User department expectations that the IT Department modify the programs of the ERP system to suit current business practices were unrealistic. • There was a perception that end users had unrealistic expectations of the role of IT. IT staff did not feel they had the manpower to re-program all the standardized reports. • Previous software systems had been developed in-house and the programmers were familiar with the program code. The ERP was off-the-shelf software and they were unsure exactly how it worked. It would take a great deal of time to learn how the software worked. • They felt they were in a Catch-22 situation. The ERP system would require users to be more active in entering data to the system and retrieving it for upper administration. In the centralized legacy system environment, the IT Department had almost total control over the systems and data. There was a concern that they would be blamed for problems that occurred because of the stupidity of the end users.

Table 2. Problems reported by management in the ERP implementation

Project Team Leader	• Team members did not adequately learn how their sub-units interacted with other sub-units in the system. • There was a lack of support from the vice president.
Vice President	• There was disappointment in the project team leaders who failed to get team members working together on the project.

Changes in the Information Technology Environment

To fully understand the complaints identified in the study, it is necessary to take a look at the profound impact technology changes have on organizations moving from the centralized legacy system environment to the distributed ERP environment. Prior to the develop-

Table 3. Problems reported by end users in the ERP implementation

Employees	Summary of Issues
Team Members from the User Departments	• Members were extremely overwhelmed with the complexity of the new system. The new ERP system was much larger and designed to integrate data that was kept in previous stand-alone systems in the past. Members could not understand how all the data came together in the system and the documents provided by the vendor were hard to understand. They expected the team leader to learn how the system worked and then educate them. • There was a general belief that the ERP system did not add value beyond the current system. • The ERP system did not handle business processes in the same manner. Members did not believe they should be asked to change how they did things. They wanted the system to be modified to adapt to them rather than the other way around. • Standardized reports from the current system would not be available in the new system and user departments believed they were being asked to take on too much responsibility in extracting data and creating reports. They reported not having adequate technical skills to do this. • Staff believed they were already overworked and that it was unfair that they were being asked to implement the ERP system without any release time or additional compensation.

ment of distributed network computer technology, software applications were developed and maintained on mainframe computers with languages such as FORTRAN or COBOL. Mainframe computers were used to store data, process data for standardized applications (i.e., payroll processing), and provide standardized data reports that were used primarily for control purposes.

The hardware consisted of a large mainframe computer, often taking up the space of an entire room, which was located in the Information Technology (IT) Department.

Most of the data processing was completed by computer programmers located in the IT Department. Other employees who needed to enter data into the system used dummy terminals that functioned only as data input machines. Data were stored on magnetic tapes that had to be physically mounted in order for a program to access and process the data.

Software was developed largely by computer programmers in the IT Department at the request of user departments that needed new application programs or specialized reports. Computer program modifications were difficult and time consuming and modifications in one program often required the modification of several other programs. The labor intensity, required to create and modify programs, limited the programming requests that the IT Department could handle.

Data were stored in hierarchical, or branch-like, databases, making it difficult to retrieve. For instance, to report the average salary of all people who were employed in 1975, the programmer would have to know the names of those individuals before a program could be written to extract the current salary data. This required that programmers have knowledge of the data element and the location of the data element. Additionally, updates were done in batch mode in which data were stored in a holding file and then uploaded to the database periodically at specified times.

As a result of these technology structures, other organizational structures were affected. For instance, since the technology did not lend itself towards integrated computer applications and programs were normally developed or modified as a result of a user department's request, applications were geared toward the data needs of a specific department rather than the organization as a whole.

Since data were hard to access, they were of limited strategic value. Upper management did not understand technology and received little direct benefit from the technology (i.e., strategic information) so it often maintained a hands-off position with the IT Department.

This had the impact of empowering the IT Department in its dealings with user departments. User departments were beholden to the IT Department. The IT Department had broad authority over the computer system and was responsible for determining which data would be collected and who could have access to the data. Once the micro-computer became available, user departments often tried to deal with inadequate support from the IT Department by developing shadow systems in which they re-loaded data from standardized reports so that it could be manipulated and summarized in alternative formats.

The evolution to the distributed data processing environment has enabled organizations to integrate data into comprehensive systems which are accessible to multiple users via networked hardware. These technology changes have had a tremendous impact on organizations. Hardware now consists of some configuration of networked mainframe, mini-, and micro-computers. Mainframe computers are no longer required; however, many organizations still choose to have a large centralized system to store application programs and large datasets. In most user departments, employees are each outfitted with a micro-computer which is linked to a server. Data are stored in multiple formats including mainframe drives, micro-computer hard drives, diskettes, CDs, and flash drives.

Since the technology of the distributed processing environment allows organizations to integrate data from business units into a comprehensive organization-wide system, most software is large-scale and complicated. Organizations are often opting to purchase packaged software systems, such as ERP systems, rather than develop them in-house. Because these systems are standardized, some program modifications are required to accommodate differences to suit the needs of the organization. User interfaces, such as the graphical user interface (GUI), which incorporate drop-and-click menus, make systems relatively easy to use. Query languages, such as Standard Query Language (SQL), allow users to manipulate data for analytic purposes and to produce reports in desired formats.

Data are now stored in relational databases which resemble tables of rows and columns. In this format, data are much easier to access and manipulate. The database contains multiple files linked together by primary keys. This eliminates the need to re-enter data in many different stand-alone systems. This limited data redundancy leads to better accuracy within the database. Integrated ERP systems focus on business processes rather than the duties of one particular business unit or department. Because the technology is easier to use, departmental users complete many of the functions once performed by the IT Department. Users are now able to manipulate the data and produce reports in formats that are useful to them. This has eliminated the need to keep shadow systems.

With easier-to-use systems and the ability to extract data in usable formats, managers now view data as a strategic resource. At the same time, IT has less control over user departments that can now access and manipulate data without the help of the IT Department. Tables 4 and 5 provide summaries of the features and the resulting impact on operations in both the centralized legacy mainframe environment and the distributed ERP environment.

Table 4. Features of centralized legacy environments

Features	Resulting Impact
Hardware • Centralized system • Single location, in IT Department Software • Difficult to use programming languages Data Management • Hierarchical database structure Business Applications • Developed by IT staff • Built around the needs of a department	Computer applications are: • Inaccessible • Non-integrated • Inflexible • Difficult to use • Geared toward a business unit or department Roles • Upper management has little involvement with IT • IT Department has almost complete control over computer applications

Table 5. Features of distributed ERP environments

Features	Resulting Impact
Hardware • Distributed system • Integrated • Multiple locations, in IT and user department Software • Easy to use programming languages Data Management • Relational database structure • Integrated data files Business Applications • Purchased software products • Built around business of the organization rather than a single business unit	Computer applications are: • Accessible • Integrated • Flexible • Easy to use • Geared toward a business process Roles • Upper management is very involved with IT • IT department has limited control over computer applications

Evaluating the ERP Failure

A look at the problems identified shows that most of the complaints were related to changes in business processes and tasks and employee roles. These problems resulted largely because of the transition from the centralized legacy environment to the distributed ERP environment. However, the problems cannot be viewed only as the growing pains that take place with a transition to a new technology environment.

In public organizations, such as universities and other state and local agencies, there are forces which exacerbate the difficulties of this transition. Limited financial resources, complicated bureaucratic organizational structures, and numerous stakeholders with competing interests all add to the difficulty.

Workflows in the new distributed ERP environment are geared toward university-wide business processes rather than tasks completed by a single business unit. Computer applications in the legacy environment focused on tasks done at the departmental level, thus fitting well with the highly bureaucratic structure in public organizations. Computer applications in ERP systems focus on business processes rather than the isolated tasks completed by individual departments thus requiring interaction between departments.

One of the reasons for the project failure was that the team members attempted to use skills they were familiar with that had been successful in the legacy environment. They began the implementation by trying to understand how the ERP system handled the tasks for which their departments were responsible. When it was clear that the new system organized and manipulated data according to business processes rather than the isolated tasks carried out by their individual departments, they became frustrated and overwhelmed. Rather than working together to identify how their individual departmental tasks should come together in the new system, team members from the user departments looked to the IT Department to resolve the problem.

An example may help to clarify the problem. In the legacy system, when the university created a new position or filled a vacant position, the budget office assigned it a position number and loaded the data to a position table. Note that the position and the employee filling the position are two different things. When a position became vacant and a department contacted HR to advertise and complete the hiring paperwork, the HR clerk called the budget office to get the position number and then manually wrote the number on all the corresponding forms. There were difficulties with the process because the budget office would reuse position numbers and the only way to track how many different employees had been in the position number was to look at a set of note cards in the HR Department. This did not bother the budget office however, because their only reporting requirement was to provide a summary report for the general assembly identifying how many positions were vacated per year.

The ERP system did not collect data by individual departmental task (i.e., posting position numbers) but rather by process (i.e., hiring an employee). Since the ERP system worked at the process level, it utilized a unique position number so that if an accounting clerk position (position number 415) was vacated, that position number stayed with the accounting clerk position rather than being reassigned to a completely different position such as a groundkeeper. The strength of the ERP system is in integrating data from various units into a coherent system that can be used by all departments that interact in a particular business process. In this case, it is hiring an employee. So, while the budget office may manage the position numbers, the Civil Rights/Diversity Department may collect EEO6 data, and the HR Department may keep track of employee certifications and educational degrees.

In the legacy environment, departments acted independently and were often unsure what data other departments collected. For the ERP implementation to be successful, the project team members from the user departments would have had to work together to identify each of the roles that their offices were to play in the hiring process. Crossing departmental lines and working together is more difficult in public organizations with formalized hierarchical structures. In these bureaucratic organizational structures, communication is often formal and complicated making ERP implementation more difficult.

Another reason for the ERP failure is related to the changing role of the IT Department. In the legacy environment, the IT Department had almost complete control over the computer system, and the data stored in it. In the ERP environment, the IT Department is responsible for maintaining the hardware and software but has less control over purchasing decisions and how data are used. Upper management, realizing the strategic nature of information, has moved to have greater control over information technology in the ERP environment. At the same time, users can now manipulate data and prepare reports in desired formats. Together, these changes have reduced the authority and control that the IT Department has over computer and information technology.

In public organizations, where the CIO position is buried at a lower level in the organizational chart to buffer it from political changes, the IT Department has less institutionalized power and authority. At SCU, the CIO reported to the vice president for business and finance instead of to the CEO or president which would be typical in a non-governmental private-sector organization.

In the legacy environment, this did not pose a problem because the IT Department had almost total influence and authority over data and the computing environment. To retrieve data from legacy systems, expert programmers needed to identify the data and its location before a query could be written. In the distributed ERP environment, user-friendly query languages such as Standard Query Language (SQL) or Query by Example (QBE) help users develop fairly-sophisticated queries very simply, often with the use of drop-down menus. Users from the IT Department voiced concerns about being blamed for problems in a system that they had little control over.

The IT team members were also overwhelmed with the complexity of the off-the-shelf ERP system. Since they had not written the actual program code, they were unsure about how difficult it would be to make modifications to the programs. Team members from the IT Department repeatedly emphasized that the ERP implementation should remain as "vanilla" as possible. In other words, program modifications should be limited to those that were absolutely necessary and not those designed to make the new system work like the old system.

In public organizations with limited funding, resources are not available to hire additional staff. The IT team members were concerned that they would be required to take on work that they did not have time to do. One major controversy was over whether the standardized reports from the old system would be re-developed by the IT staff for the new system or whether user departments would be expected to use the query language to develop their own standardized reports. Both sets of employees, the end users and the IT staff, were concerned about not having the resources to complete this task.

The lack of funding also led to other problems. Team members were expected to implement the new ERP system in addition to their regular work duties without extra compensation. It was unrealistic of the vice president to expect this of the team members. Yet, the vice president had little choice given the underfunding situation at the university.

Current Challenges Facing the Organization

At this time, upper administration at SCU is still trying to understand the magnitude of the ERP implementation failure. There has been significant turnover of the original project team members and efforts to revive the project are taking place behind the scenes. SCU hopes to re-establish a project team once it has secured adequate funding to move forward with the project.

Before doing so however, SCU should fully analyze the factors which led to the project failure. First and probably most important is that adequate resources have to be made available for new technology. While SCU did not believe it had the resources to compensate project team members for their increased efforts, overall losses due to cancellation of the project were higher than the cost of providing stipends or additional personal leave days for team members.

Second, the distributed ERP technology environment, while offering substantial benefits, is not easily adopted in public organizations. Public-sector organizations will find that moving to a business process model of doing business will be more difficult because of their highly bureaucratized organizational structures and formalized channels of communication. However, since citizens' demand for accountability will only increase, public organizations have to develop new paradigms for bringing forth the new technology environment. It is no longer possible to use older more traditional methods when implementing new technologies.

Table 6. Managing the change process for IT staff

Old Role	New Role	Management Actions to Facilitate Change
• IT staff have total control over the hardware, software, and data in the organization. • IT staff determines who can access the system and what data they can have. They determine which data will be stored in the system and what type of reports will be made available.	• IT staff move from the controller role to the service role. • Functional departments now determine what data needs to be stored in the system and they are responsible for extracting the data for ad hoc reporting. • There is widespread access to the data.	• Upper management should take an active role in understanding and overseeing the IT needs of the organization • Upper management should reassure the IT staff of their importance to the organization (as a service entity) • Upper management should use disciplinary action to deal with IT managers who are reluctant to share control of the system with user departments and managers

Finally, the project team leader and upper management need to understand and facilitate the change management process. The organizational culture in many public organizations is based on the longevity philosophy. Employees are in it for the long run and are hesitant to get in over their heads and commit themselves to jobs that become too difficult to complete year after year. Tables 6 and 7 provide summaries of ways in which managers can facilitate the change process to help the IT staff and employees in the functional user departments.

In its next effort to implement the HRS module of the ERP package, several actions should occur. Adequate resources need to be allocated to the project so that project team members have the time to complete the implementation process. This may require juggling duties among existing employees to free up team members or using funds to hire temporary employees to cover some of the workload. Managers need to develop realistic expectations and convey these adequately to project team members. To facilitate the change process, managers need to be aware of the difficulties in moving from the centralized legacy environment to the distributed ERP environment and then educate employees about the difficulties. Team members should be encouraged to network with peers in other organizations who have implemented ERP systems and should be provided with adequate resources for formal and

Table 7. Managing the change process for functional department end users

Old Role	New Role	Management Actions to Facilitate Change
• Users have little control over the computer systems • Users are responsible for data entry • Reports are developed by IT staff • Users who want data reports in alternative formats must re-enter the data from a printout into a spreadsheet	• Users determine what data should be collected to meet reporting requirements and satisfy the needs of upper management. • Users enter data, insure the integrity of the data, and extract data for customized reports • Users are involved in implementing IT systems.	• Managers need to inform user departments of their changing role and the importance of information to the organization • Managers must provide adequate resources for staff training • Staff, who do not wish to update skills to accommodate changing roles, should be encouraged to find new positions

informal training. Finally, employees who are so resistant to change that they become disruptive of the process should be re-assigned to other areas of the organization or encouraged to find employment elsewhere.

References

Bretschneider, S. (1990). Management information systems in public and private organizations: An empirical test. *Public Administration Review,* September/October, 536-545.

Erlikh, L. (2002). Leveraging legacy systems in modern architectures. *Journal of Information Technology Case and Applications Research, 4*(3), 175-189.

Griffith, T., Zammuto, R., & Aiman-Smith, L. (1999). Why new technologies fail. *Industrial Management, 41*(3), 29-34.

Hoffer, J. A., George, J. F., & Valacich, J. S. (2005). *Modern systems analysis and design.* Upper Saddle River, NJ: Pearson Prentice Hall.

Joshi, K. (2005). Understanding user resistance and acceptance during the implementation of an order management system: A case study using the equity implementation model. *Journal of Information Technology Case and Applications Research, 7*(1), 4-22.

Lucas, H. C., Walton, E., & Ginzberg, M. (1988). Implementing packaged software. *MIS Quarterly, 12*(4), 537-549.

Newcomer, K., & Caudle, S. (1991). Evaluating public sector information systems: More than meets the eye. *Public Administration Review, 51,* 377-384.

Paper, D. (1999). The enterprise transformation paradigm: The case of Honeywell's industrial automation and control. *Journal of Information Technology Case and Applications Research, 1*(1), 7-29.

Sharma, R., Palvia, P., & Salam, A.F. (2002). ERP selection at custom fabrics. *Journal of Information Technology Case and Applications Research, 4*(2), 127-146.

Author's Biography

Kimberly Furumo is an assistant professor of MIS at the University of Hawaii at Hilo. Her research interests include ERP, IS project management, human-computer interaction, and virtual teams. Her work appears in the Communications of the ACM, the Journal of Computer Information Systems, the Interdisciplinary Journal of Information, Knowledge, and Management, the Journal of Information Technology Cases and Applications, the International Journal of Electronics Marketing and Retailing, the Proceedings of the Hawaii International Conference on System Sciences, the Americas Conference on Information Systems, and the annual meeting of the Decision Sciences Institute. Prior to joining the faculty, Dr. Furumo worked in business and IT areas. She has been a member of several IS project teams.

Chapter IX

To Shop and Buy in L.A.:
Mining Cost Out of Old Processes in Building a New Supply Chain for the City of Los Angeles

Paul W. Taylor, Center for Digital Government, USA

Executive Summary

This case study focuses on the modernization of purchasing practices and policies by a large city government. It hinged on harvesting savings from existing processes as the sole means of funding the introduction of a new enterprise procurement or supply chain technology system. The case demonstrates the essential role of changing organizational behaviors, re-engineering processes, assessing risk, and judging the level of benefits that can realistically be achieved through the introduction of new information systems.

Background

Founded in 1781, the City of Los Angeles, California began as a distant outpost under Spanish rule. Two centuries later, Los Angeles had a solid claim to being the second largest city in the United States by population, which was estimated at 3.96 million persons in 2005. The city's 470 square miles contain 11.5% of the area and 38.7% of the population of the County of Los Angeles.

Best known as home to the film, television, and recording industries, the largest employers in the city include health care (Kaiser Permanente, Cedars-Sinai, Providence), aerospace and technology (Northrop Grumman, Boeing, Lockheed Martin, SBC Communications), education (University of Southern California, California Institute of Technology), finance (Bank of America, Wells Fargo, Washington Mutual, CitiGroup), logistics (FedEx, UPS) and retail (Kroger, Vons, Target). Significantly, government as a sector is second only to trade, transportation, and utilities in size as an employer.

City History and Structure

Under the state constitution, charter cities are generally independent of the state legislature in matters relating to municipal affairs, and in their ability to raise revenues. The city is a charter city originally incorporated in 1850 with its most recent charter adopted in 1999. The city is governed by the mayor and the council. As the chief city executive, the mayor is responsible for administration and service delivery. For its part, the city's full-time 15-member council is the legislative body which levies taxes, authorizes public improvements, and approves contracts among other functions.

The city provides a full range of public services, including: police; fire and paramedics; residential refuse collection and disposal, wastewater collection and treatment, street maintenance, traffic management, storm water pollution abatement, and other public works functions; enforcement of ordinances and statutes relating to building safety; public libraries; recreation and parks; community development, housing, and aging services; and planning through the 40 departments, bureaus, and commissions that rely on the council for its operating funds. Five other departments—including the water and power utility, harbor, airport, and two pension systems—have an arm's length relationship to the rest of city government. These five outliers are under the control of boards appointed by the mayor and confirmed by the council.

By fiscal year 2005-06, the city's budget was pegged at $5.985 billion, which includes $3.3 billion for departmental expenditures. A decade earlier, members of the council were openly skeptical about the efficacy of those expenditures. They knew that over a dozen city departments were spending almost a billion dollars on goods and services. They also knew the departments were storing over $53 million of inventory in almost a hundred warehouses that dotted the city. They feared that the bureaucracy had become bloated, that the city had too much of what it did not need and not enough of what it did need—and no disciplined way to tell the difference.

The penultimate act in challenging the city's old approach to so-called materials management came when an office supply superstore opened right across from City Hall.

Setting the Stage

An errand to buy a box of computer diskettes changed the way the City of Los Angeles manages its relationships with 10,000 suppliers and 40 agencies, and how it accounts for spending $800 million of taxpayer funds each year.

It was a winter morning in 1994. Then Councilman Joel Wachs asked a member of his staff to pick up a few disks at the Staples office supply store across the street from City Hall. The box of 3.5 inch disks was ultimately less important than the accompanying receipt, which lived on in legend. It was a single slip of paper that illustrated everything that was wrong with the city's procurement processes. Through the city, the price was higher, the process slower and more complex, and the administrative overhead significantly more burdensome than walking across the street. (A contemporary 1994 audit report by the Los Angeles City Controller's office detailed the same story.)

Greg Nelson was the staffer who ran that errand and who explained his eventual rise to Wachs' Chief of Staff by recalling, "I just kept volunteering to do everything that nobody else wanted to do." So began a landmark re-engineering of the city's antiquated purchasing system that began with the catalytic event involving Wachs and the box of diskettes. What followed were two years of assessment (1994-1995) which validated internal work that had documented the trouble with city practices in the mid-1980s, another four years of business process re-engineering and system re-design (1998-2002) before the launch of a new supply chain management system.

Case Description

The supply chain system would become known as the City of Los Angeles Supply Management System (SMS) but not before years of investigation, analysis, and finding the will to change the organizational behavior of a large city government best known for the fierce independence of its departments.

The Department of General Services was in a unique position to cannibalize itself in order to give itself a future. Importantly, it also had the discretion and mandate to pursue business process improvements, with or without additional funding from council. As it had done in all of its functional areas, it set aside study funds from its operating budget (which was less reliant on council allocations than line agencies because of the margins it maintained on its business operations) to review and improve its own performance.

The city selected Jon K. Mukri to overhaul the procurement program at the Department of General Services. Mukri, a 22-year veteran of the U.S. Navy, had been on point to get tons of the right stuff to the right people in the right places—including large gray cities that float.

"Coming from the navy, navigating political waters was nothing new," Mukri recalls, "but it only took 5 hours on the job to realize that this was going to take everything I had." At the outset, the long three-phase business strategy—(1) assessment, (2) re-engineering, and (3) implementation—appeared daunting and success was a long way off. Mukri knew that Wachs could provide the needed political cover to change the way the city did business. "He wanted to see it happen," says Mukri, "He knew it was broken but didn't know where."

The Department of General Services knew where it was broken. The agency had detailed its material management bottlenecks a decade earlier in a *Warehouse Report and Operations Analysis*. The report was a classic dust collector. There was no political will in 1985 to act on the recommendations, and problems rarely get better with age. That was also true of the city's record with technology projects which, Mukri says, had devolved into a "long history of failure". In fact, the city had the unenviable reputation for not being able to implement large-scale technology improvements although most city staffers could point readily to a string of failures that dated back 20 years or more.

Mining Cost Out of Old Tired Processes

A change in language—from "materials management" to "supply chain management"—hinted at what lie ahead. The second largest city in the country had a lot to work with. The point was, it had too much of too many things.

Fourteen separate agencies operated 94 warehouses with a combined inventory worth $54 million. City agencies had over 2,000 contracts with suppliers, and suppliers had multiple contacts with each agency. It made placing orders hard; it made getting paid harder. There was no way of knowing whether agencies had sufficient budget to pay for orders until after the fact, and the warehouses were great places to hide stockpiles of excess material bought to spend down year-end fund balances. Much of the excess was never used.

The political ramifications of fixing all of this seemed obvious, but turned out to be deeper than Mukri and his evolving team imagined. Wachs and Nelson urged them forward, and an initial round of meetings with city council members and agency heads suggested potential support that stopped well short of buy in. Ron Deaton, the city's Chief Legislative Analyst, was central to their success. "Early on," says Mukri, "Ron saw the utility of what we wanted to do but he had also seen so many failures before." There was only one other requirement: it all needed to be funded through hard dollar savings. There was no new money.

The requirement for self funding brought urgency and sobriety to the planning process. A plan that promised potential savings would not do. The plan had to deliver real savings—because there were new bills to pay. The plan developed by the Department of General Services purposely set out to under promise and over deliver. It brought a disciplined approach to assessing the existing procurement processes, re-designing them, and implementing a system to make the re-design real.

The members of the department's team were hand chosen to manage the project, work relationships within the city and with suppliers, and bring General Services' unique expertise to bear—namely, intimate knowledge of the city's procurement processes. "We were the experts on the business requirements," says Bob Jensen, Assistant General Manager for the Supply Services Division. "We knew how things worked and how they were supposed to work. We also had to live with the results, so we dedicated a procurement supervisor, payment manager and warehouse manager to the project 24/7. They were matched with technical and functional leads from our private partners."

The first of the private partners was the company now known as Deloitte Consulting, which conducted a third-party assessment of the city's material management processes and developed a set of recommendations for change. Deloitte Partner Dana Jennings says that L.A. had the same problems as many other cities, but differed significantly in scale. "It suffered from poor, fragmented, paper intensive purchasing processes, none of which were integrated with other city systems," says Jennings, "It was effectively broken, and there was no way to leverage the city's considerable buying power."

Some 704 interviews and other city-wide research resulted in fully-annotated reports from Deloitte that consumed six linear feet of shelf space. They identified as much as $250 million in realizable savings in the city's supply chain. The city targeted a $100 million slice, focusing on changes within those agencies under the direct authority of the city council. Much of the difference between the two figures was a function of three proprietary agencies—the Department of Water and Power, the Port of Los Angeles, and Los Angeles World Airports—which chose to remain independent and pursue administrative efficiencies through other means.

To reach the targets and make the self-funding model work, Deloitte recommended consolidation of space, contracts, and staff. "We had resounding support for change [within General Services]," says Jennings, "combined with healthy skepticism [among agency heads who said] start with somebody else's warehouse."

Jennings worked with Mukri and Jensen in building support with city council members, agency heads, and key staffers. The outreach campaign included as many as 400 meetings with people one-on-one, and in public meetings. "In the early years, there was no trust. Momentum and continuous success began to change that," observes Jennings, "Jon [Mukri] and Bob [Jensen] kept clearing road blocks and taking on battles across the system."

There was also significant work to be done with the city's 10,000 suppliers, which were frustrated by chronic late payments and burdensome paperwork. Female and minority business owners were also concerned that their hard fought gains in earning city business would be lost because of the planned changes. Deborah Ramos, Director of Operations Support for General Services, says the supplier relationships and outreach was "almost embarrassing". She began having meetings of her own, asking how suppliers big and small "wanted to do business with the city, where they struggled, where they were hindered." In response, Ramos drafted "straightforward amendments to the [city's] administrative code to reduce paperwork and reduce burden for everybody", while at the same time increasing opportunities for the smallest suppliers. The council approved the changes.

Jensen says that, over time, all those meetings went from "detractors pounding the table" to those same people leaning back in their chairs and saying, "you finally got the system to work."

Changing Organizational Behavior

The system worked, in large measure, because people were working differently. "Of the city's 42,000 employees, a third of them were painfully involved in this change," says Mukri, "they had skin in the game early on." At the operational level, an evaluation of 22 procurement-related job classifications indicated that the skills and responsibilities in 14 of them needed to be changed.

The point was not lost on Local 347 of the Service Employees International Union (SEIU) and the American Federation of State, County and Municipal Employees (AFSCME), whose members raised concerns about potential job losses and other ramifications of the job and compensation review.

The bellwether for personnel changes was the transfer of 366 staff from 14 separate agencies to create a new procurement organization within General Services, the purpose of which was to integrate warehousing, purchasing, and accounts payable on behalf of all council-controlled departments.

"The jobs were getting better and higher skilled," says Jensen, "commodity buyers became strategic procurement analysts working on higher value activities." The unions came to see the advantages. Mukri says, "we were actually professionalizing our workforce, and that was good for everybody."

IT-Related Training: Last Among the Cobbler's Children

Training the workforce with the new skills proved difficult, as were contending with rumors and dealing with misunderstandings of the project's intent and process. Mukri concedes that the city should have invested more in change management, and worked harder to get training and communication right the first time. The steering committee, careful to a fault with expenditures, took back the $1.5 million earmarked for change management—a move that Jensen believes "jeopardized the project more than any other single factor."

Still, the training program was developed and delivered internally. Trainers trained trainers, overcame an initial no show rate of 32% among trainees, and developed both advanced and remedial training modules for unforeseen shortcomings along the way.

At one end, a new certified user program created pride among users while ensuring that they could demonstrate competence on SMS. At the other end were employees who were confronting a desktop computer for the first time. Thirteen warehouse workers chose retirement over learning how to use the new automated system. Meanwhile, General Services scrambled to address a training need that had taken them by surprise—how to use a mouse.

By 1998 when the city entered the implementation phase, the city team had coalesced around a shared vision of what was now possible in making America's second largest city a better and smarter customer. It had built trust with customers and suppliers alike, who were increasingly confident that a change of this magnitude would actually work.

Jensen remained philosophical throughout, even when harboring doubts of his own. "They say a project manager can lose a third of his credibility during a project like this. The good news is that he can earn it back."

The third phase—implementation—was where reputations were made, lost, and restored. Mukri believes the discipline of the self-funding model maintained unblinking focus on savings targets, "It all helped me, especially on the really tough calls." The funding plan penciled out; the team just had to do it. "It" was the rationalization of warehouses, optimization of staff, and the transformation of procurement. Mukri says the department is on track to realize a "ten-fold return on self funding."

A city of 3.7 million people, 42,000 employees, and more than a few entrenched interests were watching in 1998 when it came time to build the system that would make the changes real. Mukri and Jensen had an ace—a big ace—up their sleeves as the third phase began. "We had full transparency on our requirements," says Jensen, "we knew them best because we owned them, and we had documented every requirement for all of our 230 processes." Mukri adds, "You've got to know your processes. If you don't know, you can't find software to complement them" (see Figure 1).

Los Angeles found its complement in PeopleSoft Supply Chain Management, which—owing to industry consolidation—is now a product offering from the Oracle Corporation of Redwood Shores, CA. "The city's well-defined requirements fit well with our methodology," says PeopleSoft Customer Service Executive Cindy Denny, "executive sponsorship was in place … and we were able to help them get the cost savings they had identified, tune their processes, and increase accountability for every transaction."

The supply management system was implemented on a centralized city-wide file server architecture. "Our database network platform was unique, nobody had done it this way for a system as large as ours," remembers Flora Chang, the SMS Director of Systems. "People told me it couldn't be done, but the architecture passed the load testing again and again, so we did it anyway."

"Every department had their own file servers—some thick, others thin," according to Jensen, "There was a lot of risk to the enterprise approach but there was not enough money to do it any other way. Flora had to be right, and she was."

" Integrated functions between purchasing, receiving and accounts payable have given users much improved procurement analysis capabilities and greatly reduced the procure-to-pay cycle time.," said Chang. "The system turned the vision of the reengineering project into reality."

To those ends, the city selected AG Consulting (a unit of Automatic Data Processing, Inc.) as its integrator for the PeopleSoft implementation, while drawing on the programming strength of the city's Information Technology Agency (ITA). Together with the city's quality assurance consultant (Logicon), the watch word—or flavor—was "vanilla".

Figure 1

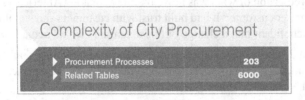

Complexity of City Procurement

| ▶ Procurement Processes | 203 |
| ▶ Related Tables | 6000 |

The vanilla approach was designed to fundamentally change the way the city procured goods and services while keeping changes to the software to a minimum. "That's why we did the huge variance analysis in phase two," contends Jensen. "We changed our processes so we could stay as vanilla as possible, except where the city ordinances required something specific. I think we got it right."

Results

The proof is in the bottom line. The $28 million project generated an initial return on investment of $37 million—nearly 130%—with an additional $3.6 million of savings each year in personnel and contract savings. The technology-powered transformation enabled America's second largest city to reduce warehousing by 40%, slash inventory levels by 50%, and cut the number of purchasing contracts by more than 50%. Furthermore, the city now earns early payment discounts on 92% of all invoices—exceeding its own targets by 12% (see Figure 2).

Ultimately, the solution helped change the way Los Angeles manages relationships with 10,000 suppliers and 40 agencies, and how it accounts for spending more than $800 million of taxpayer funds each year.

The lion's share of the initial return was through warehouse consolidation, the number of which was winnowed at a rate of eight per year since the peak of 94 in 1995. By 2002, the city was operating only 58 warehouses including a new distribution center for commodities. In that time, inventory levels were cut in half—from a high of $53,968,878 to $27,512,508. Supply Services Manager Bill Griggs says the hardest part of the change was "proving there

Figure 2

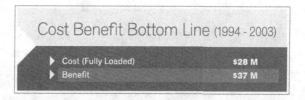

Figure 3

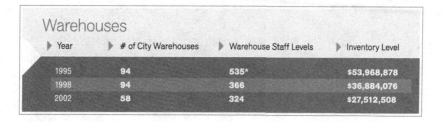

would be no loss of service to customers who had lost control of their own warehouses." He says customer agencies are now "happy and satisfied", and are taking advantage of automated reporting "to track performance and manage more effectively because its all visible and its all in real time" (see Figure 3).

The number of contracts held by the city has also been slashed, with just over 900 remaining in what had been in a crowded field of more that 2,000. Through the consolidated mega-contracts, the cornerstone of strategic sourcing, General Services takes the aggregated demand from the whole city to the marketplace. Supply Services Manager Kenneth Desowitz explains that the city can "make sure there is enough competition" to get the best value on a wide range of goods and services. In some categories, participation by minority and female-owned businesses has climbed from the low single digits to 25% with the shift to mega-contracts. "People didn't believe it," says Desowitz, "and the city was saving money" (see Figure 4).

Ramos says that suppliers of all sizes took note of the "smoother, cleaner and more efficient" processes through the new supply management system (SMS). The volume of invoices

Figure 4

Performance of Mega Contracts

Category	Estimated Savings	Actual Savings
Janitorial	9%	14%
Paper	6%	7%
Tools	9%	7%
Lab Supplies	7%	10%

Figure 5

Payment Performance Aging of Invoices

Category	November 2001	November 2002
> 30 Days	16,000	709
> 90 Days	13,000	501

Figure 6

Supply Management System (SMS) Traffic

Total Annual Orders	125,000
One Time Order / Year	3,000
Payments Annually	220,000

processed through SMS grew 43.5% year over year and the consolidated warehouses are operating at an enviable 96 to 98% efficiency rate. Jensen says that "you can see the health of a supply chain in accounts payable", pointing to the sharp drop in payment times from an average of 42 days to only 7 days.

Bea Padiangan, the Chief Accountant for SMS Payment Services, agrees, saying that the results add up to increased savings for the city. The city's goal had been to earn early pay discounts on 80% of all payments with SMS. The department has been earning early payment discounts on an average of 92% of all invoices, and reached a record 96% earlier this year. The prompt payment discounts had saved the city $3 million by November 2002, with another million earned through such discounts in the following quarter (see Figures 5 and 6).

While insisting that they are still not done, Mukri is visibly pleased with the results to date in terms of performance and accountability—all of which would have been "a shot in the dark before SMS."

Author's Biography

Paul W. Taylor, PhD, is the Chief Strategy Officer at the Center for Digital Government. Prior to joining the Center, Dr. Taylor served as deputy director of the Washington State Department of Information Services (DIS) and the Chief of Staff of the Information Services Board (ISB). He is a contributor to the journal, Public CIO, the author of a number of book chapters and juried journal articles, and his column—called signal-to-noise—appears each month in Government Technology Magazine.

Chapter X

Technology Contracting in the Public Sector

Milton L. Petersen, Neal, Gerber & Eisenberg LLP, USA

Executive Summary

Many different types of large, complex technology-related initiatives (such as the implementation of modern enterprise resource planning systems) are now becoming more popular in the public sector, posing formidable challenges to the organizations undertaking them. This chapter examines, from the point of view of a practicing information technology attorney, various different challenges facing public entities in technology contracting, drawing on examples from various public-sector projects, as well as from relevant private-sector experiences. Observations and suggestions are provided with regard to the entire contracting process, from preparing for a project, networking with colleagues, and drafting an RFP, to the types of contractual provisions that might be appropriate in technology agreements, to suggested negotiation processes and strategies, to steps to take after the contracts are signed.

Introduction

As is readily apparent from many individual case studies and examples, contracting for information technology (IT) products and services in the public sector poses some daunting challenges. In some ways, the challenges of IT contracting can be even greater in the public sector than for similar contracting activities in the private sector.

While each public-sector entity, and every technology project or initiative, has its own unique characteristics and peculiarities, there are certain aspects of the process of contracting for IT products and services that apply to nearly every technology project. Rather than providing a case study of the experiences of a specific governmental entity in a particular technology project or initiative, this chapter discusses the process of technology contracting in general, providing examples, observations, and suggestions gleaned by a practicing technology attorney from a number of public sector (as well as some relevant private sector) projects or transactions.

Background: Challenges Particularly Relevant in the Public Sector

Certain types of large technology-related initiatives that have become relatively commonplace in private industry, such as the implementation of modern enterprise resource planning (ERP) systems and the outsourcing of technology and customer relationship management (CRM) business processes and operations, have only recently begun to become more popular in the public sector. The slower pace of adoption of these types of technologies and technology initiatives by governmental entities doubtlessly results from a variety of factors, many of which likely relate to basic or fundamental differences in the nature, structure, purpose, and goals of government from those of private industry.

Governments, by their very nature, are political and territorial. A government's purpose and mandate is to serve its constituents. This can, for example, make the delegation of duties to private enterprise and ever-sensitive employment-related issues (such as, for example, in the context of a proposed outsourcing) of significant concern in the public sector. And, while the basic premise of a private-sector service provider is to charge the consumer or purchaser for services rendered, governments must wrestle with questions of whether they can, or should, charge their citizens for accessing basic services, such as those often automated through e-government initiatives (Bray, 2005).

Large technology initiatives can also be very expensive and not without considerable risk, making them particularly daunting for many governmental entities, especially smaller ones. Justifying and obtaining the required approval and funding of major expenditures by public entities can be difficult, especially without reliable evidence of the type and extent of the benefits that can reasonably be expected to be achieved. No one wants to be a guinea pig, and if few similar projects have yet been successfully completed by similar entities, then it is difficult to cite concrete results that have been obtained. Differences in business models and practices may also, in some cases, make software packages developed for the private sector less than ideally suited to the public sector (Songini, 2005), resulting in even greater risks for "early adopter" governmental entities.

Another significant challenge particularly relevant in the public sector is that, while details of many of the dealings of private enterprises are routinely kept confidential, transactions in the public sector are to a large extent just that—public. By design, the public hearings and meetings involved in the decision and approval process, and the accessibility and visibility created by freedom of information (or "sunshine") acts and similar legislation and rules, make the dealings of governmental entities largely open to all, like laundry to be aired in public.

Similarly, public-sector projects are often much more highly publicized, and, as a result, subject to much closer public scrutiny, than those in the private sector when things go awry or if shortcomings are perceived. As one author has observed, "[p]ublic sector ERP overhauls often make headlines when the projects devolve into extensive debacles" (Cowley, 2005). While IT projects in the private sector may also make headlines if circumstances get bad enough, commercial entities, both IT vendors and customers, usually have much greater ability, as well as significant financial incentives, to minimize publicity. Conversely, "[b]y its nature, the public sector seldom gets to fail quietly," and, as a result, "[w]hen it comes to troubled IT projects, it seems that the public sector is over-represented" (Songini, 2005). This high degree of transparency, both in the contracting process and in project implementation, may make public-sector decision makers even more risk averse (Thomas & Jajodia, 2004) and may have a chilling effect in general upon technology contracting in the public sector.

The slower rate of adoption of technology in the public sector may also be compounded by the fact that public entities are generally not directly subject to the competitive pressures of the marketplace. As a result, some public entities may have little automation currently in place and may suffer from "antiquated and convoluted processes that consume substantial amounts of time and effort" (Sonde, 2004). Although such a situation could potentially lead to greater results or returns, it may also have the effect of making the political, organizational, cultural, and technological hurdles that an IT project must clear that much higher. It also means that public entities are often likely to have less (and fewer) tech-savvy personnel and much less experience in negotiating large and complex technology contracts (Songini, 2005), especially in comparison with the sophisticated IT vendors that they may be dealing with.

While commercial entities are certainly not free from internal turf wars and related strife, they each generally have the single overarching goal of maximizing profits. Public-sector entities, on the other hand, often lack such a clear, unifying goal. Instead, they frequently have multiple, complex, and sometimes competing or conflicting organizational goals (Thomas & Jajodia, 2004), making it that much harder for enterprise-wide technology projects to even be initiated, organized, or undertaken, let alone successfully completed, in the public sector.

In addition, complex technology projects are generally long-term commitments. Implementation can often take years to complete, frequently spanning elections, changing political tides and office-holders, and shifts in priorities and availability of funds. Once the contracts relating to a public-sector technology project have been signed, maintaining the focus and momentum of the project over time poses a whole set of further challenges, even if implementation otherwise goes smoothly.

Nevertheless, while the challenges facing public-sector entities in technology contracting are significant, complex, and often daunting, they are not insurmountable. Although there have been some highly-publicized failures, there have also been many successful, highly complex, government technology projects. Understanding the challenges in advance and structuring and adhering to a process that not only addresses them, but wherever possible uses them to advantage, will help ensure that any given government IT project is among the success stories, rather than the failures.

Setting the Stage: Preparing for Your Project

Gathering Your Requirements

The first step in undertaking any technology project is determining, documenting, and analyzing your organization's unique needs and business requirements. This can be a large and difficult task. However, among our clients, the most successful large and complex technology projects are frequently those in which the client did a good job of determining and analyzing its business requirements in advance. Of course, anything can be taken to extreme, and we have seen cases in which clients become so bogged down in the minutia of detailed requirements gathering that their projects never get off the ground. In the context of an ERP software evaluation, it can be beneficial, and more efficient, to define requirements in the form of mandatory business process scenarios that are unique to the organization and that must be supported by the ERP software package (Thomas & Jajodia, 2004).

Gathering business requirements often involves obtaining the cooperation, participation, and input of seemingly countless different agencies, departments, groups, and individuals within your organization. As noted previously, different departments and groups may often have their own, sometimes conflicting, goals, priorities, and agenda. Nevertheless, if you are seeking to implement an organization-wide technology solution, such as an ERP system, you need to work with all of these groups, understand their particular business needs and requirements, and obtain their participation and buy-in to the project from the start. High-level executive sponsorship will likely be needed to accomplish this, and, in our experience, having an effective and committed high-level sponsor throughout the project can be critical to success. As others have noted, political will is key in getting a technology project off the ground (Bray, 2005).

Far too often we see projects in both the public and private sectors in which particular groups within the client's organization are not adequately involved (or, just as importantly, have the perception that they were not appropriately consulted or given adequate opportunity to provide input or participate) early in the project. These groups then become "splinter cells" that never fully commit to the project, are constantly looking for reasons (some would say excuses) to abandon or disassociate themselves from the project, and, as a result, fail to appropriately adopt and utilize the technology, or the related business processes, when implemented. To achieve success and the intended return on the large investment that technology projects often involve, you need your entire organization's cooperation, participation, and commitment. Without these, neither good technology, a good vendor, good business consultants and lawyers, nor good contracts will save your project.

For example, in one project in which a mid-sized county was implementing a county-wide integrated justice system, one group within the county's organization indicated very early in the project that it believed that one particular vendor's product met its needs much better than the software package that was ultimately chosen and implemented by the county and its project team. The disaffected group was forced to accept the decision. But, when minor problems began to be encountered well into the course of the project (as problems of greater or lesser magnitude almost certainly do at some point during any large, complex implementation), this group immediately began to publicly clamor for abandoning the project and switching to the other vendor's product. Satisfying everyone is always difficult and a solution may not have been simple or easy to find. Still, it might have been much more cost effective for the county's project staff to have spent more time early in the project in trying to understand the dissatisfied group's needs and finding a way to appropriately fulfill those needs with the chosen product, rather than having effectively alienated this group and been forced to do extensive damage control later on.

Technology itself is seldom the key or critical challenge in any IT project. Rather, it is how an organization prepares for, implements, and manages the change that the technology will drive or require in the organization that will likely be critical to the success of the project.

Determining Project Scope

Another important issue to begin considering early in your technology project is the scope of the project and the approach that will be used in addressing and implementing that scope. For example, in an ERP project, consider which business processes will be "in scope" and whether all of those business processes will be addressed and implemented at once (a "big-bang" implementation) or whether they will be addressed in phases. In a phased approach, core ERP functionality might be implemented, and the corresponding legacy systems replaced, in an initial phase of the project, with additional, less central functionality being addressed in one or more subsequent waves of activity.

Many organizations are first tempted to try to do everything at once, rather than breaking up the project and initially addressing only some subset of the ultimately intended scope. While there may be business reasons or circumstances that make such a big-bang implementation very attractive (or, in extreme cases, almost a necessity), be aware of the risks, pressure, and stress that your organization would likely be subject to in expanding (or perhaps exploding) its universe in such a rapid fashion. We have seen sophisticated private-sector clients, with large, experienced, highly-knowledgeable IT staffs and top-notch integrators, struggle desperately with the demands of broad scope, big-bang implementations. Assess your organization's capabilities (along with your risk tolerance and budget) honestly and fairly early in your project, and then select a realistic and achievable scope.

There is nothing like success to build support for a follow-on project. One client, a large Southern school district, wanted to develop and implement an enterprise data warehouse a few years ago, but was concerned about the size and competency of its internal IT staff, as well as the organization's capacity to manage and adapt to change. After much consideration, they broke the project up into logical segments or smaller projects, each with a manageable scope, and attacked them serially. With each successive project, not only did their IT staff develop additional skills and competencies, as well as confidence (to the point that they were using outside consultants and integrators much less by the later stages), but the support in their user community swelled larger, and obtaining necessary funding became easier, with each success. It was not long before the district was taking on an ERP implementation.

Project scope is a multi-dimensional concept. To fully define your project, there are various other aspects of project scope that you need to consider in addition to, as mentioned earlier, the "functional scope" and the "process scope" (and the scope of services and deliverables relating to each those concepts). For example, you will need to flush out the "technology scope" of the project. In addition to the hardware and software that will be the primary focus of the project (for example, the ERP product suite being implemented and the hardware platform that it will run on), the technology scope includes things such as interfaces that will be required (both to other information systems within your organization and to applicable third parties and their systems), bolt-on or add-on products to be implemented, and any network upgrades that may be needed.

The "data scope" of a project, what and how much existing or historical data will be ported into a newly implemented system, must also be determined. This is especially important in public-sector projects, as public entities often tend to convert larger volumes of data (partly due to regulatory and fund accounting concerns) than do private entities in similar IT implementations (Thomas & Jajodia, 2004). While data conversion usually does not occur until later in a project, it is often a costly, complex, and time-consuming process, and vendors and integrators generally do not include data conversion time and costs in their proposals. So, be sure to carefully consider and plan your data conversation process, as it is frequently a source of added cost and delay.

Similarly, the "entity scope" of a project can be very important in public-sector deals, as larger governmental units sometimes provide or make IT systems or services available to what can be a broad-ranging array of smaller, separately organized, public entities. For example, in one instance, the county implementing a new ERP system had previously been serving literally hundreds of small public entities of various types and descriptions, with the list of these entities almost constantly changing. The county needed the right to let these entities access and utilize the new ERP system, as hardly any of these entities would have been able to afford to implement similar systems themselves. This issue unfortunately did not come up until quite late in negotiations, and the software vendor was shocked, to put it mildly, when it learned of the county's plans. To the vendor, it appeared as if the county wanted the right to operate a service bureau, a concept not usually well received by software licensors. The issue was eventually amicably resolved, in this particular case, by carefully (and fairly broadly) describing in the ERP software license the different types or classes of entities that the county was permitted to serve or allow to use the system. However, while surprises can, at times, result in some of life's richest moments, they are almost never a good idea in technology contracting. Determine and address the scope of entities that your project needs to cover early in the project.

The "geographical scope" of an IT project (that is, the geography in which the implemented IT systems will be used) is usually not that much of an issue in public-sector deals, as public entities generally have a fixed geography. However, there are instances in which entities outside of the geographical boundaries of the area served by a governmental or other public-sector entity will need to be able to access and use the IT systems that are being implemented. This is even more likely to be the case as telecommuting becomes more widespread. To avoid surprises and inadvertent mistakes in the eventual contract (such as a geographical limitation in the license grant) that could lead to additional cost, determine early in your project the various different locations at or from which the system being implemented will need to be used.

Ultimately, nailing down project scope is critical to successfully completing your IT project on-time and within budget. The situation might, in some ways, be compared to a common strategy long successfully employed by auto dealers and salespeople in selling cars. The dealer first finds out which of the four key issues of sales price, trade-in allowance, down payment, and monthly payment (the "four-square") are the most critical or give the prospective customer the most pain (the "pain points"). Then, just like pinching one particular area of a long, thin balloon, the pain point (or points, as long as fewer than all four) can be squeezed down to what is acceptable to the customer, and the money, just like the air in the balloon, simply flows on to slightly (or perhaps not so slightly) inflate the other, remaining deal points. The customer's best tactic against this strategy is, of course, to make all of the four square issues pain points and to set limits in advance that he or she will not exceed on each point. Then the deal will either be made at those pain point limits or the metaphorical balloon will burst and the customer will have to shop for either another dealer or another car.

Similarly, in technology contracting and IT projects, there are three critical, inter-related factors that are potential pain points—scope, time, and price. Generally, if you decrease the scope of the project, it can probably be completed in less time, for less money. But increase the project scope, and it will likely take more money to complete—significantly more, if you still want it done in the same amount of time. IT projects are notorious for cost over-runs, something that not many of our clients, especially public-sector clients, can deal with well. To avoid cost overruns, you need to do your best to determine in advance just what the scope of your project (in all of its various aspects and dimensions), and the required time-line for performance of the project, will be. Only then, generally speaking, can you hope to accurately predict (or, better yet, be able to fix) the project cost. You need to do your shopping for vendors, and to know whether your budget balloon is going to burst, before you sign the contract, not be caught be surprise later.

Networking with Other Organizations

As noted previously, the high degree of transparency, openness, and visibility in both the letting and the performance of technology contracts in the public sector can pose significant challenges, as well as risks, to an organization. However, this same characteristic can be put to very good use by public entities in the planning phases of a project, before entering into a contract.

In thinking of how private enterprises share information regarding their experiences in technology projects, I am reminded of how a former boss always responded over the telephone when asked to provide a reference for a certain former employee. The response was always the same: "You'd be lucky to get Joe to work for you." Only if you were already familiar with Joe's working habits, or were present when the remark was made to notice the wry smile, and sometimes the wink, that accompanied it, could you perceive the true meaning of that statement.

Private-sector businesses tend to be much more cautious than public entities in sharing information about their experiences in technology projects, especially if things did not go all that well. Competitive and confidentiality concerns, worries about bad press, stock prices, and even lawsuits, a desire to preserve an existing, even if troubled, business relationship, and various other factors, often have a chilling effect on the open sharing of information between private enterprises, at least at management levels.

In the public sector, however, information often tends to be shared much more freely. Unlike the tight-lipped nature of highly competitive private industries, there frequently seems to be a collegial spirit among public entities, a willingness to share information to help others succeed. While there generally are still some confidentiality issues to be aware of and concerned with, much information is public available, or at least freely obtainable, and can be openly shared. So why not share what you can to help out the city, county, or school district down the road?

A characteristic common to many of the most successful public-sector technology deals that we have been involved with is that the clients have been incredibly thorough from the very start of their projects in doing due diligence regarding what they are undertaking, including learning from colleagues at other public entities who have engaged in similar projects or implemented similar technologies. These clients attend IT and public-sector conferences and seminars and specific vendor or product-user group meetings. They search and correspond over the Internet, monitor newsgroups and bulletin boards, and basically do everything they can possibly think of to learn all they can about the relevant technology and vendors, the experiences of others with regard to specific products and vendors, and any other dos, don'ts, and other tips that they can find. As a result, they come into their project with their eyes wide-open, incredibly well-informed, and aware of potential pitfalls and ready to address them.

Strictly from a lawyer's perspective, some of the most useful or helpful pieces of information that clients can obtain from or through colleagues at other public entities are copies of the agreements that those entities have signed with the same vendors that are being considered for the client's project. Existing agreements such as these are generally public documents and capable of being freely shared. That may not always be the case, however, and it should be investigated before anything is disclosed. In addition, in some cases, in order to maintain an existing relationship or get a new one off to a good start, it can be a good idea for the entity that is a party to an existing agreement with the applicable vendor to inform the vendor that it is going to share the agreement, or to even politely ask the vendor's consent to do so, before any documents are shared. Some particularly sensitive information, such as pricing, can always be redacted, if need be. If all else fails, consider filing freedom of information act requests for the agreements that other public-sector entities have executed with your prospective vendors. Speaking from experience, knowing what a vendor has previously agreed to in other deals can often be extremely useful in negotiations.

Keep in touch with the networking contacts that you make early in your project. Additional issues will likely come up as your project unfolds on which they may be able to provide useful information. For example, they may not only be able to provide helpful insight about different vendors before and during your vendor and product evaluation process, they may also be able to comment on the capabilities and qualifications of particular individuals who worked on their projects, and whom the vendor is now proposing to assign to your project, when you get that far. Listen open-mindedly to what your contacts and colleagues have to say. We have repeatedly seen cases in which comments made by other entities regarding their experiences (whether about particular vendors, products, or specific individuals) fore-shadowed, to a greater or lesser degree, troubles that were later experienced in the client's project. Along those lines, when evaluating prospective vendors, and again when a vendor proposes specific individuals to be assigned to your project, be sure to ask for lots of refer-ences, including specifically asking for references from failed or troubled projects. While the vendor will doubtlessly be selective about the references it provides, you should be sure to follow-up and check those references. What you learn can be very telling and might help you avoid major problems later on.

Forming Your Project Team

It has been said that "good company in a journey makes the way to seem the shorter" (Walton, 1847, Part I, Chapter I). Certainly, in our experience, wisely selecting the members of your project team, as well as those of your negotiating team, can make a world of difference in how long it takes to complete your project, or contract negotiations, as well as in the bumps and potholes in the road that you encounter along the way.

As noted earlier, public-sector entities often have a relatively small number of tech-savvy personnel. Keep in mind, however, that while familiarity with technology (especially the particular technology being implemented) can be important in large IT projects, an under-standing of your business and your existing business processes (especially in ERP projects) is an equally necessary skill set for your project team (Thomas & Jajodia, 2004). Of course, having good organizational, communication, and project management skills is also very im-portant, especially for project team members in leadership roles. While there will likely still be other competing organizational goals, choosing the right individuals for your project team can help make your project into a unifying goal that helps transform your organization.

When forming your project team, carefully and honestly assess your current personnel and your budget. Take a long-range view, remembering that once project implementation is complete, you will likely need qualified people to staff critical positions relating to the management and operation of the new technology or, with respect to an ERP project, the re-designed or re-engineered business processes. In our experience, project team members who are onboard from the inception of a project often become highly invested and take ownership in the project. That can make them tremendous assets, not only during project implementation, but also once the implemented technology is up and running in produc-tion. Training is nearly always a key factor in IT projects (Sonde, 2004), and the on-the-job training that your project team members acquire during project implementation can make them invaluable trainers and resources for others in your organization.

For example, one of our clients, a populous Western county, appointed its assistant county auditor as the project manager for its ERP project. He had a take-charge attitude and was the perfect choice. His background in public accounting gave him broad knowledge of, as well as deep interest in, many of the relevant business processes, along with prior exposure to several popular ERP software packages. On his initiative, and as the county had only a sparse IT staff, during the planning phase of the project the county recruited and hired two highly-qualified individuals with extensive backgrounds with the ERP software suite that the county planned to select and implement. As an example, one of these individuals had worked in project management of complex ERP projects for a large, highly-respected consulting firm for a number of years. At least from the viewpoint of the county's outside legal counsel, this strategy worked extremely well for the county. Because of their knowledge and familiarity with the subject matter, these members of the county's project team were incredibly valuable in getting the project off the ground quickly and in helping the county obtain good contracts with both the ERP software vendor and the consulting firm used in the ERP implementation. The project manager obtained contractual precedents from at least a half-dozen other counties, giving us a very good idea of terms the vendors had previously agreed to. And thanks in large part to the project management person the county hired, the county's implementation services contract includes the most thorough and detailed statement of work that I have yet encountered in an ERP deal, helping to firmly nail down project scope. At last report, the project was going quite well, and the county planned to move the individuals hired during the project planning phase into key operational roles appropriate to their skills once project implementation has been completed. That way, the county expects to retain some of the invaluable expertise developed during project implementation, rather than having it all walk out the door once the final check has been written to the consulting firm helping with ERP integration. In sum, selecting appropriate and highly-qualified project team members, and (if necessary and feasible) recruiting and hiring new employees with much needed skill sets to fill key roles in your project team, can be an effective and efficient way to help guide your project to success.

Drafting the RFP

Once you have gathered and analyzed your business requirements, determined an achievable project scope, networked with colleagues at other public-sector entities, completed other due diligence activities, and have at least the core of your project team identified, you will need to start preparing a request for proposals (or RFP) for sending out to prospective vendors. For some IT projects (such as ERP projects, which commonly have a software licensing component that can be viewed as separate and divisible from the implementation services component), you may actually need or want to prepare more than one RFP.

Drafting an RFP is an extremely important part of your project. A well-written RFP frames your project, as well as the responses or proposals that you receive back from interested vendors, and sets the tone for contract negotiations. Just as with gathering your business requirements, many different groups and individuals throughout your organization will need to provide input to a RFP. Organizing and presenting the resulting, broadly-ranging material can be quite challenging. Consider engaging business consultants with knowledge and experience specific to the type of project that you are undertaking to assist in RFP preparation and contract negotiations.

Especially with public-sector entities subject to competitive bidding rules and processes, it can be very helpful to structure certain parts of the RFP in the form of questions, soliciting specific information and leaving space in which the vendor can respond. At least certain portions of the proposals that you receive back from prospective vendors should then be formatted consistently, so that the responses that vendors provide to specific questions may be relatively easily compared with one another, on as objective of a basis as possible. You should also attach your business and functional requirements to the RFP (this is often done in the form of a "functional requirements matrix") and have each vendor respond in a consistent manner, indicating which of those requirements the vendor can fulfill or satisfy and how it would address the others. These responses can be very important and will also need to be structured so that they may be easily compared among vendors.

Similarly, the RFP should establish a common or consistent structure and process to be followed by the prospective vendors from the time they receive the RFP through execution of a negotiated contract. Many IT vendors are very sophisticated and are used to taking the upper hand early in dealing and negotiating with prospective customers. The RFP is where you need to take control and define the process to be followed. In the RFP, designate one individual as the sole contact person for your organization with regard to all communications with vendors. Describe the precise process to be used by vendors in seeking clarifications and asking questions regarding the RFP, as well as the process that you will use in answering questions and providing any supplemental materials (being sure to copy all vendors on any additional materials or information that you distribute, regardless of which vendor may have requested the materials). Prescribe the manner and form in which proposals or responses to the RFP are to be submitted, the number of copies that are to be provided, to whom they are to be addressed, and the date and time by which they must be received. If you plan to have vendors give presentations and respond in person to your questions regarding their proposals, the RFP should indicate when those sessions will be held.

RFP preparation is also the point at which legal counsel should begin to be involved in your project. There are important legal terms that need to be included in an RFP—some unique to your organization, some specific to your project and the technology to be obtained and implemented, and others more general in nature. While your internal legal counsel will be needed in any event to provide or review terms in the RFP that are specific to your organization, many public entities, as noted previously, lack experience in negotiating large and complex technology contracts. This can put you at a serious disadvantage if you are dealing with sophisticated IT vendors who negotiate complex contracts specific to their technology every day. Just as mentioned earlier with regard to possibly hiring individuals with key technical and business skills, backgrounds, and experience that your organization otherwise lacks, if you do not have the requisite legal expertise, you should give serious consideration to engaging outside legal counsel with particular knowledge and skill in the area of technology contracting.

Our clients tell us that engaging outside legal counsel who practice exclusively in the area of technology law adds significant value in negotiating technology deals. Good technology contracts have many terms and provisions that are not common in other types of agreements. Your legal counsel needs to be familiar with these technology-specific provisions, just as, you can be sure, your IT vendors' lawyers and negotiators will be. Technology attorneys stay abreast of trends and changes in IT contracting and the IT industry and can advise you accordingly. IT lawyers also negotiate repeatedly with the same general set of IT vendors, giving them unique insight as to the terms that any particular IT vendor will typically agree to, and to what extent specific terms might be negotiated, in contracts. This unique insight and experience can be tremendously valuable, especially if it is specific to the particular vendors that are bidding on your project, just as noted previously with regard to obtaining contractual precedents from other public-sector entities.

If you are on a very limited or tightly-constrained budget, you might discuss with the technology lawyers that you would like to engage possible ways to keep legal fees down. For example, while legal fees are generally charged for time worked at an hourly rate that varies with the skills and experience of the individual lawyer, we frequently negotiate blended hourly rates with our public-sector clients that apply regardless of the particular lawyer required for any given legal services. For legal services that are somewhat predictable (such as, perhaps, with regard to the initial drafting of a standard form agreement to be included in your RFP and distributed to prospective vendors), your technology lawyers may be willing to agree in advance to a fixed fee. We have also agreed to other alternative or somewhat unusual arrangements from time to time with public-sector clients. For example, we worked on a school board's ERP project in what was much like an advisory or consulting capacity, with the school board's internal legal counsel doing the bulk of the legal drafting and handling the actual negotiations, and with our participation on an on-call or as-needed basis. This helped keep legal fees down for the school board, while still making technology-specific legal knowledge available to their negotiating team. For one county hospital's project, we agreed to a somewhat similar arrangement, creating the initial drafts of the agreements, then providing advice and counsel to the hospital's internal lawyer while she was handling negotiations.

At any rate, in addition to the important legal terms that are needed in the body of an RFP, many of our clients have found it very advantageous to include a proposed standard form agreement as an attachment or exhibit to your RFP. While this is especially true for RFPs that relate to technology services, it may not always be required or desired for RFPs (or portions of RFPs) that relate to the licensing of software or software systems, especially if you are dealing with large, established software licensors (who will likely insist upon starting from their own form agreements, their own "paper", in negotiations). The standard form agreement distributed with the RFP should contain all of the terms and conditions of your preferred contracting position, to which you are ready to agree. Again, be sure to involve attorneys familiar with technology contracting in preparing the proposed form agreement. Far too often clients have not engaged us until after they have already distributed proposed terms and conditions, and the proverbial horse was already out of the barn.

While we have heard that some outside legal counsel prefer not to be involved in technology contracting projects until their clients have negotiated the best deal they can by themselves, in our experience, such an approach often results not only in a much less favorable contract for the client, but also in legal fees that are actually higher than what they might otherwise have been, especially considering the results that are achieved. In general, it is much more difficult, and far less cost-efficient, to try to correct or improve a flawed situation later than it would have been to have obtained appropriate legal assistance sooner. Many of our clients can attest through experience that involving legal counsel early in the contracting process is a wise and efficient use of resources.

In the RFP, require each vendor to respond to the proposed standard form agreement in a prescribed form and manner, with the vendor indicating the precise changes that it would require to each section of the agreement in order to have a document that it would be willing to sign. You might require vendors to respond with proposed changes to your standard form agreement with what are often referred to as "issue papers". With this method, each prospective vendor must submit a separate issue paper for each section or paragraph of the form agreement that it proposes to change, with the precise language of the proposed change shown in "redlining" (using, for example, Microsoft Word's "track changes" feature). Alternatively, especially if you are dealing with less sophisticated vendors, you might instead require the vendor to simply submit an entire redlined, revised draft of the agreement, showing all of the changes that the vendor proposes. Either way, the goal is have the vendor indicate, in precise contractual language to which it is willing to agree, every single change that the vendor proposes to your standard form agreement. This scenario allows you to fairly and objectively compare not only the business terms that each vendor offers in its proposal, but also the legal terms and conditions to which each vendor is willing to agree. Clients are often surprised to find marked differences among the legal terms that vendors are willing to agree to, and having the ability to identify those differences and make objective comparisons before determining which vendors to proceed to negotiate with can be very useful. As differences in legal terms can translate into costs and risks for your organization, they can also help justify decisions in competitive bidding situations.

Specify in the RFP that vendors are not permitted to make wholesale changes to your form agreement (such as, for example, replacing whole sections of the standard form agreement, or even the entire standard form agreement, with the vendor's own standard language). Similarly, prohibit vendors from simply inserting inconclusive comments (such as comments indicating that certain terms must be further discussed) in the standard form agreement. Require specific contractual language—"words on paper". And reserve the right in the RFP to reject a vendor's entire proposal if the vendor does not conform to the required process regarding proposing changes to your standard form. Then stick to your guns. While you might uniformly allow vendors who submit non-conforming responses a second chance, you need to take a firm hand and retain control over the process. Once you lose control, it can be tough to regain.

The specific terms and conditions to include in the standard form agreement that is distributed with the RFP will vary with your particular project (and possibly with each different component of your project, such as, for example, a software license agreement versus an implementation services agreement). However, as a general rule of thumb, keep in mind the old saying that "an oral agreement isn't worth the paper it's printed on." If there is something that is important to you in the project, make sure that it is appropriately addressed in the contract.

The importance of determining and defining your project scope is discussed earlier, and your contracts with vendors will ultimately need to accurately reflect that scope. While the details of the project scope in an implementation services contract are often laid out in a statement of work or similar document that is developed during negotiations (with additional statements of work sometimes to be developed during the course of the project), a high-level description of the project and how it will be structured (for example, the anticipated phases of the project) is often included in the body of the services agreement, with many of the other contract provisions crafted to appropriately reflect the intended project scope, structure, and approach.

A software license agreement also needs to appropriately reflect the scope of the project, granting the public entity all of the rights to the software that it needs to accomplish the goals and purposes of the project. For example, each aspect of project scope that is discussed earlier needs to be addressed. The specific software modules and programs that you license need to adequately address the functional scope and process scope for your project. The license grant needs to be appropriately drafted to cover the necessary entity scope and geographical scope, including not only the right to let all appropriate entities and end users access and use the software, but also the right for your organization to engage third parties (such as integrators, outsourcers, and other consultants) to help implement and possibly operate the software, in whatever locations are appropriate. Software license agreements also need to address the support and maintenance obligations of the software vendor, including any specific service levels (such as commitments regarding problem response and resolution) and corresponding performance credits that are to apply.

In your services agreement you will want to include provisions regarding the personnel that the vendor will assign to the project, their required qualifications, and any security and background checks that must be conducted and passed before they are assigned. Be sure to reserve a right for your organization to have any particular vendor personnel removed from your project, for any reason, upon request. Personality conflicts often arise, along with many other issues, and if someone the vendor assigns does not work out, you need the vendor to assign someone else.

You should also specifically identify the vendor's project manager or director, as well as other key personnel that the vendor will assign. Limit the vendor's ability to remove or re-assign these individuals, and provide for a period of overlap if they are re-assigned. Provisions regarding administration of the project, such as status reports to be provided, status meetings to be conducted, and participation in steering committee meetings, should also be included.

Your agreements should also specify the required time frame for performance in the project, preferably tying payments of fees to the vendor to achievement of identified critical milestones. This helps align the objectives of the parties, a very important concept in negotiations. You want to get the project completed, and the vendor wants to get paid. Tying the concepts together achieves both parties' objectives.

It is important that an acceptance testing or verification process be included in both software license agreements and implementation services agreements. Acceptance testing, or (sometimes less sensitive to software vendors, because of revenue recognition concerns) verification, allows your organization a limited period of time in which to test and verify that the applicable functional requirements have been met and that the implemented software and systems otherwise meet all applicable acceptance criteria and specifications, with the vendor obligated to correct within a specified period of time any defects and deficiencies that are discovered.

Both software license agreements and implementation services agreements need to contain appropriate representations and warranties by the vendor. While some of these may be fairly common in any type of agreement (such as representations regarding the vendor having all necessary authority and approvals to enter into and perform under the agreement, as well as representations and warranties regarding no pending or outstanding claims or litigation, no conflicts of interest, compliance with laws, and the like), there are also many that are somewhat specific to technology agreements. For example, in a software license agreement you should have a warranty regarding the software providing the features, functionality, and capabilities to efficiently fulfill and satisfy the functional requirements that were included in the RFP (and which should also be attached as a schedule or exhibit to each agreement), and in an implementation services agreement there should be a warranty regarding the vendor implementing the software so that all such functional requirements are met or satisfied. Similarly, there should be warranties regarding no material or frequent defects, and no viruses or other disabling devices, in software and deliverables that are provided, the quality of documentation and services that are provided, and, in implementation agreement, the possession of all appropriate technical certifications necessary for performance.

It may also be appropriate to include warranties regarding the adequacy and sufficient capacity of hardware and network components that the vendor recommends or provides, as well as the availability and response times to be achieved by the software and systems that are implemented. There are many horror stories of systems being implemented only to immediately require hardware upgrades to make them run in a usable manner, resulting in significant, unexpected, additional cost, and these "performance warranties" help avoid that problem. Warranties regarding the integration and compatibility of the implemented software and systems with other software and systems, and that the implemented software and systems will not result in data loss or corruption, can also be useful and valuable.

Many other provisions that are commonly termed "legal boilerplate" in an agreement should also be tailored appropriately to technology projects in general and to your project in particular. Among others, this includes provisions regarding such things as confidentiality, intellectual property rights, indemnities, and insurance requirements. The limitations of liability should be carefully crafted, with appropriate exceptions or carve-outs specified in which the limitations do not apply (such as, for example, with respect to breaches of confidentiality, any indemnities [especially intellectual property indemnities], and in the event the vendor repudiates the agreement or simply refuses to perform, with an exception for repudiation helping to avoid an "efficient breach" in which the vendor determines it would be cheaper to walk away from the deal than to complete performance). While the concept of limiting the potential liability of a vendor may be unfamiliar to public entities in certain contexts, it is something that, unless you are dealing with an extremely unsophisticated vendor, will probably be difficult to avoid in technology contracting, where it is an almost universal practice. The specified exceptions or carve-outs to the limitations of liability need to protect your organization where exposure is greatest, and your organization needs to further protect itself by negotiating appropriate limits on its own potential liability.

The larger and more complex the technology project, the more likely it is that disputes and difficulties will arise at some point. The agreements that you negotiate with your vendors need to anticipate problems and provide for an effective dispute resolution procedure, as well as an appropriate disentanglement or transition process upon termination. Many clients have found it quite helpful to require, as the final step before resorting to litigation or arbitration, the vendor's chief executive officer (or another senior-level executive) to engage in discussions on-site at the client's location in a last attempt to resolve the dispute. Nevertheless, some disputes cannot be resolved, and your agreement needs to commit the vendor, before the situation becomes acrimonious, to assist in disentanglement (that is, in the transitioning of the project to your organization or to another vendor, or in your organization's winding down of the project) at specified rates or for pre-determined fees.

Your organization may have specific requirements that need to be addressed in each of different types of contractual provisions discussed previously, as well as other specifically required contractual language. Your internal legal counsel will likely be familiar with any special or unusual contracting requirements of your organization, such as, perhaps, requirements regarding involvement of minority-owned and female-owned business enterprises or issues like "nuclear-free zones". Again, surprise is usually a bad thing in technology contracting, and these requirements need to be flushed out in advance.

Of course, it is always important to try to obtain the most favorable agreement that you can for your organization. However, in our experience in assisting clients not only during the negotiation process but also during actual project implementation and performance, the most favorable agreement is often one that is relatively fair and balanced. After all, as the ancient Greek Solon observed more than 2,500 years ago, "men keep agreements when it is to the advantage of neither to break them." We have seen a number of projects in which the vendor has been squeezed so tightly on price, or has otherwise reluctantly accepted terms so unfavorable, that the project was fraught with bitter disputes and disagreements from the very start. A balanced approach is often the most efficient in the long run, both in negotiations and after the contract is signed. You might want to strongly consider taking a balanced approach, both in preparing the form agreements that will be included in your RFP and especially later in negotiating specific contractual terms.

Contract Negotiations: Possible Approaches and Strategies

The Negotiations Schedule and Process

One negotiation strategy that has often worked quite well for our clients in both the public and the private sectors is to develop and strictly adhere to a detailed, pre-determined negotiation schedule. This schedule should either be included in the RFP that you prepare and issue, as described earlier, or provided for in the RFP and distributed later, when you have narrowed the field of prospective vendors to a reasonable number (we would suggest at least two, and perhaps three, four, or possibly even more, vendors). The negotiation schedule should provide for a fixed number of rounds of negotiations, with each vendor still in consideration during any given round of negotiations being given the same opportunity (i.e., the same, fixed amount of time) to negotiate the terms of the proposed agreements with your organization. Again, treating each vendor equally, and having documentation of that fact, can be of significant value in competitive bidding situations.

For example, for the first round of negotiations, you might schedule two days of negotiations with each vendor. The negotiation session on each day would be of fixed duration, running from, say for example, 9:00 a.m. until noon and again from 1:00 p.m. until 5:00 p.m. At the start of the first session with each vendor, your negotiating team would quickly go over the proposed changes that the vendor previously submitted, through the process described previously (whether in issue paper form or in the form of a redlined agreement), on a section-by-section basis. For each section of the agreement, you would indicate whether the vendor's proposed changes are acceptable to your organization, whether you expect that they might be acceptable with some modifications, or whether they are unacceptable and rejected. The vendor would then have the remaining scheduled time to use as it sees fit and to discuss whatever terms or provisions that it chooses with you. The limited available time encourages the vendor to concentrate on important issues, rather than wasting time in long, pointless discourses, and avoids error-prone late-night cram sessions.

Within a specified number of days after the last negotiation session with each vendor during any given round of negotiations, the vendor would be required to resubmit its proposed changes to the agreement, again either in the form of issue papers or a redlined revised agreement. Your negotiating team would then review each set of newly revised proposed changes, and one vendor would typically be eliminated (although that might not always be the case, depending upon the number of vendors included in the first round of negotiations). This process would then be repeated for another round of negotiations with the remaining vendors, until, for the final round of negotiations, only two vendors remain.

This process allows for public-sector entities to take advantage of one of the key forces of private enterprise and capitalism—competition. In each round of negotiations, each vendor is aware of its competitors that are still in consideration, allowing you to play each vendor, and its proposed contractual positions, off against the others, maximizing your leverage. The results of this process are often dramatic and surprising. Significant concessions are frequently obtained that likely would not otherwise have been, and the winning bidder or vendor is often not the one that might have been expected or favored when negotiations commenced.

While the extent to which this process is followed may vary from deal to deal, depending upon time constraints and other issues, the ultimate goal is to obtain two complete agreements or contracts for presentation to your board or other decision-making body. The most favorable contract of the two may then be chosen and executed. And, to some extent, if things do not work out with the chosen vendor, you have a fully-negotiated fallback position to turn to with the second-place vendor.

Contrary to what many clients may fear prior to trying this parallel-negotiations approach, it is generally both effective and efficient. If you manage your schedule well, negotiations are often completed in less time than it normally might have taken. Once a client has used the parallel-negotiations approach, we often find that they are so pleased with it that they insist on employing it again in subsequent deals. Many vendors have even indicated that they find the process fair, expedient, and efficient. In one instance, when two fully-negotiated contracts were presented to one quasi-public entity's board and the board selected one particular vendor, the vendor that was not selected called to say how pleased it had been with the process, even though ultimately unsuccessful in its bid.

The Negotiating Team

Just as, as noted earlier, carefully and wisely selecting the members of your project team can be extremely important, the composition of your negotiating team is also critical. Each key stakeholder group within your organization should be represented, if possible, but the size of your negotiating team probably should not exceed five or six people, including your attorneys. If your negotiating team gets much larger than this, then it becomes very difficult to quickly reach consensus on issues and make decisions. So, just as with your project as a whole, high-level management commitment and involvement will likely be needed.

The members of your negotiating team need to collectively be able to effectively and expeditiously deal with all types of issues, business, technical, and legal. Above all, your negotiating team needs to be empowered to make these decisions, subject, of course, to final review and approval of upper-most management and your board or other decision-making body. There is nothing that throws negotiations further off track, or that sooner undermines the effectiveness of your negotiating team (and therefore your leverage in the deal), than having to repeatedly re-open issues that you thought had already been settled, because one particular group's viewpoint is not adequately represented on your negotiating team or the approval of what had been thought to be an acceptable position is unexpectedly withheld or delayed. While it is not infrequent that there will be some final, minor issues still to resolve after when you first think negotiations have been completed, you want to try and minimize these occurrences, especially if negotiations have been difficult. You do not want your vendor to back away at the last minute from favorable terms that you thought were negotiated and agreed upon.

Other Comments on Negotiations

Negotiations of technology contracts can be tedious, difficult, and time-consuming, even when using the negotiation process described previously. However, you need to view this process as an extension of the discovery and due diligence process that you conducted at the start of your project. As an attorney, a large part of one's role in contract negotiations is to raise issues, ask questions, point out inconsistencies, and facilitate discussion. Many detailed contractual provisions, and many of the minutes spent in negotiations, serve to help establish a common understanding between the parties of just exactly what each of them will do in performance under the contract. It is certainly better to discover any misunderstandings before you sign the contract rather than afterwards. Again, as repeatedly noted earlier, surprises tend to be a very bad thing in technology contracting.

It can be very difficult at times to remain patient through negotiations when the parties seem at loggerheads. Yet, as Gandhi (who had been a successful lawyer and whose policies of civil disobedience required great patience) once said, "Honest disagreement is often a good sign of progress." Once each party knows the other's position, you can assess the situation and available alternatives and try to find a resolution. Once you find that resolution, it is generally not hard to document it in a mutually satisfactory form. It is seldom the agreed-upon, negotiated positions reached in settling issues during negotiations that cause problems in performing under an agreement. Problems usually arise from issues that you did not discover or anticipate.

Challenges Likely to Face an Organization After Contract Execution

Ideally, once contract negotiations have been completed and the contracts have been signed, they can be filed away, never again to see the light of day, and the project will happily proceed to a successful conclusion. Of course, especially with complex technology projects, that seldom, if ever, happens. Problems are almost certain to occur during the course of any complex technology project, and you need to anticipate and be ready for them (just as, you can be sure, any experienced IT vendor will be doing).

You need to leverage and expand upon the knowledge and expertise that was developed during the pre-implementation phases of the project (i.e., during due diligence, RFP preparation, and contract negotiations). Try to keep the same project team members assigned and focused on the project, putting the knowledge that they have gained to work. It is also important that the individuals responsible for managing your project are familiar with the contracts that you laboriously negotiated, so that they know what your vendor is obligated to do and can make sure that the vendor actually does that. We have frequently seen vendors essentially try to re-write certain contractual obligations during performance or implementation, getting a customer or client to agree to, approve, or sign-off on something less than what the vendor was really obligated to provide.

Structuring the project so that there can be small "wins" or accomplishments to announce frequently during the course of project implementation can also help keep support for the project throughout your organization, and project momentum, strong. In our experience, it is especially important to have a dedicated, active, even tenacious project manager who stays on top of implementation activities from the start. It seems that once a project is allowed to start to stray off-course, it can take Herculean efforts to get it back on track.

We have also found that sophisticated vendors are often very good about documenting when customers or clients fail to fulfill their obligations under a contract, even with regard to seemingly minor points. We have seen vendors produce logs that indicate every instance in which the customer failed to do something it was required to do, such as, for example, make a certain person or resource available on a particular day. However, clients seldom are nearly so diligent in recording their vendors' shortcomings. In response, and as a result of discussing these situations with clients, we have sometimes created simple problem report forms that the clients instruct their project team members to complete and submit with regard to errors, delays, or failures by their vendors. Completing and filing these away at least creates a documented record of a vendor's failings, if the project goes awry. And a documented record like this can be very useful in litigation.

While the challenges that you face in negotiating the contracts for your technology project will be significant and complex, they frequently pale in comparison to the whole new set of challenges encountered in actual project implementation. Nevertheless, the knowledge and experience that you gain in preparing for the project, as well the common understandings that you reach with your vendor and the solid contracts that you obtain in negotiations, will help you surmount the challenges of implementation.

References

Bray, R. (2005, October 1). Municipalities struggle to make e-gov pay. *Summit, 8*(6), 6-8. Retrieved February 7, 2006, from http://www.summitconnects.com/Articles_Columns/PDF_Documents/200510_03.pdf

Cowley, S. (2005, December 12). Growing Nevada county starts $62M app overhaul: Clark County replaces mainframe software with mySAP ERP suite. *Computerworld*, *35*(50). Retrieved February 7, 2006, from http://www.computerworld.com/print-this/2005/0,4814,106915,00.html

Sonde, T. (2004, February 1). 11 ways to leave your legacy systems behind – Far behind. *Government Procurement*, 12. Retrieved February 7, 2006, from http://www.govpro.com/ASP/viewArticle.asp?strArticleId=103341&st=4

Songini, M. L. (2005, September 26). Public-sector blues: Why do so many public IT projects seem to go wrong? *Computerworld*, *39*(39). Retrieved February 7, 2006, from http://www.computerworld.com/printthis/2005/0,4814,104877,00.html

Thomas, G. A., & Jajodia, S. (2004, July 1). Commercial off-the-shelf enterprise resource planning software implementations in the public sector: Practical approaches for improving project success. *Journal of Government Financial Management*, *53*(2). Retrieved January 30, 2006, from http://www.westlaw.com

Walton, I. (1847). *The complete angler; or The contemplative man's recreation*. New York, NY & London, England: Wiley & Putnam. Retrieved February 7, 2006, from http://www.gutenberg.org/dirs/etext96/tcang10.txt

Author's Biography

Milton L. Petersen is a member of the Information Technology Practice Group, at Neal, Gerber & Eisenberg LLP, a law firm in Chicago. Mr. Petersen focuses his practice on information technology-related transactions, including enterprise resource planning, outsourcing, systems integration, software development, e-commerce, and technology licensing transactions, technology consulting and services agreements, and information privacy and confidentiality-related issues. Mr. Petersen deals with both public and private-sector clients, ranging from entrepreneurs and very small entities to large governmental organizations and Fortune 100 companies. Prior to law school, Mr. Petersen worked as a computer and network performance consultant in the information technology industry.

Chapter XI

GovBenefits.gov:
A Case Study in Government-to-Citizen Interaction

Curtis Turner, U.S. Department of Labor, USA

Executive Summary

This case study examines how 10 federal agencies came together in the fall of 2001 to implement an e-government initiative as part of President George W. Bush's Presidential Management Agenda. The initiative, known as GovBenefits.gov™, is a Web site that connects citizens to 1,000 (390 federal and 610 state government) benefit and assistance programs. Through a series of personal interviews and an examination of program documentation, the case study explores the people, technology, and processes used to launch and maintain the Web site. The author arrives at five lessons learned, which are: (1) Establish a clear value proposition; (2) Develop shared risk and rewards; (3) Develop tangible results quickly; (4) Use creativity to get the word out; and (5) Don't stop innovating.

Background

In late 2001, President George W. Bush unveiled his administration's management agenda. A key feature of the agenda was the launching of 24 e-government (E-Gov) initiatives designed to leverage technology to make government more efficient and effective. Among the 24 programs envisioned was a Web site that would consolidate dispersed information about government benefit and assistance programs into one easy-to-use Web site. Today, that vision is a reality with GovBenefits.gov, a Web site that connects citizens from all walks of life to 1,000 (390 federal and 610 state) benefit and assistance programs. The Web site consolidates information spread across 40 million federal government Web pages (Hernon, Dugan, & Shuler, 2003) to help connect citizens with their government. Launched in 2002, under the leadership of the U.S. Department of Labor (DOL), GovBenefits.gov is an inter-agency program that today brings together 16 federal agencies as partners (partners, funding partners) to provide citizens with a single point of entry to benefit and assistance programs.

GovBenefits.gov accomplishes its mission through collaboration and shared risk taking by using a formalized governance structure. The multi-agency governance system allows the DOL to share in the risks and rewards with the 16 federal funding partners, but more importantly enables the partners to have significant input into the direction of the program beyond just writing a check. Furthermore, over time the program has developed the technological infrastructure to move from a development-intensive effort to a state of normal operations or "maintenance mode" while preserving the ability to scale the program up or down through the use of flexible Web architecture. The impetus for GovBenefits was borne from the President's vision to utilize e-government to make government more effective.

President's Vision

During the summer of 2001, President George W. Bush's Director of the Office of Management and Budget (OMB), Mitchell Daniels, began a process to identify strategic E-Gov opportunities as part of a broader effort to outline the specific elements of the President's Management Agenda (PMA) (Office of Management and Budget, 2003). The PMA seeks to reform government to be more citizen-centered, less bureaucratic, and more market-driven. A focus of the PMA is the use of E-Gov technologies to achieve these goals. Through a task force dubbed the "Quick Silver Task Force", a group of 80 senior federal officials collected information from numerous federal employees, citizens, and their own professional expertise to identify possible E-Gov initiatives. The initial information gathering process yielded more than 300 suggestions, including many E-Gov projects that were already underway or in the planning stages. From the list of 300 projects and ideas, an objective evaluation and scoring process reduced the number of initiatives to 24 that would become a part of the PMA (Office of Management and Budget, 2003). The President outlined his vision for e-government in a memo to federal agencies:

My administration's vision for Government reform is guided by three principles. Government should be citizen-centered, results-oriented, and market-based. These principles have been woven into the five Government-wide reform goals outlined in my Administration's Management Agenda: strategic management of human capital, budget and performance integration, competitive sourcing, expanded use of the Internet and computer resources to provide Government services (Electronic Government or E-Government), and improved financial management. Effective implementation of E-Government is important in making

Government more responsive and cost-effective. Our success depends on agencies working as a team across traditional boundaries to better serve the American people, focusing on citizens rather than individual agency needs. I thank agencies who have actively engaged in cross-agency teamwork, using E-Government to create more cost-effective and efficient ways to serve citizens, and I urge others to follow their lead. (Bush, n.d.)

Setting the Stage

Prior to GovBenefits.gov, if a citizen wanted to find federal or state assistance he or she had to know about the specific benefit program and know which government entity to contact for information about the program. According to the Catalog of Federal Domestic Assistance (CFDA), prior to the creation of GovBenefits.gov there were more than 1,500 government programs for federal domestic assistance, as well as the many benefit programs managed by state and local government agencies (Listing of All Programs, n.d.). Information for those programs is generally available through the Internet. However, the information spans across 40 million federal government Web pages (Hernon et al., 2003). As a result, citizens had to know the complex government organizations to find relevant benefits. Without an easy-to-use, single source of information a citizen's search for benefits would often result in frustration instead of assistance. In addition, government staff assisting citizens would spend time interacting with a citizen before finding out that the citizen did not meet the

Table 1. GovBenefits.gov funding partners

Original Federal Partners
Department of Labor (managing partner)
Department of Agriculture
Department of Education
Department of Energy
Department of Health & Human Services
Department of Homeland Security
Department of Housing & Urban Development
Department of State
Department of Veterans Affairs
Social Security Administration
Partners Added After the Launch
Department of Commerce
Department of Interior
Department of Justice
Department of Transportation
Department of Treasury
Small Business Administration

basic criteria for the award or entitlement. Or, they would discover that the citizen really needed to be communicating with a different federal or state organization. This fragmented government-to-citizen benefit communication process is characterized by inefficiencies and frustration.

GovBenefits.gov Solution

The OMB established GovBenefits.gov in early 2002 as an E-Gov initiative to connect citizens with their government. The GovBenefits.gov mission is to provide improved, personalized access to government benefit programs, such as Medicare/Medicaid, Food Stamps, or Social Security Disability Insurance.

The initiative was defined as a partnership of 10 federal agencies, with the DOL selected to manage the effort. In many ways, the DOL was the logical agency to sponsor and host the program given the agency's traditional role of assisting the unemployed. Moreover, GovBenefits.gov is aligned with the DOL's broader mission declared by Congress in 1913 when it created the agency "to foster, promote, and develop the welfare of working people, to improve their working conditions, and to enhance their opportunities for profitable employment" (U.S. Department of Labor, n.d, ¶ 2). Connecting people with the resources they need directly fosters the welfare of workers and their families. This alignment with the DOL's mission helps the program maintain high-level support within the Department. The DOL worked with its partner agencies and the OMB to develop a business case that outlined the project's goals, objectives, specific milestones, and performance metrics.

Shortly thereafter, the DOL sought contactors to support the development and marketing of the site. Through a competitive solicitation, the global strategy and technology firm Booz Allen Hamilton (Booz Allen) was selected as the prime contractor to support the program, and BAE Systems was selected to provide Independent Validation and Verification (IV&V) and system security services. To maintain support from the partners and gain momentum, the project quickly went from business case and a discussion of concepts to a live Web site in just 96 business days on April 29, 2002.

The following case study examines four key aspects of this E-Gov program. First, we provide an explanation of the technology behind the Web site and the rationale for the technology choices. Second, we review the development of a governance structure that enables the program to sustain itself over the long term. Third, we review the public outreach efforts to increase site traffic. Fourth, we review the program's outcomes and results. Finally, the case study outlines five key lessons learned. The next section outlines the approach to the GovBenefits.gov solution.

Case Description

At the time of the site's launch in April 2002, the site featured 55 programs, representing all of the original partners, and worth over $1 trillion in annual benefits to citizens (U.S. Census Bureau, 2005). As of January 2006, the Web site has, over time, grown to 390 federal programs and 610 state administered programs. The content has attracted more than 19 million visitors and generated nearly 4.3 million referrals to government benefit programs and the site regularly receives more than 350,000 visits each month (GovBenefits.gov Total Visits, n.d.). To make the site accessible to the widest population, the site incorporates technology to assist citizens with disabilities and was translated into Spanish to serve the nation's fast-growing Hispanic American population. To achieve these results required a focused Program Management Office (PMO).

While existing DOL staff could have possibly managed the program as a special project from within the Chief Information Officer's office, DOL's senior leadership recognized the need to coordinate with other agencies and the logistical challenges of getting the Web site up and running in a short time frame. As a result, the DOL established a separate PMO to launch and maintain the Web site.

Program Organization

In almost any program or project, effective program management is essential. As the managing agency for GovBenefits.gov, DOL's Assistant Secretary for Administration and Management and Chief Information Officer, Patrick Pizzella is the senior DOL executive responsible for the execution of the GovBenefits.gov vision. In early 2002, Pizzella and his leadership team established a PMO for the project, which included the hiring of a full-time program manager to supervise the development and implementation of the site. Figure 1 highlights the organizational structure of the program.

The PMO provides direct oversight and control of the project to ensure it meets the strategic objectives and specific milestones established by the OMB. In an interview with former DOL Program Manager Denis Gusty, the program manager serves as the primary day-to-day interface with the funding agency stakeholders as well as other government entities such as the OMB and the General Services Administration (GSA) (personal communication, January 16, 2006). Six functional teams provide the daily support for the program.

The six functional teams include:

- **Project Management\Controls:** Responsible for all project controls including scheduling, procurement, budgeting, and reporting.

- **Product Management:** Responsible for managing the content on the site and performing testing activities to ensure quality and accuracy.

- **Configuration Management:** Responsible for managing the workflow for updating the Web site.

- **Development:** Responsible for all technical and software-related components of the Web site.

- **Change Management:** Responsible for working with partners on their Memorandums of Understanding (MOUs), coordinating partner meetings, marketing, and public outreach. Responsible for managing site requirements, Spanish translation, usability testing, site graphic design, and layout.

Figure 1. Program organizational structure

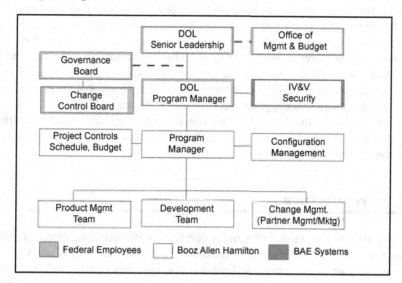

- **Independent Verification and Validation (IV&V):** Responsible for independently testing all software for operational and security requirements.

As noted in Figure 1, the DOL provides one full-time program manager to oversee the day-to-day management of the program. Contractors Booz Allen and BAE Systems provide the remaining staff and expertise necessary to execute the vision. The Booz Allen Program Manager serves as the primary interface with the DOL Program Manager for supporting the PMO. Five of the six functional teams are staffed and managed by Booz Allen, and the sixth team, IV&V, is staffed by BAE Systems and reports directly to the DOL Program Manager. While the program did experience turnover throughout the project at all levels except the DOL Senior Leadership level, the project progressed because of solid transition plans, central document repositories, and continuity of contractors. Although individual contractor staff transition on and off the project, the institutional knowledge is passed down from person to person.

Technology

Site Hosting

An early decision that had to be made was how and where the Web site would be hosted. According to Gusty, the DOL could host the site but would need to procure additional hardware that would have taken time and money to complete (personal communication, January 17, 2005). Another option was to have GSA host the site through their existing contract with AT&T since GSA/AT&T had spare capacity and could quickly accommodate the DOL's needs. The decision was made to go with GSA because the hosting agreement was already in place and the lower costs associated with sharing the hosting resources with GSA were beneficial to the DOL. The downside to the decision was that the product management team could not make real-time content updates to the site and that the update schedule was dependent upon the other applications GSA hosted. In late 2005, due to contractual changes at GSA and the continued growth of the site, the DOL began investigating alternative hosting providers that could provide increased service through more frequent site updates and enhanced scheduled maintenance.

Site Architecture

Shortly after the hosting decision, the project team started gathering comprehensive requirements to determine the site architecture. Requirements gathering is the process whereby key stakeholders are consulted and provide their input as to what should be included in the creation of the application. During the requirements gathering process, considerations for compatibility with the hosting provider, scalability of the architecture, ease of use, and cost were considered. In the end, according to Justin Gaspard, a Development Team leader, the team decided to build GovBenefits.gov using the Sun Java™ 2 Enterprise Edition (J2EE) programming language because of, in large measure, the DOL's interest in partnering with GSA to host the site at significant cost reduction (personal communication, November 23, 2005). At the inception of GovBenefits.gov, GSA agreed to host GovBenefits.gov on the servers used for its government portal Web site, Firstgov.gov, which was written in the J2EE programming language. Therefore, the logical decision was to develop GovBenefits.gov in the same language to create a seamless shared hosting environment. Using a different programming language could have caused delays or complications in getting the site up and running in under 100 days as well as created possible longer term technical support issues with GSA. In addition, as a mature language, J2EE is widely supported in the software development community compared to other programming languages, such as Perl or Python®, which were also considered. Overall, according to Gaspard, the decision to use J2EE was relatively easy to make considering J2EE's portability, cost-effectiveness, and robustness as a programming language (personal communication, November 23, 2005).

In January 2006, the site underwent an upgrade to a flexible portal-based architecture. Previously, any layout or cosmetic changes had to be modified via time-intensive and thereby costly recoding processes. By transitioning the site to a portal-based platform, upgrades and changes to the site are faster with essentially "drag-and-drop" capability. This translates to lower operating costs for the site. In addition to easier maintenance, another major outcome of the upgrade is the ability to share the GovBenefits.gov portal technology with other government agencies. The innovation known as "Customized Connections" allows states and other federal agencies to offer the GovBenefits.gov search technology and benefit information on their own Web sites without creating a duplicate database or Web site. GovBenefits.gov successfully demonstrated the ability to reuse the site's architecture in April 2006, when the program unveiled the first customized connection with the U.S. Department of Veterans Affairs.

The core function of GovBenefits.gov is the eligibility screening questionnaire that evaluates a person's situation against all of the different program criteria. According to Gaspard, the completed questionnaire pre-screens at an 80% (or better) accuracy level. Thus, if a user completes the questionnaire, there is an 80% likelihood of the user being eligible for the programs displayed in the results list. The site can not be 100% accurate for all users or programs because the site includes competitive scholarships, fellowships, and grant programs that have subjective judgment or criteria that can not be captured in the questionnaire. In addition, some benefit programs require highly-personal, case-specific information that is beyond the scope of the questionnaire. Achieving 100% accuracy was also challenging because eligibility questions differ across agencies, so a common eligibility question such as personal income is defined a specific way for one agency but differently for another, thus causing a conflict for the database. Nevertheless, users who complete the questionnaire have a sense of the programs for which they are most likely eligible, which in the past would have required users to visit each Web site independently, find the eligibility information, and then try to determine if they were qualified.

Content Management System

Another important aspect for the program was how to keep its content current. There had to be a mechanism for entering new benefit program information in a standard and timely way. According to DOL Program Manager Curtis W. Turner, the DOL, in consultation with its contractors and other entities, selected the Vignette® Enterprise Content Management System as the Web-based software platform to maintain content on the GovBenefits.gov Web site (personal communication, November 22, 2005). Although the Vignette system required some customization to meet the program's content management requirements, such as limiting the use of pop-up windows when the site does not use them, the system was able to accommodate most of the requirements established by the DOL. For example, Vignette provides an integrated graphics interface much like Microsoft Word; however, its limited capability still requires the user to edit some HTML code by hand. The key feature to Vignette is it creates a standard data entry interface for content to be entered and then published on the Web site.

Concurrent to the ongoing use and testing of the internal content management system, the development team began further customizing Vignette for use externally by the federal partners. An important milestone in the progress of the program was deploying an external content management system allowing partners to manage their own benefit information on the site. A key reason for implementing external content management was also to save maintenance costs by having the benefit agencies, rather than the project team, manage program content.

Independent Verification and Validation (IV&V)

Considering the multitude of federal government security regulations, independent security verification and site testing were important elements to be incorporated into the project from the very beginning. As the name implies, the IV&V Team is a separate team from the Booz Allen Team. This allows the IV&V Team to test the site and security independently of Booz Allen's development work, which bolsters the integrity of the entire development process. In addition to independently testing the site prior to any update to the public, the IV&V Team is responsible for monitoring and ensuring compliance with all privacy and security regulations.

Governance: Multi-Agency Partnership

A unique aspect of this program has been the inter-agency collaboration between the DOL and the other 15 federal agency funding partners. The program initially included 10 funding partners (Table 1), including the DOL; however five additional agencies have since become funding partners. As of January 2006, the site featured programs from all 16 funding agencies and nine other federal non-funding agencies. As of April 2005, the site also includes more than 500 programs administered at the state level that receive federal funding such as food stamps and Medicaid.

According to Gusty, early in the program's development there was resistance toward the project, skepticism of the DOL's motives, and resentment of the OMB's directive that partner agencies would be required to help fund the project (personal communication, January 16, 2005). While some agencies saw the benefit the program would bring to their respective agency others were less enthusiastic. One early partner was the U.S. Department of Education, represented by Harry Feely. In conversation with Feely, the Department of Education's early position regarding GovBenefits.gov was positive, but there was concern about the cost of implementing the solution (personal communication, January 12, 2006). In contrast to the Department of Education's willingness to participate, several partners were disinclined to join the program (Gusty, personal communication, January 17, 2001). To demonstrate progress and overcome the natural inclination to not part with financial resources, the DOL set a deadline of 100 days to get the Web site up and running to prove to the partners that the program could and would be a success.

Because skepticism was anticipated, the DOL began an active stakeholder management relationship program, dedicating two full-time contractor resources to three key tasks. First, the stakeholder managers ensured the project was in regular communication with the agency partners through conference calls and e-mails. Partners were provided with monthly reports detailing program expenditures as well as performance metrics related to the agencies' programs listed on GovBenefits.gov. Second, the program established a governance structure that allows partners to have a stake in the decision-making process. Third, the program encouraged active participation by the partners through working groups and other program-related activities.

In the infant stages of the program, the DOL Program Manager held weekly conference calls with the funding partners to keep them apprised of the site's progress. After the first 100 days, partners received weekly e-mail updates with information on new content, new partners, visitation statistics, awards, and relevant program updates. This regular and timely communication helped to assure the partners that they were getting a return on their financial investment. As the program evolved, the regular e-mails transformed into monthly electronic newsletters.

The program manager also conducted a series of "Road Shows". Throughout the early development stages of the program, the DOL's Program Manager would meet with decision makers from partner agencies at their offices and present the GovBenefits.gov program and its value proposition. These road shows along with regular partner communications laid the foundation for long term buy-in to the program.

Table 2. GovBenefits.gov governance structure and roles

	Governance Board Charter	Change Control Board Charter
Objective	Provide oversight and guidance, making recommendations for both business and financial strategies and timetables, ensuring Partner Agency consensus, providing executive sponsorship for GovBenefits.gov outcomes in the Partner Agencies, and resolving inter-agency issues.	Oversees the support and maintenance of the GovBenefits.gov site. Approves new questions proposed for benefit programs, maintains site objectives. All policy and process for the site are reviewed by the CCB annually.
Chair	Managing Partner while in development, with the option of yearly rotation afterwards	Managing Partner while in development, with the option of yearly rotation afterwards
Voting	Funding partners in good standing Member representatives will be authorized to make decisions on behalf of their agency	Funding partners in good standing Member representatives must be empowered to represent agency viewpoint in all decision-making
Non Voting	OMB, agencies that have provided program content but are not funding partners	OMB, agencies that have provided program content but are not funding partners
Frequency	Monthly	Monthly or more frequently if necessary
Decision Process	Consensus-based Where consensus cannot be reached a majority vote is required, 1 vote per agency. Majority of the Governance Board and the Managing Partner must agree, if there is no majority, or if the Managing Partner does not agree with the majority, then no action is taken based on that decision. 6 members including the Managing Partner make a quorum.	Consensus-based Where consensus cannot be reached a majority vote is required, 1 vote per agency. 6 members including the Managing Partner make a quorum.

Source: GovBenefits.gov Governance Plan

In 2004, during a week-long strategic planning session, the DOL and its partners institutionalized the GovBenefits.gov program through the formation of a governance structure (U.S. Department of Labor, 2004a, 2004b). A permanent governance structure was needed to increase the partner's involvement in decision making and strategic direction. During the week-long strategic planning session, the partners developed the overall vision for the governance structure as well as identified the program's near-term goals and priorities. These goals included developing a fee-for-service funding model, improving the ease of use of the site, and reducing the cost of operating the site (U.S. Department of Labor, 2004a).

As a result of the strategic plan, the partners created two governing bodies for the program: a Change Control Board (CCB) and a Governance Board (Table 2). The CCB is made up of designated representatives from each funding partner agency and oversees the support and maintenance of the site. The CCB established a monthly meeting cycle whereby representatives meet at the DOL headquarters and review progress toward specific milestones and provide input on a tactical basis.

The second governing body created was the Governance Board consisting primarily of the Chief Information Officers (CIOs) from each funding agency. The Governance Board provides strategic and financial guidance to the program. In addition to the CIOs, representatives from the OMB are invited to participate in the meeting to provide a broader E-Gov perspective. Initially, the Governance Board met monthly to provide strategic direction for the project; as the project matured the meetings were scaled back to quarterly. According to Feely, the governance system that was established provides each agency with an equal voice in the decision-making process, which is important for sustaining support for the program (personal communication, January 12, 2006).

A key function of the partners is to set the strategic direction for the program. This is accomplished in two ways. First, each year the CCB members, DOL leadership, and the contractors collaborate to develop a strategic plan that outlines the broad direction and goals for the year. According to Turner, the strategic planning process provides the partners an opportunity to have specific input into the direction of the program, whether it's adding new content or functionality to the site or other changes (personal communication, December 5, 2005). The second method for partner input is through the annual submission of the OMB 300, also known as the OMB Business Case. The OMB 300 outlines the performance milestones and time-line for achieving them. Jointly outlining goals and milestones ensures the DOL, the partners, and the OMB are all in agreement as to what the program should accomplish for the year.

Table 2 highlights the structure of the two governance bodies. As an example of the two Boards' work, the CCB convened a special working group to establish a fee-for-service funding model for the program identified as a goal in the strategic plan. Initially, OMB established the financial contributions from the partner agencies to the program. As the program evolved, the partners, in consultation with the OMB, sought to devise a permanent funding structure to sustain the program that would be equitable and formulaic so as new partners were added their funding contribution could be easily determined. Through a consensus process, a funding model was developed that took into account the number of programs represented on the site and the dollar value of those programs. Once the model was agreed to by the CCB working group, it was approved by the full CCB and then forwarded to the Governance Board for formal approval. In June 2005, the Governance Board approved the new funding model for implementation in fiscal year 2006 (U.S. Department of Labor, 2005).

To further create a sense of institutionalization for the program, representatives to both boards are provided formal advanced agendas and briefing packets, a regular meeting schedule is set, and meeting minutes are taken and reported out at the next meeting. Although each is a small detail, combined they add to the professionalism and institutionalization of the program. In addition, informal working groups are used to complete specific tasks. The working groups further the camaraderie and shared sense of purpose by the partners. For example, in 2003, a working group was convened to identify state administered programs that could be added to the site. The outcome of the working group led to hundreds of programs added to the site in 2004. By the program's third anniversary in 2005, the site featured more than 1,000 programs based on the work completed by the working group in 2003. In 2005, another working group was formed to review the online questionnaire. The group reviewed all 145+ questions and found more than 40 questions that could be eliminated or combined with others. Fewer screening questions make the site easier to use for citizens. The working groups have meaningful impact to the site and further partner commitment.

While informal working groups and monthly board meetings helped to develop a shared sense of purpose and mission for the program, a formal element was still required. In order to have their programs listed, all of the federal funding partners are required to sign an MOU with the DOL. The MOUs outline each agencies' responsibilities for providing funding, designating personnel to attend board meetings, and agreeing to supply and maintain content for the site. The DOL is required to maintain the site, support the program financially at a higher level, and provide the partners with monthly financial and performance reports, as the second party to the MOU.

Marketing: Getting the Word Out

An overarching theme to the GovBenefits.gov program has been communications, internal and external. Critical to maintaining support from the funding partners was communication about the program's results and progress. Equally critical to success was communicating to the public the availability of GovBenefits.gov as a free resource for finding benefits and assistance programs. Over the life of the program, between two and five full-time contractor personnel have been dedicated to developing a national marketing campaign to promote the site to the public, with an average annual materials budget of $125,000. This requires the marketing team to execute outreach tactics with the highest impact at the lowest possible cost. The team leveraged relationships with its federal partners to help spread the word by requesting links on their Web sites and providing articles for their agency newsletters. In addition, the program actively sought partnerships with non-profit agencies and other government entities to increase awareness. However, the site features so many programs with an almost universal audience that the marketing team narrowed the scope of its national outreach efforts to targeted audiences. The team selected seven audiences to focus its efforts:

- Senior citizens
- Veterans
- Low income
- Unemployed workers
- Farmers
- Students
- Case workers serving at-risk populations

These audiences were selected because they are the mostly likely to find benefits related to their personal situation, or, as in the case of case workers, are in a position to use or recommend GovBenefits.gov to their clients. With these audiences identified, the marketing team develops an annual tactical marketing plan focused on delivering the GovBenefits.gov message across multiple channels (online and off-line). Based on this framework of audiences and channels, the marketing team employs a wide array of tactics to increase the number of impressions. An impression is counted when one person saw or heard the GovBenefits.gov message one time. The goal is to maximize the number of impressions that are converted into actual visitors to the Web site.

Online Marketing

When most people think of Internet marketing, the first thing that probably comes to mind is either banner ads or pop-up ads on Web sites. However, marketing on the Internet encompasses a wide range of activities beyond banner ads. Given the generally low response rate banner ads yield in driving people to Web sites compared to other tactics, a company or government agency must saturate the Internet with banner ads to obtain impact—and that costs money. In fact, a marketing gap analysis report prepared by Edelman Communications in 2005 suggested it would cost at least $375,000 per year just for banner ads to achieve some basic level of online presence (Edelman Communications, 2005). Without a large multimedia advertising budget, the GovBenefits.gov marketing team instead pursues low-cost tactics to build online awareness.

The most frequent online marketing tactic pursued is the acquisition of links to GovBenefits.gov. Since major search engines such as Google and Yahoo! use the number of links to a site as a key element of search engine rankings, increasing the number of links to GovBenefits.gov became an important long-term goal to obtaining and maintaining a high rank within the major search engines. In July 2004, the site recorded nearly 1,000 links to GovBenefits.gov and, as of December 2005, Google reported more than 4,500 sites linked to GovBenefits.gov. The marketing team increased the number of links by continuously asking organizations to place links on their Web sites to GovBenefits.gov (Link Popularity Check, 2006). As of September of 2006, if someone used Google.com and searched on the term "government benefits", GovBenefits.gov was returned as the first listing and was returned as the third listing when searching just on the term "benefits".

As another online tactic, the marketing team uses e-mail to reach potential users and intermediary groups. Specific e-mail campaigns communicated the GovBenefits.gov message to groups such as librarians, county clerks, and others who were in a position to promote the site to the populations they serve. These intermediary groups in turn promoted the site by adding links to their own Web sites and in many cases included information about GovBenefits.gov in their own newsletters. In one example, the marketing team sent an e-mail to 11,000 listserv subscribers through the DOL's Center for Faith-Based and Community Initiatives office. The e-mail generated requests for more than 25,000 GovBenefits.gov brochures in just one week (C. Turner, personal communication, January 5, 2006). As previously mentioned, the program sends out a monthly e-mail newsletter to agency partners and interested stakeholders. The newsletter reinforces the GovBenefits.gov message and keeps the Web site in front of people.

Off-Line Marketing

Given the limitations of conducting an online campaign without paid advertising, the program also engages in off-line marketing. The off-line tactics most commonly used fall into four categories: public relations, media/advertising, direct marketing, and event marketing. In order to maximize the materials budget, the marketing team consistently seeks "free" media coverage through traditional public relations techniques, submitting op-ed pieces to newspapers, and leveraging media resources within the DOL. Because GovBenefits.gov has a unique value proposition of connecting citizens to federally-funded benefit programs, many news outlets see the story as an interesting use of technology that directly impacts the average citizen.

Public Relations

Public relations is defined many ways, but essentially involves the art and science of crafting and "pitching" a message or story for the media to use in a news story or article. The marketing team provides editors and reporters with sample articles, quotes, and story ideas that feature GovBenefits.gov. For example, in the fall of 2004, the National Funeral Directors Association published an 800-word informational article about GovBenefits.gov. According to Turner, the article was a good fit for the magazine because funeral directors are increasingly providing customized services and support to families during a time of grieving. The GovBenefits.gov team drafted the article and submitted it to the editor. Two months later, the article was published almost verbatim (C. Turner, personal communication, January 6, 2006). The result of the ongoing public relations effort has been hundreds of stories being published in magazines, professional trade journals, newspapers, and association newsletters with little or no direct materials costs besides the labor time to draft and pitch the articles.

Media/Advertising

The development of a public service announcement (PSA) is another frequently used tool in public education and outreach campaigns. Recognizing the potential for high impact, the marketing team, in collaboration with the DOL's Audio/Visual Team, created a TV PSA using testimonials gathered from non-profit agencies and individuals who had successfully used GovBenefits.gov to find benefits. In addition, the program produced a radio PSA in English and Spanish to promote the site. The DOL distributed the PSAs to hundreds of cable TV and radio stations. Since the PSAs began airing in 2004, 11.9 million TV viewers have seen the GovBenefits.gov message and more than 2.5 million have heard the GovBenefits.gov message on the radio (WestGlen Communications, n.d.). The total cost to produce both the TV and radio PSA was $60,000, a modest investment with high impact given the cost of other outreach methods.

In October 2005, the marketing team also secured free or "public service" outdoor advertising space at five locations on the Washington, D.C. subway system for a one-month period. The five outdoor ads cost $5,000 to print and included 200 ads for the rear of Washington, D.C. buses. During the campaign, approximately two million people saw the ad; as a result, the cost was relatively inexpensive (K. Reynolds, personal communication January 10, 2006). However, in spite of the large exposure, visitors to GovBenefits.gov remained flat for the month. This outcome caused the marketing team to reconsider the effectiveness of outdoor advertising on such a limited scale.

Direct Marketing

One of the standbys of traditional marketing is the tri-fold brochure, which is durable and designed for quick reading. The marketing team developed a tri-fold brochure and full color poster in both English and Spanish for use in direct marketing efforts. Since the program's launch, the marketing team distributed several hundred thousand brochures and posters to a variety of targeted sources, including Career One-Stop Centers, Goodwill Industry stores, libraries, unemployment centers, and many other locations (E. Mezile, personal communication, December 15, 2005). Most often the recipient receives a cover letter introducing the GovBenefits.gov program along with a small sample of brochures and/or posters. Included in the package is a response card that recipients may return to the DOL to request additional materials at no cost to the recipient. The program achieved cost savings by sending brochures on a per-request basis versus sending packages of brochures to a recipient who might not agree to distribute them.

Event Marketing

Event marketing is a traditional tactic that facilitates one-on-one interaction between the GovBenefits.gov brand and potential site users. The GovBenefits.gov team executes event marketing by attending conferences, trade shows, speaking engagements, and conducting one-on-one meetings with potential and existing partners. Conferences and trade shows have been effective in reaching potential users; however, conferences tend to be more expensive on a per-contact basis. As a result, the marketing team generally attends only one to two conferences per year.

Each year in April, the DOL hosts an anniversary event at the DOL headquarters to celebrate another year of the GovBenefits.gov program. The anniversary events feature high-level officials from the DOL as well as officials from partner agencies. Each year, the event culminates in the unveiling of a new feature of the Web site or important program announcement, such as the debut of 400 new federally-funded, state administered programs. By unveiling a new feature or site upgrade several things happen. First, the event forces the entire team to innovate and brainstorm new options for the site. Second, the event creates a hard deadline for the upgrade since the anniversary is always celebrated on or very near April 29, the original launch date. Third, the event raises awareness among stakeholders, the E-Gov community and within the DOL, highlighting accomplishments from the past year.

Program Oversight and Measuring Results

The PMA outlines three government reform themes: making government more results-oriented, efficient, and citizen-centered (Office of Management and Budget, 2002). Therefore, delivering results to the public is the top priority. Before the project was even launched, the DOL and OMB developed what is now known as the OMB 300. The OMB 300 refers to the section of the OMB's guidelines for major capital programs including information technology investments like GovBenefits.gov. The OMB 300 requires agencies to undertake a thorough review of major IT investments on an annual basis and establish measurable goals, milestones, and outcomes for each investment.

Program Oversight

Each quarter the program reports to the OMB its progress toward meeting its milestones in three areas—deployment, resources, and schedule. Within each category are specific milestones, such as deploying a new version of the site by a particular date or increasing site traffic by a specific percentage. According to Jack Koller, a former OMB E-Gov manager, meeting or exceeding the milestone for the period receives a green rating, small lapses or minor delays receive a yellow rating, and major delays or cost overruns receive a red rating, indicating a serious risk to the program (personal communication, December 1, 2005). Projects that consistently receive red ratings face increased scrutiny. Koller further indicated that funding partners are also rated on their own management scorecards by their timeliness in fulfilling their financial and content obligations to GovBenefits.gov (personal communication, December 1, 2005). In addition to aligning with the PMA, the program consistently received all green ratings on its performance scorecard.

In addition to the OMB's scorecard, the OMB provides additional oversight to all of the 24 E-Gov initiatives by assigning each project to one of four OMB Portfolio Managers. This structure provides additional oversight as well as coordination between E-Gov initiatives. The portfolio manager role provides a strategic, multi-agency view and supports agencies in their efforts to share information and resources.

Partner Oversight

As previously discussed, when the DOL first launched the site there were just 10 federal agencies. As of summer 2005, the program represented 16 federal funding agencies. This is evidence that the DOL properly managed the program. Although the federal government is large, the federal IT community is relatively small, and agency CIOs talk among themselves. If GovBenefits.gov had developed a poor reputation and failed to deliver on its promises, new partners would have stayed away from the project. Instead, over time the program welcomed six more funding agencies and hundreds of additional benefit programs. Finally, in a discussion with Dennis Egan from the U.S. Department of Agriculture (USDA) and member of the GovBenefits.gov CCB, if GovBenefits.gov had performed poorly, existing partners would have refused to sign their MOUs with the DOL (personal communication, December 22, 2005). According to Edward Hugler, to date, the DOL has been successful in securing continued funding commitments from the partner agencies (personal communication January 19, 2006).

Site Traffic

While meeting key OMB milestones is critical to continued OMB support, increasing site traffic is also very important to the DOL leadership and the partners. From 2002-2005, GovBenefits.gov cumulative site traffic reached more than 19 million people, and the site referred more than 4.3 million users to partner agency programs (GovBenefits.gov Total Visits, n.d.).

Public Outreach Results

Measuring the effectiveness of a given marketing tactic against another tactic is difficult; however, the marketing team regularly evaluates the outcome of a given tactic to ensure the program is pursuing activities with the most overall impact. According to Turner, "From a pure cost perspective, the PSAs presented the best value to the program, generating over 13 million impressions for approximately $60,000 to produce both the TV and radio PSAs" (personal communication, November 30, 2005). The PSA cost less then $0.005 per impression, whereas conferences cost the most, at approximately $1.25 per impression, but may yield meaningful relationships and personal contacts to help spread the word about the site. Historically, the event with the most impact occurred in 2004 when the "Dear Abby" column mentioned GovBenefits.gov as a valuable resource (Van Buren, 2004). Web site traffic more than doubled for several days, yet this outreach method costed the program nothing to produce. Several other events triggered similar spikes in site traffic including most notably President Bush mentioning the site during a press conference regarding Hurricane Katrina relief efforts in early September 2005.

Awards

The program actively sought E-Gov and Web site awards to affirm the program's value to the partners as well as maintain support for the program within the DOL. Because of the continuous efforts to innovate and deliver citizen value, the program secured more than a half-dozen government excellence and E-Gov awards. Receiving awards provides additional validation to funding partners that GovBenefits.gov is both a well-managed program and one that provides value to its users.

Challenges and Lessons Learned

Throughout the evolution of the GovBenefits.gov program there have been challenges and risks that threatened the program. The GovBenefits.gov team successfully managed and mitigated those challenges and, through extensive interviews with past program managers, agency partners, and key contractor staff, arrived at five lessons learned.

Lesson Learned #1: Establish a Clear Value Proposition

Before launching an E-Gov initiative, articulate and communicate a clear and convincing value proposition to the stakeholders involved. Cross-agency collaboration is possible, but the program has to answer the "What's in it for me?" question first. An early part of the GovBenefits.gov success was the ability to demonstrate to its funding partners that by participating they would receive something of value in return. According to Egan, benefit program managers from the USDA saw GovBenefits.gov as another avenue for reaching potential beneficiaries, and potential applicants coming from GovBenefits.gov are more likely to be eligible for USDA programs, making it a win-win for the department. To achieve this buy-in however, the GovBenefits.gov team actively communicated with partners through in-person "road shows", regular teleconferences, and e-mail updates to communicate the GovBenefits.gov value proposition and project status. This buy-in however was not universal, as previously mentioned by Gusty; in fact some early partners were reluctant to support the program. Today, to maintain buy-in from the partners, the program actively involves partners beyond the formal monthly meetings through the use of special working groups, such as the fee-for-service working group and the questionnaire working group. The working groups and other activities allow the partners to contribute to the program.

Lesson Learned #2: Develop Shared Risk and Rewards

For an inter-agency E-Gov initiative like GovBenefits.gov to be successful it is critical to create shared risk. GovBenefits.gov established shared risk by working with the partners to create a governance model that allowed partners to have a decision-making role but accept some of the risk associated with the program. Partners balance their risk by contributing to the development of the annual OMB business case outlining specifically what the program will accomplish and when. This gives the partners some authority over the direction of the program. In addition, by funding the program, partners place a portion of their budget at risk; however, the program mitigates the risk with monthly financial reports and regular communication about the project. The program also shares in the reward of delivering a citizen-centered, easy-to-use portal for citizens to access benefit programs. Partners benefit from receiving citizen referrals of users who are more eligible for their programs. GovBenefits.gov became a new outlet for partner agencies to communicate with the public about their programs. Today, the partners continue to support the program strategically and financially.

Lesson Learned #3: Demonstrate Tangible Results Quickly

GovBenefits.gov was up and running in 96 days. This demonstrated to the partners that GovBenefits.gov was well managed and serious about meeting its mission. Additionally, GovBenefits.gov had the distinction of being the first of the 24 E-Gov initiatives to go live, which helped to garner additional attention and support for the program. This achievement was accomplished with a well-defined software development life cycle methodology, weekly team meetings between all of the teams, implementation of a thorough project schedule using Microsoft Project, clearly defined requirements, and support from senior DOL leadership that encouraged the site to develop quickly. Today, the program maintains a rigorous adherence to the project schedule to meet deadlines along with regular inter- and intra-team meetings to monitor progress and risks to the program. Communication is the key to mitigating risks early and finding solutions. Moreover, the DOL's senior leadership continues to provide strong support for the program.

Lesson Learned #4: Use Creativity to Get the Word Out

Even with a modest public outreach budget, the program uses creative partnerships with community groups, such as Goodwill Industries, state Career One Stop Centers, and community- and faith-based organizations to spread the word. The program maximizes free press by supplying sample news stories and articles to media outlets on a regular basis and following-up with reporters and editors to pitch the GovBenefits.gov story. Today, the marketing team continues to pursue high-impact, low-cost tactics that maximize exposure of the GovBenefits.gov message and brand, and drive more than 350,000 people per month to the site (GovBenefits.gov Total Visits, n.d.).

Lesson Learned #5: Don't Stop Innovating

A challenge that remains is the need to innovate and remain relevant to users visiting the site, which may contrast with the strategic direction to transition the Web site to maintenance mode. In the near term, future upgrades to the site will likely consist of logical progressions that do not require substantial changes and enhancements. For example, the deployment of a portal architecture in January 2006 enabled the program office to offer Customized Connections to other government entities. The future beyond Customized Connections is not yet chartered; could the next step be a one-stop location for users to actually apply online for benefit programs? It is possible; however, major data sharing and privacy hurdles must be resolved before it can be a reality. However, the infrastructure to provide expanded site capabilities is now in place. The new portal architecture enables future upgrades to occur without major investments. Moreover, the decision-making infrastructure is also in place. If the Governance Board decides to expand the site's capabilities it also has the ability to fund the incremental development costs through the fee-for-service funding model.

Conclusion

In the fall of 2001, a group of senior government executives brainstormed how to effectively harness the power of the Internet and the potential of e-government to improve the lives of citizens and make government more effective. Out of that process, GovBenefits.gov was born. In just 96 days, the Web site that connected citizens with 55 federal benefit programs accounting for more than $1 trillion in benefits was created. Over the course of four years, the program has grown and now represents more than 1,000 federal and federally-funded, state administered programs. From the GovBenefits.gov experience, a new model for inter-agency cooperation and collaboration was born. While some thought it was impossible for ten federal agencies to agree on anything, let alone agree to fund a single Web portal for benefit information, the funding partners collaboratively formed a governance structure and funding model to support the mission of the program. Through this, a scalable, citizen-centric Web site capable of growing with the needs of the programs was developed and deployed to the public. So long as the current 16 federal funding partners maintain a shared vision for the program, and the program continues to deliver results that are meaningful and citizen-centric, success will follow.

Acknowledgments

I would like to recognize the many people who contributed to this case study. Thank you to Patrick Pizzella, Ed Hugler, Elana Mezile, Martina Harris, Keisha Reynolds, and Kimberly Wingard for their reviews and input into the case study. A special thank you goes to David

Haradon for your research and assistance drafting this work. Finally, I would like to thank all of the contributors to this case study including: Denis Gusty, Dennis Egan, Harry Feely, Jack Koller, Christine Fantaskey, Justin Gaspard, and Tamara Burrell, for providing their valuable insight.

References

Bush, George W. (n.d.). *The importance of e-government* [Memo]. Retrieved January 17, 2006, from http://www.whitehouse.gov/omb/egov/g-2-memo.html

Edelman Communications. (2005). *E-gov marketing plan gap analysis.* Unpublished report, Office of Management Budget.

GovBenefits.gov Total Visits (n.d.). [Data file]. Washington, D.C.: U.S. Department of Labor.

Hernon, P., Dugan, R. E., & Shuler, J. A. (2003). *U.S. Government on the Web: Getting the information you need* (3rd ed.). Connecticut: Libraries Unlimited Inc.

Link Popularity Check. (2006). Retrieved January 25, 2006, from http://www.marketleap.com

Listing of All Programs. (n.d.). *Catalog of federal domestic assistance.* Retrieved January 17, 2006, from http://12.46.245.173/pls/portal30/CATALOG.AGY_PROGRAM_LIST_RPT.show

Office of Management and Budget. (2002). *President's management agenda.* Retrieved December 10, 2005, from http://www.whitehouse.gov/omb/budget/fy2002/mgmt.pdf

Office of Management and Budget. (2003). *E-government strategy.* Unpublished report, Office of Management and Budget.

U.S. Census Bureau. (2005). *Consolidated federal funds report, Fiscal Year 2003.* [Data file]. Retrieved from U.S. Census Bureau Web site, http://harvester.census.gov/ cffr/index.html

U.S. Department of Labor. (n.d.). *Start-up of the department and world war I, 1913-1921.* Retrieved January 25, 2006, from http://dol.gov/asp/programs/history /dolchp01.htm.

U.S. Department of Labor. (2004a). *GovBenefits.gov strategic plan – Phase II.* Unpublished report, U.S. Department of Labor.

U.S. Department of Labor. (2004b) *Program governance concept of operations.* Unpublished report, U.S. Department of Labor.

U.S. Department of Labor. (2005). *GovBenefits.gov Governance Board Meeting Minutes,* June 2, 2005. Unpublished report, U.S. Department of Labor.

Van Buren, Abigail. (2004). Letter to *Dear Abby.* Retrieved January 23, 2006, from http://www.uexpress.com/dearabby/?uc_full_date=20040930

WestGlen Communications. (n.d.). *GovBenefits.gov 2005 public service campaign results*. Unpublished report, U.S. Department of Labor.

Author's Biography

Curtis Turner *joined the U.S. Department of Labor in July of 2005 to manage the Presidential Management Agenda's, E-Government initiative, GovBenefits.gov. Curtis spent nearly 29 years with the United States Postal Service, where he played key roles in shaping and developing that agency's Internet Channel and flagship Web site: USPS.com. Mr. Turner brings a wealth of talent and experience to the GovBenefits.gov program for marrying information technology and marketing to provide services to citizens and reduce government cost. Leading the program team for the GovBenefits.gov, he strives to establish one place online where citizens and benefit program professionals can go and easily find federally-sponsored programs that meet any individual's needs. Mr. Turner has a Master's degree in business administration and lives in Northern Virginia.*

Chapter XII

Tampa, Florida Internet-Based Customer Service Center

Steven M. Cantler, City of Tampa, Florida, USA

Executive Summary

The City of Tampa, Florida developed and implemented an innovative Web-enabled enter-prise-wide solution, addressing basic requests for services with centralized citizen access to four major areas: submission of requests, opinions, recommendations, and inquiries; online payments; public records research; and automatic re-direction to non-city agency services. The TampaGov Customer Service Center resulted from a need to effectively track and manage the wide variety of service requests and communication exchanges between citizens and the city staff who serve them. Three primary issues were addressed: (1) Citizens are confronted with daily life events and do not know which government agencies to contact; (2) Citizens want access to government services at their convenience (24/7); and (3) Citizens want to know what is happening to their request. To be successful, the project needed to provide a flexible, comprehensive method of communication and collaboration with citizens. This objective was met.

Background

About Tampa, Florida

Tampa is the largest city in Hillsborough County, the county seat, and the third most populous city in Florida. Tampa is located on the west coast of Florida, approximately 200 miles northwest of Miami, 180 miles southwest of Jacksonville, and 20 miles northeast of St. Petersburg. In 2003, the population of the city was estimated at 313,000 (United States Census Bureau, n.d.), approximately one-third of the total for Hillsborough County.

Tampa's economy is founded on a diverse base that includes tourism, agriculture, construction, finance, health care, government, technology, and the port. The Tampa Metropolitan Statistical Area (MSA), consisting of Hillsborough, Pinellas, Pasco and Hernando counties, is a growth market. In 2004, the Tampa MSA population was estimated at 2,563,000 (Greater Tampa Chamber of Commerce, n.d.a). This places the Tampa MSA in the top 25 nationally, second among Southeastern metropolitan areas, and the largest in Florida (Greater Tampa Chamber of Commerce, n.d.b).

City of Tampa Government

The City of Tampa has a mayor-council form of government. The mayor and seven council members are elected by the voters of Tampa to serve for terms of four years. The Mayor's Office renders services required of the executive branch of city government including administrative functions and public relations. The mayor provides direction to department heads, administers city ordinances and council resolutions, meets with the public, and provides information on matters of community concern. The City Council, the legislative branch of city government, is responsible for enacting ordinances and resolutions that the Mayor of Tampa administers as the city's chief executive. The council's goals are to provide responsible legislation, ensure the safe, efficient, and fair operation of city government, and to provide for the general health, welfare, and safety of the citizens of Tampa.

The city delivers a full range of municipal services as provided by state statute and city charter. These include public safety, water, wastewater, solid waste, parking, public improvements, cultural, recreational and general administrative services. For fiscal year 2006 (FY06), which began October 1, 2005, 4,958 (City of Tampa, n.d.b) full-time positions were budgeted to provide the necessary services to citizens. The FY06 budget totaled $674 million. The revenue sources included: 58% from taxes, 37% from user fees (water, solid waste, wastewater, and parking), and 5% from bonds and other sources. The targeted expenditures included: 47% for public safety, 14% for parks and recreation, 12% for capital improvements, 11% for central government, 10% for public works, and 6% for debt service.

City of Tampa Information Technology Services

Information Technology Services (ITS) supports city operations through a network of business applications, the Web site and intranet, electronic mail, and desktop applications, for more than 3,500 employees at the city's 35 locations along with connections to other government and commercial networks. The ITS staff is composed of approximately 85 employees, of which about half are allocated for business applications support, and half are dedicated to network and systems operations support.

Setting the Stage

Enterprise Customer Service Vision

In the mid-1980's, the city administration undertook its first strategic information planning effort to identify and assess projects that could leverage information technologies. This endeavor identified "action orders" as the initiative with the greatest potential benefits.

In 1968, AT&T introduced 911 as a nation-wide emergency telephone number. Similar to 911, the action orders concept was to provide a convenient method of receiving, routing, and re-directing the multitude of non-emergency service requests from citizens, to ensure each request reached the appropriate service provider. This initiative was to aid in promoting government transparency, specifically an operating environment in which citizens would not need to know how government is organized to address daily life event issues. At the time, very few government agencies had this vision. And it was not until 1996 when Baltimore was the first to implement use of 311 for non-emergency police calls and city services. Unfortunately, the action orders project was not scheduled, as the funding to establish a city-wide communication network was not available.

City of Tampa Internet Presence

The City of Tampa Web site officially launched on September 18, 1996, with the delivery of static content primarily from six departments. Since its inception, the city has taken incremental steps in maturing its Web site service offerings. In early 1999, the site was re-structured and major efforts were undertaken to make the site more than a minimal Internet presence. All city departments were engaged to publish information about their services and business processes. To this end, ITS established a Web contributors group to assist and educate participants in Web technologies; and this effort resulted in involvement from more than 40 agencies. Initially, the focus was strictly on quality content, that is, current and accurate information.

In 2000, the site emphasis changed from static to dynamic, database-driven information resources. In 2001, the site was branded as TampaGov. It experienced another major re-design to provide a consistent appearance and to transition to more of a citizen-centric focus.

The site also began providing revenue collection services, such as utility bill payments and parking ticket payments.

In 2002, the emphasis shifted to interactive online services along with the continued expansion of a citizen-centric focus. These efforts received national attention, as Tampa's use of information technology was recognized for excellence and leadership in the local government arena. Specifically from the annual assessment activities provided by the Center for Digital Government, TampaGov was awarded 1st Place in the 2002 Best of the Web, and Tampa was awarded 1st Place in the 2002 Digital Cities Survey.

In the four-year span from 1999 through 2002, the Tampa Web site emerged as a major avenue for citizens to acquire information and conduct business. By the end of 2002, more than 10 million page requests had occurred during the year. More than one million dollars in revenue had been collected via the site. And approximately 10,000 e-mails were originating from TampaGov each year.

Case Description

Business Problem Trigger

As citizen use of the Tampa Web site increased, the nature of electronic communication to city officials began to change. Via the mail-to links on the site, citizens were sending service requests to operational departments, and in many instances, a timely response was expected. Due to this cultural change, a significant operational problem emerged. ITS Web support staff started receiving follow-up requests from citizens indicating their original Web-based communication had been unanswered. And with the mail-to link strategy, it was not possible to determine if the target employee(s) had received, read, and responded to the incoming messages. Additionally, research identified that numerous e-mails were being sent to the wrong agency, as citizens either guessed which department would handle their concern or would merely pick the most convenient mail-to link they could find. As a result, in 2002 ITS management initiated a project to address these issues.

TampaGov Customer Service Center Solution

From the detailed problem analysis, it was evident that a solution could not merely provide simple message status tracking, but also needed to incorporate message re-directing and routing. Specifically, with the TampaGov Web site serving as an enterprise communication network hub, the 1980's concept of action orders could be incorporated.

Thus the TampaGov Customer Service Center arose from a need to effectively track and manage the wide variety of service requests and communication exchanges between citizens and the City of Tampa staff who serve them. Three primary issues were targeted: (1) Citizens are confronted with daily life events and do not know which government agencies to contact to address their service needs; (2) Citizens want access to government services at their convenience 24/7, not merely when government agencies are staffed during typical business hours; and (3) Citizens want to know what is happening to their request—"What is the status?"—and want to provide feedback during the service assessment/delivery. More specifically: Did the agency receive the request? Once received, was the request read? Once read, were actions taken? Was the request completed?, and so forth.

With the project objectives identified, ITS personnel initially sought out a low to no cost commercially available solution. At the time, few alternatives existed that were specifically designed for local government. Tampa's research identified Motorola's Customer Service Request system as offering the best fit, however it was cost prohibitive. Management did not provide capital funding for this endeavor; therefore ITS Web technologies staff turned their efforts to the process of internally designing, coding, and testing this new messaging facility. A small project team was assembled, with the majority of the development activities handled by two employees—one lead analyst that designed the facility and one senior analyst that did all the programming. The system was developed using Microsoft technologies, that is, Microsoft SQL Server as the data repository and Microsoft Active Server Page (ASP) coding for Web page processing. The initial development effort was completed over a six-month period, and it was accelerated by using design principles that allowed for the flexible implementation of services via dynamically-created entry forms and custom city responses.

The design was approached primarily from the citizen's perspective. The citizen facing Web pages and related navigation paths were constructed to provide easy access to a service of interest. In part, this was accomplished by categorizing areas of interest such as report a problem, request a service, ask a question, provide an opinion, and make a payment. Services were also grouped by keywords to aid in locating the appropriate service quickly. These techniques allowed services to be organized logically vs. exclusively by organizational responsibilities. For example, a citizen that wants to request removal of a dead animal from a road no longer needs to be aware of or determine who is responsible. No longer necessary is the issue of whether to contact Animal Control, which is a county agency, or Solid Waste or Transportation, which are city agencies. Instead, merely searching for and locating the dead animal removal service, will guarantee the request is routed to the appropriate authority.

Although some technical challenges were encountered during the development process, including e-mail integration and the requirement for complex administrative views, the major barrier that needed to be breached was in educating the staff on the benefits to be derived. Specifically, some supervisors and business analysts were concerned the deployment of a city-wide online message tracking and routing system would result in significantly more work and less efficiency. Workshops were provided to demonstrate the new system capabilities; and during these sessions, the benefits from providing tangible audit trails of the citizen and staff communication became apparent to even the most skeptical. The written documentation resulting from use of the system was superior to relying on the recall of staff from telephone or face-to-face conversations. For common requests requiring a standard action, consistent responses were possible with less effort. And managers could independently monitor activity based on facts as opposed to varying personal perspectives.

In February 2003, the core design and related programming were completed and the pilot implementation launched. A small select group of departments participated in the pilot phase, as this part of the installation was used to confirm the system operated as intended and to identify the impact to existing business procedures. The pilot duration was originally scheduled for three to four months.

Mayor Pam Iorio took office on April 1, 2003, and the Customer Service Center initiative became a cornerstone component of the new administration. The Customer Service Center directly supported one of the mayor's (five) strategic focus areas specifically, "Efficient City Government Focused on Customer Service" (City of Tampa, n.d.a). As a result, the mayor fully supported a comprehensive city-wide deployment. The pilot duration was extended to ensure additional management functions identified by the new administration were included, and to ensure technical and procedural training was provided to all front-line customer service responders. The enterprise-wide implementation occurred in November 2003.

TampaGov Customer Service Center Features

The TampaGov Customer Service Center provides centralized citizen access to four major areas: submission of service requests, opinions, recommendations, and inquiries; self-service payments; self-service public records research; and automatic re-direction to non-city agency services. The system delivers centralized access to common civic activities such as reporting a pothole needing repair or missed garbage pick-up, expressing a position on a zoning request or other community issue, paying a utility bill or parking ticket, or researching crime activity. The Customer Service Center presents the citizen with choices based on life event issues vs. having to know which department or agency is responsible for handling their needs. The system accomplishes this by providing flexible methods of finding a desired service, including keyword searches, popular categories, and organizational structure. The purpose of enabling a multitude of pathways is to deliver access as quickly as practical using the citizen's perspective. For example, a citizen interested in tax-related services can search for "taxes", and the resulting selection list would include business tax services from the City of Tampa, property tax services from Hillsborough County, intangible tax services from the State of Florida, and income tax services from the Internal Revenue Service.

Each type of request reflects the specific requirements and business language used by the service department responsible. When a request is submitted, the system generates a tracking number and an access key associated with the request; using these identifiers, the citizen can independently follow-up as needed to aid in determining what actions have resulted. The system routes the request to the responsible department and employee(s). Once received, the recipients are presented with a list of processing actions customized to reflect the business responses appropriate for the request type. As actions are taken, system features assist the staff in providing consistent, professional responses including the use of predefined or standard replies. Actions are recorded, and the status of the request is updated as appropriate. The system notifies the citizen when actions occur, keeping them informed as their request is being processed.

Citizens can request services without organizational knowledge. They can track city actions. They can provide follow-up information as conditions change. And they can withdraw their request if the service requirement is no longer needed. In many instances, the system allows citizens to remain anonymous yet still provide two-way communication with city officials.

This is particularly appealing to those with public safety concerns in fear of reprisals from others.

Employee actions are extremely varied, so the system was designed with diverse alternatives including: delegating the request; transferring the request to another department; posting comments and notes; notifying the citizen or other employees of issues; changing the request status; and spawning new requests. In addition to custom-specific responses, the system provides employees with standard actions and responses based on the type of request. Employees may choose the method by which they are notified of service requests (e-mail, digital pager, neither). And employees can organize and search requests by different data fields. For example, one employee may choose to manage their list of requests by sorting the list based on the request date, while another employee may prefer to view requests based on request status, that is, issues needing action first and closed requests last. Using search filtering, an employee could determine if a code enforcement issue, such as an overgrown lot or a building code violation complaint, had been previously reported.

Independent of the Internet, requests continue to originate using traditional methods. Citizens mail, fax, phone, and walk in to city offices. Regardless of the notification method, employees can proxy on behalf of the citizen to enter requests into the system. In instances when a citizen calls a city department with a concern, the employee can enter the request into the system, and then provide the caller with the system generated tracking number and an access key. With the tracking number and access key, the citizen can independently check on the request via an Internet connection, or the citizen can call any city office and ask about the status.

Employees can also create requests either for internal business communication purposes or as they encounter a service requirement from the field. For example, the system has been used to capture employee responses to training session surveys, asset inventories, and other requests for information that are accessible only by city staff. Employees may be authorized to not only submit the request but also collaborate in the communication. In these instances, employees may choose to participate in the actions being taken. This provides access to the same business functions available as the (other) employees who are typically responsible for handling the request.

The system also addresses management concerns, such as: "Did the request get to the appropriate employee? Was a response made; Was it timely, consistent, and complete? Are there conditions that need attention?" It aids in monitoring, managing, and reporting on the business communications. Real-time summary and detail statistics reports are available for quick insights into what service levels are being delivered. Since actions are tracked, the Customer Service Center reports on status and average response duration. The standard reports can be filtered using desired selection criteria to provide immediate access to conditions of interest. Specifically, requests can be selected and sorted by various dates, service types, and status values. The data repository can also be searched by citizen contact information or by the message and response details. Printer-ready reports are dynamically produced when needed. The reports contain all information regarding the tracked communication. Management can also initiate requests or inquiries. Requests can incorporate other management tracking requirements of interest. A due date may be assigned to a specific message instance or automatically generated based on the service type. One or more meetings may also be associated with the request. Management can alter the authorizations of those involved with the collaboration; therefore, authorized responders can be added or removed as needed.

The system aids in the accountability objectives of the city administration. It gives citizens the capability to track the progress of their requests. It helps departments to provide consistent customer responses, to assess service response times, and to coordinate actions when multiple agencies are involved. And, management gains immediate access to service delivery information, improving communications along with activity monitoring and reporting.

In addition to communications management and tracking, the Customer Service Center also incorporates direct linking of citizens to online payment services, online records access, and to more than 100 services managed by other (county, state, and federal) government agencies. The links established to other jurisdictions were identified and incorporated based on previous citizen requests and the known availability of access to the services. When a non-city service link is selected, the citizen is informed that a transfer of request ownership will occur along with the fact that Tampa's Web site conditions, privacy policy, and security policy will no longer apply.

TampaGov Customer Service Center Implementation and Impact

The Customer Service Center successfully met its intended goals. The pilot program in February 2003 represented only three city agencies and less than 20 services. When full implementation occurred in November 2003, the system immediately expanded to include approximately 50 agencies and 200 services. The initial rollout of the Customer Service Center required a full-time administrator to educate staff, to review service requirements, and to integrate existing business processes. The administrative activities evolved to a part-time facilitation and support role. The ongoing administration of the Customer Service Center resulted in the formation of an advisory committee, with representatives from several departments to monitor activities and to recommend enhancements. Additionally, key employees were identified to forward requirements to the administrator, to enforce standards, and to share new information.

Prior to city-wide implementation and after coding and testing of the system was complete, a training program was established to aid in a successful deployment. Internal staff developed and administered the training. Different levels of training sessions and materials were created to accommodate several target groups including business analyst responders and service managers. For citizens, a streaming video introducing the Customer Service Center was created, and the video is available for viewing directly on the facility home page.

Since its introduction through 2005, more than 700 city employees have been trained, over 82,000 communication exchanges have been tracked, and access to more than 400 services has been provided. Via the TampaGov Customer Service Center, citizens submit opinions, problems, and service requests. Requestors can send follow-up information, change their contact information, or even remain anonymous. Citizens can readily determine what is happening to their request; determine whether it was received and read; and track other actions taken. In 2005, activity included 39,539 service requests, 93,325 follow-up actions, and 1,718,877 sessions of self-service research and payments.

Via the TampaGov Customer Service Center, citizens quickly locate and access services without regard to, or knowledge of, the government agency responsible for the service delivery. TampaGov provides direct access to the areas of its jurisdiction; and also provides efficient re-direction to county, state, and federal agencies for government services outside its authority; the result is a one-stop service environment. For example, a citizen seeking "tax"-related services could use the keyword search to quickly locate business tax services (from the City), property tax services (from Hillsborough County), state tax services (from the State of Florida), and federal income tax services (from the Internal Revenue Service). In 2005, more than 100,000 service requests were re-directed to other agencies.

By making access and delivery of services more efficient, the tangible benefit from this e-government initiative is evident. Since service activity is logged, management has the capability to quantify the benefit impact. In 2005, a projected savings of 67,366 hours of citizen's time and 104,068 hours of staff time occurred. These estimates were derived by calculating the estimated timesavings for citizens and employees from four types of requests: self-service payments, self-service research sessions, requests from city-managed services, and re-directed requests to other agencies. Field studies were used to approximate the average time saved for each of the four types of requests. Via the TampaGov Customer Service Center, citizens access government services 24/7. At their convenience, citizens submit and track service requests, research public records, and make a variety of payments for government-delivered services. In 2005, citizen use of the Customer Service Center occurred 56% of the time during normal business hours and 44% during non-business hours.

The Customer Service Center activity is evidence of citizens empowered as integral partners in the collaboration process and having direct access to government services. Citizens recognize the utility of the TampaGov Customer Service Center and how it aids in providing quality service delivery. Citizen appreciation for the system is reflected in feedback sent to the city.

"Well done! The e-mail communication with city departments is just great! I have used it and the response has been almost immediate and completely effective. I am most impressed with this service and wish to say 'Thank you'." (Scott T, Tampa, Florida)

"Enjoyed using the correspondence system, It shows people that you are working on their problems or concerns in a timely manner." (Wendell D, Little Rock, Arkansas)

"Thank you for your quick response. I appreciate your timeliness and attention to my request!" (Christy A, Tampa, Florida)

"I love this new email tool! Great job, City of Tampa! I am getting responses, replies and results! Excellent way to let your citizens communicate and keep track of what's going on! This is fantastic! And, as a neighborhood association president, this new tool will help me streamline my questions of the city on behalf of our residents." (Emmy R, Tampa, Florida)

"I'm ecstatic about the thoroughness of your website. It has good continuity and should be the epitome for other cities to follow." (Peter D, Bedford Heights, Ohio)

The access to and delivery of needed services via this initiative has provided substantive personal level impacts. Many examples can be used to illustrate satisfactory outcomes for common requests; but consider the following two incidents (via the actual transcripts), which convey new opportunities to satisfy human interests. These experiences have positive outcomes, facilitated primarily by the ease of access, with use of the Internet as the communication backbone.

Example 1: Australian High School Boys Jazz Band Traveling to Tampa

10/6/2003 11:46 PM Message Submitted

In January the Jazz Band from our school, the North Sydney Big Band (one of Australia's leading Youth Jazz ensembles), will be visiting the Tampa area. We are looking for performance opportunities in public places. Could there be any possibility of a performance in the Franklin Street Mall? We are in the area January 8 to 11. I would be happy to send you more information. I really hope you can help—it would be great! Thanks, and best regards,

Saul Richardson, North Sydney Boys' High School

10/7/2003 8:13 AM Message Read by Xxxxxx Xxxxxx, Special Events Coordinator, Parks and Recreation

10/7/2003 9:13 AM Note sent by Xxxxxx X. Xxxxxx

Dear Mr. Richardson:

I can see several opportunities to have them perform in our downtown area. On weekdays we schedule performances at one of our downtown Parks (Lykes Gaslight Square Park) between Noon – 1:30 p.m. Thursday 1/8 or Friday 1/9 is currently available. Also, we are conducting an Antique Car Show in downtown Tampa on Saturday, 1/10, and having them perform sometime during that event (11 a.m. – 3:00 p.m.) would also be a nice addition to our activities. Before I can commit to scheduling, however, I would need to know how much it would cost to have the Jazz Band perform here. Please let me know your requirements and schedule and we'll see if we can work out the arrangements. Sincerely,

Xxxxxx X. Xxxxxx

10/7/2003 9:06 PM Message Read via TampaGov

10/9/2003 12:06 AM Note from Saul Richardson

Dear Xx Xxxxxx,

Thank you for your interest and quick response! There would be no cost involved: we are happy to perform for free. Our tour is already fully funded from here, so we need nothing extra. Of the dates you mention, Saturday January 10 at the antique car fair

would suit us best—maybe two hours, broken into 2 sets, at any time during the event. We are happy to provide all equipment needed if that suits you, just need access to power. Otherwise a drum set would make our arrangements a little easier. Thanks again, and best regards,

Saul Richardson, North Sydney Boys' High School

10/9/2003 8:02 AM Message Read by Xxxxxx Xxxxxx, Special Events Coordinator, Parks and Recreation

10/9/2003 12:14 PM Note sent by Xxxxxx X. Xxxxxx

Dear Mr. Richardson:

This is great! What I think would work best would be to have the band scheduled for a performance between 12 Noon – 1:00 p.m. (that gives our crowds about an hour to arrive) then we could have them do the "finale" between 2:00 p.m. and 3:00 p.m. (which would also give the young men a chance to get lunch and check out the car show and other displays). This is a really exciting opportunity for us. Getting back to logistics, we have plenty of power at Lykes Park (we have numerous 20 amp/110 volt outlets). But what about seating for the band? How many chairs would we need for them? Also, how do you arrive? Do you have busses? If so, I can provide them with parking access if I know how many to provide for. Do you have any type of requirements you can send me? I want to make sure they have the best possible experience when they're here. As for the drum set, let me know the specifications on that so I can start looking for it. (I'm not sure I can find one, but as least I'll have time to look between now and January.) If you have a web site, please send me the address. Sincerely,

Xxxxxx X. Xxxxxx

10/10/2003 1:05 AM Message Read via TampaGov

10/10/2003 1:28 AM Note from Saul Richardson

Dear Xx Xxxxxx,

Thanks—those times are perfect. We will arrive in one bus. 12 chairs is all we would need. There are 25 musicians in the band, most of them stand up to play. We could bring a drum set with us from Australia—we may need it somewhere else—but if you can find one it would include bass drum, 2 tom toms, 1 floor tom, high hat stand, snare drum on stand, drum stool and at least 2 cymbal stands. Our website is www.nsbjazz.com. If you like I can either email or post some promotional and background material about the group. Best regards,

Saul Richardson

10/10/2003 8:54 AM Message Read by Xxxxxx Xxxxxx, Special Events Coordinator, Parks and Recreation

12/19/2003 7:10 PM Note from Saul Richardson

Dear Xx Xxxxxx,

Our group will soon be leaving for the USA, so I would like to confirm some of the details of our performance scheduled for January 10. Firstly, for our part, we are bringing our own drum set with us so that is taken care of. Secondly, can you give directions for me to pass on to our bus driver as to the exact performance location and where the bus can unload and park. Thirdly, is rain an issue? Is the performance space under cover? Thank you for you time and help with this. we are really looking forward to performing in Tampa. Closer to the performance date I will email you a contact mobile phone number for us, as soon as we have confirmed one. Best regards,

Saul Richardson

12/29/2003 10:22 AM Message Read by Xxxxxx Xxxxxx, Special Events Coordinator, Parks and Recreation

12/29/2003 2:58 PM Attachment Added by Xxxxxx Xxxxxx, Special Events Coordinator, Parks and Recreation

Car Show Festival Map 03 CAR SHOW 1103 (1).pdf 100958 (bytes)

12/29/2003 3:19 PM Note filed by Xxxxxx Xxxxxx, Special Events Coordinator, Parks and Recreation

Dear Mr. Richardson:

Sorry for the delay, I was out of the office last week. I have attached a map of our car show from November (we hold them in the same location each month). The street address of Lykes Gaslight Square Park would be 400 N. Franklin St. (zip code is 33602—should you or the driver want to do a Yahoo Map or MapQuest search for it over the internet.) It lies at the intersection of Franklin St. and Kennedy Blvd. Kennedy Blvd. is a state road (also known as State Rd. 60) but is one-way west bound as it passes through Tampa. I will arrange to have some additional parking meters bagged along Kennedy Blvd. (immediately adjacent to Lykes Gaslight Square Park) for the bus to use for its parking. There is no shelter in the park, so, inclement weather would be a problem for us. I don't have any back up indoor venues available. Fortunately, our current 7-day local weather forecast looks good (mid-70's during the day, around 60 degrees at night—with only partly cloudy skies). We've had a few cold fronts move through in Dec., but most have been short-lived. I'm hoping the temperate weather continues. I can't tell you how happy we are to have your band play for our January 10th Classic Car Cruise. I look forward to hearing from you in person. Sincerely,

Xxxxxx X. Xxxxxx

12/30/2003 3:44 AM Message Read via TampaGov

1/15/2004 1:32 PM Closed by Xxxxxx Xxxxxx, Special Events Coordinator, Parks and Recreation

No further action anticipated. Event occurred 1/10/04. The Jazz Band was FABU-LOUS!

1/17/2004 4:12 PM Message Read via TampaGov

Example 2: Swedish Sons Seeking Lost Father

8/1/2004 7:26 PM Message Submitted

Hi! My name is David Reynolds and I am looking for my American father Frank Reynolds. For about 3 years ago I lost contact with my father who lived in Tampa. He was in a car accident and had been taken care of at a hospital. I wonder if someone can help finding him again. He was born in Macon, GA. Hightower is our family name but he was adopted by the Reynolds as child and lived in Edgefield, SC. He was born on 1948-12-31. I really hope anyone can help me. I have not seen my father in 24 years now. I am planning to visit Tampa soon to track him down, but It will be difficult. Best regards,

David Reynolds, Sweden, Stockholm city.

8/2/2004 2:26 PM Message Read by Xxxx Xxxxxxxxx, Police Sergeant, Police

8/2/2004 2:28 PM Note sent by Xxxx Xxxxxxxxx, Police Sergeant, Police

There are numerous persons with that name in Tampa. Please supply a date of birth or something else to narrow the search.

Sgt. Xxxxxxxxx

8/2/2004 4:34 PM Message Read via TampaGov

8/3/2004 2:21 PM Note by David Reynolds

Hi again. This is all I know about my missing father Frank. Full name: Frank (Richard) Reynolds ... He is 55 years old today. His sister lives in South Carolina. Her address is: Mrs Ethel Janice Lane Matthews. 422, Bausket Street, Edgefield, S.C. 29824. My father has many sisters, I only knew some few names as Pearl, Ronelle,,, My father was adopted by the Reynolds family that lived in Charleston, S.C. Please help me in anyway it is possible. Can I find him in other sort of ways? From,

David Reynolds

8/4/2004 7:28 AM Message Read by Xxxx Xxxxxxxxx, Police Sergeant, Police

8/4/2004 7:37 AM Closed by Xxxx Xxxxxxxxx, Police Sergeant, Police

> *Mr. Reynolds,*
>
> *I found your father's information based on an arrest in Tampa on 06-18-04. The information is public record and can be found by going to www.hcso.tampa.fl.us and clicking online inquiries, then clicking arrest inquiry. Enter Reynolds, Frank in the space for the name and leave the rest blank. Click inquire and persons with that name will come up. The top one is your father. Click the blue i next to his name for his most recent information. I could find no phone number for his address.*
>
> *Sgt. Xxxxxxxxx*

8/4/2004 10:20 AM Message Read via TampaGov

8/4/2004 10:30 AM Note by David Reynolds

> *Thank you very much Sgt. Xxxxxxxxx. This was not good news but better then nothing. I can see that my father still keep getting in problems with the law. Thank you very, very much for all information on my father. Keep on working for a better society, best wishes to you.*
>
> *David Reynolds*

8/4/2004 10:46 AM Note by David Reynolds

> *Hi again! Well, I shall send him a letter. But could you if you have any contact with him forward that his sons, Victor and David Reynolds are looking for him and that he can email me. We have money and can pay a flight here to Sweden and take care of him. If he lives on the street he will not survive. My address.*
>
> *David Reynolds*
> *Smedsbacksgatan 7*
> *11539 Stockholm*
> *Sweden.*

8/4/2004 12:57 PM Message Read by Xxxx Xxxxxxxxx, Police Sergeant, Police

8/4/2004 1:09 PM Note sent by Xxxx Xxxxxxxxx, Police Sergeant, Police

> *Mr. Reynolds,*
>
> *If I have contact with him I will pass that on.*

8/4/2004 2:45 PM Message Read via TampaGov

8/4/2004 4:47 PM Note by David Reynolds

> *Hi again! I hope no one there will get tired of me writing. Me and my brother will leave Sweden on august 12 and arrive at Tampa city the 13 august. I hope I can talk*

with Sgt Xxxxxxxxx or any other officer at duty concerning finding Frank Richard Reynolds, our father. We have not seen him in 23-24 years. I was just 3 years old when he left us and went back to U.S.A. He was abused as child by his adoptive father and now have problems with drinking. We will help him the best way we can. Bye,

David Reynolds

8/5/2004 7:29 AM Message Read by Xxxx Xxxxxxxxx, Police Sergeant, Police

8/5/2004 7:34 AM Note sent by Xxxx Xxxxxxxxx, Police Sergeant, Police

I am assigned to the office of the Chief of Police in the main police station, located at 411 N. Franklin Street. My contact number is (813) xxx-xxxx and I am on duty Monday through Friday, 8 a.m. to 3 p.m.

Sgt. Xxxxxxxxx

8/5/2004 2:21 PM Message Read via TampaGov

8/19/2004 2:48 PM Note by David Reynolds

Hello Sgt Xxxxxxxxx!

We have now found frank and I am grateful for all your help. Much thanks,

Reynolds brothers

8/19/2004 2:51 PM Message Read by Xxxx Xxxxxxxxx, Police Sergeant, Police

8/19/2004 2:53 PM Note sent by Xxxx Xxxxxxxxx, Police Sergeant, Police

I am happy to have been of some help.

Sgt. Xxxxxxxxx

8/24/2004 12:52 PM Message Read via TampaGov

These examples illustrate new possibilities enabled with the introduction of contemporary communication measures for citizens seeking assistance to their daily life challenges.

Current Challenges Facing the Organization

Integration with Back-End System Operations

Prior to the Customer Service Center implementation, several departments utilized back-end systems to manage their service requests. For example, Code Enforcement uses a management system to track their cases, inspector actions, fines, and so forth. The Customer Service Center design did not attempt to integrate with these systems, and the systems were not abandoned. Instead some departments duplicate information submitted via the Customer Service Center, by copying it into their back-end systems. Further, as actions including incident closures occur within the back-end systems, department staff is challenged to synchronize the results in the Customer Service Center. As each back-end system has its own unique characteristics, constructing common generic interfaces may be difficult. If and when this requirement is prioritized and resources are allocated to address it, eXtensible Markup Language (XML) use is expected to help facilitate a solution.

Centralized Call Center

Tampa is assessing the establishment of a consolidated call center for non-emergency-related citizen requests. The Customer Service Center could provide the necessary centralized data repository required for this venture. An expansion of features to include a knowledge base containing common problems and solutions would be desirable. Ideally, Tampa would incorporate 311 as part of this strategy, however the county has jurisdiction over a 311 deployment.

References

City of Tampa. (n.d.a). *Efficient city government.* Retrieved December 20, 2005, from http://www.tampagov.net/dept_Mayor/strategic_areas/efficient_city_government.asp

City of Tampa. (n.d.b). *FY2006 annual budget, The budget process.* Retrieved December 20, 2005, from http://www.tampagov.net/dept_Budget/FY2006_budget/files/budget/Intro%20thru%20Construction%20Programs%20(1-13).pdf

Greater Tampa Chamber of Commerce. (n.d.a). *Community profile of Tampa Bay – Economic development information.* Retrieved December 20, 2005, from http://www.tampachamber.com/ed_commprofile.asp

Greater Tampa Chamber of Commerce. (n.d.b). *Demographics of Tampa Bay – Economic development information.* Retrieved December 20, 2005, from http://www.tampachamber.com/ed_demographics.asp

United States Census Bureau. (n.d.). *Tampa (city) quick facts from the U.S. Census Bureau.* Retrieved December 20, 2005, from http://quickfacts.census.gov/qfd/states/12/1271000.html

Author's Biography

Steven M. Cantler *is Information Technology Services Project Manager, City of Tampa. He has over 20 years of government service; responsibilities included lead analyst and project manager roles for database and security administration, host systems technical support, PC/LAN/WAN operations support, and new technology research and development. Accomplishments include: established database administrator role for Tampa including the creation of database business standards and procedures; designed and constructed the primary support systems for Tampa's online applications including security administration, data archiving, report creation, and error handling; created network management controls in the areas of software licensing, server performance, and virus protection; designed and implemented Tampa's intranet; and architected Tampa's Web presence. He has been recognized by Government Technology Magazine in 2004 and by the Center for Digital Government in 2003 as one of the most innovative, hard-working, trend-setting leaders in the nation.*

Chapter XIII

Conquering the Invasion of Technology:
E-Government and Property Tax Collections in the Stonewall County Tax Commissioner's Office

Saundra J. Reinke, Augusta State University, USA

Dwight D. Johnson, Augusta State University, Georgia, USA

Executive Summary

This case study evaluates the offering of online property tax collections to constituents within Stonewall County, Georgia. It addresses the costs associated with offering such a service, whether or not the county's citizens would use such a service, and the approval and/or absorption of convenience fees by the county. Most of the events in the case study are based on real-life events but the names have been changed to preserve anonymity.

Background

Stonewall County is a rapidly growing community which boasts a population of over 100,000 and is seen as a desirable county in which to live and work. The county's rapid growth, cost-conscious management, and high-quality public services have established it as a model community for efficiency in government. While the county is experiencing major growth, a top priority for the county is to provide the public with the best possible services at the lowest possible cost.

Stonewall County is operated under the council-manager form of government. Governed by the Stonewall County Board of Commissioners, the commission consists of four districtly elected commissioners and one county wide elected commissioner who serves as the chair. The County Administrator, Samuel Sturgis, has served for over 15 years in this position. Mr. Sturgis, a veteran of county management, works well with the commissioners to guide the county towards their shared vision of providing quality, low-cost services to the public. Within the government, there are also several elected constitutional officials. These constitutional officers receive their funding from tax revenue approved by the county commission. Over the past years, there has been a contentious relationship between these constitutional officers and the Board of Commissioners regarding various financial and political issues. The Board of Commissioners does not always see fit to approve the budget that would further facilitate customer service in the Tax Commissioner's Office.

The major source of revenue for the county is property tax collections. In Stonewall County, property tax bills are generally mailed to taxpayers in September and are due by mid-November of each year. In 2004, approximately 46,000 property tax bills were mailed out. These bills consisted of personal property which includes boats and boat motors, business furniture, fixtures, equipment, inventory and supplies, as well as tracts of land and the structures and improvements located on them. In Stonewall County, taxes can be paid in person, by check or cash, placed in the drop box located at the government campus or mailed.

Ad Valorem Tax, on the value, in relation to property tax, is the next largest source of revenue for Stonewall County. The basis for Ad Valorem Taxation is the fair market value of property, which is established as of January 1 of each year. The tax is levied on the assessed value of the property which, by law, is established at 40% of fair market value. The amount of tax is determined by the tax rate (mill rate) levied by government jurisdictions (one mill is equal to $1.00 for each $1,000 of assessed value, or $.001).

Property taxes are collected by the County Tax Commissioner, Josephine E. Johnson, a constitutional officer elected for a four-year term. She is responsible for receiving tax returns filed by taxpayers and/or designating the Board of Tax Assessors to receive them. She also accepts and processes Homestead Exemption Applications and serves as an agent of the State Revenue Commissioner for registration and titling of motor vehicles. She performs all functions related to billing, collection, and disbursement of property and Ad Valorem Taxes collected in the county.

Overall, her main duty is to collect and disburse property taxes to the various entities that make up Stonewall County. Property tax collections are the focal point that most citizens see and feel on a "first-hand" basis. Consequently, the management of her operation attracts much public attention and scrutiny. While Tax Commissioner Johnson agrees with the Board of Commissioners that the best possible services should be offered to the public at the least cost, she has had a volatile relationship with the county administrator. These conflicts have oftentimes played out in the local paper, the *Stonewall Star*. Ms. Johnson believes that these conflicts, and the accompanying publicity, have not been good for either the county or her office. Consequently, she is eager to bolster both the public image of her office, and improve her relationship with the county administrator and the Board of Commissioners.

The Case

Online Tax Collection

In 2000, as a result of taxpayer congestion within the tax collection office and an overall push by the county to become more customer-oriented and interactive, Tax Commissioner Johnson implemented a credit card collection process for "real estate" or real property tax collections. The county administrator and the Board of Commissioners enthusiastically endorsed this new initiative. They saw this as progressive, and an opportunity to reduce the county's operating costs.

An Interactive Internet Interface was implemented that allowed citizens to pay their property taxes by credit card over the Internet. A convenience fee of 3% of the tax amount was charged by a contracted third-party vendor. As an example, the fair market value of a property is $150,000.00; this includes all improvements and structures located on the property; the assessment value of this property would be $60,000.00 or 40% of the fair market value. This is then multiplied by the millage rate making the total amount of the bill $1,507.80 (Assessed value $60,000 multiplied by the millage rate 0.02513). The amount of the convenience fee would be $48.23 (3% of $1507.80 plus the three-dollar transaction fee) making the grand total for property tax paid for this parcel to be $1,556.03.

Unfortunately, things have not worked out as expected. While the implementation of the online tax was a more progressive approach to tax collections, in 2003, only eight citizens took advantage of the Internet service. The amount collected for the first month of the tax season amounted to a mere $5,447.38. To make matters worse, the cost of operating the Tax Commissioner's Office has not decreased as expected, instead it has actually increased.

The New Official

John Hood is the newly appointed Deputy Tax Commissioner for Stonewall County. He has been in local government for about five years and is working on his Master's in public administration at the local university. Ms. Johnson hired Mr. Hood because he had previously worked in the private sector and has a good working knowledge of Internet collection alternatives. She is deeply concerned by the low response to the online payment option, and to the fact that the operating costs for her office have gone up as employees worked to implement the new online payment system. After reviewing the previous year's collection rate via online tax collection, Mr. Hood began his research.

Administrator Sturgis as well as the Board of Commissioners are strong proponents of online services and expect this method to work and further the county's efficiency. Johnson and Hood agree wholeheartedly, and sincerely want to see online tax collections not only succeed but to increase tax collections and become a model for other county services. Since online services offer an additional, convenient option for citizens who wish to complete their transactions, Internet payments should be used readily by citizens and patrons of the county. But this is not happening. Mr. Hood's initial research concluded that very few people were using online services, they were not saving the county any money, and a new strategy was needed.

Hood chooses to do three things to try to determine why citizens are not using this innovative service. First, he contacts other county tax commissioners' offices to see what online services they are offering and how well they are working. Second, he decides to survey taxpayers. Finally, he decides he should look at how tax collections are processed to see what, if any, new efficiencies Internet collection might provide.

In contacting other tax commissioners, he learns several important facts. First, although 21 of the 22 commissioners surveyed had a Web site, only 11 allowed citizens to pay their taxes online. Surprisingly, most counties were not even allowing citizens to use a credit card! Second, a county very similar to Stonewall recently began absorbing the convenience fee associated with online payment and noticed a spectacular increase in the use of the online option. In 2001, the first year this county had online tax payment, citizens paid the convenience fee and only nine citizens paid online. In 2002, when the convenience fee was waived, 499 citizens paid online, and tax collections soared.

Hood thinks this last point may be important, so he decides to include a question about the convenience fee in his survey of taxpayers. Since Tax Commissioner Johnson is in a hurry for the results, he decides to survey customers in the Motor Vehicle Tag Office about their feelings on property tax collection options. Over a two-week period, 4,599 customers completed his short survey. An astonishing 80% of respondents indicated they would like to pay online. However, 90% of those who said they would like to pay online indicated they would NOT be willing to pay a convenience fee in order to pay online.

Mr. Hood and Tax Commissioner Johnson, conclude that the convenience fee is a serious obstacle to citizen use of the online payment option. Since she is eager to make online collections successful, she directs Hood to research what exactly needs to happen in order for online services to succeed. He finds that offering online services includes several aspects.

The County Information Technology (IT) Department tells him that a Web design and maintenance company has to be hired to design any Web site and teach others how to view the information necessary for their department functions. Currently, the IT Department does not have the budget or necessary skills to perform such a task; therefore, this work has to be outsourced. Between discussions with the IT Department and online research, Johnson finds that before the inception of the site, the county must think carefully about the profit and loss margin of such a project.

Stonewall County may find online services would not be cost effective. While the profits would prove to be worth the risk long-term, the county must be willing to absorb start-up costs, including additional staff, during the first years of operation. The county could assume the convenience fee and consider the site as a liability until such time as a determined number of patrons use it. As the number of transactions completed online increases, the need for a bigger staff will decrease. A staff decrease will, of course, lessen the amount of revenue needed to facilitate the operation of the Tax Commissioner's Office. The cost of online services must be identified in relation to the benefits. If the benefit will never exceed the cost of doing business online, the plan will never be successful. This is a step that Stonewall County did not take before implementing online tax payment. With this in mind, Hood feels it is imperative that the county determine what it hopes to gain from online tax collection, and set some performance standards for the operation.

Hood's research also finds several drawbacks to online services that he believes should be acknowledged. Public demand for e-government is measured by the percentage of people with Internet access. Many, primarily low-income people do not have Internet access (McNeal, Tolbert, Mossberger, & Dotterweich, 2003). Information poverty is another hurdle to the success of e-government. This is a result of a dichotomy between those with easy access to an abundance of information and those who do not know how and where to find it. Finally, funding for public agencies is never adequate for the varied and constantly increasing demands for new online processes (Jaeger & Thompson, 2004). Although Stonewall County has a generally affluent and highly-educated citizenry, there are pockets of poverty. As a result, Hood concludes that there will always be a need for methods of payment other than just the Internet.

Finally, he reviews the procedures the Tax Commissioner's Office uses to manage tax payments. He discovers that there is no direct electronic interface between the third-party vendor handling credit card payments and taxpayer's records. In other words, the third-party vendor is notifying the county of the citizen's payment, and the payment is then handled in exactly the same manner as any other payment. A direct electronic interface would save staff time, and ultimately reduce payroll, but there is a possible drawback. Hood learns that another county that did have such a direct interface encountered a serious problem when the third-party vendor had a security breach. As a consequence of that problem, citizens' personal data, including credit card numbers, were lost to unscrupulous thieves who stole hundreds of thousands of dollars using citizens' credit cards. That county is still trying to recover from the scandal.

Johnson's Dilemma

Based on Hood's research, Tax Commissioner Johnson knows that for online property tax collection to work, the county must absorb the convenience fee, and be willing to invest in additional staff while the system is still in its infancy. She also feels the county should at least weigh the pros and cons of direct electronic interface for processing credit card payments. At the same time, she wants to create as little conflict with the commission as possible. Currently, the Board of Commissioners has served for several decades. Each of them has agendas that are important to them as well as their constituency. The county administrator and Board of Commissioners' goal is to have online tax collections increase while reducing operating costs. Johnson's biggest task will be convincing each commissioner that the absorption of convenience fees will benefit the county. The tax commissioner has built a friendship with the Chairman, Juleb Early. An elderly gentleman that has the respect of the entire Board of Commissioner's, Mr. Early has agreed to help Ms. Johnson in her efforts.

Additional Reading

Brannen, A. (2001). E-government in California: Providing services to citizens through the Internet. *Spectrum*, Spring, 10.

Jaeger, P. T., & Thompson, K. M. (2004). Social information behavior and the democratic process: Information poverty, normative behavior, and electronic government in the United States. *Library & Information Science Research*, 26, 94-95.

McNeal, R. S., Tolbert, C. J., Mossberger, K., & Dotterweich, L. J. (2003). Innovating in digital government in the American states. *Social Science Quarterly*, 84(1), 60.

Wholey, J. S. et. al. (Eds.). (1994). *Handbook of practical program evaluation*. San Francisco: Jossey-Bass Inc.

Authors' Biographies

Saundra Reinke is an associate professor and director of the MPA Program at Augusta State University. She has published in Review of Public Personnel Administration, Journal of Public Affairs Education, Journal of Military and Political Sociology, Public Integrity, and has work forthcoming in Public Productivity and Management Review. In addition, she has authored two case studies, several book reviews, one book chapter and has two book chapters forthcoming.

Dwight D. Johnson currently holds a Bachelor of Arts Degree in communications, public relations and advertising, and a Masters of Public Administration from Augusta State University. He has several years experience in public sector management with an emphasis on taxation of property. Mr. Johnson is a member of the Georgia Political Science Association, American Society for Public Administration, and the Governor's Office of Highway Safety. He is a member of Pi Alpha Alpha which is a National Public Administration Honor Society. Recently, he was awarded a Five-Year Certificate from the University of Georgia's Carl Vinson Institute of Technology for County Tax Officials and an Award for Excellence presented by Randolph P. Strong, Brigadier General, Commanding General, Fort Gordon, Georgia.

Chapter XIV

Alaska Federal Health Care Access Network:
Deploying Telemedicine Services in the 49th State

Bogdan Hoanca, University of Alaska Anchorage, USA

Executive Summary

The case describes the development of the Alaska Federal Health Care Access Network (AF-HCAN), a consortium providing telemedicine in Alaska. Given the state's vast geographical areas, the lack of infrastructure in the remote villages, and the extreme climate, AFHCAN faced particular challenges in ensuring access to quality health care across its target area. Using federal funds, a consortium of federal, military, and private organizations developed an intuitive, easy to use, custom-developed software and an integrated (cart-based) hardware platform. Low utilization levels following the initial deployment, prompted an organizational change from delivering a software/hardware product to delivering a turn-key system (including training). The system has been successfully deployed to 260 sites in the state. Users with limited computer literacy levels and even with limited English language skills are able to use the systems successfully. Overall, both patients and heath providers report high levels of satisfaction with the system.

Background

If one were to purposely design the ideal testing environment for telemedicine applications, it would probably look a lot like the State of Alaska. Vast areas, sparsely populated by an ethnically-diverse mixture of peoples, harsh weather conditions, and extreme life challenges combine to make this the case. Providing access to quality medical care in such an environment requires a partnership of government, military, for-profit enterprises, and non-profits. Through a seven-year effort, a consortium of government, for profit, and non-profit organizations deployed in Alaska the largest telemedicine network in the world. There are challenges remaining, but they seem much less daunting than the initial deployment.

By the time the first Russian explorers arrived there in the early 18th century, Alaska had been inhabited for tens of thousands of years by a mix of Eskimo and Indian people, living off the land through a combination of hunting, fishing, and gathering of local plants. By the end of the 18th century, Alaska was already an important source of fur for Russian traders. Throughout the second half of the 18th century and the first half of the 19th century, Russians established settlements and built forts and churches, forging inland mainly in the Western Alaska. Later on, in 1867, the United States (US) of America purchased Alaska from the Russians. Eventually, in January 1959, Alaska became the 49th state to join the U.S. (Alaska Blue Book, 1994). This history is still reflected in the wide cultural and ethnical diversity in the state.

Alaska has one seventh of the area of the United States of America, but it was home to only slightly more than 627,000 people at the last census (Alaska, 2000), only 0.2% of the U.S. population. About half of the population lives in the three main urban centers, within relatively easy access to modern health care facilities. The other half lives in remote areas, mainly in tiny villages, many of which have fewer than 100 inhabitants. A third of the state area is north of the Arctic Circle, and the mountains in the state include 17 of the 20 highest peaks in the U.S. Most of the villages are not on the road system, and can be reached only by airplane and seasonally by boat. Roads in Alaska are few, and only connect some of the major population centers. Often, these roads are closed in winter for extended periods due to snowfall, avalanches, or other extreme weather.

The power grid largely follows the road system. Most of the isolated villages off the road system have their own power generation facilities. Because of the small scale of the operations, as well as the extreme weather, power delivery is rather unreliable, and power outages are frequent and often long lasting. Backup power is expensive, because transportation costs are high to bring generators and fuel to the villages.

The plumbing infrastructure is also outdated. Most of these villages are built on the tundra, a soft soil with high water content. The top layer of the soil melts in summer and is frozen in winter, making it difficult to build heavy structures for year long usage. In fact, the soil can even melt in winter due to heat loss from the bottom of heated buildings. For this reason, most buildings have no foundation, but rather are built on stilts. Consequently, flush toilets and running water are rather uncommon in rural Alaska, although they are becoming more widespread.

The population itself is highly diverse, including in addition to the usual racial mix in the United States a large number of descendents of the ancient inhabitants of the area, collectively known as Alaskan Natives. This single designation is misleading, because Alaskan Natives include several widely different cultures speaking more than 20 languages (classified into seven language families). In addition to the language differences, dress, art, hunting and fishing techniques and tools, and social customs are strikingly different as well. The major ethnic sub-groups are Yupik and Cupik in the West; Inupiak in the North; Athabascan in the Central areas; Aleut and Alutiiq in the Southwest; and Eyak, Tlingit, Haida and Tsimshian in the Southeast.

Following the Alaska Native Lands Settlement Act (ANCSA) in 1971, Alaska Natives have received collectively 1/9th of Alaska's land and almost a billion dollars in cash in exchange for land claims to most of the state's territory. Much of the land in the state is still federally owned. The Act created 13 native corporations. Twelve of them are regional in nature, and received land and financial resources. These corporations represent shareholders living in the respective regions. A 13th corporation includes natives not living within any of the regional corporations' areas and is endowed only with financial resources, but no land. These corporations are significant economic players in the state and in the U.S., in general. Their mandate is to create jobs for their members, to provide financial dividends (some of several tens of thousands of dollars per year), as well as to provide public goods to their members. Several of these corporations are involved in providing health care, educational opportunities and elder care.

Health care facilities in Alaska are highly concentrated, mainly in the largest urban center, Anchorage, which includes the Alaska Native Medical Center (ANMC), the Providence Health System, and the Alaska Regional Hospital, as well as a large number of smaller private practice offices. The other large population centers and regional hubs all have medical centers serving the people in the vicinity. Most villages have a medical clinic, but these clinics are usually staffed with health aides or nurses. The next section describes in more detail the existing medical facilities in the village clinics.

Setting the Stage

The earliest use of telemedicine was probably in 1925 when an emergency supply of Anti-Diphtheria serum was delivered to Nome, Alaska via dog sled. The journey over 700 miles of frozen tundra is now the theme of "the Last Great Race", the Iditarod. Eighty years later, although airplanes are now available along with modern communication technologies, it is still challenging to provide access to quality health care in small remote villages.

There are village clinics in almost every community in Alaska, but in the smallest villages, the low number of residents cannot justify the expense of one or more medical doctors on staff. Even if money would be available, the remoteness and relative isolation of villages makes it difficult to retain medical personnel. The lack of city type of entertainment, the lack of basic creature comforts in some villages, and the difficulty in accessing professional information and peers makes doctors move on from village clinics to larger facilities after only a small number of years. To increase retention, efforts are underway to train local village residents as nurses or community health aides (discussed more in-depth next). These people are much more likely to stay in the village and provide continuity of medical care than are medical personnel raised and trained outside the village or the state.

When medical help is needed, village residents go to the village clinic and get help from the local health care providers. Before telemedicine, when the problem was too complex to be handled locally, residents had to travel to one of the regional medical centers or even to Anchorage. This is expensive (hundreds of dollars per travel), disruptive for family life and also often impractical depending on the type of medical problem. Serious medical emergencies pose even more problems and require air medical evacuation, a very expensive solution (up to tens of thousands of dollars). Moreover, because of the relatively small number of planes available for medical evacuation, there might not be enough planes to attend to all emergency cases at any given time. The problem is compounded when the nature of the emergency does not allow the patient to be moved, let alone jostled around on a plane flying through turbulence for several hours. Air travel is more dangerous in Alaska than in the rest of the U.S.: according to the National Transportation Safety Board, between 1990 and 1998 there were an average of one accident every other day, resulting in more than 350 victims. Finally, weather makes access uncertain for many of the winter months—most of the year in some of the Northern areas of the state.

A third option is available at times. A few times a year, doctors fly into villages to attend to routine medical care. Still, for most of the year, the patients must choose between limited care locally or the expense and hassle of travel to a larger medical facility.

Telemedicine in various forms emerged as the solution to providing care to distant communities. According to the latest report on telehealth in Alaska (AFHCAN, 2004), the earliest attempts to use telemedicine were made in 1967, using short-wave radio. This technology proved to be too unreliable and was replaced by satellite communications in 1971, upgraded to another type of satellite link in 1974, then replaced by long distance calls through the voice telephone network in the 1980's, slow scan television in 1985, followed by facsimile transmission. In the 1990's, the focus moved to using data networks, through a combination of research grants and government funds. The funding sources included the National Telecommunication and Information Administration, National Library of Medicine (NLM), Alaskan Indian Services, the Department of Defense, Veterans Affairs, and the U.S. Coast Guard. The military and Coast Guard funding was in support of their personnel on remote bases, some located close to villages.

In 1994, the Alaska Telemedicine Testbed Project (ATTP) brought together the University of Alaska Anchorage (which is part of the state-wide university system), AT&T Alascom (a local carrier), and Providence Health System (the largest health care provider in the state). The state, Alaska Native organizations, and some private companies also joined in the effort. By 1996, through a grant from NLM, ATTP developed and installed a telemedicine network in 26 villages. As part of the project, they developed both hardware and software to support otolaryngology (ear, nose and throat, or ENT) and dermatology. The ENT application was chosen because it "exhibited no evaluation bias for gender and age" (Pearce, 2001).

Two major findings of the pilot program were to show that first, patients as well as providers perceived telemedicine to be at least as good as existing treatment options, and secondly, the telemedicine option did not reduce the turnover in health care providers in village clinics (AFHCAN, 2004). The pilot program introduced the concept of a modular, cart-based hardware platform, with a computer and medical peripherals, as well as a digital camera for transmitting images of the patient. Another important concept was that of "store and forward" via the public switched telephone network, which allowed practitioners in the village to enter a case in the system and forward the case to a doctor for examination at a different time. One of the major problems with earlier systems was that doctors or radiologists were not always available to consult with the health aide while the patient was in the clinic. Additionally, store and forward can easily operate with lower bandwidth connections and even with dropped connections, often the case in Alaska due to weather conditions.

Case Description

In 1998, the Senior State Senator, Ted Stevens, initiated an effort to deploy telemedicine state-wide. Funds were made available to develop and deploy the technology to 235 sites in the state. The number increased to 248 sites by 2004 and to 260 sites in early 2006. The consortium that developed the telemedicine solution is the Alaska Federal Health Care Access Network (AFHCAN), which started as an initiative of the Alaska Federal Health Care Partnership (AFHCP). In turn, AFHCP is a result of collaboration efforts among the Department of Veteran's Affairs (VA), Department of Defense (DoD), Department of Homeland Security (U.S. Coast Guard—USCG), Indian Health Service (IHS), and the Alaska Native Tribal Health Consortium (ANTHC). AFHCP's mandate is to ensure access to quality health care to federal beneficiaries.

AFHCAN's mission is to "improve access to health care for federal beneficiaries in Alaska through sustainable telehealth systems" (www.afhcan.org). The federal beneficiaries are those of the agencies that comprise AFHCP. Of the AFHCAN sites, only 3% are accessible via the road system. The rest require air access, and 74% require small planes for access. Another 3% are only accessible via helicopter or have limited or special requirements even for air access.

AFHCAN is managed by the Alaska Native Tribal Health Consortium (ANTHC), a tribal organization, established in December 1997 to manage health services in the Alaska Native Health System. ANTHC also manages and operates the Alaska Native Medical Center (ANMC)—the largest and most modern medical center delivering services for Alaska Native beneficiaries. In providing health care to the Alaskan Natives, ANTHC works with regional health corporations including Bristol Bay Health Corporation, Maniilaq Health Corporation, Norton Sound Health Corporation, and Yukon Kuskokwim Health Corporation. In deploying telemedicine to its client organizations, AFHCAN had to work closely with 43 autonomous organizations throughout the state, including three U.S. Air Force bases, six U.S. Army sites, and eight U.S. Coast Guard locations.

In developing the telemedicine network, AFHCAN used technical standards developed by the Alaska Telehealth Advisory Commission (ATAC). ATAC was formed in late 1998 to evaluate, document, and assess telehealth services in the state. The commission included high-level executives from the major health care providers in the state (including the ANTHC), from major telecommunications carriers and from regulatory and government bodies in the state. The core principles under which ATAC operated required all entities that become involved with telehealth to ensure equal access to all Alaskans, to cooperate with all the other entities in ensuring interoperability of the systems, and to plan to make sure the long-term financial viability of the systems was assured.

AFHCAN developed the hardware, software, and the connection network, but the actual telemedicine services were to be provided locally by the clinic at the site, in collaboration with remote medical specialists (most of them at the ANTHC). Because AFHCAN's mandate does not include operating the equipment, providing the connectivity and training was initially left to the organization operating the clinic. This attitude changed after the project staff realized that technology by itself does not address the telehealth needs of the population. More details on the organizational changes induced by this transformation are next, in the section about training.

The telehealth system allows health providers in local village clinics to collect patient information into an electronic case and to transmit the case to a medical specialist at a remote location via a secure network. The case can include text, as well as images taken with a digital camera or with a medical imaging device, as well as other clinical data, for example, electrocardiograms (ECG). Once the patient data is entered into the case, the case is submitted to a remote server (process referred to as "store and forward" in AFHCAN literature). The doctor who will review the case receives an e-mail alerting her that there is a case waiting to be processed. When she has time in-between patients, the doctor logs on to the system, reviews the cases waiting for her, makes comments and suggestions for treatment, and sends the commented cases back to the providers in the village. After the doctor has sent the processed case back, the provider in the village receives an e-mail message alerting him that the case is ready.

Deployment Challenges

AFHCAN started as a four-year project, 1999-2002, but was later on re-organized and extended for two more years with funding from Indian Health Services. Since 2005, AFHCAN has been re-organized as a business managed by the ANTHC, and is working towards becoming profitable through the sale of telemedicine products and services within and outside Alaska.

AFHCAN spent 1999 on planning initial development. The work was done by a Steering Board (acting as Board of Directors), the AFHCAN Project Office, and by six committees (Business, Legal, Clinical, Informatics, Technology, and Training). In the beginning, the project employed two software developers to develop the custom software and a team of technicians to assemble the cart's hardware. With sustained efforts, 10 carts were manufactured per week, and prepared for deployment to the remote sites. For network connectivity, collocation facilities were set up with to local telecommunications carriers, General Communications Inc. (GCI), and AT&T Alascom by mid-2002.

According to Stewart Ferguson, Ph.D., Director of the AFHCAN project, deployment of the hardware started on December 15, 2000. The first shipment of cart parts was sent to Selawik, in the Central-Northwest part of the state, loaded on two long sleds. In spite of all the planning, new challenges emerged. Jostled around along the bumpy sled ride, a reinforcement bar had broken through the single-cardboard box in which it had been packed and was lost in the snow. The fact that the bar was white did not help either, and the deployment was delayed for a full day, to allow the air delivery of a replacement bar from Anchorage. The deployment team learned quickly that packing the equipment securely is of paramount importance (and they moved on to using double thickness boxes).

Although the equipment was delivered quickly to the remote sites and although those sites were reported as "deployed", the actual readiness of the "deployed" sites varied considerably. Some sites received equipment, and the equipment was assembled by AFHCAN on site. Other sites had both the equipment and the training. Other sites had equipment delivered to a local distribution site, with the intent of assembling and connecting the equipment at a later time. Finally, some sites lacked connectivity, but still used equipment for training and for later submission of recorded cases.

Hardware

AFHCAN worked with physicians and local providers to incorporate user feedback into the design of the telehealth equipment, both hardware and software. Through several stages of upgrading the initial workstation, the equipment is now mounted on a rugged cart on wheels, allowing the equipment to be wheeled from one room into another in the clinic, even across uneven floors and doorsills. The profile of the cart is narrow enough to allow passage through most doorframes. The AFHCAN report (AFHCAN, 2004) compares the challenges of the mechanical design of the cart with those of the Mars Rover. Significant care went into the selection process for the switches for the cart and even in the selection of the stool for the health care provider.

To handle the power outages, the initial cart design included an uninterruptible power supply (UPS), but these devices were not robust enough to handle the challenge of the unreliable electrical power in the villages. The latest version of the cart includes an insulating transformer which is expected to last much longer. According to the AFHCAN Web site, the cart can continue to operate on the on-board battery for up to 70 minutes following a loss of power.

An unexpected challenge was the power cord management. The early version included a power cord management drawer, but this drawer often attracted children who liked to play with the cords. The latest solution encloses the cords in a rugged box, out of sight and out of reach of children.

The cart connects to the local server via an encrypted wireless link, to avoid the added complication and reliability problem of a wired network connection. The 300 feet range of this wireless connection is sufficient for most village clinics. The wireless access point is a Cisco Aironet 1230 AG Series IEEE 802.11 a/b/g device.

The peripherals on the cart were selected to be easy to use and also rugged. Each peripheral requires only a one-button operation from the central touch-screen display. The Welch Allyn 300S video otoscope is used to take images of the patients' ear, nose, and throat (and mouth). An intuitive electrocardiogram (ECG) device, the IQMark Digital, allows data acquisition via 4 or 12 wires. A tympanometer and an audiometer are also included, the Earscan by Micro Audiometrics. Additional devices on the latest version of the hardware include a miniature dental camera, Evolution M-series by Digital Doc; the Midmark Diagnostics IQmark spirometer, to measure lung capacity; and a vital signs monitor, including pulse, temperature, respiratory rate, blood pressure, and oxygen saturation in the blood.

The cart includes a computer, selected for low power and high performance, and with room for expansion (a number of extra ports and card slots). A media reader accommodates a variety of storage media, as well as a dock for a digital camera. The "diagnostic quality" touch screen display allows high quality imaging, has a long lifetime, and can be cleaned with standard glass cleaners. All connected devices are programmed to adapt and to self configure. For example, the scanner on the cart will recognize the document size and orientation and optimize its settings accordingly.

The system integration efforts have led to a robust cable management design that avoided unnecessarily exposing cables, ensuring that exposed cables are resistant to pulling, do not drag on the floor, and are not in danger of being crushed against walls. In fact, the entire cart is resistant to being pushed against walls, and items are securely attached. The AFHCAN literature claims that a cart was salvaged from a burning clinic, moved to a nearby building and continued to operate without any problem.

More recently, a wall mounted version and a briefcase version of the hardware have been developed as well.

Software

In addition to the challenges relating to weather, lack of reliable electrical power and geographical isolation mentioned earlier, user interface issues were particularly challenging. Many of the health providers in the village sites were not very technically literate and many of them spoke local languages more readily than English. The resulting system was able to handle well most of the challenges.

The software was designed to be easy to use, and to involve a minimum of technology literacy on the part of the user. Touch screen controls are color coded, and include a pictorial reminder of the function (for example, a miniature scanner icon on the button for activating the scanner). The software runs on Microsoft Windows™, but the computer boots directly into the AFHCAN software. This way, users do not need to be familiar with PC operating systems, with internals of medical devices, and do not even need to be very well versed in the English language. Each device only requires a one-button activation and no setup. According to AFHCAN, once the user logs on, any medical device can be accessed within three or fewer screen clicks. The screen text is also customizable, based on a file that can be translated into other languages and can allow different character sets.

The software was designed to allow room for user error, and also to save time. A health care provider can work on practice cases using the cart, because it is easy to take data and discard it. Not all measurements are automatically logged. Whether for real cases or for practice, the provider and the patient receive instant feedback on the measurement taken, because images get displayed on the screen and can be viewed as they are attached to the case. To save time, several of the fields comprising a case have shortcuts, where the provider can check boxes, which in turn generate text comments that are entered into the case. This saves time and effort, as the provider does not need to type long strings of text on a keyboard. Additionally, the software keeps track of the identity of various health care providers who enter information on each case.

The software is customizable to fit an existing clinical workflow. Cases can be sent to individual medical doctors or to departments (groups). Consultants (doctors) can be advertised locally or enterprise-wide. The software allows for establishing electronic trust relationships between two or more organizations. Electronic trust relationships follow the trust relationships between actual organizations and allow a more streamlined flow of information between sites flagged as "trusted". For example, remote locations can be set up to receive automatically code updates from a trusted distribution point.

To be able to handle unreliable connectivity, the software was developed to be highly resilient to connection drops. The early version of the system required an initial connection to the remote server to create a case, and then allowed the provider to continue to enter the case even if the connection was dropped. The latest version allows the case to be initiated and entered entirely off-line, and submitted in the background when connectivity is available.

Another benefit of the simplicity of the software is the fact that providers still feel comfortable with it even at low levels of usage. According to AFHCAN, more complex telehealth systems are not sustainable below a certain level of usage, below which users lack reinforcing of learned skills and forget how to use the equipment. In contrast, many users of the AFHCAN system report good performance even at low usage rates of one to five cases.

Connectivity

The network was designed to comply with the HIPAA Privacy and Security Requirements. It uses satellite connectivity over a wide-area network (WAN) providing connectivity with bandwidths ranging from 128 kb/s to 1.544 Mb/s (T1). Most of the sites have T1 connectivity. Two Alaska-based telecommunications carriers, General Communications, Inc., and AT&T Alascom provide the links. The same WAN is also used for teleradiology, telepharmacy, health care-related video conferencing, and Voice-over-IP.

Data is signed by the sender and encrypted using the public key of the destination site. A "server-to-server" technology allows connections through most firewalls. Data is distributed across 40 servers throughout the state. The servers synchronize contents every five minutes.

Training

As in any new system deployment, training of the users has had a significant impact. The initial budget for training was $2.35 million, primarily for training of the Community Health Aides/Practitioners (CHA/Ps). CHA/Ps make up for 66% of the health care personnel in the villages. They are local village residents, nominated by the village council, and who undergo basic training in advanced first aid, CPR, taking a case history, and in assessing and diagnosing a patient. Challenges in training CHA/Ps included bridging both a cultural gap (when the trainer was not Alaskan Native) and a computer literacy gap. For any issues beyond their training, the CHA/Ps report to and rely on nurses and physicians at regional centers and in Anchorage. The CHA/Ps provide almost 500,000 consultations per year in 200 villages statewide. According to AFHCAN, these providers must have finished eighth grade, but many did not finish high school (the median education level is 11th grade).

The AFHCAN pilot study started with an emphasis on assembling and delivering telemedicine carts and software to remote sites. As carts were delivered and placed into service at most of the target sites, most of the target sites were declared "deployed". In spite of available technology, the equipment experienced low utilization rates initially. Surveys administered by the University of Alaska Anchorage in 2003 and 2004 indicated that lack of connectivity and lack of training were the main reasons for the low usage rates. Based on this new information, a major re-organization followed, with a change of focus, moving away from simply delivering hardware and technology, and moving towards delivering true telemedicine capability, a "Whole Product Solution".

The changes in the organizational structure (Figures 1 and 2) entailed moving the WAN outside the AFHCAN office, because of its functions beyond the AFHCAN network. Managed by ANTHC, the WAN is also used to deliver tele-radiology, tele-pharmacy as well as tele-behavioral health services. The technical group (Fig. 1) became the operations group (Figure 2), positioned to deliver a Whole Product Solution, in other words, a system that

Figure 1. AFHCAN organization in 2002

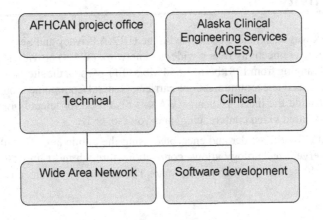

Figure 2. AFHCAN organization FY 2004

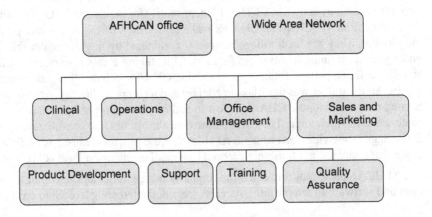

is tested, supported, and ready to be used for delivering health care. Two more software developers were hired, along with a hardware engineer and a full-time tester. Additionally, a newly-created Sales and Marketing Group (Figure 2) was created to interface with customers and to identify new sources of revenue. A significant effort was made to develop a training force. As of 2005, AFHCAN offered 24/7 professional support, as well as training and certification, both in Anchorage and on site at village clinics. Teams of training professionals have regular travel scheduled to remote locations to train system users.

Project Evaluation

According to AFHCAN, current telemedicine applications include Pediatrics, Cardiology, Family Practice, Trauma Registry, ENT, Dermatology, and Same Day Surgery. A success story of same day surgery was featured in the ATAC 02-03 Annual Report (Alaska Telehealth Advisory Council, 2003). The story is about a case of pregnancy complications requiring surgery in a village location where no surgeon or anesthesiologist were available. Extreme weather, as well as the length of the flight itself made air evacuation impossible. In the end, the local family practitioner completed the surgery successfully, coached via videoconferencing equipment by surgeons in Anchorage. Future applications of telemedicine are expected to include Surgery, Urology, Women's Health, Orthopedics, and Neonatal Services.

Both patients and providers see the technology as very beneficial in providing access to quality health care. Eighty percent of providers agree or strongly agree that telemedicine has improved the quality of health care, the patient satisfaction, that it makes their job more fun and that it helps in communicating with a doctor. Studies have also shown that telemedicine offers similar quality of service to that of face-to-face encounters. One much-quoted study is for a particular type of ear procedure, where comparison between in-person follow-up and telemedicine-mediated follow-up showed equal performance.

The current list of providers of telemedicine through AFHCAN and the ANMC include two cardiologists, one dermatologist, emergency room physicians, one endocrinologist, ENT physicians, two ophthalmologists, several pediatricians, one neurosurgeon, one podiatrist, a urologist, two surgeons, a women's health doctor, as well as a team of instructors that accept test cases from CHA/P's in the field.

The usage of the telemedicine system has increased steadily. In the latest publicly available report, 2003 figures indicate more than 8,000 cases filed for the year (Figure 3). Part of this increase was due to deployment to additional sites. More recently, the increase has been fueled by higher utilization at existing sites. From 2004 to 2005, although only five additional sites were deployed, the year-over-year increase in the number of cases was 50%.

As shown in Figure 4, most telemedicine cases reported to date use the video otoscope. The device is the most expensive among the equipment on the cart, accounting for more than 30% of the cart price. The digital camera is used for dermatology applications, but also for family practice. The scanner is also much used, more so than initially thought. Finally, the ECG is not much used, but is probably extremely important in the small number of critical cases where its use is required.

According to AFHCAN data, 45% of providers submitted five cases or fewer. Approximately 8% of the providers submitted 250 or more cases, some having submitted as many as 1,000

Figure 3. Number of cases archived 2001-2003 (Source: AFHCAN, 2004)

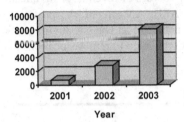

Number of cases archived

Figure 4. Percentage of cases using the medical devices on the AFHCAN cart (Source: AFHCAN, 2004)

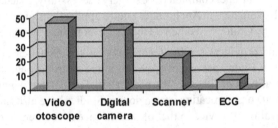

Percentage of cases using devices on the cart

or even 2,000 cases. The actual usage of the carts is much greater than these figures would indicate, because of the use of carts for unreported observations. Such uses not only help train the providers, but also help reassure patients by providing visual feedback, which in turn is reported to have reduced the use of antibiotics and to have increased patient compliance with the prescribed treatment plan. The unsaved cases make up 50-150% of the saved cases.

The priorities of AFHCAN listed cost reduction as the least important goal. The main goals were providing access to health care and increasing the quality of the care offered. Still, cost reduction was a clear benefit of the project. According to AFHCAN data, store and forward telemedicine removed the need for travel 34% of the time, caused travel 8% of the time, and did not affect the need for travel 59% of the time. For 37% of the 13,307 encounters archived 2001-2003, and for a conservative $200 roundtrip price, the money saved in airfare only is a staggering $2.8 million. Considering the requirement for a travel companion for the patient, as well as additional expenses associated with lodging, per diem and time away from work and family, the savings could be even higher. A study quoted on the AFHCAN Web site estimates that for every dollar of telemedicine services reimbursed by Medicaid, patients saved an average of $4.41 in travel expenses. The site also estimates that ENT services provided via telemedicine amounted to half a workload of a specialty physician, who would have had to travel across the state.

The organization has received numerous awards for the development and deployment of telemedicine. In May 2004, AFHCAN received the American Telemedicine Association President's Awards for the Advancement of Telemedicine. The same year, in December, AFHCAN received the TETHIE Award for "Most Innovative New Technology Device for Diagnosis".

Critical Developments

According to interviews with key players in the development of the telemedicine network (Key Informant Interviews; see AFHCAN, 2004), there were several events that proved to be critical for the project's success. The formation of ATAC was critical for providing funding, ensuring sustainability, and recognition for the program. ATAC's efforts were also acknowledged in relation to the passage of the Telehealth Improvement and Modernization Act of 2000 which allowed telehealth services to be reimbursed by Medicaid. "Store and forward" types of services were specifically mentioned in the Act for Alaska and Hawaii-based telemedicine.

Congressional funding was also critical, and the use of Universal Service Funds made affordable otherwise prohibitively expensive WAN links, by subsidizing carriers to deliver services in remote areas. A typical cost of $12,000 per month for a T1 line in rural Alaska is reduced to a mere $900 by the USF subsidy, according to the AFHCAN report. Finally, good technology choices, based to a great extent on prior experiences with projects like ATTP and Department of Corrections' telepsychiatry project were essential as well. In particular, the use of touch screens and the choice of rugged devices and system integration options were very important.

Future Trends

The Key Informant Interviews also outlined future issues that AFHCAN will need to address. Several regulatory issues include the interstate medical practice (in particular licensing), limitations on the use of USF funds, as well as security and privacy issues. Among the IT-related challenges, ongoing training, and the need for written (and possibly online) manuals were recognized as critical for increasing the number of providers and their level of comfort with technology. Additional challenges identified the need to bring new applications online, and to increase the quality of existing ones. One interviewee made the case for a need to transform telemedicine from a communications tool (a remote specialist coaching local practitioners) to a clinical tool, allowing the remote specialist a more active role.

Some of the offshoots of the program are in telemedicine initiatives in the private sector. General Communications, Inc., one of the carriers that provides the AFHCAN WAN, is now offering a connectivity product geared to supporting telemedicine applications (ConnectMD, n.d.). The secure (HIPAA compliant) managed network service enables real-time applications, as well as exchange of data, voice, and video.

Another issue still open is that of the clinical workflow. Cart usage at DoD sites was much lower than at IHS sites, in part because the AFHCAN system did not fit in the existing workflow. Many DoD sites had physicians on staff, who did not require much use of the telemedicine cart in their daily work. When physicians needed access to an outside special-iot, they expected a response in real time, which is not what the system had been designed for. Moreover, the lack of an online directory of specialists further reduced the usage. Some physicians also complained about the absence of additional medical devices they would have liked to use on the cart, in particular ultrasound systems. Finally, many DoD personnel believed that the archived cases were property of the ANTHC, so they felt limited in their ability to use archived cases to conduct outcome assessment. Veterans Administration us-age of carts was also reduced, because of the lack of compatibility between the AFHCAN software and the VA records system. VA reported the system as beneficial for improving quality and decreasing costs associated with connectivity, as well as for strengthening rela-tions with local communities. Finally, the Coast Guard was somewhat slow to incorporate the use of the cart in their workflows, but commented that the system would pay for itself with even one single use.

The issue of cost is still central for the future of telemedicine. According to a participant, even the low cost and high durability technology developed by AFHCAN is still "too expen-sive to be replicated in the private sector and too expensive to be maintained in the public sector." The AFHCAN cart costs $24,000 (more than 30% of which is the cost of the video otoscope). Most participants expect to see decreased federal subsidies for telemedicine in the future, making cost reduction essential for the sustainability of the project.

To this order, AFHCAN is now considering selling hardware and software solutions to other entities outside Alaska. Negotiations are underway with NORTH Network, an orga-nization that provides telemedicine services at more than 100 sites in Ontario, Canada, and with a Pennsylvania Health Care System that manages 40 sites. The U.S. Food and Drug Administration recognizes AFHCAN as a manufacturer of Medical Devices, and recognizes the hardware and software as medical devices. Full FDA certification of the equipment is required for AFHCAN to be able to acquire liability protection for selling the system outside of the U.S. federal government. UL and CE certifications of the system are underway and are expected to facilitate further sales in the U.S. and European Union. Finally, the strategic plan developed in early 2004 called for AFHCAN to reorganize as a business operation able to take contracts outside the AFHCP.

List of Acronyms

AFHCAN—Alaska Federal Health Care Access Network

AFHCP—Alaska Federal Health Care Partnership

ANMC—Alaska Native Medical Center

ANTHC—Alaska Native Tribal Health Consortium

ATAC—Alaska Telehealth Advisory Commission

ATTP—Alaska Telemedicine Testbed Project

CE—Conformité Européenne—"mandatory European marking for certain product groups to indicate conformity with the essential health and safety requirements set out in European Directives" (www.cemarking.net).

ECG—Electrocardiogram

FDA—Food and Drug Administration

HIPAA—Health Insurance Portability and Accountability Act of 1996

IEEE—Institute of Electrical and Electronic Engineers

IHS—Indian Health Services

NLM—National Library of Medicine

UL—Underwriters Laboratories, Inc.

VA—Veterans' Administration

WAN—Wide-Area Network

References

AFHCAN (Alaska Federal Health Care Access Network). (2004). Evolution & summative evaluation of the Alaska federal health care access network telemedicine project. Retrieved February 13, 2006, from http://www.alaska.edu/health/Telemedicine/Telemed.htm

Alaska. (2000). Census 2000: Alaska profile. Retrieved January 10, 2006, from http://ftp2.census.gov/geo/maps/special/profile2k/AK_2K_Profile.pdf

Alaska Blue Book. (1994). *Alaska blue book, 1993-94* (11th ed.). Juneau: Department of Education, Division of State Libraries, Archives & Museums.

Alaska Telehealth Advisory Council. (2003). Alaska Telehealth Advisory Council FY 2002 – 2003 annual report. Retrieved January 18, 2006, from http://www.hss.state.ak.us/dph/chems/ATAC/pdfs/ATAC%2002-03%20Annual%20Report%20Final.pdf

ConnectMD. (n.d.). ConnectMD – Case studies. Retrieved January 31, 2006, from http://www.connectmd.com/product_case_study.html

Pearce, F. W. (2001). Alaska telemedicine testbed project. *Telemedicine and Telecommunications: Options for the New Century*. Symposium Sponsored by the National Library of Medicine, March 13-14.

Author's Biography

Bogdan Hoanca *is an assistant professor of management information systems at the University of Alaska Anchorage (UAA). Before joining UAA, he co-founded, started-up, and sold a company that builds components for fiber optic communications. He also helped start and consulted with a number of other start-up companies in optical fiber communications. Bogdan received a PhD in electrical engineering from the University of Southern California in 1999. His current research interests revolve around technology, in particular e-learning and societal implications of technology, as well as privacy and security.*

Chapter XV

YerelNet
(Local Network):
A Web Portal and
Web-Enabled
Communication Platform
for Turkish
Local Governments

Mete Yildiz, Hacettepe University, Beytepe, Ankara/Turkey

Executive Summary

This chapter presents the case study of YerelNet (Local Network, in Turkish), which is a Web portal and a Web-enabled communication platform for local governments in Turkey. The project was initiated for gathering reliable, complete, and updated data about Turkish local governments. The chapter first describes the background of the case, the Turkish administrative system, briefly. Then, it presents the nature and important actors of, as well as the strategic decisions made within the project, together with problems experienced and solutions found by the project staff. The chapter ends with the critical evaluation of the case as an interesting application e-government in a developing nation, with small IT budgets and particular cultural challenges.

Background

Country Background

In order to understand the case under study, it is essential to examine the context in which the case occurs, which is, the social, political, and administrative systems of the Republic of Turkey. Turkey stands at the crossroads of Europe, Asia, and the Middle East. On a land slightly larger than the State of Texas (814.578 square kilometers), it hosts a population of 71.3 million people (United Nations Development Report, 2005).

Turkey is a unitary state, governed by a unicameral parliamentary democratic system. Mustafa Kemal Atatürk founded the Republic of Turkey on October 29, 1923. Its capital is the City of Ankara. Turkish citizens exercise their sovereignty directly by the elections, and indirectly by means of the legislature, executive, and judiciary. The principle of "separation of powers" prevails among these three organs.

The administrative system of Turkey was modeled after France. It is highly centralized. The country is divided into 81 provinces. These provinces are administered by a group of civil servants appointed by the center. The highest ranking of these appointed civil servants is the provincial governor. In addition to the central/national government, that is, the ministries in Ankara, there are almost 40,000 local government units throughout the country. About 35,000 units are villages, 3,225 units are municipalities, about 1,000 of them are local government associations, and finally there are 81 provincial local governments.

Legislative power is vested in the Turkish Grand National Assembly. The Assembly is composed of 550 members of parliament who are elected directly by the citizens every five years. Elections are held under the general direction and supervision of the judiciary, according to the principles of free, equal, secret, direct, universal suffrage, and public counting of the votes.

Executive power and function is exercised and carried out by the President of the Republic and the Council of Ministers. The President is the head of the state. He supervises the proper and harmonious functioning of the state organs. The Turkish Grand National Assembly elects the President for a term of seven years among its members or among citizens, who are eligible to be deputies.

The Council of Ministers consists of the Prime Minister and the ministers. The Prime Minister is appointed by the President among the members of the Turkish Grand National Assembly. The ministers are appointed by the President among the members of the Turkish Grand National Assembly or among those eligible for election as deputies. The Prime Minister and the ministers assume the duty upon a vote of confidence taken from the Turkish Grand National Assembly. Judicial power is used by means of the independent courts. The principles of state of law, independence of the courts and judges, and the guarantee of judges' rights are taken as the basis of using this power. The Constitution has divided the organs of judiciary as legal, administrative, and special. The legal and administrative judiciary are of two tiers.

The host organization of the project under investigation, TODAIE, or with its abbreviation in the English language, PAITME (Public Administration Institute for Turkey and the Middle East) was established in 1952, with an agreement signed between the Turkish Government and United Nations (Omurgonulsen, 2004). The institute reports to the Office of the Ministry of Interior. According to the Law Number 7163, which is the founding law for the Institute,[1] this agency is responsible for educating government employees, conducting research in the field of public administration, publishing public administration books, periodicals, and documents that may be useful for government agencies, encouraging the professional development of the theoreticians and practitioners of public administration, and finally, acting as the coordinator agency for the research efforts in the area of public administration in Turkey and the Middle East.

Case Background

YerelNet (Local Network, in Turkish; hereafter named as so) is a Web portal and a Web-enabled communication platform for local governments in Turkey. It is the brainchild of PAITME's Center for Local Government Research and Education. The Local Network Project was developed in order to solve the problem of gathering reliable, complete, and updated data about Turkish local governments—a problem, which has been troubling PAITME for a long time (Ayman Guler, 2001).

Collecting complete and current information about local governments had long been planned (Yildiz, 2004). Before the implementation of the Local Network Project, neither the exact numbers of local government units (municipalities, provincial local governments, villages, and derivatives of these three main local government types, such as local government associations and local government financial enterprises), nor the amount of technical and personnel resources that local governments are using were exactly known by the national government. Data gathering, however, is not an end in itself, but it is a means for better planning, decision making, and public policy analysis about the Turkish system of government, on the one hand, and a critical tool for encouraging and enabling transparency and accountability in using government resources, on the other.

The project staff decided to create a Web portal, which would function both as an electronic bulletin board on which local governments can post their information, and citizens can read and react to them. The intention was to have the Web site work as a screen, behind which a powerful database that stores and organizes all kinds of data and information received by the system existed.

The Local Network Project staff decided to use the Web as the medium of interaction, in order to reduce the costs of coordination and collective action between local governments, as Web site format decreases the cost of information dissemination and retrieval. Having a single Web site for all the local government units in a country may create several positive externalities. First, it may enable best practices and most efficient standard operating procedures spread from successful local governments to others. Second, it may encourage greater transparency and accountability by making citizen involvement in the affairs of local governments easier. Finally, increasing interaction both among and between the providers and users of local information and services may ease the generation of collective action by citizens and local government.

The main features of the Local Network Project are presented in Table 1.

Table 1. Features of the Local Network Project

Level	Local
Funding	Domestic State Planning Organization (90,000 New Turkish Liras = US$ 67,000 a year, according to 2006 exchange rates)
Software	Open-source
Technical Support	In-House, contracted in
Outsourced to	Teclinn Private Firm (Individual contracts for each IT expert)
Decision-Support Systems	Being planned
Paperless Office/ Document Mgmt. Sys.?	NO
Databank/ base	YES
Internet/Intranet	Internet only
MERNIS compatible?	N.A.
Type	G2G, G2C, G2B
Set up Cost	90,000 New Turkish Liras = US$ 100,000 (according to the average exchange rate in 1999-2001)
Began	1998
Completed	2001, ongoing
Pilot Project	NO

Source: Adapted and revised from Yildiz, 2004.

Case Description

Content and Objectives of the Local Network Project

The Local Network Project was planned in the years 1999 and 2000, and the Web site, which can be visited on the Web at *http://www.yerelnet.org.tr* (for a screen shot, see Figure 1), began to function in January 1st, 2001. The Web site currently (as of February 2006) holds data about 3,225 municipalities, nearly 35,000 villages, 81 provincial local governments, and more than 1,000 local government associations.

Financial support for the project came from the Turkish State Planning Organization in yearly increments. The main direct costs incurred were the financial payments for human and technical resources to set up and maintain the Web site. In its first three years (1999 to 2001), the total cost of the project had been approximately 90 billion Turkish liras[2] (Ayman Guler, 2001).

The main stakeholders of the project included Turkey's local governments, academics, students, the private firms doing business with local governments, and citizens. Local governments were responsible for providing up-to-date and reliable data about themselves. As mentioned earlier, the objective of this data collection effort was to provide a pool of local government data for planning, decision, and public policy-making at the national level goverment. Academics and students gained the opportunity to use data generated by the project in their scholarly works and homeworks. Some academicians worked actively in creating and organizing content, as can be seen in Figure 1.

Project objectives were three-fold: First, the management philosophy of the Local Network Project is to share government information for free with all the interested parties. The idea of freedom of access to information is evident in the policy of providing government information without any kind of access fee. Increasing political communication and interaction among local governments, and between governments and citizens have been attempted to be accomplished by the provison of electronic discussion forums, and online question and answer sections on the Web site.

A second objective was the creation of a transparent system of local governments, in which the citizens would have access to many types of local government information, which in turn, will enable them to participate in local and national level government's decision-making processes. Participation in the local decisions was expected to increase the accountability of local governments toward its citizens. One way of encouraging administrative transparency

Figure 1. Screen shot of the Local Network Web site

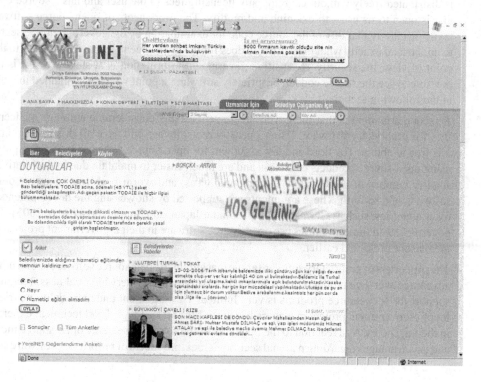

and accountability was to provide laws and regulations, results of local and national-level elections (including the old elections since 1963), local bids and tenders, local government budget information, transcripts of local assembly decisions, and publications and press coverage on Turkish local governments on the Local Network Web site. Such detailed information about monetary and political processes in local governments was real "news" to the ordinary citizen.

A third and final objective was to create a system that would serve as an online on-the-job training center for elected and appointed local government employees. Such a system would also function as an online library that would include handbooks that would provide basic information, problems and solutions regarding the fiscal and personnel structures, and infrastructure of Turkish local governments, detailed information about legal developments in Turkey, and international developments that are relevant to Turkish local governments.

Strategic Decisions

There are several decisions which contributed to the success of the Local Network Project. First, the management team's decision to use open-source software for the Local Network Project has both financial and technical repercussions. Although the use of open-source software made the Local Network structure much more flexible by making future add-ons easy to implement, the real advantage of open-source software use was to contain the cost of the project.

Open-source software, which is used by an increasing number of governments world-wide, is distributed freely without charging any licensing fees to the user and has a source code that is open to its users to examine and modify. The proponents of open-source software argue that the availability of the source code for examination by the government is essential to understand exactly what that software does for the government agency. According to this point of view, the security of sensitive government information is at stake when it is not possible to see the source code in proprietary software, a point which is explained in detail in the following sections.

A second argument is that the government agencies pay considerable amounts of license fees for proprietary software. Using open-source software will save all this money since it is free to obtain. The third and last argument for open-source software is that computers using open-source products crash less and are much easier to maintain due to the relatively smaller number of hacker attacks, computer virus, and worm problems in open-source software, and so forth. These arguments are supported by showcasing the developments in other countries, such as Germany, Brazil, China, Japan, and South Korea (Sum, 2003). The governments in these countries use open-source software in their e-government projects for the reasons presented earlier.

The supporters of proprietary software argue that although open-source software has an initial advantage over their products of not paying license fees, it has a very big weakness. Technical support for open-source products is very limited. This argument understandably worries a lot of e-government project managers because of the lack of high-level technical expertise in their agencies. As a reaction to the openness of the source code in the open-source model and its advantages regarding national security issues, producers of proprietary software such as the Microsoft Corporation, decided to share their source code with foreign governments. Microsoft even argues that, since the source code is open only to the government but not to third parties as it is in open-source, this is even more secure for the government since third parties may or may not have ill-intentions.

Another dimension of this debate is ideological. The underlying philosophy of the open-source movement is developing the source by improving it and then sharing it with others to use and develop. This approach, which defies both ownership and intellectual property rights, creates an alternative business model to that of proprietary software. Such an alternative worries software companies and threatens their existence. The characterization of the open-source software as "digital socialism" by some of its supporters and opponents may create uneasiness in politicians and e-government project managers (Yildiz, 2004).

The Local Network Project Management Group made a second strategic decision by temporarily integrating the members of a small private IT firm to its organizational structure as independent contractors. Such an arrangement proved to be useful against the classical principal-agent problems of adverse selection and moral hazard, by enabling Local Network managers and staff to continually observe the IT company workers' true intellectual resources and monitor their work habits and actual performance. The place of the contractors in the organizational chart is shown in Figure 2.

This structural arrangement and the use of open-source software, thus, not paying any money for software licenses, enabled the Local Network Management Team to cut costs dramatically (Yildiz, 2004).

A third strategic decision that helped the project team to minimize the financial cost was the decentralized nature of the data inputting system. Each and every local government unit—except the villages—such as municipalities, and provincial special districts, were

Figure 2. Organizational chart and communication patterns for the Local Network Project Management Team

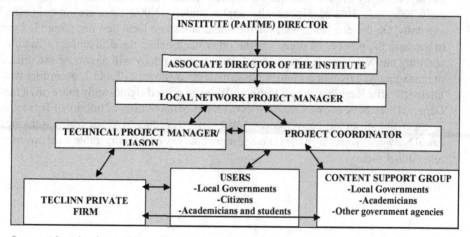

Source: Adapted and revised from Yildiz, 2004.

given a login name and password. Each unit inputted their own data into the system by using their own hardware and software. Thus, the project did not need to incur the cost of providing the technical infrastructure for each local government unit.

Recent Developments

The most recent developments in the Local Network Project are the increasing use of online discussion forums, plans to distribute local news throughout the country via the Local Network Web site, customization of the Web site for different groups of users, and plans for increasing capacity of Web site use (Personal Interviews, 2005).

First, online forums are increasingly available for Local Network users. These forums are used for the discussion of local issues and to provide both negative and positive feedback about services provided by local governments. In other words, the project's government-to-citizen orientation is becoming as important as that of government-to-government.

Second, the Local Network aims to be the distributer of local news throughout the country, beginning from 2006. To this end, the project staff has been negotiating an agreement with national broadcasting agencies for the purchase of local news content. These news will then be screened and processed by a software in Local Network, and relevant local content will be provided to the users of the Web site. The availability of more local news coverage to the citizens on the Web site is expected to increase both the number of Local Network users and access to local information. The selection of the news agency and the distribution of local news through Local Network Web site will be put into effect by the end of February 2006 (Personal Interviews, 2005).

A third important recent change in the project is the customization of the Web site. In other words, the content can be rearranged in a way to answer the information needs, and maximize the utility of specific groups of users. The Local Network Web site now has six different customization features for different types of users, such as citizens, local government workers, and local government experts.

Finally, currently the Web site has the capacity to accommodate 50,000 users a day. As of early 2006, only 30% of this capacity, approximately 15,000 users, are accessing the Web site daily. On the one hand, additional content and more local news coverage is expected to increase the number of users. On the other hand, when the difficulties of funding and updating the Web site are kept in mind, increasing capacity will aggravate the difficulties of managing an expanding system. Nevertheless, as shown in Table 2, according to Alexa Internet Traffic Rankings, Local Network Web site is used significantly more often than the General Directorate of Local Authorities (a branch of the Ministy of Interior of Turkey, which is responsible from local governments) Web site. According to Alexa Traffic Rankings, the Local Network Project Web site is visited more than any other comparable local government-related Web site.

Table 2. Traffic rankings of some Turkish Web sites (number of visitors) *

#	Website Addresses (HTTP://WWW)	Project/ Host Organization	TRAFFIC RANKING/ DATES		
			09.14. 2005	01.24. 2006	02.14. 2006
1	yerelnet.org.tr	Local Network Project (A Project of the Research and Training Centre for Local Administrations, at PAITME)	38.094	32.529	24.496
2	yerelbilgi.gov.tr	Local Information (A Project of the General Directorate of Local Authorities)	No data	No Data	418,741
3	icisleri.gov.tr	Ministry of Interior Web site	49.517	40.377	40.921
4	ankara-bld.gov.tr	Ankara Metropolitan Municipality Web site	231.500	192.321	513.930
5	mahalli-idareler. gov.tr	General Directorate of Local Authorities (A Branch of the Ministry of Interior) Web site	477.478	220.602	178,510
6	beper.gov.tr	Municipal Performance Measurement (A Project of the General Directorate of Local Authorities)	1.157.529	839.269	905.770

* *A smaller rank means more visitors. For example, having number 1 as the rank means being the most visited Web site of the Internet.*

Source: Courtesy of Local Network Project staff. Data taken from Alexa Web site rankings on the stated days from www.alexa.com.

Case Evaluation

The Local Network is the first example of its kind, as an online local government information management and sharing system. The project has been recognized both nationally and internationally. Nationally, it was one of the finalists of the 2004 E-Turkey competition, in the e-government category. As data in Table 2 suggest, the Local Network Web site is visited more than other comparable Web sites. Thus, it can be argued that the users of local government information find the Local Network Project useful and successful as well.

As a sign of success at the national level, the Local Network Project initiated the creation of a similar project within the Ministy of Interior, under the name of Yerel Bilgi (Local Information). A protocol was signed between PAITME and the Ministry of Interior for the establishment of Yerel Bilgi on April 4, 2001. The protocol gave the duty of project planning to the Center for Strategy of the Ministry of Interior. PAITME and the General Directorate of Local Authorities was given the duty to implement the project. After a while, the General Directorate preferred to continue the project alone.

Internationally, the World Bank chose Local Network as an exemplary application for similar projects in the Eastern European countries. Romania and Hungary showed great interest in the project, and wanted to replicate its structure and results with the help of Turkish expert personnel (Gumussuyu, 2001).

The Local Network Project is a good example for the application of e-government at the local government level. It includes government-to-government (interaction between the national government and local governments, as well as among local governments), government-to-citizen (providing local government information to citizens and academicians), and government-to-business (posting local government bids and tenders online) e-government interaction types.

The Local Network is also unique for its use of a private Information technology firm by absorbing that small firm temporarily into the organizational structure of the government agency that sponsors the project. The use of open-source software to contain costs is also unique among the national level Turkish e-government projects.

The Local Network has the power to transform the interaction between both citizens and local governments, and local governments among themselves by providing local government information (and in the future, local government services) on its Web site. It also is a huge step towards transparency of local government operations that is long considered as hotbeds of corruption and inefficiency. Finally, this project serves a considerable size of the Turkish population. Almost everybody in Turkey does some business with local governments in their daily lives. Therefore, the impact factor of the Local Network Project is quite high.

Current Challenges Facing the Project

There are six major challenges that the Local Network Project faces (Personal Interviews, 2005). First and foremost, the sustainability of government funding is a huge challenge. The government funds of 90,000 New Turkish Liras (approximately $67,000 as of February 2006), annually awarded to the project, may be given to the host agency for the last time in 2006. In the future, the project staff may have to rely on advertisement revenues and other income-generating ideas such as finding sponsors, in order to survive without government funding.

A second challenge is the management of ever-increasing content. As the content of the Local Network Web site increases, security of contents became more of an issue. In order to ensure the security of the contents, the project management team plans to employ a technical security expert in 2006. Another negative externality of the increasing amount of content is the inadequacy of the existing content developers to update the content regularly. The solution to this problem is to employ more content managers, and this requires more money. Still, with limited resources, the Web site design has been changed three times within the last two years. The content is changed in order to accommodate the flow of new information, and to increase the ease of access.

A related problem that Local Network faces is the slowness of some local governments to update their content. Since they have no authority on local government personnel, who update the content, the Local Network staff should find other ways to encourage the local government officials to update their information regularly.

A fourth challenge is the possibility of people committing crimes while they are using the Local Network System. For example, as more users interact through the online forums of the Local Network, intense quarrels, reaching to the point of online fights, increasingly occur between the users. The project staff can occasionally be asked to come to the police headquarters, or to bring the transcript of the online fight to the public prosecutor.

A fifth challenge is the low level of Internet penetration and technology ownership in Turkey. Without ample opportunities to access e-government services, the provision services is not very meaningful. As it can be seen in Table 3, data from the 2005 State Statistics Institute Survey show that PC ownership is less than 12%, and Internet connection levels are quite low. Still, increasing cell phone penetration may present a solution to the problem of access: Project managers of e-government initiatives should begin to consider making their Web sites and services cell phone-compatible, as cell phone ownership (72%), and Internet connection via cell phones (3.21%) are higher than most other categories. Cell phones, together with Internet cafes, may help to alleviate the problem of digital divide in Turkey (Yildiz, 2002, 2006).

Finally, there is an interesting situation in the Local Network Case. On the one hand, it is a highly visible project from the citizen's point of view, as the feedback pouring from e-mail and telephone messages as well as high levels of membership in online forums demonstrate. On the other hand, the Local Network was recognized as a successful project by international actors such as the World Bank, but interestingly it was largely ignored by the Turkish e-government community and the media (Yildiz, 2004). Nevertheless, the Local Network is the living proof that a comprehensive project can be managed with open-source software, with the low cost of the overall project, and high quality of technical support.

As a conclusion, it might be argued that the Local Network Case is an interesting case involving electronic government in a developing nation, with small IT budgets, and particular cultural challenges. The case underlines the importance and complexity of the integration of local e-government to higher levels of e-government, such as state and federal governments in federal administrative systems, and national governments in unitary systems within a consistent e-government development policy, keeping in mind environmental and cultural variables.

Table 3. Technology ownership by Turkish households in 2005 (%)

TECHNOLOGY	PERCENTAGE OF OWNERSHIP	PERCENTAGE OF INTERNET CONNECTION WITH THE TECHNOLOGY
Television (including cable and satellite transmissions)	97.74	0.05
Cell/Car Phone	72.62	3.21
PC	11.62	5.86
Game Console	2.9	0.02
Portable computer	1.13	0.74
PDA (Personal Digital Assistant)	0.14	0.08

Source: DİE Hanehalkı Bilişim Teknolojileri Kullanımı Araştırması (State Statistics Institute Household IT Use Survey) 2005, Retrieved on December 1, 2005 from, http://www.die.gov.tr/TURKISH/SONIST/HH-Bilisim/hhbilisim.html.

Acknowledgments

The author would like to thank the previous and current members of the Local Network Project Staff for their openness for sharing their information and insights with me.

References

Ayman Guler, B. (2001). *E-Turkiye: Yerel yonetimler*. Transcripts of the discussion panel in the 7th Internet Conference in Turkey. Retrieved October 17, 2005, from inet-tr.org. tr/inetconf7/oturumlar/yerel-yonetimler.doc

Gumussuyu, C. (2001). *About the research and training center for local administrations*. Unpublished Manuscript. Public Administration Institute for Turkey and the Middle East, Ankara.

Omurgonulsen, U. (2004). Turkiye'de lisans duzeyinde kamu yonetimi ogretiminin kurumsal gelisimi ve sorunlari. In M. K. Oktem, & U. Omurgonulsen (Eds.), *Kamu Yonetimi: Gelisimi ve Guncel Sorunlari* (pp. 27-83). Ankara: Imaj Yayinevi.

Personal Interviews. (2005). Interviews with the Local Network Project Staff, December 28, 2005, Ankara, Turkey.

Sum, N.-L. (2003). Informational capitalism and U.S. economic hegemony: Resistance and adaptations in East Asia. *Critical Asian Studies, 35*(3), 373-398.

United Nations Development Program. (2005). *Human development report*. Retrieved January 3, 2006, from http://hdr.undp.org/reports/global/2005/pdf/HDR05_HDI.pdf

Yildiz, M. (2002). Bir kamu politikasi araci olarak internet kafeler (Internet cafés as a public policy tool for achieving universal service and bridging the digital gap in Turkey; in Turkish). *Amme Idaresi Dergisi (Turkish Journal of Public Administration), 35*(2), 232-254.

Yildiz, M. (2004). *Peeking into the black box of e-government policy-making: The case of Turkey*. Unpublished doctoral dissertation. Indiana University, Bloomington.

Yildiz, M. (2006). The state of mobile government in Turkey: Overview, policy issues and future prospects. In I. Kuschu (Ed.), *Mobile government: An emerging direction in e-government*. Book chapter submitted for review.

Endnotes

[1]   For the founding law for the PAITME, see http://www.todaie.gov.tr/tmev1.asp.

[2]   About $100,000 according to the average exchange rate of the years 1999 to 2001, which is 888,000 Turkish Liras (0.88 New Turkish Liras).

Author's Biography

Mete Yildiz is an assistant professor at the Political Science and Public Administration Department of Hacettepe University in Turkey. He worked as an associate instructor (2001-2003) and a visiting lecturer (2003-2004) at the School of Public and Environmental Affairs at Indiana University, Bloomington. His research focuses on government reform, with special emphasis on technology use (e-government and m-government), public policy, and digital divide (especially the potential role of Internet cafes and mobile phones in bridging it). Yildiz is the co-founder (with Jon Gant) and was the organizer of the E-Government Workshop at Indiana University (2001-2003). During his stay at Indiana University, Yildiz attended the NSF-funded WebShop at the University of Maryland (Summer 2002), and worked as the managing editor of The Information Society Journal (2001-2002). Yildiz holds a Master's degree in public administration from University of Southern California in Los Angeles, USA, and a PhD in public affairs from Indiana University-Bloomington.

Chapter XVI

The New York State Web Site:
Accommodating Diversity Through a Distributed Management Structure

J. Ramon Gil-Garcia, University at Albany, SUNY, USA

Sharon S. Dawes, University at Albany, SUNY, USA

Executive Summary

How does a very large and diverse state government with a long history of decentralized IT management go about creating a high-quality state-wide Web site? This case describes New York State's distributed approach to Web site development as well as the strategies, benefits, weaknesses, and continuing challenges of a distributed Web management structure.

Background: About New York State and Its Government

New York is the third most populous state in the U.S. with about 19 million people in 2000, making it one of the biggest potential markets in the nation for e-government services. Compared to residents of other states, New Yorkers are generally well-educated and relatively affluent. The state's population has a high proportion of computer owners and Internet users. At the same time, New York State government is a large and diverse enterprise that offers a wide variety of public information and services. This combination of factors suggests New York is an ideal location for comprehensive citizen-oriented Web services. However, despite a long history of IT applications in individual agencies that support government programs, New York is a latecomer to *state-wide* IT policy and management, including state-wide e-government. It was the last major state to create a central IT agency following decades of almost complete decentralization of IT functions and services.

From the inception of state government computing in the 1950s through the early 1990s, New York's information technology policies, systems, and staff were almost entirely de-centralized among scores of state agencies. Spending oversight was exercised by the Division of Budget for major new systems or hardware acquisitions, and the Office of General Services held most of the state's telecommunications contracts and operated a data center that served some of the small- and medium-sized agencies. But, beyond these two aspects, individual state agencies had substantial autonomy with respect to how they chose and deployed information technology, how they designed and implemented systems, and how they staffed these functions.

The mid-1990s brought two major developments that led to dramatic changes in the way New York State government used and managed IT. First was the election of Governor George Pataki whose policy agenda emphasized making state government smaller, more efficient, "business-like", and "business-friendly". These policies led to the creation of organizations and activities that had significant influence over the future direction of IT management. The second development was the emergence of the World Wide Web with its promise of convenient public access to government information and services "anywhere, anytime". State agencies embraced the Web as one way to streamline government operations as well as a means of increasing access to information and services.

Setting the Stage

When Governor Pataki took office in 1994, he began an evaluation process designed to bring the far-flung array of state IT assets under more standardized and centralized control. Among his early actions was a decision to consolidate more than three dozen agency-based data centers. Inevitably, this effort generated considerable concern on the part of the operating agencies and raised questions that went far beyond the data centers themselves to the heart of the relationship between decentralized agency operations and central coordination and control. These concerns included:

- What role will agencies play in planning, implementing, and evaluating the effort?
- On what basis will consolidation be designed?
- Which agencies will be affected and when?

- What functions will be consolidated? What ones will remain with the agencies?
- Who will manage the implementation process?
- Who will manage data center operations?
- What will agencies have to pay for and where will the money come from?
- What benefits can agencies expect?
- How will jobs be affected?

A consultant report led to a series of legislative hearings on this topic, with much concern about the proposed location of the center away from the state capital, and the impact consolidation would have on agency missions and the state IT workforce. Eventually, the plan was put in abeyance while a Task Force on Information Resource Management was created within the Governor's Office to bring about more gradual change in IT management. The task force drew its 30 staffers from the agencies themselves and adopted an ambitious change agenda in which the agencies were invited, and expected, to participate. A number of inter-agency committees and special projects were launched to begin to map out preferred technology standards, coordinate geographic information systems, and adopt state-wide IT policies. Policies were adopted on such topics as inter-agency data sharing, use of Social Security Numbers, appointment of agency security officers, relationships with local governments, and other topics (State of New York, Office for Technology, n.d.).

In 1997, the task force became formalized in state law as the NYS Office for Technology (OFT) (State Technology Law, L.1997, c. 430, § 28), making New York the last major state to create such an organization. The statement of Legislative Intent notes:

"It is important that New York state create a distinct office for technology to strategically manage its technological resources such that the planning and development of such resources occur on a statewide basis, in accordance with the business needs of the state and in a manner which positions the state for the future... It must foster the appropriate public access to useful information and promote the full protection of the rights of citizens. It must harness the economic benefit of emerging technologies in a cost effective manner, standardize practices to foster efficiency, facilitate the exchange of information within and among agencies, and seek to address the needs of businesses and local governments as well as state agencies. Finally, the management of New York state's technological resources must occur collaboratively and in conjunction with state and local government agencies..."

Thus, OFT was born and has continued to grow and take on new responsibilities. Its initial focus was limited to coordination and policy making. During 1998-99, OFT took on responsibility for orchestrating the state's preparations for the Year 2000 date change (Y2K). This successful effort was an early exercise in communication and coordination among all state agencies under the central leadership of OFT. Data center consolidation proceeded as well, but at a fairly slow pace and with a high degree of agency participation. Eventually, OFT's scope of responsibilities expanded to include operation of the consolidated data center, the state-wide telecommunications network, and other operational functions such as development of a state-wide Financial Management System. By 2005, OFT had grown to more than 600 employees with a budget of about $250 million, both figures about three times the national average (NASCIO, 2002).

In January, 2002, five years after the creation of OFT, Governor Pataki signed Executive Order 117, establishing the position of chief information officer (CIO) of New York State to oversee, direct, and coordinate "the establishment of information technology policies, protocols and standards for State government, including hardware, software, security and business re-engineering; [as well as] overseeing and coordinating the development, acquisition, deployment and management of information technology resources for State government."

Organizationally, OFT reports to the CIO. Accordingly, although infrastructure, computing, and networking are the primary areas in which OFT interacts with other state agencies, it also has continuing responsibilities in the development of IT policies for the state. OFT and the Office of the CIO work together in establishing state-wide policies and the overall IT strategy for the state, working with the assistance of a state-wide CIO Council representing the agencies and local governments.

Similar to other states, New York's legislature has the power to mandate the provision of certain information or services online. It also has the ability to impose requirements about privacy, security, accessibility, usability, and other topics. However, the involvement of the legislature in technology concerns is actually quite low. While some specific legislation has been passed such as the Electronic Signatures and Records Act of 1999, and the Internet Security and Privacy Act of 2002, neither house of the legislature has a specific committee for IT oversight and no individual members have taken on IT management as a particular area of interest. In contrast to most other states, New York's IT initiatives have been almost exclusively conceptualized and supported by the executive branch.

Nevertheless, a handful of state and federal laws shape the way New York uses new technology. The Electronic Signatures and Records Act (ESRA) gives legal status to most electronic documents and authorizes the use of electronic signatures for many binding business transactions. However, ESRA also requires that any information that a state agency puts in electronic format must still be available in a paper form. For example, the state government telephone directory is available on the Web, but printed copies must also be prepared—the number of printed copies can be greatly reduced, but not totally eliminated. OFT organized and carried out an extensive public-private consultation process to develop the regulations and guidelines for ESRA implementation.

The Internet Security and Privacy Act requires that every state agency Web site presents its privacy policy. For instance, an agency must say what personal information is collected and if and how it will be disclosed. Agencies that collect personal information from citizens such as the Departments of Health, Motor Vehicles, or Tax and Finance have to be especially careful in observing privacy requirements. There are also some specific security requirements for agencies in certain public domains such as criminal justice and law enforcement. For all agencies, the law requires that if a personal record of an individual is disclosed, that person must be notified. To comply with the law, OFT created a model policy which many agencies adopted voluntarily rather than create their own.

At the federal level, two laws have had a strong influence on the way the state uses information and technology. The Health Information Portability and Accountability Act (HIPAA) has a pervasive impact on information and services provided through the Web. It includes provisions about security and privacy for health-related information. The Department of

Health and several other state agencies collect and maintain this type of information. OFT, through its data centers, hosts much of this information and therefore needs to be knowledgeable about HIPAA's requirements and deadlines.

Finally, New York State accessibility standards were developed considering Section 508 of the federal Rehabilitation Act. While Section 508 does not apply directly to states, a committee of state agency IT professionals in New York developed and recommended an accessibility policy and supporting practices using 508 as a guide, and OFT adopted these recommendations as a formal policy for all state agencies.

Case Description

In June 2000, as a result of the governor's initiative called "Government without Walls", the Office for Technology began working in conjunction with the Governor's Office to develop an integrated and consistent state-wide Web presence. However, by the time OFT began this work, most agencies already had Web sites, some of them quite extensive. All of them contained information about the agency and its program, and some offered online services. In all, there were already more than 170 services and transactions online. In addition, each agency made its own decisions about priorities, content, and format.

Because so many agency Web sites and services already existed, OFT did not attempt to create one comprehensive Web site for state government, but rather initiated an effort to create a main page or state portal from which people could have access to information and services provided by individual agencies. This distributed approach was a realistic one, given the situation, but it brought with it some important challenges. These included a lack of dedicated central funding, decentralized decision making about content and priorities, inconsistent technical skills and infrastructures among the agencies, and no single authoritative source of leadership.

As a practical matter, the project began with a review of all the services that the individual state agencies offered and the development of a strategy to move them online. One of the e-government project managers observed, "we were already up the first rung of the ladder of informational websites. We [now] needed to move towards integrated, coordinated, seamless, knock-down-the-walls of the government's bureaucracy of agencies and deliver services and transactions and eventually integration and customization."

Although competition among the states was beginning to emerge thanks to academic and commercial studies that ranked the quality of state e-government efforts, New York declined to make big promises. "We did not set any dates," said one OFT manager. "At the time the federal government and some states were saying 'we will have all critical (whatever that means) services, or 200 services, or whatever, available on line by such-and-such a date.' We didn't do that. What we did was we used the agencies and it was always a collaborative approach with the sixty-plus state agencies and with their executive management. We identified as a unit, all together, what were the state's priority services and transactions."

According to an OFT executive, the effort started by "creating an inventory of what services and applications were out there ... identifying for those things that are not on line, are there any plans to do so? What would it take to move them online? So that was all part of a discovery process that led into creation of what was called the 'top 75' … prioritized applications that exist in state government and identifying and tracking over time how those applications were being moved online. As some would be moved, then others that were in the queue would be moved up to the top 75." Some observers thought this process did not yield a set of truly state-wide priorities, but rather was a laundry list of agency-level priorities already in progress. Nevertheless, agencies appointed e-government coordinators to oversee these efforts and progress toward bringing those priority areas online was tracked and reported quarterly.

In addition, there was an effort to create the NYS portal and to work with all the agencies to establish a process to manage links to their Web sites and to keep information up-to-date over time. An additional goal was to reduce the "stove pipes" image, at least on the Web. As the first step in this effort, OFT held a contest for a common state-wide banner that would appear at the top of the Web sites of all state agencies. The winning entry was created by a staffer at the Department of Motor Vehicles. The interactive banner contained links to the governor's home page, a list of citizen services, and a list of business services. Another button provided access to a functional state-wide map. Adopted in September 2000, the banner was the first effort to coordinate the look and feel of agency Web sites without affecting their content or operation.

Use of the uniform banner was required as part of an effort to create a brand for NY and a recognizable image for the Web site. The banner is functional and users can click on

Figure 1. Agency home page using the New York State banner

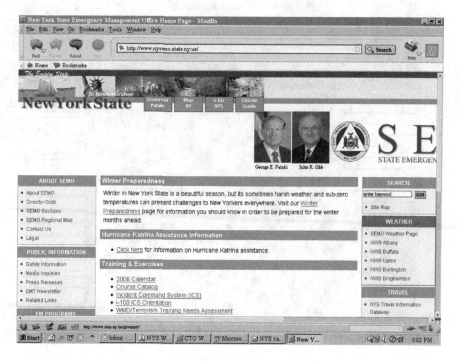

its picture and four buttons and go to different sections of the state portal (Figure 1). Of course, not everyone was excited by this idea. Most agencies had already invested a great deal of time and effort in designing their own Web sites. One agency Webmaster said, "I thought chairs were going to be thrown" at the meeting where the banner was announced. "I mean, people get very vested in their design." Nevertheless, the banner solved an important problem—giving authenticity to state government Web pages. OFT wanted people coming to state Web sites to be certain they had reached an official page. The banner "was like a trademark, a branding of it … so you know you're on an official website."

While some agencies objected to the banner, others agreed it was a good idea. One CIO observed that, "Using the state banner is a positive thing" for citizens, who should not have to figure out how government is organized. "I [also] think the state portal concept is a good one… it's a good idea to separate out the state portal and then allow the agencies to go out and develop their own websites based on their needs. Obviously, the needs of a tourism agency are going to be different from the needs of a revenue agency or a health department."

Evolution of the New York State Web Site

According to an OFT leader, the mission of New York State Web site (see Figure 2) is "to enable end-users, which in this case would be the citizens of the state, to be able to get to the

Figure 2. New York State Web portal

information they need as quickly and easily as possible." Another OFT manager described the mission as "to provide an easy to use … alternative for folks to conduct their business, to live and work, and … grow businesses in New York State. To bring people to New York State, to help them find government rules and regulations and licensing and all those things, and … find their way through the maze, and do it easily."

The state-wide portal was unveiled in March 2001. Before that date, New York's "home page" was not much more than an alphabetical list of the state agencies. If visitors knew which agency they needed, they could click on the agency name and go to its Web site. Everyone agreed that this was not even minimally acceptable in terms of usefulness or usability, and it certainly did not project the image of a state in touch with its citizens or on the leading edge of technology.

In designing the more functional portal, various attempts were made to get citizens' opinions and expectations about the initial design of the Web site. Regional meetings were held with citizens, but they were not well-attended. To compensate, OFT staff held focus groups among its employees, conducted surveys, and tried to get feedback during the annual Government Technology Conference, where OFT had an information booth.

At one point, an inter-agency group was charged with the responsibility of laying out the state-wide Web site design using a "life events" framework. Some found this quite appealing as a way to organize a citizen's access to government. One participant described how such a framework "organizes things around life events like weddings or deaths, sending a child to college, getting your driver's license, paying your taxes."

However, the life events strategy was later discarded in favor of a simpler approach that used topical categories to help citizens, businesses, and other potential audiences navigate through the New York State government. This topical approach required much less integration and was judged to be more amenable to the fact that so many agency Web sites were already in place.

In addition, New York adopted some guidelines about how agency Web sites should be structured, but, except for the banner, they are flexible and not mandatory. According to an OFT leader, this approach is only partially successful because it works like a federation in which each agency can make most of the decisions regarding its own Web site. As a result, "there is great heterogeneity. So that translates into lots of different ways [to manage the Web site] … that first page layer of an [agency] website has a common footer and format across the state. And great liberties are taken on that because there isn't one place that's designing all of it. Each agency gets to feel almost a compulsion to put their artistic sense into the design of the look and feel."

The launch of the portal in 2001 was supposed to be phase 1 of the e-government effort. Phase 2 was planned to be a more integrated and customizable Web portal. The effect of the 9/11 terrorist attacks took a heavy toll on this ambition. An OFT staffer noted, "… we knew there was $50 million in the governor's 2001 budget, $25 million for infrastructure, $25 million for application development for services or transactions that would be spread out to the agencies with the infrastructure being built centrally here at OFT. After 9/11, none of that money passed—there was nothing for new initiatives and there hasn't been since."

Services and Audiences

The NYS portal is organized in five main sections: (1) Governor Pataki, (2) map-NY, (3) e-bizNYS, (4) Citizen Guide, and (5) a search function. In most pages within the portal, there is also an option for citizens to send feedback or ask specific questions using an online form that goes to OFT staffers for answers. Through this option, citizens ask questions about where to find specific information or services. However, these questions also provide ideas for improvements. For example, if there are many questions about a particular topic, OFT tries to make that section of the portal more clear or to add more information.

In addition to the five main sections, the portal presents categories such as "Health Care" and "Doing Business" at the left hand side of the screen. The purpose of these categories is to provide initial guidance to visitors. Agencies decide in which categories each of their links should appear. By design, these categories are not mutually exclusive. Because people search for information in different ways, some links can be found in two or more categories. Each category contains links to specific information and services in the respective agency Web sites. Most of these links go directly to specific applications or forms (e.g., a driver license renewal). The objective of this design is to get to the information or service a person is interested using the fewest possible number of "clicks". The portal is therefore a categorizing and indexing tool that links to specific information and services maintained outside the portal.

Thus the entire NYS Web site includes pages developed by many different agencies within the executive branch. The Assembly and the Senate have their own pages, and these pages are also linked to the state portal. Most of the online services are provided at the agency Web sites. From these Web sites, people can conduct electronic transactions such as filing taxes, renewing a vehicle registration, or making a reservation for a state park. Some services can be paid using a credit card or other electronic payment. Many downloadable government forms are available as PDF files, but due to accessibility issues, they are also usually available in other formats (e.g., HTML).

Web Site Management

The New York State Web site is managed by a combination of outsourcing and in-house development (see Figure 3). The front page and the governor's pages are managed by the Governor's Office through outsourcing (with the exception of the most static links such as the New York State Constitution). The formal contractual relationship is between the vendor and the Governor's Office. However, OFT has a working relationship with the vendor, which consists mainly of coordination efforts in relation to the design and content of the Web site, including making sure that standards are followed.

Most of the other Web pages, including online transactions, are developed and managed directly by state agencies. In fact, no services are provided directly through the portal as the portal has not been designed to do so (e.g., it lacks the necessary security). OFT manages the portal categories and the major sections that link to other agencies (map-New York, e-business, and citizen's guide). Similar to other state agencies, OFT also has its own Web site.

Figure 3. Web site management overview

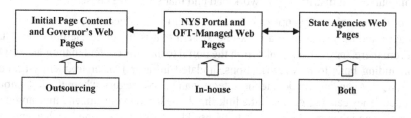

The portal was developed by OFT as an index and database in ColdFusion, a software developed by Macromedia. It has a search engine that can look for information within the portal database, but cannot search for information and services at the agency Web sites. That is, if the information is contained in the links that agencies include in the portal database, then it can be found with the search engine. By contrast, if the information is at an agency Web site, but has not been added as a link to the portal database, the search engine cannot find it.

Part of the NYS Web site is hosted by private vendors, and part of the Web site is hosted by OFT. Most agency Web sites are hosted internally, and most of the content is updated by the respective agencies. Web site hosting and content management are not centralized, and agencies can make their own decisions about which strategy to follow (in-house, outsourcing, or a combination). According to one OFT manager, there are relatively few instances of agencies outsourcing the hosting of their Web sites.

The Office for Technology (OFT) plays the role of overall Web administrator and works in conjunction with the Governor's Office, which is the content owner of part of the initial page and the governor's pages. OFT is responsible for uploading and keeping current information in several pages of the portal as well as in its own Web site.

At OFT, two units have direct responsibilities for the Web site. One is responsible for the content and acts as the liaison between OFT and other agencies in the state government. This coordination takes place through the e-commerce/e-government coordinators in each state agency. The other unit at OFT is responsible for application development. This includes some state-wide applications, applications developed for small agencies, and internal applications for OFT operations.

The distributed management approach has allowed OFT to operate with a very limited staff for Web site design and maintenance. During the development stage, four people were coordinating content, three or four programmers were working full-time, and there was support from the networking unit in terms of managing bandwidth and potential Web site traffic. According to several estimates, the total staff time currently devoted to the NYS Web site at OFT is probably no more than the equivalent of one full-time employee. However, at least one person is responsible for the Web site at every state agency. This person can be the CIO, the Webmaster, or the public information officer, among others.

This distributed approach has both pros and cons. For OFT, it entails "coordination across 60-some agencies and making sure that they all are good at managing their links, keeping them up to date, not letting them go bad, adding new ones ... some are very good, some are very bad and it's kind of staying on top of it. But the advantage of distributed [management], of course, is it distributes the workload and that's why we chose it."

For the agencies, this approach requires them to introduce their own content to their Web pages and then to go into a back-end system that is linked to the portal and its database. From there, they can add links from the portal to the new content in their agency Web pages, including links to new transactions, updated information, or frequently-asked questions (FAQs). Agencies can decide the category and sub-category where the link should be classified. They can also decide if the link should be listed in the citizen guide and/or e-business section and they enter keywords to be used by the search engine. Each agency has its own processes and rules about who can write and edit links at the agency level. Each agency has "a publisher", who many times is the Public Information Officer. The publisher approves either new information or modifications to the existing content. Finally, the information is published overnight when the New York State Web site is updated. For instance, for a new Motor Vehicle transaction, "they enter the link and the key words; how people should find it from the state portal to connect to that. And so then it appears as a new Motor Vehicle transaction. They'll go in and put it under the transportation, vehicle category. They might put it under e-business in terms of a transaction. It could [also] go on Map New York if there's a geographic component to it …".

OFT and other state agencies can run reports to identify broken links and other problems, and the results are sometimes discussed among the agencies involved in order to fix the problems. Agencies can also see how much traffic they are getting from the portal. They work with OFT in solving the problems encountered. In addition, some multi-agency groups have helped to solve specific problems such as categories with too many links. One of these joint efforts culminated in the creation of the small business portal, which is a portal-within-a-portal to help people to start new small businesses. This portal follows a logic similar to some initiatives at the federal level that attempt to identify and coordinate "lines of business" among agencies performing similar functions or serving similar constituencies, with the purpose of sharing resources. However, it does not integrate information or services behind the scenes. Rather it presents links to various independent services organized in a logical way.

Benefits of the NYS Web Site

The New York State Web site offers alternative ways for citizens and businesses to interact with the state. A great deal of information and many services are available through the Web site 24 hours a day, 7 days a week. One person summarized the benefits succinctly: "I mean, 262 services and transactions were online a year ago. Well, there's 262 benefits right there."

This represents an increase in convenience for citizens, businesses, and other stakeholders. People can get information more easily and they can find very diverse information and services in one place. For example, senior citizens and students can find government programs through the Web. Similarly, a person can get information and make reservations for state parks, apply for an EasyPass for paying tolls on the New York State Thruway, or they can file their taxes electronically.

Businesses can conduct business with the state electronically. For them, the Web site represents an opportunity to get through some of the necessary "red tape" and perform transactions conveniently. At the same time, the Web site has the potential to promote economic development for the state by providing easy access to business opportunities such as state government contracts for vendors. For example, "if a business wants to do business with the state ... in the past they would send in a letter to get on the bidders list and it might take 60 days to get on the bidders list ... today you can do that with the Office of General Services by going online, identifying the products or services that your company provides and then you are on automatically ... that day you can bid for any relevant bids that may be going out...".

Unlike citizens or businesses which usually want one-time transactions, local governments are more interested in having online applications that help them with their daily relationships with the state and their respective work processes. A few applications have been developed to help local officials do their jobs. These are secure operations restricted to specific users such as tax assessors. This area has received much less attention, but slowly, more applications like these are developing.

State government also benefits from the Web site in terms of effectiveness and citizen satisfaction, as well as some efficiencies. However, cost savings are not comparable to Web services in the private sector because, among other restrictions, government cannot go totally online and still serve everyone it needs to serve. Other benefits for state agencies include the ability to communicate with their constituencies in a more effective way. As an OFT staffer noted, "I think all agencies realize that the use of their websites is a very significant communications media for them." Government Web sites cannot only communicate administrative information and provide electronic services, they also have the potential to help government in communicating a more integrated and consistent image to citizens, businesses, and other stakeholders.

As of 2005, the format and design of the state Web site had undergone some minor changes, but the supporting database and overall framework remained basically the same as the portal that was launched in 2001. However, the number of services increased every year and by the end of 2004, there were 295 services and transactions available through the Web site, not including static information (State of New York, Office for Technology, 2004).

Current Challenges

In managing the current Web site and preparing for the future, New York State is facing several challenges. Some clearly stem from the state's distributed Web management approach, others are more general issues associated with many government IT applications.

Challenges of the Distributed Web Management Approach

The distributed approach has considerable coordination challenges. For instance, keeping information current in the whole Web site is a widely-distributed responsibility and not every agency performs it well. "There are a couple of agencies that just aren't updating and it's just old information. The technology's not the problem. Getting people to just update their sites and keeping it fresh is really the [challenge]." One agency Webmaster agreed, observing, "I think there are a lot of agencies that don't have ways of keeping their site current. You'll go out and find a lot of sites where the information was posted once and never touched again. We're very careful to avoid that, I mean, our PIO will go home and spend three hours a night looking at the website and tell you if something's out of date. But there's [usually] a disconnect between program people, Web people, and IT people." And the bigger the agency, the bigger this problem becomes as geographically-dispersed operations, vendors, and committees, as well as multiple organizational layers and units become involved.

For New York State, the Web site is the image of the state government and many agencies work hard to provide relevant and current information, as well as transactional services. However, not all agencies have the same capabilities and organizational priorities. Therefore, their level of engagement and compliance with state-wide policies and objectives varies tremendously. A manager at OFT noted that the biggest challenge is "staying in synch and coordinating with the governor's office and different [agencies], because you are all different organizations and priorities sometimes differ ... The [state] CIO's office goes a long way to help clarify the state's technology priorities and the governor's but each agency still manages its own budget. So if you're managing your own money separately, you're going to have your own priorities."

Another important challenge is to make more information and transactions available on the Web. This is especially difficult when no new funding has been available for several years. As budget and workload demands increase, some look to the state Web site as a potential way to improve efficiency. Similar to the private sector, agencies seek online alternatives that can help them save money and provide better services. When they can be made, cost-savings justifications are important because e-government initiatives compete for resources with other priorities such as education, health, and public safety.

However, as a CIO of a large agency pointed out, budgetary restrictions also negatively affect the ability to make things available through the Web. "Since you have basic services you have to provide, I think with reductions in budgets, the push toward the Web has been reduced. You have to be able to balance your use of the Web with all of the other services you're trying to provide as an agency." Another manager observed, "I think that [the state] needs to commit resources and not just human resources. They need to commit dollars to this. They need to say that this is important and they need to show that this is important by committing funding—and if they don't fund it, you get what you pay for."

Offering services through multiple channels presents additional financial and operational pressures. Even if state government has certain services online, it is also required to provide paper-based and walk-in service. Therefore, while the state can reduce access to these other channels when it has a Web-based version, it still has to offer these low-tech alternatives.

Security and confidentiality are also challenges for the New York State Web site. The Web site is the public image of the state and can potentially help government to interact with citizens, businesses, and other stakeholders. As an OFT leader explained, "It's the governor's face; it's the governor's picture; it's the governor's addresses and words and documents. And insuring that that stuff cannot be altered in any way or accessed and changed in any way, is a huge challenge for us." In addition, many agencies keep and manage citizens' personal information. Developing policies and procedures which balance access and confidentiality is not easy. The CIO of a large agency said, "… the biggest thing from our perspective is the confidentiality of information. We can't put everything out there." A number of agency CIOs say that until there are widely accepted and reliable identity and user authentication mechanisms, the number of transactions they can offer the public is unlikely to grow.

Content ownership and management also present problems. One manager observed, "The first [challenge] is ownership and what I mean by that is who owns what? Who owns the content, who owns the update of the content and the management of the content? So how is that all kind of managed, because what I've found, not only in state but in [other organizations], nobody really wants to own anything or they want to own everything, so there's no real clear delineation between the ownership of the items at hand." Moreover, many organizations struggle with finding the "right" organizational location for Web leadership. In some, the IT shop plays that role, in others the public information office or the Commissioner's Office. Content may be managed in a highly-decentralized way within agencies or it could go through a strict (and highly-controlled) vetting process.

Usability and accessibility present ongoing obligations. A state Web site is designed for the general public. Different users have different skills and capabilities as well as different needs and interests. Given New York's status as a major gateway for immigrants, this challenge also includes providing information and services in multiple languages. As an OFT leader observed, the biggest challenge for New York State is to create a Web site that can be easily used by the majority of people: "It's very difficult to develop a website that can be easily accessed by 95% of the people 'cause everybody's trying to do it differently; everybody thinks differently. I think that's the challenge for us now. How do we build something that can be used by everyone easily."

Skills and Staffing Challenges

Due to the independent development of agency Web sites during the first years of Web use, New York State agencies do not have standard skills or infrastructure. A Webmaster said, "[the state] was late in coming and as a result … many agencies had gone forward … however they could do it and it's particular to their agency […] And because it was implemented in different ways in different agencies with different personnel, there's no common skill base; there's no common training, and it's totally ignored in the title structures that Civil Service comes up with."

This lack of standardization in the workforce skill set has resulted in some important limitations. An OFT leader recognized that skills are hardly transferable at this point "…because the roles and responsibilities of each …of the job categorizations are so open and so variable. It's that whole issue of moving from Agency A to Agency B. You may not have the same skill sets, because Agency A did this and Agency B did that. So one of the things the [state] CIO is trying to work on is, are there specific job skills and qualifications that we want to standardize at each of these levels so that it would allow people to move from agency to agency much easier."

Specialized training for Web site design is still a challenge. Web site development requires certain skills such as programming in basic HTML or developing transactional applications in Java, or familiarity with accessibility tools. Such skills are not always readily available. While some staff are trained in proprietary packages, such as Oracle portal, or authoring tools like Dreamweaver, much less attention is given to training people in the underlying principles of Web technologies.

Civil service rules about hiring and promoting strongly affect the ability of state agencies to hire and retain IT employees. First, they influence the hiring process because employees generally have to start at the entry level and it is very difficult to hire people at higher levels with certain technical skills. For instance, one manager complained that,

"It's very difficult for us to be competitive when we hire. Right now, the kids coming out of school, they don't want to work in state government 'cause we pay probably half or a quarter of what they can get in private industry. And I don't blame them. So they go somewhere else and we cannot be competitive in our starting salaries."

In addition, civil service rules have an impact on retention because sometimes very good employees are not very good at taking tests or at managing others. However, promotion is usually based on management skills and specific tests. An OFT leader explained how "the inability to be flexible in the area where people who aren't good at taking tests but do a wonderful job on a day to day basis, can't really be moved forward because the test is the thing that keeps them from progressing."

The Challenge of National Rankings

Finally, comes the influence of national rankings of state Web sites. Like their counterparts all over the country, OFT leaders and managers closely monitor national rankings that report the quality or functionality of state Web sites. In recent years, several groups of researchers, associations, and private companies have developed these very public report cards on e-government in the states (Council of State Governments, 2002; Gant, Gant, & Johnson, 2002; Lassman, 2002; NASCIO, 2002; West, 2001). Some of the methodologies evaluate the whole state Web site, others mainly assess the state portal, and a third group attempts to assess each state's overall e-government strategy. Despite their differences, states tend to view them all as overall yardsticks of their e-government performance. An OFT manager observed,

"Whichever [ranking] you looked at, whether it was the Brown or the Digital Government one or whatever, New York State was slipping ... if you look at the states and their various websites and portals ...you have to keep changing; you have to stay up there; you have to stay fresh; you have to add content; you have to add transactions; you have to add better ways to access the data, better search engines, more languages. And if you don't, you're not keeping up, and it's a poor reflection on the state."

New York State, in fact, shows inconsistent results in the rankings. In "State and Federal E-Government in the United States" developed annually by Darrell West at Brown University (2000-05), New York has been among the top 15 states in e-government functionality in the last six years (2000=2nd; 2001=7th; 2002=11th; 2003=8th; 2004=4th; 2005=14th). However, it dropped from a high of 2nd in 2000 to a low of 14th in 2004. In the Center for Digital Government rankings, New York's position has been only middling, ranging between the 16th and the 33rd place (1997=24th; 1998=33rd; 1999-2000=32nd; 2001=16th; 2002=21st; 2004=Not Available. Only top-25 states were reported; New York was not one of them). However, even in this ranking, New York State was recognized with a Sustained Leadership Award, which "recognizes states that have made the most progress in digital government as measured in the first five years of the Digital State Survey from 1997 through 2002."

Rankings are problematic for all states because, regardless of their accuracy, they are the most public and most politically visible measures of performance. Rising higher is cause for celebration, stories in the press, and wide public attention. Low scores, or worse, declining ones, bring both internal and external criticism, not the least of which comes from the governors themselves. Each year, New York tries to learn from the examples of higher ranking states and to do what it can to improve the state's scores the next time around.

References

Council of State Governments. (2002). *The book of the states* (2002 ed., vol. 34). Lexington, KY: The Council of State Governments.

Gant, D. B., Gant, J. P., & Johnson, C. L. (2002). *State Web portals: Delivering and financing e-service*. E-Government Series. Arlington, VA: The PricewaterhouseCoopers Endowment for The Business in Government.

Lassman, K. (2002). *The digital state 2001*. Washington, DC: The Progress & Freedom Foundation.

NASCIO. (National Association of State Chief Information Officers). (2002). *NASCIO 2002 compendium of digital government in the states*. Lexington, KY.

State of New York. (1997). *State technology law*. Retrieved from http://www.oft.state.ny.us/OFTRulesRegs/OFT_Enabling_Legislation.htm

State of New York, Office for Technology. (n.d.). *NYS information technology policies, standards & best practice guidelines* [Web page]. Albany, NY. Retrieved from www.irm.state.ny.us/policy/index.html

State of New York, Office for Technology.(2004). *Statewide plan for implementing e-commerce/e-government in NYS. "A government without walls"*. June 2004 Update. Albany, NY. Retrieved from http://www.oft.state.ny.us/archive/ecommerce/the_plan.htm

State of New York, Office of the Governor. (2002). *Executive order 117*. Albany, NY: Governor's Office of Regulatory Reform. Retrieved from www.gorr.state.ny.us/gorr/EO117_fulltext.htm

West, D. M. (2001). *State and federal e-government in the United States, 2001*. Providence, RI: Brown University.

West, D. M. (2002). *State and federal e-government in the United States, 2002*. Providence, RI: Brown University.

West, D. M. (2003). *State and federal e-government in the United States, 2003*. Providence, RI: Brown University.

West, D. M. (2004). *State and federal e-government in the United States, 2004*. Providence, RI: Brown University.

West, D. M. (2005). *State and federal e-government in the United States, 2005*. Providence, RI: Brown University.

Authors' Biographies

J. Ramon Gil-Garcia is a post-doctoral fellow at the Center for Technology in Government and is also on the faculty of the Rockefeller College of Public Affairs and Policy at the University at Albany, State University of New York. Dr. Gil-Garcia is the author or co-author of articles in various journals including The International Public Management Journal, Government Information Quarterly, European Journal of Information Systems, Journal of Government Information, and Public Finance and Management. His research interests include electronic government, inter-organizational information systems, quantitative and multi-method research approaches, information technology in organizations, and public management.

Sharon S. Dawes is the director of the Center for Technology in Government (CTG) and associate professor of public administration and policy at the University at Albany/SUNY. Her main research interests are cross-boundary information sharing and collaboration and government information strategy and management. Most of this work has been supported by the National Science Foundation, U.S. Department of Justice, Library of Congress, and State of New York. A fellow of the National Academy of Public Administration, she holds a PhD in public administration from the Rockefeller College of Public Affairs and Policy at the University at Albany.

Chapter XVII

Bureau of Housing Services (BHS)

Luis Felipe Luna-Reyes, Universidad de las Américas-Puebla, México

Theresa A. Pardo, Center for Technology in Government, University at Albany, New York, USA

Felipe Burgos Ochoátegui, Universidad de las Américas-Puebla, México

Rocío Moreno Sanabria, Universidad de las Américas-Puebla, México

Executive Summary

One of the main problems of information systems development in multi-agency, inter-organizational projects is sustaining willingness to participate across many different and differently organized entities with multiple, and in some cases, mutually exclusive operating assumptions. This case describes such an environment. The New York State Bureau of Housing Services faces the dilemma of using its authority to compel homeless service providers to share information needed to develop a new information system versus seeking providers' support to develop the system through collaboration.

Introduction

We were driving back from New York City (NYC) to Albany, and as always, we were taking advantage of the ride to debrief from the morning's presentation. We were coming back from a presentation about the Homeless Information Management System (HIMS) to the New York City Homeless Providers Ad hoc Technology Committee. Unfortunately, this time the results were not very encouraging. Their skepticism was visible through their gestures and body language; "what's in it for us" was the question they wanted answered. The frank questions asked made by John,[1] a representative of Homeless Volunteers, kept repeating in the back of our heads.

I can understand why it is helpful for the state to do this project, but I find it hard to understand why it would be helpful for our individual organizations—What benefit is it for my group and others to participate? How will client-specific information be protected? Who will have access to the data once we turn it over to you, even the sample data you are requesting for the pilot stage? What happens to it at the next level and how will it be stored and utilized? Who will have access to what data? For what purposes will the data be used? Will resource allocation and funding decisions be based on the data? Will we be ranked, judged, or otherwise evaluated through use of these data?

Others in the committee were also concerned about how this system would benefit them and why should they participate. Only 5% of the homeless service providers in NYC were automated so committee members knew there would be costs to participation—"Who will bear the costs of the development, implementation, operation, and maintenance of the system? Will the confidentiality of our clients be violated? Will the same agreements that ensure confidentiality of data in traditional state systems be extended to this system?"

We needed "real" provider data to develop the HIMS prototype, so we had to find a way to obtain that data. Mary, one of the team members, thought we should not be so concerned about the providers' concerns given that our office funds all their programs, and in some sense we owned their data, and could require them to give us what we needed to develop the prototype. Charles, on the other hand, felt that if we were to include the providers in the development process to ensure that the system had value both to the state and to them then they might give their data more willingly. The status of regulations related to the providers' confidentiality and privacy concerns remained a concern—one that would need to be addressed if we were to move forward.

In short, we agreed—the committee had asked us for "a mission statement for the project and a statement from New York State specifying how any data provided by the homeless shelters to the Bureau of Housing Services (BHS) will be used, who will have access to it, and what protocols were being developed to monitor this use." At that point, we all turned to Rod—the Bureau Director and the final decision maker on this questions; would we use the authority of BHS to require submission of the client data necessary to build the prototype, or should we prepare the mission and confidentiality statement to answer providers' concerns as a first step in securing their voluntary participation and commitment to a collaborative effort?

Setting the Stage

New York State's involvement in the regulation of homeless shelters can be traced back to 1977. In that year, BHS assumed responsibility for the program. Among their activities, BHS staff wrote regulations and certified and audited shelters. By 1999, the shelters funded by BHS were providing emergency shelter and support services to nearly 29,000 homeless people per year (CTG, 2000). Overall, program costs were estimated to be $350 million in 1999, of which $130 million were spent on service programs. The programs offered through these shelters included a comprehensive services eligibility determination process, case management, and direct services and referrals. Programs associated with substance abuse and domestic violence were also provided through a series of partnerships with other state agencies such as the Office of Alcohol and Substance Abuse (OASAS), and the Division of Housing and Community Renewal (DHCR) (Sloma, 1999).

BHS shares responsibilities to oversee shelter and service programs with local authorities. In New York City, the oversight of these shelters is shared with the New York City Department of Homeless Services (DHS); outside New York City, county social services agencies play this role. A particular challenge to the program is the fact that 80% of the homeless population in New York State is concentrated in New York City, Westchester, and Suffolk Counties (Sloma, 1999).

Homeless services in New York State are offered by a complex array of providers. Shelter providers in New York City are divided into two categories. The first category serves families and children, and the second focuses on single adults (Powers, 2001). Some of these shelters are operated by the city, but the majority are not-for-profit organizations. Some of these are small facilities that provide services only to a few families or single adults, while others are major international organizations such as the Salvation Army or the American Red Cross. The diversity of size, mission, programs, and case management strategies among these organizations increased the challenge of creating sharing understanding about the value of sharing information through a common system.

The New York City Homeless Shelter Directors Ad Hoc Technology Committee was initially created as a coalition of providers to stop the implementation of NCHOR, a case-management system mandated by NYC DHS. "DHS adopted the position that compliance was part of the service provider's contractual obligation to the city, with no additional support or budget relief extended to provider agencies. This implementation methodology quickly resulted in front-line staff frustration and disillusionment, missing or inaccurate data, lost productivity, redundant processes (sometimes including entry of the same data on the same client into multiple "mandated" systems, as well as the provider's own manual or digital systems), and an overall decrease in resources available to client service delivery [..] Collapsing under its own weight, the implementation failed" (Radcliffe, 2003). The failure of the NCHOR system was also attributed to the fact that "those who participated in the pilot were dissatisfied with the off-the-shelf application. [...] The system, developed by a researcher who wanted all the data, including case notes, was not useable or useful for case workers who did not follow social worker logic and required multiple screens for data entry" (Powers, 2001, p. 115). This previous experience was closely linked with the providers' concerns about the implementation of the HIMS project.

BHS Information Problem

Staff of BHS spend about 50% of their daily activity responding to information requests about homeless programs (OTDA-BSS, 1997). The inquiries come from sources as varied as the Governor's Office, the legislature, the press, the agency commissioner, advocacy groups, and even school children. All of them are interested in various aspects of homeless programs. Although BHS has several electronic information resources, the information held in these systems was primarily administrative in nature. The best example of these systems was the Welfare Management System (WMS). Further, the systems themselves were different in design and purpose. Data held in them could only be used to answer questions such as—how many people did we shelter and feed. As the BHS staff liked to say—how many people got "three hots and a cot"?

Other important questions about the impact of homeless programs could not be answered because important data resided only in the heads of providers and others familiar with the programs and in paper-based quarterly reports submitted by shelters to BHS. For example, program managers and caseworkers believed that, through the services they provide, homeless people were becoming more self-sufficient, thus reducing public assistance costs. However, no program performance data existed to either support or challenge this belief. Program managers only had access to aggregated information used mainly for evidence of compliance and payment purposes. Assessments of the effectiveness of the services were anecdotal.

Knowledge about trends in outcome-based evaluation of government services, customer-focused marketing, and new technologies such as data warehousing and the World Wide Web led BHS staff to begin to consider how these new trends could help their efforts to understand more about the impact of their programs. They began to consider the feasibility of a system designed to support the evaluation of services and to assist in the identification of the best mix of services for any given population. Having a system with the information needed to answer questions about program outcomes would help them not only to reduce time needed to answer to specific questions, but also to improve their planning and decision-making processes. Such a system, however, would need to draw together information in new ways from a diversity of sources and formats; some of it even in paper form.

This new system also had the potential to serve as a tool to assess individual shelters and programs, affecting BHS funding decisions. Given previous experiences with other funding agencies, providers were aware of this potential use. Thus, they were concerned not only about the confidentiality of their clients, but also about future funding for their programs.

Building a Case for HIMS

At the end of 1997, BHS began working in partnership with the Center for Technology in Government (CTG) to examine the particular challenges government managers face when using information. The information challenge facing BHS was expressed as follows: "The impact of the programs and services and implemented over the past decade is unknown. Government agencies have not been willing to commit the funds and resources to determine whether service and residential programs are effective rather investments have focused on compliance and enforcement. It is unclear whether desired outcomes such as fostering self-sufficiency, reducing or preventing reoccurrence of homelessness, reducing dependence on public assistance, and improving overall life skills are realized. Government agencies need to develop a comprehensive evaluation system that is capable of assessing multiple factors which impact on homelessness of families and single adults. Although most of the necessary information on homelessness clients exists in paper records, a uniform database needs to be developed to allow matching against existing databases, such as employment and labor files, the Welfare Management System (WMS), the Medicaid Management Information System (MMIS), etc." BHS believed that an information resource could be developed to "assist in directing resources, funding and program revisions."

The BHS team was looking for answers to a series of questions related to the feasibility of the system such as, what are the main problems and costs associated with data cleansing and matching, and what is the perceived value of the system among the user community. BHS staff and staff from the Center for Technology in Government engaged in a series of workshops to conduct a feasibility analysis for the project. During this series of workshops, important stakeholders for HIMS were identified including local government partners. Current practices in homeless management systems were also identified. The workshops also involved the high-level design of interfaces for the prototype system. One workshop participant characterized the meetings as "guided sessions... they are all based on the same type of facilitation rather than group decision conferencing."[2] Through this work, the BHS staff developed a much better understanding about their information problem and some ways to tackle it.

Two very important workshops were held on October 19 and 20. During these meetings, CTG and BHS staff established the time-line and elicited initial data issues for the development of the prototype. The team planned to develop the HIMS prototype in 11 months, starting in November 1998 and finishing in September 1999. The first two months were for design; the next five, to the development itself; the next three to evaluation. The last month was for writing a final report. During these planning sessions, it became clear that a critical milestone in the development process was the acquisition of data from local partners.

The project team included two important groups; the BHS staff and the Audit & Quality Control (A&QC) group as those responsible for the WMS. Conversations in these workshops were oriented to developing mutual understanding about current information resources. In particular, what was already held by the state and how it was organized and used. As one of the members of the team commented:

A&QC knew the Welfare Management System... and the BHS staff knew the program side... and what we were doing was pulling information from both of them with the purpose of them understanding each other... A&QC knew WMS, Welfare Management System, but they didn't know what the data were used for. So those meetings were spent diving into topics such as what data are stored in the WMS, and then, BHS talking about how they use that data, why it is collected [..] So we spent a lot of time learning about their whole world, and they were learning each other's perspectives. (names of the actors removed)

During the October 20 meeting, the team explored possible data sources, mechanisms to collect data, and the assumptions underlying the data. Participants identified several sources of data besides WMS that could or should be included in the prototype development: HOMES (detailed information about NYC facilities), SCIMS (database containing single-adult services for NYC facilities), and FACTORS (case management system), the New York City Department of Homeless Services (DHS) database, payment claim systems, and of course, financial and case-management data from state-funded shelters.

All data sources belonged to different organizations, and most of them were necessary to be able to show the value of the system through the prototype. A member of the team commented that, "data would be integrated in the prototype so that users can assess the value of the data, identify associated data quality issues, and identify and build tools to support the use of the data [...] In short, the prototype would be designed to provide a 'little slice of reality'."

The discussion was organized around three main topics—costs, service evaluation, and outcomes. The team began to understand the costs of current information access and decision making practices. They began to frame the costs of future alternative strategies. The discussions also focused on developing a common set of outcome indicators. The team began to realize that a common set of outcome indicators would require some specification and adoption of data standards. Length of stay, dependency on public funds, recidivism, and utilization of services and impacts of the welfare reform were identified as system-wide high priority data elements and efforts were undertaken to see if standards could be established.

As a result of the workshops, Rod and his team had a shared understanding of their "service objective", as well as three parallel tracks of activity. The service objective of the team was "the development of a uniform database to provide management with the information needed to track homelessness and to more effectively manage the program" (OTDA-BSS, 1997). The three tracks of activity were generally understood to be the development of the HIMS prototype of a data warehouse system, the development of a prototype set of standard definitions and data elements, and the development of a prototype model for evaluating homeless services and measuring system effectiveness. The central part of the strategy was the prototype, conceived as a "proof of concept" or "saleable item", which also would be at the heart of system development as an iterative, evolutionary process.

To accomplish the tasks, it was becoming more and more clear that a fourth cross-cutting focus of effort involved securing the participation of those organizations in direct contact with clients and with the data necessary to drive HIMS. To secure this involvement, the BHS staff were making presentations about the HIMS concept in as many places as possible. They presented the project ideas to representatives of the NYC DHS, Suffolk County, and Westchester County Departments of Social Services, to Directors of Shelters for the Homeless, and to the NYC Human Resources Administration in the second half of 1998 and in January 1999. These organizations were owners of the main data sources needed to build the prototype.

As a result of these initial conversations, some government agencies were willing to share their data to build the prototype. In the case of homeless providers, the team identified an existing network called the New York City Homeless Shelter Directors. The network represented the interests of 60 member agencies providing services for families, children and single adults. A number of years earlier this group had formed an Ad hoc Technology

Committee. This committee appeared to be the natural point of contact with the provider community. The mission of the Ad hoc Technology Committee was to promote the use of information technology to track and improve service delivery. The committee also advocated for government policies that ensured providers' ability to improve their technological capabilities. Finally, as expressed in their mission, "through the promotion of shared resources and expertise among the members, we strive to allow them the opportunity to access the most efficient and reasonably priced products and services available." Some potential benefits of HIMS would be aligned to the main objectives of the committee. Having a shared information repository, for example, would be a valuable source for benchmarking and best practices identification.

The BHS staff met with the Ad hoc Technology Committee in January 1999. The reaction to the HIMS proposal was grounded in many experiences of that committee in particular the ANCHOR initiative and a previous attempt by NYC DHS to link funding decisions to program evaluations. Given their previous experiences, shelter providers were cautious about "help from the state" and unclear about how it might benefit them and their clients directly. They were also concerned about the potential of this system to harm their clients through breaches in confidentiality.

Current Challenges Facing the Organization

The project setting is a multi-government, inter-organizational one, involving state, county, and city regulatory agencies and the non-profit and local government homeless service providers that receive financial support from the state. The inclusion of provider data in the HIMS prototype was crucial to efforts to assess the costs and benefits of the services provided to the homeless population. The proposed system had substantial threat potential for two reasons: (1) the system could be used to provide oversight agencies with enhanced ability to control or even eliminate programs, and (2) new data capture, management, and use strategies raise a number of questions about client confidentiality.

Although Rod and his group—as a funding agency—had the right to require the necessary data be provided by shelter staff, the BHS team understood that the Ad hoc Technology Committee has successfully stopped the implementation of other proposals such as the case-management system—ANCHOR. Taking on this committee might be problematic.

Acknowledgments

The research reported here was supported by National Science Foundation Grant #SES-9979839. The views and conclusions expressed in this chapter are those of the authors alone and do not reflect the views or policies of the National Science Foundation.

The authors acknowledge the contribution of professors John Ickis, and Julio Sergio Ramírez from INCAE Business School for their advice for structuring the chapter as a teaching case.

References

CTG. (Center for Technology in Government). (2000). *Building trust before building a system: The making of the homeless information management system.* Retrieved June, 2002, from http://www.ctg.albany.edu/guides/usinginfo/Cases/printable_bss_case.htm

Milter, R. G., & Rohrbaugh, J. (1985). Microcomputers and strategic decision making. *Public Productivity Review, 9*(2-3), 175-189.

OTDA-BSS. (New York State Office of Temporary and Disability Assistance-Bureau of Shelter Services). (1997). *Proposal to the using information in government program.* Unpublished manuscript. Albany, NY.

Powers, J. (2001). *The formation of interorganizational relationships and the development of trust.* Unpublished dissertation. Albany, NY: University at Albany.

Radcliffe, L. (2003, January). *How should we deal with funder-mandated data collection in human services?* Retrieved from http://www.uwnyc.org/technews/v6_n3_a2.html

Sloma, R. (1999). *A managerial evaluation of homeless services: An interim report.* Working paper. Albany, NY: Center for Technology in Government.

Endnotes

[1]   The case is based upon a real project, but the names of all participants have been disguised.

[2]   Decision conferences are "computer-supported meetings in which several decision makers develop an explicit framework or structure for organizing their thinking about an important, non-routine policy or program choice" (Milter & Rohrbaugh, 1985, p. 183) making an explicit effort to combine the strengths of intuition and analysis enhanced by the presence of a facilitation team. UIG workshops followed the facilitation scheme of decision conferences, but the use of computers was limited to capturing thoughts and drawings from team conversations.

Authors' Biographies

Luis Felipe Luna-Reyes is a professor of business at the Universidad de las Américas in México. He holds a PhD in information science from the University at Albany. Luna-Reyes is also a member of the Mexican National Research System. His research focuses on electronic government and on modeling collaboration processes in the development of information technologies across functional and organizational boundaries.

Theresa A. Pardo is deputy director of the Center for Technology in Government at the University at Albany, SUNY. She is on the faculty of Public Administration and Policy and the Information Science Doctoral Program at the University. Her research in government information strategy and management focuses on information technology innovation in the public sector, strategic planning for information technology, electronic information access programs, and interorganizational information integration.

Felipe Burgos Ochoátegui is dean of the School of Business and Economics at the Universidad de las Américas in México. Dr. Burgos is currently a member of the Business Faculty at the Universidad de las Américas, and also a member of the graduate faculty of Texas Christian University in Fort Worth, Texas. His research interests are related to operations management, quantitative methods, and the effect of cultural factors on the implementation of quality processes.

Rocío Moreno Sanabria is a professor of business at the Universidad de las Américas Puebla in México. She is a PhD in business science from the University La Salle. Her research is in e-commerce, strategic planning for marketing, and service marketing.

Chapter XVIII

A Collaborative Communications Center and Public Safety Data Systems

Jerome A. Schulz, Independent Consultant, USA

Richard Tuma, Waukesha County Communications Center, Wisconsin, USA

Executive Summary

During 2004 Waukesha County, Wisconsin, implemented a collaborative 9-1-1 public safety communications center. This case study describes the implementation of the Waukesha County Communications Center (WCC) and illustrates the challenges involved when multiple governments collaborate on a project involving complex technology. The implementation of the new center provided an opportunity to move to advanced technology for all of the aspects of dispatch work. The project also provided an opportunity to implement an integrated criminal records system for all participating municipalities. The biggest difficulties the WCC faced in the implementation process were a delay of several months in the switchovers from the old centers due to addressing problems and also some difficulty in achieving response time on calls that was acceptable to the center's partners. By late 2005, the new center had a number of plans in place to address these and other issues that commonly face projects of this magnitude.

Background

About the Communications Center

The new Waukesha County Communications Center serves as the 9-1-1 public safety answering point (PSAP) and dispatch center for the County Sheriff, 28 of the county's 37 municipalities, and a number of fire departments and fire districts. The center also acts as the primary PSAP for all wireless calls within the county, and wireless calls found to be for other centers are in turn transferred to those centers with information previously not available to them. The county also provides radio services to most municipalities in the county with a 13 channel, 800MHz trunk radio system with seven receive/transmit locations.

About Waukesha County

Waukesha County includes 576 square miles of suburban and rural areas at the western edge of the Milwaukee metropolitan area. The 2004 population of the county was 377,193, making it the third largest county in the State of Wisconsin. An elected County Executive administers the operations of the county while a 35-member part-time County Board is elected by district and serves as the legislative branch. Six department heads are also directly elected: the Sheriff, Clerk of Courts, County Clerk, County Treasurer, District Attorney, and Register of Deeds.

The Adopted Operating plus Capital Budget for the county for 2006 was $251,215,355. The county has a variety of sources of revenue including property tax; the 2006 county property tax levy was $87,595,762.

All areas within the county are included within one of the county's 37 cities, villages, or towns. Each municipality develops its own budget independently of the county. Like the county, the municipalities have the authority to levy property taxes. Almost all municipalities have their own police forces, although five of the municipalities also contract with the County Sheriff for police patrol. The municipalities are also responsible for fire protection, which they provide though a combination of full-time and volunteer fire departments and also several shared fire districts.

Local Governments are Collaborating

Local governments are increasingly seeking to collaborate with each other as a way to improve service and reduce costs. Some areas in which local governments in Wisconsin have collaborated have been:

- Police services, such as the Sauk-Prairie Police Department, serving the villages of Sauk City and Prairie du Sac, Wisconsin;

- Fire services, including the many joint fire districts around the country; and
- Library services, such as the Hudson Area Joint Library, serving the City of Hudson, Village of North Hudson, and the Towns of Hudson and St. Joseph, Wisconsin.

One especially attractive area for collaboration is the operation of public safety communications centers. Local governments are increasingly moving to collaborative communications centers because the collaborative model can provide several major benefits:

- Higher quality service to the public through more comprehensive staffing, use of more sophisticated procedures and technology, and so forth;
- Reduced costs through economies of scale and the elimination of inefficient dispatch centers at smaller governments;
- Ability to adopt sophisticated yet expensive technology due to economies of scale;
- Freeing of smaller municipalities from the headache of having to seek and implement their own solutions;
- Easier sharing of ongoing activities and criminal records with neighboring municipalities;
- Greater ease in scheduling staff, especially for 24 by 7 coverage; and
- Increased ability to provide sufficient staff for disasters or serious incidents.

The Pursuit of More Sophisticated Technology is a Driver for Collaboration

Recent years have seen great advances in the technology available for public safety dispatch functions. This advanced technology offers the potential for improving service to the public, especially in the sometimes life and death situations involved in public safety dispatch work.

But the implementation of this technology can be very challenging, not to mention costly, for smaller communications centers. And so, being able to take advantage of more sophisticated technology through a shared communications center is a main driver for collaboration.

As shown in Figure 1, there are at least three major types of technology typically found in a modern communications center:

- Telephone systems for communication with the public, which ideally supports:
  - o   Enhanced 9-1-1 (E-9-1-1) capability for automated phone number identification (ANI) and automated location identification (ALI) of calls from landline and Voice over IP (VoIP) telephones.
  - o   Wireless E-9-1-1 capability to provide the caller's phone number and the location of calls from cellular telephones.

Figure 1. Typical communications center technology

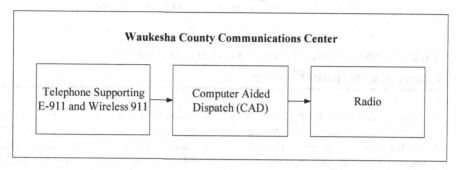

- Computer-aided dispatch (CAD) software to support processing of calls. Modern CAD systems gather data related to the call, automate the protocols dispatchers use in various situations, and document the handling of the call for statistical and record-keeping purposes.
- Radio systems for communication with public safety responders.

But achieving collaboration can be made challenging by political hurdles, which can include legitimate concerns that the service in consolidated centers may not be as responsive as that which is enjoyed in the smaller centers being consolidated.

The Goals of the Case Study

This case study traces the evolution of the Waukesha County Communications Center, with a particular focus on how the new center leads to more effective technology use through initiatives such as a common police records management software vendor. The case study also discusses problems that were encountered during the implementation of the center and how these problems were overcome.

Setting the Stage

County Leadership was Stable

One factor that has helped bring about collaboration within Waukesha County is that the county leadership has been very stable. At the time of the initiation of the WCC effort, Dan Finley had served as the County Executive since 1991, following three years as the County Board Chairman, and James Dwyer had served as County Board Chairman since 1994. Dan

Finley left office in 2005 and Dan Vrakas now serves as the County Executive. Many of the county department heads and senior managers also had long tenures.

The County Sheriff had Provided a Shared Communications Center

The county also had a strong history of collaboration for public safety services. For many years, the county sheriff had managed a sophisticated communications center that provided dispatching for the Sheriff's Department plus seven municipal police departments and eleven fire and emergency medical services (EMS) departments on a contract basis. The CAD system used by the Sheriff's Center provided an interface for criminal records data to the sheriff's records management system, although not to the similar systems at municipal police departments. Many of the municipalities within the county chose to operate their own communications centers, and some of these municipal centers in turn provided dispatch services to other municipalities.

However, there was occasionally dissatisfaction with the level of service provided by the Sheriff's Communications Center. This dissatisfaction was one of the motivations for several municipalities to leave the Sheriff's Communications Center in 1979 and form the Lake Area Communications System (LACS) collaborative communications center. Over time LACS came to serve eleven fire departments and four police departments (Pewaukee Fire Department, 2006).

County Radio Services Provided Services

The County Radio Services Division also provides radio services to the county sheriff as well as to almost all of the municipalities and public safety agencies within the county. As with the communications center, a benefit of collaboration for radio services has been access to more advanced technology. One example of this was the implementation in the 1980s of mobile data terminal (MDT) technology. The sheriff plus most municipalities participated in the shared MDT system, which allowed officers in their patrol cars to perform functions such as driver's license checks and criminal background checks. This collaboration allowed Waukesha County municipalities to enjoy MDT technology years in advance of many larger cities. In 2006, the MDT system infrastructure is being replaced at no cost to the member agencies because the county took the initiative to replace this system and sought federal grant funds for this purpose.

A Sense of Independence

So for some time, the county's municipalities have been willing to collaborate with the county and other municipalities to seek better services. However, the municipalities also have retained a sense of independence and have felt free to pursue other alternatives, with the formation of LACS probably being the best example.

Wireless 9-1-1 Becomes an Additional Driver

During the late 1990s and early 2000s, the need for wireless 9-1-1 services that would accommodate cell phones became an additional driver for collaboration.

Since the 1990s, the growth in the use of cell phones has been explosive. The use of cell phones has not only grown but cell phones are replacing conventional phones, as is shown in Figure 2 (Federal Communications Commission, 2000-2005). In fact, for a few years there have been more cell phones than residential and small business phones in the U.S.

The problem that began to surface in the 1990s was that there was not yet a good system for providing 9-1-1 service for cell phone users, and as the number of cell phone users increased this became a major concern. The traditional enhanced landline 9-1-1 system implemented in most localities in the 1980s and early 1990s uses data from telephone company records to provide the communications center with the home address of a caller using a landline phone. In the most sophisticated applications, this address could be interfaced into the CAD system to show the location of the caller on a computerized map using geographic information system (GIS) technology.

But even if a 9-1-1 system could provide the home address of the owner of a cell phone in a similar way the owner of the phone would not necessarily be home at the time of the call. So a solution was needed which would pinpoint the actual calling location of the cell phone.

Technology quickly developed to provide several levels of support for wireless 9-1-1 calls:

Figure 2. Growth in the U.S. of cell phones vs. residential and small business phones

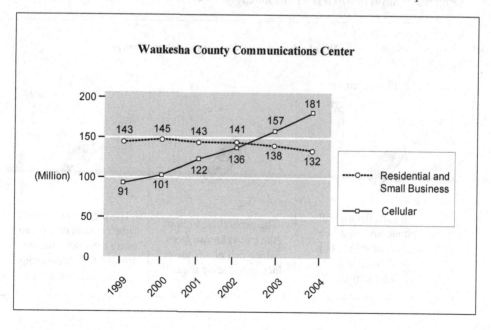

- **Phase Zero:** Wireless calls from a large area served by a mobile telephone switching office (MTSO) go to a central communications center for further routing, although precise data on location is unavailable and the call is routed without even the originating cell phone number.

- **Phase 1:** The communications center receives the caller's ten digit phone number and also information on which cell phone tower is picking up the signal, which locates the cell phone within a mile or so of its location.

- **Phase 2:** Provides the same data as a Phase 1 call plus the location of the caller expressed as latitude and longitude. The Phase 2 technology uses either a handset solution, which takes advantage of global positioning system (GPS) ability on the caller's phone, or a network-based solution, in which the signal from the phone is measured from three or more call tower locations.

Figure 3 illustrates the difference between these phases.

Having a collaborative communications center that serves a larger area lessens the risk that a call is initially picked up by an inappropriate PSAP, as of course does the evolution to Phases 1 and 2. A collaborative center also spreads the burden of the related investment for the technology to allow the 9-1-1 PSAP to accept and use the data provided by Phase 1 and Phase 2 technology. The Phase 2 technology includes the ability to display the cell phone location on a computerized map using the latitude and longitude received from the wireless 9-1-1 system.

The State of Wisconsin had wanted to encourage consolidation as a way to provide better wireless 9-1-1 service and took two actions in the late 1990s and early 2000s:

Figure 3. Phases of wireless 911 technology

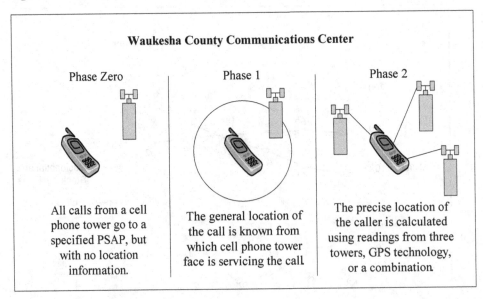

- The state mandated that each county designate a single communications center to answer all wireless 9-1-1 calls for the county.

- The state instituted a surcharge on cell phone bills and devoted this revenue to grants for communications centers to implement wireless 9-1-1 technology.

Waukesha County was the first county in the State of Wisconsin to implement Phase 2 technology, and within nine months the WCC worked with all seven cellular carriers doing business in the county to enable acceptance of Phase 2 data.

Case Description

The desire for a combined communications center for Waukesha County began growing in the late 1990s.

The County Focuses on Strategic Initiatives

During the 1990s under the direction of the county executive and the County Board, the county made an increasing use of strategic planning and developed a succession of several multi-year plans. The use of strategic planning was one of several factors that caused both county and municipal decision makers to become more likely to consider additional things they could be doing to provide more effective government for all in the county.

As a result, the county took on a number of projects which were strategic in nature and which involved cooperation with other jurisdictions. One example was the development of the county's Workforce Development Center. The center was developed in cooperation with Waukesha County Technical College and was built on the grounds of the college. The goal of the center was to provide "one stop shopping" for job training and services related to the State of Wisconsin's welfare reform system.

Another instance of collaboration was the merging of the county's wide area computer network with that of the City of Waukesha, where most county facilities are located.

Positive Experiences with Trunked Radio Project Sets the Stage

However, the strategic project that did the most to set the stage for the WCC was the installation of a county-wide trunked radio system. Although the county had provided a shared radio system for some time, the system used traditional technology in which each municipality operated with a separate frequency.

Even prior to the events of September 11th and the Katrina hurricane, county and municipal leaders realized that they could benefit from a radio system that would offer better sharing of frequencies to allow greater interoperability across jurisdictions and across the entire area of the county. An additional driver for change was the looming need to change out much of the hardware in the system anyway due to frequency reallocations (i.e., frequency "refarming") mandated by the Federal Communications Commission.

The technology selected to address these issues was an 800 MHz "trunked" radio system. The way trunked radio works is that a section of frequencies is managed in common by the system, which dynamically assigns frequencies to callers as needs require. The many users of the system share a number of talk groups. The system can then assign more frequency to a call group if there is a spike in activity, and, most importantly, can assign additional frequency to mutual assistance call groups during an incident spanning municipalities.

An additional advantage of a county-wide trunked radio system is that should a user drift away from his or her normal area they are picked up by new antennas, whereas in the previous system a radio lost coverage as it strayed from the towers that serviced its frequency. Initial budgeting for the trunked radio system took place in the late 1990s, and implementation of the system took place in 2000 and 2001. By the end of 2001, the charter members of the trunked radio system were actively using the new system.

Although the trunked radio project was generally a success, an issue arose during the implementation that was a harbinger of problems for the WCC: when the system did not work satisfactorily municipalities would work energetically to advocate for problems to be addressed—and would also be willing to air their complaints in the media. And in Waukesha County, it is fairly easy to get your story "in the paper", since for some years the local *Waukesha Freeman* newspaper and the larger, regional *Milwaukee Journal Sentinel* have been in a bit of a circulation war in the Waukesha County area, and both papers cover local government news more extensively than might otherwise be the case today.

The main complaint by municipalities in the trunked radio implementation concerned "dead spots" in the system coverage. The southward progression of the Ice Age glaciers ground to a halt in the area around Waukesha County, digging out kettle-shaped valleys and depositing "moraines" of gravel hills. The resulting hilly terrain of the county presents a supreme challenge for radio coverage. As radio users encountered dead spots with the new system they articulated their complaints, which were sometimes picked up in news stories that cast an unfavorable light on the new system.

County and local officials worked with the system vendor during 2001 and 2002 to re-design towers and address these problems. Ultimately, these and other problems were overcome and the trunked radio system has become quite popular, with all but one of the municipalities now choosing to participate.

Communications Center Discussion Begins: The Issue of Governance

As the radio project began moving towards implementation the stars seemed to be aligning for the communications center project; county officials were considering advancing such a project, and there was also growing interest among officials in the county's many municipalities in moving to a more comprehensive collaborative communications center.

In late 2000 municipal officials began meeting with the county sheriff to begin discussion of a collaborative center. These sessions included presentations from officials of successful collaborative centers in the nearby Chicago area. However, a movement into the communications center project did not immediately stem from these talks.

Part of this slowness had to do with consideration of governance for the new center. There were two main possibilities for governance.

- The State of Wisconsin allows for the creation of *shared commissions* in which several governments can in effect set up a new unit of government that would be overseen by an appointed board.

- An alternative governance model would be for a *single government to sponsor* the center, and in this case the sponsor would almost have to be the county.

The advantage of a shared commission was that it would avoid the perception among the partners that the county was playing a parental role. But the disadvantage of a shared commission was the extra time and overhead involved in initially establishing the commission and then maintaining it over time. Discussions continued on these two models but an agreement was not coming together.

The County Offers to Sponsor the System

Finally in 2001, the county officials stepped forward and proposed that they would act as the government to sponsor the communications center. The county began seeking formal commitments from the municipalities for participation in the center, and the county executive developed a proposal in his recommended budget for 2002 for funding for initial components of the project such as the design of the center facility. The proposal called for the primary funding coming from the county with contributions from the participating municipalities. This proposal was adopted by the County Board.

Although county officials had the ultimate authority for administering the center, they also set up a Dispatch Operations Commission under the structure of the County Board with five committees reporting to the new Dispatch Operations Commission:

- Facility and Construction
- Fire and EMS Protocols
- Police Protocols Committee
- Human Resources
- Partners

The County Advances the Proposal and Addresses Objections

Advancing the proposed project required addressing potential objections to participation in a collaborative communications center. County officials worked with municipal advocates of the communications center to defuse these potential objections. Figure 4 shows how objections were addressed in the county's proposal.

Rather than attempt to recover the complete cost of the development of the communications center from the participating municipalities, the county offered to pay for half of the development costs (e.g., costs for building the new facility) and *all* of the eventual operating costs other than components such as the costs for computer network links between the communications center and local police and fire departments. In this way, participation could not help but reduce the costs seen at the local level, and so this cost structure provided a major inducement for municipalities to participate. The costs for the municipalities were pro-rated based on the real estate assessments of the communities. The partners were given eight years to pay their shares, with no interest.

The fear that the sheriff would control the communications center and give priority to sheriff's operations is not unusual nation-wide. Rather than placing the center under the sheriff, the county proposed to set up the center as an independent Department of Emergency Preparedness, and re-locate the county's Radio Services and Emergency Management functions within the same department. And as noted earlier, policy decisions for the center were given over to the new Dispatch Operations Commission and its five committees.

Figure 4. How potential objections were addressed

Waukesha County Communications Center	
Concern	**How Addressed**
There might be increased cost to the municipalities.	The county would pay for half of the development costs and almost all of the eventual operating costs, so that participation could not help but reduce the costs seen at the local level.
The County Sheriff's Department would control the center and might give priority to sheriff's operations, etc.	Rather than placing the center under the sheriff, the county would set up the center as an independent department.
The fate of existing municipal dispatch employees was uncertain.	The county would hire local employees as county employees and "grandfather" them in at their existing seniority levels.
There was a potential for poorer service, with the belief that calls now efficiently dispatched in a smaller center would somehow receive poorer service in a larger operation	The hope was that the use of more sophisticated technology and the advantages of a larger staff would provide better service.

With similar consolidations, local employees had failed to transfer to the consolidated center, for various reasons. To address the concerns of municipal dispatch employees, the county offered to hire local employees as county employees and "grandfather" them in at their existing seniority levels, thus preserving their vacation benefits, and so forth.

The toughest concern to address, however, was the fear that participation in the collaborative center would lead to poorer service than in a smaller center under the control of the municipality. County officials stressed that the use of more sophisticated technology and procedures and the advantages of a larger staff should help provide better service, especially for 24x7 coverage and at the time of disasters or serious incidents.

Inclusion of Records Management Support Provides an Additional Inducement

An additional inducement that the county proposed was to implement shared police and fire records management systems for the center's partners. As shown in Figure 5, a modern communications center of course needs a CAD system, but additional police and fire systems such as incident tracking and police criminal records need not be within the communications center.

In the existing Sheriff's Center, for example, dispatch data was interfaced to a separate incident tracking module used by the Sheriff's Department, but there were no automated interfaces to the similar systems of the municipal partners.

For the new center, the county proposed that the scope of the project would include a unified police records management system for all partners. The new system would include CAD functionality that would be integrated with incident tracking and criminal records. The WCC would host the servers for the system, and municipalities would access the system through network links between their facilities and the center. The system that was ultimately selected was from Spillman Technologies, Inc., along with a separate fire system from ACS Firehouse. In order to address all the needs of the WCC partners, the county also commissioned an accident citation module from Spillman.

Figure 5. Typical police data systems

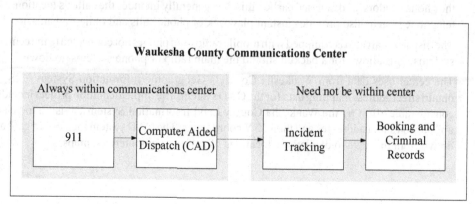

Providing these systems greatly increased the allure of participation in the center. Use of the shared systems would free the municipalities from the headache of implementing and maintaining their own records systems. And, use of the integrated system would allow all of the partners to enjoy instant integration of CAD data into their records; for example, data such as the street address of the 9-1-1 caller would be included in the incident data and would not have to be rekeyed as in the past. Also, use of a shared system provided at least the potential for sharing of data among municipalities.

The partners paid a one-time license fee for their usage of the Spillman software along with a share of the annual maintenance fee. As noted previously, use of the shared system also required each partner to install and pay for a network link with the center. Some of these links are relatively inexpensive digital subscriber line (DSL) links, which use virtual private network (VPN) technology with encryption to provide needed security.

The County Gives Up Its Existing CAD System

But in order to implement the Spillman system along with the CAD module, the Sheriff's Department had to give up its existing CAD system—the CrossCurrent CAD system. The sheriff's personnel were happy with their use of CrossCurrent, but it did not offer a complete integrated police records system.

The sheriff's move away from CrossCurrent was an example of a situation in which collaboration required some amount of some participants "going backwards" to achieve a greater good. This was also an example of an organization giving up "best of breed" systems that serve more narrow areas in order to gain the advantages of integrated systems that serve a wider scope.

Technology Components are Sophisticated

As has been discussed, one of the benefits of moving to the collaborative communications center was gaining access to more sophisticated technology. Figure 6 summarizes the technologies that ultimately came to be used in the system.

The Positron phone system initially captures the enhanced 9-1-1 data that is being sent from the phone vendors; as discussed earlier, this data generally includes the caller's location. The telephone system also provides instant playback of phone calls and radio transmissions.

The dispatch staff also is equipped with mobile radios and phones not connected to the center's systems. This allows for a backup should the main radio or phone systems go down.

The center uses data from Waukesha County's Geographic Information System (GIS) to obtain street address mapping data for the CAD system. The implementation project included considerable effort by the Waukesha County Land Information System Division to "clean up" data on street addresses and their X-Y coordinates. The CAD system then uses a geobase drawn from this data to display the locations of calls on computerized maps.

Figure 6. Technology solutions

Waukesha County Communications Center	
Application	**Vendor and Product**
Computer-Aided Dispatch (CAD) Software	Spillman Technologies, Inc.
Police Records Software	Spillman Technologies, Inc.
Fire Records Software	ACS Firehouse
Telephone System Supporting Enhanced 9-1-1 (E-9-1-1) and Wireless 9-1-1	Positron Power 100
Call Recording	CVDS ComLog
Radio Consoles	Motorola CENTRACOM Gold Series Elite
Dispatch Consoles	Watson Furniture Group Gold
Emergency Medical Services (EMS) Software	Priority Dispatch Corporation ProQA
Geographic Information System (GIS)	ESRI
VHF Simulcast Fire Paging System	Motorola transmitter using VHF frequencies
Weather Radar	Meteorlogix
Mobile Data Computers (MDCs)	IP MobileNet
Long-Term Uninterruptible Power Supply (UPS)	Liebert

Wireless 9-1-1 is Implemented

As noted previously, the State of Wisconsin required each county to designate a single communications center within the county to answer wireless 9-1-1 calls, and Waukesha County designated the new collaborative communications center as this center. Part of the work of implementation was developing the relationships with each of the seven wireless carriers serving the county that would allow the WCC to receive either Phase 1 or Phase 2 data from these carriers.

The State of Wisconsin has now begun making grants to help fund the implementation of wireless 9-1-1 technology. Since the county has already made the investment for Wireless 9-1-1 it will now be allowed to use these grants to recoup $1.5 million of its investments.

The WCC eventually progressed to Phase 1 or Phase 2 with all seven wireless carriers, and was the first of the 72 counties in Wisconsin to advance to Phase 2.

The New Facility Presents Many Advantages

An additional advantage of a collaborative center is that it allows for the construction of a sophisticated facility. The WCC provides for a measure of security due to its location in a somewhat hidden area of the county grounds; due to the function of the center, members of the public have no reason to visit the center. The building is designed to accommodate problems of civil unrest and bad weather, and has excellent perimeter security.

The building is 12,000 total square feet. The center is built with enough space to serve the initial partners with some room for growth, and it could be expanded for even additional growth. Emergency electric power for the facility is provided through an uninterruptible power supply (UPS) paired with a diesel-fueled generator.

The City of Waukesha Communications Center and the county center provide mutual "hot backup" for each other; if one center should go down the other immediately picks up the load. The county center also acts as the backup PSAP for the City of Waukesha as well as several of the other remaining centers in the county.

Staff are Consolidated and Processes Rethought

Implementing the WCC required transferring the existing Sheriff's Dispatch Center staff into the new department and then bringing staff from the partner municipalities in as county employees. Some municipal dispatchers had been doing other types of work in addition to dispatch, especially work related to records, and so had the opportunity to remain at their previous centers in some version of their old positions; for this reason and others not all municipal dispatchers transferred over to the new center.

Training new dispatchers is a special challenge. In the new center, dispatchers must receive 207 hours of classroom training plus an additional 480 hours of training-related experience. Overall, the project for the new WCC spent $275,000 on training which ultimately was extended to 1,000 individuals. This included training for municipal staff using the Spillman system.

As part of the new center, the process for answering calls was also rethought, breaking the staff into separate crews of call takers and dispatchers. Under the previous process, each dispatcher answered 9-1-1 calls plus also acted as an operator for a municipality. Figure 7 shows how the new process splits the work between call takers and dispatchers.

Figure 7. Roles of call takers and dispatchers

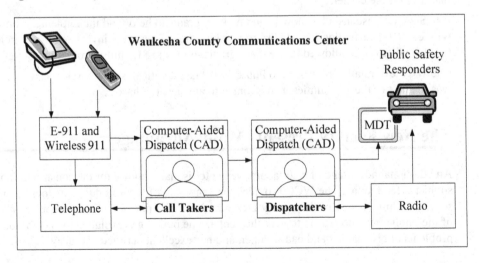

The protocols in the CAD system work automatically to bring in the dispatcher at the appropriate time; the call taker does not have to take action to bring the dispatcher in, and often the dispatcher will begin sending units while the call taker is still on the phone with the caller. During busy periods, the CAD system gives the dispatcher a queue of calls to dispatch by, and the priorities for this queue can vary by community.

This process improves the quality of the interaction, since the call taker can focus attention on the caller while the dispatcher can focus on the radio transmission with the responders. The process should also provide the potential to decrease the overall response time. However, a disadvantage is that neither the call taker nor the dispatcher has full knowledge of the incident, and so the process requires that call takers and dispatchers become skilled at communicating with each other primarily through their entry of data into the CAD system.

Municipalities Commit and the Facility is Constructed in 2002 and 2003

During 2002, the county asked municipalities to commit to partnerships in the new center. The deadline for these decisions was eventually extended to October 17, 2002.

Once the 2002 County Budget was adopted, work on the project could begin with the design of the new facility. This led to budgeting for the construction of the facility in 2003, and groundbreaking took place on April 1, 2003. The completed facility was occupied in January of 2004.

A new Director, Richard Tuma, was hired in 2003 to oversee the county's new consolidated Emergency Preparedness Department. Activity in 2003 also included procurement of the new technology.

Implementation is Delayed until Late 2004

By March of 2004, procurement and installation of the new computer and radio hardware was largely complete. The grand opening of the facility took place on May 8, 2004. An exciting development took place in July of 2004, when the center gained the ability to answer wireless 9-1-1 calls using Phase 1 and Phase 2 technologies. The center was staffed starting at this point in order to begin answering the county's wireless 9-1-1 calls with the new technology and transfer them to the appropriate dispatch center.

The date for the switch to the new center for initial users was originally planned for May of 2004. However, a number of factors delayed the implementation for several months; these included testing, training, and procedural issues.

A special problem that delayed the implementation was developing the maps for the system and also the related street address "geobase" used by the CAD software. Although the new CAD system was the first for the county that would use computerized maps in conjunction with the CAD software, the county was able to convert GIS maps that been developed by the county's Land Records Office. Developing the related geobase was more challenging, however, since now the data associated with streets had to also contain x-y coordinates to allow it to be displayed on a map, and the county needed some time to develop this data.

An additional problem was ensuring that the new CAD system could accommodate the use of "grid addressing" in some parts of the county. The grid address system, which is only used in a few parts of the U.S., builds both north-south and east-west coordinates into the address. For example, an address that would be 1234 N. Main St. in conventional addressing might be W43N1234 Main St. in grid addressing. Accommodating the use of grid addressing required a software modification by the CAD software vendor.

The implementation finally took place in several phases starting in August of 2004 with the LACS center moving in, then in November of 2004 with the Sheriff's Department, and continuing through February of 2005 with the move of the City of Brookfield center. Implementation activity in 2004 also included the migration of center participants onto the Spillman police records software.

The Center Addresses Start-Up Problems

As the center moved into its first full year of operation in 2005 considerable energy was devoted to resolving start-up problems. The switchover for the largest partner in the system, the City of Brookfield, occurred on February 21 of 2005. Less than three weeks later, on March 12, in a highly-publicized incident a disgruntled church member murdered several members of his congregation meeting at a hotel in Brookfield and then took his own life.

The aftermath of the shooting involved extensive analysis of the role of the WCC in the handling of the incident; this included an 800-page report by Brookfield officials that focused in part on the WCC. Initially, officials praised the role of the WCC in the incident, noting that it would have been very difficult to handle an incident of this scale with the need for mutual assistance from neighboring communities without the greater capacity that the center provided; for example, the old City of Brookfield center would have had two dispatchers on duty on the Saturday afternoon when the shooting occurred, whereas the new WCC had 10.

However, a follow-up report and subsequent analysis faulted the center in a number of ways for problems in handling the incident. Problems included inadequate procedures and also a failure of both WCC personnel and also personnel in the field to follow the procedures that were in place. One example was not directing personnel from other departments responding to the incident to initially report to the city's command center. Both the City of Brookfield and the WCC committed to work to improve standard operating procedures (SOPs) and to perform better training of staff in the existing and new procedures. Additional SOPs were developed and others modified so an event like this would be handled in the way the partner agencies preferred.

As 2005 progressed, an issue also surfaced regarding response times. Several factors influenced the response times that partners were seeing:

- The WCC was relatively new and was still fine-tuning procedures and working to optimize response time.

- A number of the center's fire partners had requested that the center use an emergency medical dispatch (EMD) protocol which involves asking a number of questions of the caller before dispatching a unit, partly to ensure dispatch of an appropriate unit. While use of this protocol was intended to provide a better overall result, it admittedly added to the response time. Note that the fastest response time is not necessarily the best response time; for example, "hot" responses with vehicles speeding to the scene raise the possibility of accidents, and a few extra seconds spent to determine the nature of the caller's problem may help determine that a hot response is not required.

- The WCC now had the technology to start the clock for the measurement of response time the moment a call was received. In contrast, in some of the centers that had been consolidated a dispatcher would often listen to the incoming 9-1-1 call while taking paper notes, and an automated clocking of the call would only begin when the initial entry was made into the CAD system. Also, time that had been spent receiving a call at a PSAP and forwarding it to a municipality might not have been recorded. So for this and additional reasons, a comparison on response time with the new center to what the partners had known was not necessarily an "apples to apples" comparison. On this last point, Keith Griffiths points out that:

> The latest state-of-the-art interfaces between phone equipment and computerized dispatch systems capture the exact time the phone is answered, and generally the time it takes to answer the phone. Hence, when new technology is installed in a 9-1-1 center, there is often the illusion of extended call-processing times, sometimes raising questions about the adequacy of the new hardware or software, or about the performance of 9-1-1 staff and its operating procedures. (Griffiths & Scott, 2004)

As issues regarding response time surfaced and partners complained about this problem, the center worked to improve response times, and by the end of 2005 this situation was somewhat better. However, as had been the problem with the issue of coverage in the trunked radio system, the controversy was picked up in the press, which ran a series of stories on these issues. There was also some television news coverage of the controversy.

A fire chief at a smaller municipality was particularly unrelenting in his complaints, which were reported in the press in several stories. Part of the problem was that his calls were now being serviced using the EMD protocol, which had not been used in the previous center. The chief eventually appealed to his local council to withdraw from the center, but the council overruled him and chose to remain in the center.

This incident illustrated a problem in managing a collaborative center; in their decision to participate in the combined center, municipal decision makers may overrule police and fire chiefs who may have preferred to not participate. Reasons why police and fire chiefs might prefer to not participate can include loss of the scope of their responsibilities with the dissolution of centers that they had run and loss of control of their dispatch functions with their move into a "customer" role.

In the case of one of the county's larger municipalities, the council deferred to their fire and police chief and chose not to participate, despite the allure of cost savings. But in other

Figure 8. Average dispatch response time (in seconds)

Waukesha County Communications Center				
Service	Oct 2005	Nov 2005	Dec 2005	Jan 2006
EMS	108	108	110	105
Fire	107	108	105	97
Police	N/A	N/A	N/A	92

cases municipalities participated over the objections of their fire and police chiefs. This can then create a situation in which the chiefs are reluctant participants and may be more vocal in their complaints about center problems.

By the end of 2005, response times were improving and center staff were continuing to work with the partners on improving processes. Figure 8 shows response times for this period (Waukesha County Communications Center, 2006).

Emergency Medical Dispatch Support Added to Services

In late 2005, the center completed special training and implemented special software to provide enhanced support for emergency medical dispatch, which would assist in incidents such as calls involving the immediate need to deliver a baby.

Chronology of Events

Figure 9 presents a chronology of the key events in the implementation of the WCC.

Start-Up Costs were $6.6 Million

The total start-up cost for the new center was $6.6 million. These costs had originally been budgeted at $6.9 million, so the center's implementation was about $300,000 under budget.

As noted previously, each agency paid a portion of the start-up costs, with the partners paying half of the total and the county paying half. The county funded its portion of the project plus the debt for the partners with bond financing as part of the County Capital Budget.

Figure 10 shows the start-up costs for the project (Waukesha County Department of Administration, 2006).

Figure 9. Chronology of key events

Waukesha County Communications Center	
Event	Date
Field testing completes on the trunked radio system.	December 1, 2000
Implementation of the trunked radio complete for charter members.	December 31, 2001
Communications center design funds budgeted in county budget.	January 1, 2002
Municipalities commit to membership in the new center.	October 17, 2002
Communications center construction funds budgeted.	January 1, 2003
Groundbreaking for new communications center facility.	April 1, 2003
New communications center facility occupied.	January 1, 2004
Installation completes for computer and radio hardware.	March 1, 2004
Grand opening of communications center facility.	May 8, 2004
Original switch date for initial users (was eventually postponed).	May 22, 2004
Begin answering wireless 9-1-1 calls using Phase 1 and 2 technology.	July 13, 2004
Switch over for customers from LACS Center	August 18, 2004
Switch over for customers from the sheriff's center.	November 30, 2004
Added agencies from the City of Oconomowoc center.	December 17, 2004
Switch over for the City of Brookfield.	February 21, 2005
Shootings at Brookfield hotel.	March 12, 2005
Switch over for the Village of Butler	March 31, 2005
Implementation of automated EMD software.	November 1, 2005

Figure 10. Start-up costs

Waukesha County Communications Center	
Cost	Amount
Design and Construction of Facility	$3,081,303
Computer System Hardware and Software and Communications and Radio Equipment	$2,619,235
E 9-1-1 Phone System	$467,626
Training	$275,275
Contracted Services	$150,394
Total	$6,593,833

Center Achieves Stability in 2005

By the end of 2005, a total of 28 municipalities plus related fire districts and the county sheriff had joined the center; the participating police departments had 171,008 residents, which is 47.4% of the county's population. Only nine departments were not participating, but these municipalities had a population of 189,759, 52.6% of the county (U.S. Census Bureau, 2000). The municipalities choosing not to participate tended to be the larger cities in the county with mature communications centers. This participation is shown in Figure 11 on "Participating Police Departments".

In some cases these municipalities may have delayed joining the center to observe how the new center would work. Any municipalities that would join the center after the implementation would pay an initial start-up cost similar to that paid by the original members, based on the current real estate assessment of the community. New entrants would also need to make their complete contribution in the first year rather than having eight years to pay. Some of this revenue would be applied by the county to conversion costs for that municipality and the remainder would go into the general fund of the county to partly reimburse the county for its original investment.

The operating costs for the center in 2006 are budgeted at $3.8 million, as shown in Figure 12 (Waukesha County, 2006).

Has the new center reduced the total overall costs for the county and its partners? It is a little difficult to tell, partly since the "before" expenses were spread across 29 governments. The largest partner, the City of Brookfield, made the decision to participate based on the belief that it would save $525,000 a year (Johnson, 2002).

There are probably about the same number of dispatchers across all the governments, but with some lucky timing the center came online just in advance of the growth in wireless

Figure 11. Participating police departments

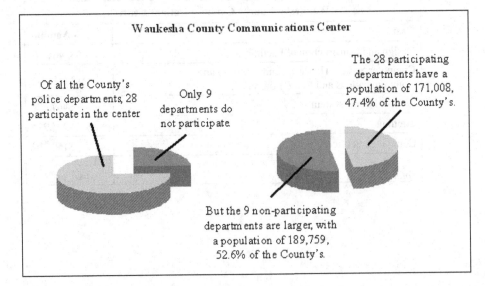

Figure 12. Budgeted operating costs for 2006

Waukesha County Communications Center	
Cost	Amount
Personnel	$3,020,980
Operating Expenses (e.g., Hardware and Software Maintenance)	$413,005
Interdepartmental Charges from Other County Departments	$322,803
Fixed Assets	$10,000
Total	------------- $3,766,788

9-1-1 calls, possibly avoiding an increase in staff and a related increase in staffing costs. What does seem certain is that despite the controversy about response times the center will provide better service, which has a value that is hard to calculate.

What other benefits has the center achieved? All participants now share in the use of more sophisticated technology, and the partners no longer have to seek and implement their own solutions. It is easier to schedule staff, due to the concentration of staff. The ability to provide sufficient staff for disasters or serious incidents has improved, as was shown in the Brookfield hotel incident.

One benefit that has yet to be achieved is sharing of data on ongoing activities and criminal records among neighboring municipalities. The use of the common records management system would seem to facilitate this sharing, but the procedures for doing this have yet to be worked out among the partners.

Current Challenges Facing the Organization

In October of 2005, the WCC received 5,461 9-1-1 calls. Of these, 1,274 were from landline phones and 4,207 were from wireless phones. Recall that the WCC receives the landline calls for the 47% of the county population but that it receives wireless calls for 100% of the county. Of the total of 5,461 calls, 46% are transferred to other centers, and almost all of these are wireless calls. The latest statistics indicate that wireless 9-1-1 calls account for 77% of all the 9-1-1 calls answered at the center.

Efforts to Improve Response Time Continue

The center management and staff have continued to work to reduce the time required to respond to calls. This effort has included meeting with the CAD software vendor to identify needed improvements in the CAD software. The WCC has also temporarily suspended use of the EMS protocol.

Staff Turnover is a Problem

The center has experienced turnover problems, which are common in dispatch work. Four dispatchers who had migrated from the older centers left quickly; one retired, one took a position as a police officer, one transferred to another county position, and one left because of an inability to do the faster-paced work. The center has seen a reduction in turnover as it has implemented some steps to better screen applicants and as it has increased its training program. The national average annual turnover rate for dispatchers is 17%, so even when centers achieve this "average" turnover rate, replacing and training of new employees is very time-consuming and expensive.

The County Works to Implement Mobile Data Computers

The computers used in the patrol cars and other public safety vehicles of the County Radio Services customers are still the descendants of the mobile data terminals (MDTs) installed in the 1980s. The MDTs are "dumb terminals" that can display data but are somewhat limited in function. The coming years will see these units replaced with mobile data computers (MDCs), which are specialized PCs that can more easily communicate with the CAD system and enable functions such as silent dispatching, in which in sensitive situations a dispatch can be sent without radio traffic.

Among other advantages, an MDC can display the complete text of a CAD system call for service and can interactively communicate with the dispatcher, thereby providing more ac-curate data as to time en route, and so forth. The MDCs will use IP Mobile Net technology for their links with radio towers.

Voice over IP Phone Calls Present a New Challenge

Having addressed the problem of wireless calls, the center needed to turn its attention to an additional 9-1-1 problem—VoIP calls. Recent years have seen an increase in the relatively new service of Voice over IP (VoIP) or "Internet" telephone service. The biggest source of VoIP use is through cable television providers, who offer VoIP phone service as part of a package that includes cable TV and Internet access. Such providers offer 9-1-1 compatibility in the same way that landline telephone companies do, by maintaining a data file linking telephone numbers to home street addresses. However, other types of IP telephone providers such as national and international services may not do this.

The WCC worked with Time Warner, the only major local cable television company of-fering VoIP, and also Vonage, a national provider, to ensure that the center would be able to receive location data on 9-1-1 calls. The growth of VoIP phone users may be dramatic; Time Warner only began offering VoIP in Southeastern Wisconsin in mid-2004 and by the end of 2005 had at least 6,000 subscribers in Waukesha County. As with wireless 9-1-1, an advantage of the WCC is that it should make it easier to manage VoIP 9-1-1 on behalf of all the partners.

More Collaboration in the Future?

The several departments that initially declined to participate might join the WCC in the future, but there is no particular movement towards that yet. But one last advantage of the WCC is that it will hopefully lead to additional collaboration initiatives in the future. As Mayor Jeffrey Speaker of Brookfield commented on the occasion of the center's opening, "The success of this will open the door to other discussions of shared services, such as public works" (Enriquez, 2004).

References

Enriquez, D. (2004). Countywide dispatch center ready to open. *Milwaukee Journal Sentinel*, May 9.

Federal Communications Commission. (2000-2005). *Local telephone competition: Status report.*

Griffiths, K., & Scott, G. (2004). 9-1-1 center operations: Challenges and opportunities. *ICMA IQ Report, 36*(6), June. Washington, D.C.: International City and County Managers Association.

Johnson, M. (2002). Brookfield leaders to vote on consolidated dispatch system. *Milwaukee Journal Sentinel*, September 30.

Pewaukee Fire Department. (2006). *Lake area communications system*. Retrieved February 15, 2006, from www.pewaukeefire.com/lacs.html

U.S. Census Bureau. (2000). *Wisconsin quicklinks*. Retrieved February 15, 2006, from http://quickfacts.census.gov/qfd/states/55000lk.html

Waukesha County. (2006). *2006 adopted budget book; Emergency preparedness.*

Waukesha County Communications Center. (2006).

Waukesha County Department of Administration. (2006).

Authors' Biographies

Jerome A. Schulz is an independent consultant in information technology for local governments and non-profit organizations. He served as the Manager of Information Systems for Waukesha County from 1993 through 1999, prior to the development of the WCC. Mr. Schulz is the author of Information Technology for Local Government: A Practical Guide for Managers, published by the International

City/County Management Association (ICMA). He also serves as an adjunct faculty member at the University of Wisconsin-Milwaukee's Department of Public Administration. Mr. Schulz holds a BA in government from Cornell University, and an MPA from Roosevelt University.

Richard Tuma *is the Director of Emergency Preparedness for Waukesha County. He previously served as the Communications Center Manager in a number of consolidated centers in Illinois, and has over 30 years of experience in the communications and public safety fields. Mr. Tuma holds a BA from the University of Wisconsin-Stout and a Master's degree from the University of Wisconsin-Whitewater. He is a member of the Association of Public-Safety Communications Officials (APCO) and the National Emergency Number Association (NENA).*

Chapter XIX

The Challenges of Building a Knowledge Management System for Local Collaboration

Yu-Che Chen, Northern Illinois University, USA

Kurt Thurmaier, Northern Illinois University, USA

Executive Summary

This chapter provides a case study of building a knowledge management system for collaboration between local governments. It describes the management and development of such a system including Web sites and online search and submission of collaborative agreements. It also stresses the importance of coordination and management support for a multi-party development team. Data quality assurance should also be an integral part of the data collection and migration from a paper-based to an electronic system. The authors hope to shed light on the interrelated components of building a knowledge management system on collaboration. Moreover, the findings of the case study inform the practice of managing a multi-party development team.

Background: The Need for Knowledge about Inter-Local Collaboration

Local government collaboration has been a topic for policy discussions among local governments in Iowa for decades. In recent years, however, it has become a hot policy topic with the legislature and governor. This case examines an effort by Iowa State University (ISU), the Iowa Department of Management (IDoM), the local government associations in the state, and the state's Chief Information Officer (CIO) to create a knowledge management system that includes converting hundreds of boxes of paper agreements into a Web-accessible database on inter-local agreements in Iowa.[1] The outcome of this project is a public policy tool that will enhance the ability of local governments to collaborate on the wide range of public services they provide, and for citizens and policy makers to be able to monitor and contribute to the public policy discussions about inter-local collaboration.

Inter-local agreements in Iowa are governed by chapter 28E of the Iowa Code, which authorizes any public agency in the state to enter into an agreement with one or more public or private agencies for joint or cooperative action. These agreements are popularly called 28E agreements, and communities formalize collaboration by using 28E agreements in a variety of areas, including economic development, traffic patrol, mental health services, water and sewage treatment, and many others. All 28E agreements are required to be registered with the Iowa Secretary of State and the local county clerk.

Until this project, nobody could describe the extent of 28E agreements, nor the scope of activities covered by 28E agreements. The Iowa Secretary of State (SOS) has approached management of the 28E statute with indifference, registering and warehousing the filings as required by the law. SOS obtains no revenue from the filings and consequently has dedicated minimal staff to the effort. Compliance with the 28E statute has been very uneven; some cities and counties are more likely than others to use the 28E statute and file their agreements with SOS. In addition to the formal 28E agreements, cities and counties may also collaborate with contracts that are not registered with SOS. These agreements are usually referred to as Memoranda of Understanding, or MOUs. Finally, public agencies, especially cities and counties, often use a variety of informal "handshake" agreements to provide public services to citizens. When the governor and legislature increased their interest in local government collaboration in 2003, policymakers found that they lacked data upon which the debate about the effectiveness and efficiency of local governments could be based. The Iowa League of Cities (League) and the Iowa State Association of Counties (ISAC) could only query members for examples to present legislators with evidence that local governments were collaborating to increase service efficiency. One researcher with an interest in a particular type of 28E agreement related the painful and very inefficient process of spending hours (several years ago) looking through boxes and boxes of warehoused agreements searching for the type of agreements he was studying.

The Public Policy & Administration Program at Iowa State University (PPA) approached the League, ISAC, IDoM and the state's CIO to suggest that these organizations collaborate to create a knowledge management system that would convert the papers filed in boxes by SOS into a Web-accessible database that would:

- Provide a database searchable by type of 28E agreement and type of participating government (e.g., county, small town, large city);
- Produce a GIS-based spatial representation of each 28E agreement;
- Provide e-mail links for designated 28E contacts;
- Provide a downloadable copy of each 28E agreement;
- Present analysis of a survey of local officials who managed 28E agreements to identify how well the agreements were increasing the effectiveness and efficiency of local public services; and
- Produce in-depth management reports (for a sample of selected 28E agreements) that discuss why and how an agreement is effective (or ineffective) based on personal field interviews with participating 28E agreement managers.

The initiation of this "28E project" was based on the premise of the positive role that information technology can play in improving public services. The use of information technology helped the federal government in modernizing its systems to better serve citizens (Fountain, 2001). It also holds the potential to save costs and deliver better value (Landsbergen & Wolken, 2001). Collaboration adds an important ingredient for successful public service delivery due to its ability to pool resources from different partners. A solid information system facilitates collaboration by providing better information coordination and exchange (Dawes & Prefontaine, 2003; Moynihan, 2005).

The 28E project would only be possible with the collaboration of the local government associations and the state agencies. In particular, the project would require many hours of labor-intensive work and financial support for a multi-year project. The state's CIO, who heads the Information Technology Enterprise in the state's Department of Administrative Services (ITE/DAS), received support and encouragement from the Governor's Office to approach the IowAccess Council (IAC) for financial support of the project. After several presentations and discussions with the council, the project was approved and funded for approximately $130,000.

The council chose to limit funding to the initial scope of the project, focusing resources on the 28E agreements filed between 1993 and 2003. The effect was to provide all of the search features in the database only for agreements filed since 1993. Although all of the agreements filed since 1961 would be kept in the database, agreements filed before 1993 would only be retrievable in a search by the year in which they were filed, the filing number in the SOS index file of agreements, or public service type; and the presented results would not provide a downloadable (i.e., scanned) copy of the agreement to the end user.

Setting the Stage: Prior Process and the Use of Information Technology

Prior to the 28E project, the philosophy of public agencies regarding 28E agreement knowledge has been one of data collection, not information resources management (IRM). Data collection fulfills the Secretary of State's obligation to be the repository of 28E agreements. An IRM approach treats information as a resource for planning and utilization to achieve an organization's goals; it elevates the importance of information to the level of human and financial resources in an organization. An IRM approach will require SOS to invest in making the information of inter-local collaboration readily available to aid public managers and legislators in their decisions.

The initial assessment of project feasibility conducted in summer 2003 determined that SOS provided limited management of the 28E filings. The basic procedure was to receive a 28E agreement in the mail from a public agency such as a county or city clerk. The agreement was date and time stamped, then affixed with a barcode and scanned as a TIFF file. Then, the agreement was logged into an index file with only seven fields, as seen in Figure 1. The index file is a text file that contains seven data fields of more than 11,000 records dated back to 1961.

The handling of submitted paper copies of 28E agreements and updating of the index file were usually done on a weekly basis. The quality control measure was a "double-key" process where the data entry was occasionally verified by another reader. SOS began to scan the submitted documents into TIFF files only in 2002; as staffing workload permitted, the office had begun to scan documents in previous years. By 2003, the office had scanned documents filed from January 2000. The scanned TIFF files were saved in a server space. The DocLoc variable (Figure 1) refers to the document locator number for scanned files.

The office had no authority to establish standards for filing agreements; consequently, the subject and description fields were often unhelpful in determining even the basic nature of the 28E agreement. For example, many subject entries are "28E agreement" or "inter-local agreement". Similarly, the description field could be equally vague. Entries such as in Figure 2 were not very useful and data conversion often required someone to find and read the TIFF version of the 28E agreement to recode the subject and description for the searchable database.

The technology used at the time was minimal in support of this paper-based process, with the goal of serving as a repository. SOS used scanners to produce TIFF files for the submitted 28E agreements. At the time of the initial assessment, SOS had a pilot project of making the index file available online. But, it was not live yet. Even if the searchable index file had been put online, the inherent challenges of making sense of the information contained in the index file would have persisted.

Figure 1. Index file fields: 28E agreements filed with the Secretary of State (pre-2006)

Filing Date	Subject	Description	Expir	Print Flag	BarCodeNumber	DocLoc

Figure 2. Example of subject and description entries in SOS index file (pre-2006)

Subject	Description
JOINT SERVICES AGREEMENT	between Polk County and the City of Des Moines

Case Description: Managing Multiple Parties with Multiple Project Components

The first step in the 28E project was for the three main actors (PPA, SOS, and ITE) to enter into a 28E interagency agreement that stipulated responsibilities of each party and financing by the IowAccess Council. The organizations brought different assets to the project. The website hosting would continue to be at SOS; they had the legal authority and responsibility for managing the 28E filings and had considerable experience with online transactions associated with their responsibilities for corporate filings under the Uniform Commercial Code (UCC). ITE brought the technical programming expertise necessary for the project; in addition, ITE staffed the IowAccess Council and had the organizational routines in place for funding council projects.

The PPA faculty at ISU provided intellectual energy, project design, and graduate students for the labor-intensive data conversion project. The PPA faculty initiated the project. The ISU team also provided the service of publicizing the project and gaining support from the users of the inter-local collaboration knowledge base. PPA had healthy working relationships with the local government associations; they, in turn, encouraged members to cooperate with the project.

The negotiation on the 28E project took more than 12 weeks, much longer than expected. Aside from having too many lawyers involved, the main obstacles related to the differing project cultures of ITE/DAS and PPA/ISU. The standard procedure for ITE was to organize and monitor projects based on one hourly rate applied to each hour spent on a project. This culture emanated from the agency's restructuring into a self-funded enterprise in a recent state re-organization, and the fact that ITE was usually the exclusive labor used on projects funded by the IowAccess Council and it was convenient for the council and ITE to account for projects in this manner.

The PPA team worked in a university culture that preferred a flat fee payment when projects provided the deliverables stipulated in a contract. The accounting system and principles of the university and ITE were dissimilar, despite both being state agencies. The university generally desires more flexibility to reallocate funds between project budget line items (e.g., between faculty and student salaries). The compromise created a monthly reporting and invoice system that presented deliverables that had been met and that required 1/12 funding in exchange. The funding deliverables match was imprecise and eventually the agreement was amended to a flat fee paid upon completion of the project deliverables, as originally desired by the university.[2]

In addition to the difference in accounting practices, there were issues concerning hosting of the Web site, site content, and control. As a standard policy, ITE is responsible for Web hosting for the first year for all projects funded by the IAC. It is to take advantage of ITE's enterprise-wide Web servers, security measures, and existing codes. However, being an independent elected office itself, SOS prefers to have every component of the information system physically under its roof. The use of an authentication module that requires use of resources at ITE proved to be controversial. After several long meetings and negotiations, SOS was able to keep full control of the system with ITE/DAS providing programming resources.

Figure 3. 28E knowledge management system at a glance

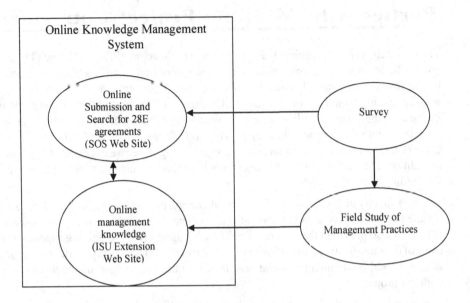

This project has three inter-related deliverables to establish a knowledge management system for inter-local collaboration in the production and provision of services (Table 1). The relationships between the three components are shown in Figure 3. Each of the main deliverables amounted to a major project itself.

Information System Design, Development, and Implementation

The objective of the information system development component was to transform the flat index file created and maintained by SOS into a searchable database accessible from the SOS Web site. There were three aspects to this project component. First, this required organizing and scanning thousands of paper copies of 28E documents dated back to 1993. Then, a labor-intensive effort of data organization and migration was launched to add value to the index file. Second, this component involved generation of several maps for geographic representation of the 28E agreements. Third, the creation of the database is being followed by programming to creating an MS SQL database and a Web site that connects to this database, working in the IT environment at SOS.

Survey of 28E Management in Local Governments

The objective of the 28E survey component was to identify the management factors that contribute to effective and efficient inter-local agreements, including the impetus for agreements, use of information technology to communicate with partners, regularity and modes of interpersonal and interorganizational communication, and underlying social networks among agreement partners. The survey also included questions about user priorities for the information system loaded on the Web. The feedback was used to guide selection of key data fields and the layout of Web pages.

Field Studies of Selected 28E Agreements

The objective of the field studies component was an in-depth discussion with local government managers of selected agreements to corroborate survey data and test hypotheses regarding the roles of network champions and elected and appointed officials; the utility of underlying social networks as the basis for effective inter-local agreements; and the roles of interpersonal and interorganizational communications in agreement success. This is consistent with the notion of knowledge sharing, a main objective of the project. Public managers can learn from best practices in inter-local collaboration, even for their specific service area. Placing these analyses into the Web information system enhances the value of the information contained in the database of actual agreements.

The final tripartite 28E agreement specified responsibilities and deliverables for the three main project components. Tables 1 and 2 were attachments to the final PPA-ITE-SOS agreement. We next examine each of the project components in detail.

Table 1. Project steps and deliverables for respective parties

Partners	Phase 1	Phase 2	Phase 3	Phase 4
Iowa State University, Public Policy & Administration Program	• Data preparation and analysis • Survey generation • Gather user inputs	• 28E practice and user input survey • Logical design and development of a relational database for data requirements	• Survey data analysis • Interviews and field trips • Generation of management reports • Generation of customized static GIS maps • Public presentations of the information system	• Customized data analysis • Enhancing management reports • Public presentations of the information system
Information Technology Enterprise	• Provide system requirements for hosting environment	• Preliminary physical database design • Preliminary interface design	• IS design • IS implementation • IS testing and installation to go live.	• IS enhancement • IS update
Secretary of State	• Consultation and collaboration • Provide 28E agreements, cooperate on data preparation • Map out hosting environment	• Consultation and collaboration	• Consultation and collaboration • Provide testing and hosting environment	• Consultation and collaboration • Operational support and testing and hosting environment

Table 2. Collaborative responsibilities of 28E project team members

Parties to the Agreement	Hosting Information System	Data Ownership	System Development	Title to Equipment and Source Code	Record keeping
Iowa State University, **Public Policy & Administration Program**			System design and development programming	Storage devices Shared source code	Maintain records of 28Es for analysis and management reports
Information Technology Enterprise			System design and development programming	Shared source code	
Secretary of State	Hosting	Secretary of State owns the data	Consultation and Collaboration for the System design and development programming	Hosting computer hardware and software Shared source code	Maintain database of agreements and management reports

Information System Design, Development, and Implementation Design and Development

The information system design began even at the stage of developing the proposal for funding by the IAC in spring 2004. General requirements for the system were negotiated at the outset with the partner organizations, implicitly a condition of their participation. The city and county associations, for example, were only interested in the new online system if it would meet the needs of their member cities and counties. For them, key elements of the system were the search abilities within the database. They wanted to be able to search for 28E agreements by type of service, type of government, name of government entity, and the year in which it was filed with SOS. They also wanted to be able to access an actual copy of a given 28E agreement. Of secondary interest was the ability to "see" the agreements on a map. The requirements of the system served as guidelines for the development of the system, particularly the transformation and enhancement of the SOS index file into a database that could provide the relevant information for the required search abilities.

The information system development component required cooperation by all three of the agencies, with initial responsibilities taken by PPA and the final programming work taken by ITE (see Tables 1 & 2). Beginning in the summer of 2004, the initial work of the project involved the transformation of the SOS data in a flat file into a relational database and then enhancement of the data to include the critical searchable variables such as entity names, service type, and contact information. The database transformation and development required 1,300 hours of labor.[3]

Data Migration and Database Design

There were numerous conversion issues. The first issue was that SOS had only scanned 28Es filed since 2000. From a total of 7,137 agreements filed from 1993 through June 2004, this left about 3,200 agreements to be scanned into TIFF files, a duty that fell to the PPA team because the SOS staff workload was full at the time. These paper agreements were sitting in boxes. Some of the agreements were filed out of order. It required time and effort to locate, organize, and scan those agreements. A PPA team member spent 148 hours on this task alone in the summer of 2004. Most of the remaining work on data migration and database design for generation of GIS maps continued in fall 2004 and into early 2005.

Secondly, given the limited number of fields in the SOS index file, one task was to identify the additional variables required for a searchable database and then to collect and enter the appropriate data for each variable. The PPA team took a user-centric perspective to identify the information needs for public managers and legislators. One of the search variables to be added was the type of public service provided by the 28E because public managers would like to know the collaborative arrangements for their responsible service areas (i.e., fire and emergency management). As a result, each of the agreements in the index file needed to be coded for the type of public service. Given the often vague descriptions of many agreements, many hours were required to open the appropriate TIFF copy of an agreement and read it to determine the service to be provided.

A third issue was the creation of a service coding system that was specific enough for users, balanced by the need for a parsimonious set to make coding easier and faster. The service code index was created by combining basic codes from a city and a county budget. The coding scheme was transformed into a drop-down box for the Web site search engine. This was a crucial step in creating the master lists of agreements by service area. These lists provided the basis for drawing cases for the third component of the project—field interviews.

A final vexing issue was coding the various public agencies with an entity ID that could be searched from the Web and identifying all the participants for each agreement with their proper code. The goal was to provide an accurate list of participants for every agreement. One main task is to develop a classification system to give each participating government entity a unique ID. Although the FIPS code was available for cities and counties, it does not apply to schools, fire departments, water districts, or other special districts. These entities were coded with a numbering scheme that was able to distinguish between two townships with the same name but located in two different counties. Townships are responsible for rural fire departments and often participate in inter-local agreements for fire service delivery. The other main task was to put together a linking table that for each agreement, every single participating entity is identified. This task required the reading of the index file and sometimes related image files with additional research.

Visualization: Static Maps with Geographic Information System

A related aspect of the information system development was the creation of the maps to visually represent the networks of 28E agreements for various types of public services in

Figure 4. Map of 28E agreements for highways and public works

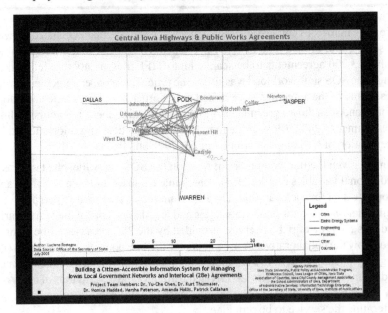

Iowa. This is an important element as requested by the potential users of the knowledge management system. This provides the benefits for policy makers to effectively learn and communicate the intensity and patterns of collaboration between local governments in various areas of public services (i.e., fire protection, emergency services).

The original conception was a dynamic link between each 28E agreement produced by the Web search engine and a map, much as one gets driving instruction maps from online map programs. It was quickly determined that this level of GIS service was beyond the resource constraints of the 28E project. Neither the SOS, nor the ITE/DAS has the GIS server or GIS personnel to take on this part of the project to serve dynamically-generated maps based on user queries. Instead, the team opted for a set of static maps produced by a GIS faculty team member in the Department of Community and Regional Planning at Iowa State University. Production of the maps with ArcGIS revealed several coding errors in the database, mainly incorrectly coded entity IDs. Consequently, the maps required several iterations to be clean and accurate. Most of the map production and error correction took place in spring 2005. A sample is provided in Figure 4.

Knowledge Management Web Site: Search and Submission of Collaborative Agreements

The third aspect of the information system development required SOS, ITE, and PPA to agree on the functionalities and appearance of the 28E Web site. Since SOS is the hosting agency, a basic design feature posed by the SOS was that the site was compatible with their existing programming and Web design. In addition, SOS was careful to insure that the online filing of a 28E was only one of several options for filing agreements, since they had no authority to compel online filing. Consequently, three options needed to be developed within the package. The ideal filing method for the future integrity of the database is that an agency files an agreement online by completing the form and uploading a scanned copy of the 28E. Alternatively, an agency can complete the form online, print the form, attach the 28E and mail it to SOS; although the data fields will have relevant information for data searches, the information will need to be entered into the database manually by SOS staff each time an agency uses this option. Finally, an agency can avoid the online system altogether and simply mail a 28E agreement to SOS without completing the online form at all; this option is least desirable from the 28E project's perspective because the agreement would then need to be read and analyzed and coded into the database by SOS staff.

Several issues arose related to the design of the Web site hosting the searchable database and online filing. Agreement was first required for the set of variable fields by which users would be able to search for 28E agreements, as established in the design phase with the user groups and as verified by the 28E survey results (discussed next). This discussion was largely the province of SOS and PPA, with a task of balancing the need for enough fields to enable a user to narrow a search as desired, with a desire by SOS to limit on the number of discrete fields a user filing an agreement would be required to enter. Given that SOS had no authority to prescribe any details beyond the vague requirements of §28E 2003, SOS was reluctant to require too many fields for the online filing, lest users rebel and refuse to use the online system.

The second issue to be decided was how to account for amendments to existing agreements. The current filing system does not distinguish between new 28Es and amendments to existing agreements. While there is no practical distinction for filing requirements under §28E 2003, the distinction is critical to an effective knowledge management system. The online filing option was designed to link the new amendment to an existing agreement in the database (which could be searched and found in advance by the user filing the agreement amendment). A report can then be generated for that agreement that lists the set of related agreement filings.

The identification of system requirements followed the process of a system development life cycle. The project team at ITE conducted several extensive meetings to identify the functionalities by using the "use case" approach and VISIO for visualization and discussion. These meetings took place in spring and summer of 2005. The three primary groups of actors identified in the use case are general public, public administrators, and SOS staff. General public can conduct search for 28E agreements by selecting years, name of participant, and specific location. In addition to what the public can do with the system, public administrators can file agreements online. They need to first register with the SOS before conducting the online filing. SOS staff has the privileges of a public administrator. Moreover, they are responsible for managing the registration process by using an authentication and password management model. The staff can also update and modify records in the master database.

Implementation

Based on the system requirements identified in the design phase in the summer of 2005, ITE and SOS began working together to implement the system. It included the development of the Web site as the front end and the design of MS SQL database as the back end. This SQL database needed to accommodate all the data elements to allow all 28E agreements to be searchable. Also, it included the information for registered users to create a function for "my agreements". So, a "public administrator" has the convenience of being able to have all the data fields filled automatically for an amendment and have a list of all agreements filed by him/her. The information system had to work in SOS information technology environment where hosting and maintenance of the 28E database was to take place.

This phase of the project was hampered by turnover within ITE. First, the ITE project manager was replaced a year into the project. The immediate consequence was only a change in the primary contact for the project while another manager was found for the project. Later, however, when the new project manager was brought on board, there were also some operational changes implemented by ITE. New weekly status reports were sent to all three partner organizations, but the most significant initial report was the loss of the ITE programmer for the project. After working several months with the SOS and PPA in 2005 to get agreement on Web-page mock-ups, the ITE programmer had just begun to program the system when he left ITE for a different job, leaving the project on hold until ITE could obtain a new programming resource. In addition, ITE used its allocation of the project funding (about $35,000) just for the planning phase and had to return to the IowAccess Council for additional financing (about $40,000) to complete the system programming. In January 2006, the mock-up Web pages were completed. SOS and ITE/DAS were then working closely to begin programming of the database and Web interface to work in the IT environment at SOS.

Another round of intensive work took place in spring 2006. ITE, SOS, and PPA worked to make some final modifications based on the viewing of the prototype. Another main task has been data quality assurance. ITE conducted several independent data quality checks to identify potential redundancies in the data. SOS checked the updated and organized data by PPA against its master records. A fully-functional system hosted in the SOS environment was ready for testing by all three parties in June. A round of user testing is scheduled to took place later in June.

Survey of 28E Management in Local Governments

The PPA research team had sole responsibility for the survey of 28E managers in local governments. The survey was designed to provide an initial evaluation of the management and operation of 28E agreements among local governments. The survey project therefore excluded 28E agreements between state agencies or between a state agency and a local government. In late summer 2004, the survey was first mailed to all local government entities that filed a 28E agreement with SOS between 1993 and 2003,[4] or about 5,300 agreements. The survey asked about the reason for establishing the agreement, satisfaction about the effectiveness and efficiency of the service delivery as a result of the agreement, and modes and frequency of interaction with agreement partners. The survey also treated the survey respondents as a user group and asked for their input on the features that should be available on the Web-accessible database. There were questions about the information they wish to get from the Web site and which item should receive a high priority. Examples of the data items for the respondent to choose from include actual agreements, description of agreements, jurisdiction information, contact information for agreements, performance indicators, successful agreements, management reports on crafting agreements, and a map showing agreements by service types. Survey generation required substantial expansion of the SOS index file to include: an entity identifier for each member of an agreement (e.g., some agreements could include all 99 counties) and an address for each entity in an agreement.

The survey involved a cover letter tailored with different signatories for each major government type. The survey design targeted key offices for each type of government that would receive the survey packet and then distribute the surveys to the appropriate department head who actually had responsibility for managing the 28E agreement. The survey packet included the cover letter, instructions, and a set of files burned to a CD. The files were organized into directories for each department with a known set of 28E agreements, and a general directory for distribution by the government contact target. Each directory contained a set of TIFF files (one for each scanned 28E agreement) and a PDF file created as a mail merge document. The PDF file was actually a continuous document with the barcode on page 1 of each survey, corresponding to a TIFF file also present in the same directory. Thus, the recipient was able to print a copy of the actual 28E agreement and the corresponding 28E survey document. Although it was much more work to copy all of the TIFF files into discrete directories, it was thought that this made it easier for respondents to evaluate the agreement, since they would not need to find a copy of the agreement in their files (if they could). Thurmaier and Wood (2002) had found that cities and counties generally did not keep good records of their inter-local agreements and had trouble finding the documents upon request. Hence, the strategy was used to side-step this potential reason for nonresponse.

Field Studies (28E Management Reports)

The PPA team also had sole responsibility to generate 28E management reports by conducting interviews on a selected sample of 28E agreements to identify success factors and draw management lessons from the agreement experiences. The research design for the management reports used a comparative case study framework. The goal was to identify 12-15 types of public services and study a sample of agreements in each category. The analysis could then try to generalize across agreements for specific types of public services.

All field interviews were based on a discussion guide developed by the 28E research team (faculty and MPA students in the Public Policy & Administration Program at Iowa State University) and approved by the Iowa State Institutional Review Board. Interviews were arranged by telephone and e-mail. Most interviews were conducted in person, although several were conducted by phone, especially when large travel distances were involved for the interviewer.

By May 2005, management reports had been written for five types of local government services: economic development, traffic patrol, city-school recreation facilities, youth services, and mental health. The ISU 28E Web site makes the reports available in full and in the form of a five-page executive summary. Four reports were completed in May 2006 covering fire response, emergency management, wastewater treatment, and annexation agreements. Three more reports are scheduled for completion by December 2006, including analysis of agreements for collaborative planning, 911 dispatch centers, and road projects.

Deliverable Outcomes

Ultimately, the 28E project is producing two related Web sites. The SOS Web site will host the official 28E online filing site and the searchable 28E data repository. Local and state agency users will be able to file original agreements or amendments. Other users, including citizens and officials from state and local governments, will be able to search the Web site for specific types of agreements, or for agreements specific to a level of government. Reports generated from the searches will allow the user to print and download a PDF copy of any agreement filed since 1993 with the SOS.[5]

The second Web site is hosted by Iowa State University. This site includes the GIS maps of agreements filed between 1993 and June 2004, by type of public service. In addition, users can find 28E management reports discussing the management issues involved in agreements for a variety of public services, including economic development, emergency management, traffic patrol, mental health, and city-school recreation facilities. Finally, the site contains basic analysis of the agreements in the SOS database as well as various analyses of the 28E survey data. Research papers analyzing the data from the survey and database will be presented at various conferences and workshops and will be archived on this site as well.

Current Challenges Facing the Project and Its Potential Benefits

Challenges

The turnover of ITE personnel made the coordination and resource allocation rather difficult. The current ITE project manager, who was not initially involved in the development of the project, has quite limited institutional memory. As a result, the most recent effort to coordinate multiple parties in signing the statement of work proved difficult when the initial agreements on the scope of the project were not incorporated. The programmer who initially developed a mock-up Web site and participated in the detailed discussions about the system requirements also left ITE. The recruitment and training of a new programmer took more than a month. Afterward, new meetings have been required to re-introduce all the members involved. There is no telling whether there will be more turnovers that may further delay the project.

Another potential problem is having another round of cost-overrun. All the initially budgeted resources for the system design and development by ITE were exhausted before programming the MS SQL database. Although more resources have been approved by the IowAccess Council for the programming side of the project, there may be a possibility of needing more resources. It is particularly the case when the system requirements are done on a consensus basis and cost implications of additional requirements are not made explicit in the meetings.

The delay due to personnel turnover, cost-overrun, and managing multiple partners may present challenges for rigorous testing. The ISU team offered to test the system and bring more updated data into the system at the same time. However, as the end of the spring semester draws near, students who can work on the project are going to graduate. It could be the case that no resources will be available for rigorous and comprehensive testing at the time of the system completion.

A potential related problem of delay is the loss of momentum and consequently the use of online filing and knowledge base of inter-local collaboration. The major events to publicize the coming of the online system were in spring 2005. It has been over a year since that announcement. It probably requires another round of campaign and training sessions to increase the use of online filing. However, one key faculty member who worked on the project will not be available to conduct those information sessions after the summer of 2006.

The sustainability and ultimate impact of the project over a long period of time also depend on the use of the system. It may require active promotion by SOS. It is uncertain whether the SOS will invest time and resources to do so. In addition, the knowledge component of the project needs to be updated periodically to be valuable to the user community. The 28E management reports are hosted by the Iowa State University Extension site. The existence and long-term maintenance of the site are not an issue. However, whether there will be resources three to five years from now to do the periodic update remains to be seen. The hope is that making the data available will raise the interest of public managers in Iowa and researchers around the country enough to provide help on periodic updates.

Data quality presents a challenge to eventual wide-spread use. When the searchable database is made available, public managers who use the system will be able to notify SOS of needed corrections. SOS will be expected to make the corrections, although it is not receiving new labor resources from the legislature to mange this new system. Consequently, corrections may take longer than users might expect. The rate of accuracy is probably above 95%. However, it is difficult to determine the extent to which people will take issues with the data entry errors. As a result, the use of the searchable database may be rather limited.

The Status of the Knowledge Management Project and Its Potential Benefits

As of January 2006, we had some basic information about formal collaboration among public agencies in Iowa. For example, from 1961 through June 2004, cities, counties, school districts, and state agencies had filed about 11,800 agreements with SOS. The 28E filing rate had been accelerating through 2001 and then started to fall. We have also learned that the 28E agreements cover all types of intergovernmental agreements between local and state agencies. The survey data suggest that the increased effectiveness is even slightly more of a reason for creating a 28E agreement than efficiency, and that most 28E agreement members are very satisfied that their agreements are achieving the stated goals and increasing effectiveness and efficiency of local government service delivery.

SOS and ITE are currently moving ahead with the implementation of the searchable Web site connected to a MS SQL database. In early June, a fully-functional system was placed in the development server at SOS. All three parties were able to test the system with the complete real data and functionalities. Another round of data quality check is scheduled to be conducted in June. User testing of the system will take place in June as well. The goal is to have the system go live in July 2006. The Web site providing management knowledge hosted by ISU extension has all of its contents ready. These two Web sites will have links for each other to serve as a complete knowledge management system for local government collaboration.

The knowledge management system, when fully functional and open to the public, will fulfill its promise. It will empower the public to learn about the use of collaborative agreements as a way to provide public services in their communities and any communities of their interest. In addition to knowing the basic statistics about the use of collaborative agreements, public administrators can learn about the best practices in managing collaborative agreements as well as using model agreement templates. The online submission of 28E agreements is also a time-saving device for submission and management of agreements. Policy makers can have an enhanced understanding of the collaboration for public service production and delivery by using flexible search options (i.e., by time period, service type, jurisdiction, etc).

References

Dawes, S., & Prefontaine, L. (2003). Understanding new models of collaboration for delivering government services. *Communications of the ACM, 46*(1), 40-42.

Fountain, J. (2001). *Building the virtual state: Information technology and institutional change*. Washington, D.C.: Brookings Institution Press.

Landsbergen, Jr., D., & Wolken, Jr., G. (2001). Realizing the promise: Government information systems and the fourth generation of information technology. *Public Administration Review, 61*(2), 206-220.

Laudon, K., & Laudon, J. (2002). *Management information systems: Managing the digital firm* (7th ed.). Upper Saddle River, NJ: Prentice Hall.

Moynihan, D. (2005). *Leveraging collaborative networks in infrequent emergency situations*. Washington, D.C.: IBM Center for the Business of Government.

Thurmaier, K., & Wood, C. (2002, September/October). Interlocal agreements as overlapping social networks: Picket-fence regionalism in metropolitan Kansas City. *Public Administration Review, 62*(5), 585-598.

Endnotes

[1]   According to Laudon and Laudon (2002), a knowledge management system has an IT infrastructure that facilitates the collection and sharing of knowledge and software for distribution of knowledge and making it more meaningful (p. 374).

2   The complications that arose from negotiating the details required under the 28E statute had a quick result. A second project funded by the IowAccess Council and ITE for work by PPA faculty was negotiated under a Memorandum of Understanding instead of the 28E statute. It was the first experiential learning of the PPA team about why cities and counties might choose an MOU instead of a 28E to formalize a collaborative agreement.

3   This includes planning and team management hours spent by the principal investigators.

4   The project eventually included the agreements that were filed in January-June 2004 as well.

5   As labor resources permit, SOS may also convert pre-1993 paper files into scanned and downloadable PDF documents, but there is no timetable for commitment to do so.

Authors' Biographies

Yu-Che Chen is an assistant professor of political science at Northern Illinois University. Dr. Chen's research interests include the management of e-government projects and IT-enabled collaboration in management networks. He has published in Public Performance and Management Review, Social Science Computer Review, Government Information Quarterly, Public Administration Quarterly, and other journals. He recently published an IBM report on the use of information technology in preventing and responding to global health-related crises. Dr. Chen teaches e-government and program evaluation courses. He serves on the national IT Committee for schools of public affairs and the editorial board for the International Journal of Electronic Government Research.

Kurt Thurmaier is a professor of political science at Northern Illinois University. He teaches public budgeting and finance, comparative administration, research methods, and intergovernmental relations. Prior to joining the academic community, he was a budget and management analyst for four years in the budget office for the State of Wisconsin. His research interests include state and local budgetary decision making, inter-local collaboration, and e-government management. His books include Case Studies in City-County Consolidation (with Suzanne Leland), and Policy and Politics in State Budgeting (with Katherine Willoughby). His publications also have appeared in Public Administration Review, Journal of Public Administration Research and Theory, Public Budgeting and Finance, and other journals.

Chapter XX

Using GIS to Generate Spatial Datasets for Public Management and Analysis:
A Description of the Enterprise Zone Fiscal Impact Project in Indiana

Jim Landers, Indiana Legislative Services Agency, USA

Executive Summary

This chapter describes the Enterprise Zone (EZ) Fiscal Impact Project conducted in 2003 by the Office of Fiscal and Management Analysis (OFMA), Indiana Legislative Services Agency (LSA). The focus of this project was to better inform policy analysts and policy-makers about the extent and nature of business activity within Indiana's 29 EZs. The most important outcomes of the project were the generation of digitized maps of the EZs and the geocoding of data from the Quarterly Census of Employment and Wages (also referred to as ES-202 data) to the EZs. The geocoding process yielded a census of business establishments in the EZs, and a dataset reporting employment levels, wage levels, and industry classification information for each business identified in the EZs. The project failed to yield much-needed information on sales receipts, income, and investment expenditures by EZ businesses. Researchers conducted a survey of EZ businesses to obtain this information, but the survey failed to yield sufficient samples to draw conclusions about EZ businesses. In addition, geocoding of tax return data was considered, but researchers determined the geocoded tax return data would not yield valid and reliable information about EZ businesses. This project has provided valuable descriptive information for EZ administrators and was utilized by OFMA staff to estimate fiscal impacts of proposed EZ tax incentives for the Indiana legislature. The case also demonstrates how analysts can utilize GIS and available data sources to create new demographic and socio-economic databases for localized and idiosyncratic geographic areas. Nevertheless, the case also suggests that widespread geocoding of existing databases containing geographic information may not lead to a GIS that validly reflects phenomenon in such areas. Thus, researchers must exercise caution in geocoding and utilizing the resulting databases for research and analysis.

Background

This section outlines the technical expertise and annual workflow within the Legislative Services Agency (LSA) which facilitated completion of the *Enterprise Zone (EZ) Fiscal Impact Project*. LSA is established by state law as the non-partisan administrative and service agency for the Indiana General Assembly. State law provides that LSA perform the bill drafting, research, code revision, *fiscal, budgetary, and management analysis*, information, administrative, and other services requested by the Legislative Council. The Legislative Council is the administrative and policymaking board for the General Assembly. It is comprised of legislative leaders of the Senate and House of Representatives and is responsible for directing the work of LSA and appointing the agency's executive director. To carry out its mission, LSA has approximately 80 employees, with some 23 attorneys, 16 fiscal researchers, two GIS specialists, and other editorial, technology, and administrative personnel.

Specifically, the project was conducted by the Office of Fiscal and Management Analysis (OFMA), one of three primary functional units of LSA. OFMA consists of a director, deputy director, and 14 fiscal analysts. Of this 16-member staff, three have PhDs, one is ABD, and nine have Master's or professional degrees. OFMA also has a continuing contract with a faculty economist from Purdue University who performs fiscal research and forecasting tasks and assists OFMA staff with such tasks. The primary function of OFMA is to produce fiscal notes for the legislation introduced by members of the Senate and House of Representatives during the legislative session. The legislature meets from January through April in budget years (odd numbered years) and from January through March in non-budget years (even-numbered years). Fiscal notes provide an estimate of the direct impact that legislation could have on state and local spending and/or revenues. OFMA fiscal analysts also routinely provide fiscal staffing for legislative committees during the legislative session.

As to the timing of the research project, the interim period between legislative sessions potentially provided a time period during which the project could be conducted. While not as intense and fast-paced as the legislative session, the interim period for OFMA staff consists of various routine and non-routine research and staffing tasks. In particular, the interim period is when OFMA staff can focus on researching current issues, and constructing, updating, and maintaining databases used for fiscal analysis and research. During the interim period

OFMA provides staffing to legislative study committees which typically begin meeting and conducting research in June or July. The run-up to the legislative session typically begins in mid-October when interim study committees are completing their work, and fiscal work relating to draft legislation for the upcoming legislative session commences. During the interim, OFMA staff also works on a variety of other tasks, including providing requested fiscal research and analysis to legislators and staff, conducting an evaluation of an executive branch program or agency, and annually compiling and publishing the *Indiana Handbook on Taxes, Revenues, and Appropriations* and the *Indiana Pension Handbook*. OFMA staff also participates informally in the consensus revenue forecasting process conducted annually during November and December. OFMA staff generates revenue forecasts for the state's cigarette tax, alcohol beverage taxes, insurance premium tax, and casino wagering tax, and assists with the forecasts for the corporate income tax, individual income tax, sales tax, and inheritance tax. Thus, the interim period is the time that special projects such as constructing the EZ business database would otherwise be conducted by OFMA. While the 2003 legislative session was a budget session ending in late April, the 2003 interim period still provided sufficient time for OFMA staff to work on the project.

As to technical expertise issues, OFMA staff has significant experience building and maintaining internal databases for fiscal research, and accessing data from various state and federal databases for purposes of fiscal research. OFMA houses multi-year taxpayer databases for the state individual income tax, state corporate income tax, and state inheritance and estate taxes. These databases are utilized to generate descriptive information and to simulate the impacts of proposed tax law changes. OFMA staff also maintains a state-wide parcel level property tax database to be used for fiscal research and analysis. The staff has also completed studies of the impact of the state-wide property tax re-assessment in 2002-2003. OFMA staff regularly access local government administrative data from the state's local government database to provide information in fiscal notes; and school finance data from state Department of Education databases to do estimates and analysis relating to the school funding formula. As a result of the estimation and database work conducted by OFMA, the fiscal analysts have substantial expertise using software programs to perform descriptive and analytical work, including Excel, Access, SAS, SPSS, and Oracle Discoverer.

Setting the Stage

This section discusses the factors that motivated the *Enterprise Zone (EZ) Fiscal Impact Project*. The project was motivated by legislation proposed in January, 2003, to significantly enhance the tax incentives that could be offered to businesses operating, investing, and employing individuals in Indiana's 29 EZs. The new incentive regime proposed in this legislation was a response to state and local tax system changes enacted in June, 2002. These changes were expected to have detrimental effects on the existing EZ tax incentive regime.

The Indiana EZ Program was established in 1983. By 2003, there were 29 EZs operated by municipal governments throughout Indiana. To establish an EZ, a municipality must apply to the state's economic development agency for approval.[1] Among several requirements that must be satisfied before an EZ is approved, the municipality proposing the EZ must establish an Urban Enterprise Association (UEA). A UEA is comprised of a 12-member association board to govern the EZ. In practice, the UEA boards employ personnel to manage and coordinate the day-to-day development activities and programs within the EZs. Historically, five tax incentives were available for businesses operating, investing, and employing individuals in the EZs. The incentives comprised:

1.   A local property tax credit for business inventory located in an EZ;

2.   A state corporate gross income tax exemption for income earned in an EZ;

3.   A state income tax credit for equity investment in an EZ business;

4.   A state income tax credit for wages paid by an EZ business to new employees who are also EZ residents; and

5.   A state income tax credit for interest income earned by financial institutions from loans to EZ businesses.

As in all place-based incentive schemes, these tax incentives serve as a recruitment tool for the EZs by establishing a material financial advantage for conducting business operations in the EZs. From 1995 to 2002, an average of almost 1,700 businesses state-wide annually claimed at least one EZ tax incentive, with the annual incentive total averaging about $37.2 million.[2] On average, about 92% of the annual tax incentive total (about $34.2 million per year) was attributable to the inventory property tax credit. The next largest incentive was the gross income tax exemption, comprising an average of about $1.3 million per year—about 3.5% of the annual tax incentive total.

While the tax incentives generate a sizeable subsidy for the recipient businesses, they also provide the primary source of operational funding for the UEAs. State law requires a business receiving EZ tax incentives to assist the UEA in an amount determined by the municipality where the EZ is located. This requirement has been implemented by municipalities in the form of a "participation fee" equal to a percentage of the tax savings a business obtains from the tax incentives. In 2003, UEA participation fees ranged from 20% to 49% of tax savings (IDOC, 2003). Participation fees paid by incentive recipients to UEAs averaged about $8.4 million per year state-wide from 1995 to 2002. Based on the distribution of annual incentive totals cited earlier, about $7.7 million in annual funding for the UEAs was attributable to the inventory property tax credit, with the gross income tax exemption accounting for an additional $300,000 annually in funding for the UEAs.

Tax restructuring legislation enacted in 2002 made substantial changes to the state and local tax system in Indiana. Two changes, in particular, had significant implications for the EZ program, both in terms of the recruitment tools available to the EZs and the funding source the incentives provided for the UEAs. The tax restructuring legislation repealed the corporate gross income tax beginning in 2003, thus, eliminating the second-most utilized tax advantage to the EZs. More importantly, the legislation exempted certain property from the inventory tax beginning in 2004, and scheduled the inventory tax for elimination beginning in 2007. The legislation also allowed for county-level elimination of the inventory tax before 2007. Thus, EZs would soon lose the incentive that had most to do with their competitive tax advantage over non-EZ areas in Indiana and that provided the overwhelming source of operational funding for the UEAs.

In response to the tax restructuring changes, legislation was proposed during the 2003 legislative session to substantially expand the package of tax incentives available to EZ businesses. Due to insufficient data about the business and economic activity taking place in the EZs, fiscal analysts from the Office of Fiscal and Management Analysis (OFMA) were unable to generate estimates of the potential fiscal impact of the proposed incentives. Ultimately, the legislation was not enacted by the General Assembly. The proposed incentives comprised:

1. A local property tax deduction for depreciable business tangible personal property other than inventory located in an EZ;

2. A state income tax deduction for incremental income generated by EZ businesses;

3. A state income tax credit equal to $1,500 per job created by an EZ business;

4. A state income tax credit for job training costs incurred by a business for training of EZ residents;

5. A state sales tax credit for purchases of building materials for projects built in an EZ; and

6. An additional state sales tax collection allowance for retail merchants located in an EZ.

During the 2003 legislative session, OFMA staff considered using data from two sources to estimate the potential state and local fiscal impact of the proposed new incentive regime. The data sources considered were: (1) existing data compiled by the Indiana Department of Commerce from annual reports submitted by businesses receiving EZ tax incentives; and (2) demographic and socio-economic data reported on a local basis by the U. S. Census Bureau, the U.S. Bureau of Economic Analysis (BEA), and the U.S. Bureau of Labor Statistics (BLS). OFMA staff concluded that neither of these sources could be utilized to validly estimate or impute the fiscal impact of the new incentive regime.

The annual reports of tax incentive recipients contain information about a recipient business's legal organization (corporation, partnership, or sole proprietorship), annual employment and wage totals, and the jobs created, incentives received, and participation fees paid by the business during the year. Annual report data spanning 1995 to 2002 was made available to OFMA, however, the 2001 and 2002 databases were incomplete. Annual report data was unavailable for years prior to 1995. OFMA staff concluded that the annual report data could result in biased estimates of business activity in the EZs and the potential fiscal impact of the new incentive regime. Potentially, the annual report sample consisted of firms that systematically benefited more than others from the existing incentive regime (in particular, from the inventory property tax credit). As a result, the new tax incentive regime, with primarily state income and sales tax incentives, could result in a much different and possibly larger response group. In addition to the selection bias concerns, OFMA staff concluded that C Corporations were likely over-represented in the report data in comparison to S Corporations and Partnerships.[3] Due to their preferred tax status, S Corporations and Partnerships have become a fast growing type of business organization (compared to declining numbers of C Corporations). Consequently, OFMA staff concluded that this significant and growing portion of the business community was excluded from the report data, which would bias any analysis or estimates relying on this database.

An array of federal government data was also available, but OFMA staff concluded these data posed different validity problems. *Census 2000* data at the block level comprised demographic count data of little use for fiscal impact analysis of business incentives. Tract level data comprised household monetary information (income and poverty measures, housing values, and rental rates) useful in describing the EZs, but did not include business data. BEA annual income data also were available at the Metropolitan Statistical Area (MSA) level, the county level, and by BEA economic areas. In addition, BLS quarterly employment and wage data were available at the county level, with reports for some cities. The richest source of business data was the County Business Patterns databases which included establishment and employment counts, industry sector information, and wage totals at the county level and MSA level. In all cases, the spatial area of measurement for these data was not coterminous with the EZs and, except for census blocks and tracts, the EZs were small relative to these geographic units. In the case of census tracts, while the geographic size was not disproportionate to EZ sizes, the boundaries of the EZs and the overlapping census tracts deviated substantially. Thus, OFMA staff concluded that measures relating to counties, MSAs, places, and even census tracts likely would not be representative of the EZs. What's more, given the variation in geographic shape and size of the EZs, OFMA staff was concerned that imputing measures from census tracts or other geographic units to EZs would be unreliable.

Figure 1. Geographic mismatch of Fort Wayne EZ and units of analysis for federal databases

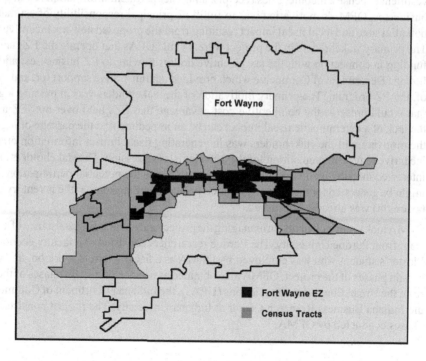

Figure 1 presents an example of the geographic mismatch between the EZs and the geographic units of analysis for the federal government databases outlined earlier. Figure 1 compares the footprint of the Fort Wayne EZ to the city limits of Fort Wayne and the census tracts intersecting the EZ. The Fort Wayne EZ is almost four square miles in size while the land area of Fort Wayne totals about 79 square miles. Allen County, where Fort Wayne is located, is about 657 square miles in size. A total of 16 census tracts overlap the Fort Wayne EZ, with the EZ representing less than half of the area of 13 of these census tracts.

Due to the shortcomings outlined previously, OFMA staff concluded that these data could not be utilized to validly estimate the extent of business activity in the EZs or the potential fiscal impact of the new incentive regime. In addition, OFMA staff concluded that relevant data on the EZs could not be developed on a valid or reliable basis within the time frame of the 2003 legislative session. As a result, OFMA's fiscal analysis during the 2003 legislative session specified that the proposed new tax incentive regime could reduce tax revenue, but that the extent of this reduction was indeterminable.

Case Description

This case describes the nine-month *Enterprise Zone (EZ) Fiscal Impact Project* conducted by the Office of Fiscal and Management Analysis (OFMA) to create a database describing the businesses and business activity in Indiana's EZs. The project commenced at the conclusion of the 2003 legislative session. The primary goals of the project were to create a census of EZ businesses containing information about wage and employment levels, investment expenses, income, sales receipts, and other pertinent information relating to these businesses. OFMA's motivation was to fulfill its principal responsibility of estimating the potential state and local fiscal impact resulting from the proposed new tax incentive regime. The primary stakeholders in the project were: (1) the UEAs that operate the EZs and obtain funding in connection with the tax incentive dollars flowing to EZ businesses; and (2) the Indiana Department of Commerce which provided administrative support for, and oversight of, the EZ program. The primary motivation of the stakeholders was in passing legislation that would preserve the competitive cost advantage that EZs held over non-EZ areas. As the lack of a determinable fiscal impact can be an impediment to the passage of legislation, the motivation of the stakeholders was in generating fiscal impact information on the new incentive regime in preparation for the 2004 legislative session. The stakeholders also were interested in using the fiscal impact estimates to gauge the potential participation fees that might be generated for the UEAs since their primary funding source (the inventory property tax credit) was already diminished.

OFMA took the principal role in managing the project and obtained the assistance of a research team from Purdue University. The Purdue researchers consisted of a faculty economist and Master's student who was employed by OFMA as a fiscal intern to work on, and manage, certain phases of the project. OFMA also obtained assistance on certain phases of the project from the Urban Enterprise Associations (UEAs), the Indiana Department of Commerce, and the Indiana Business Research Center at Indiana University. The project consisted of four phases conducted by OFMA:

1.   GIS mapping of the EZs;

2.   Geocoding employer data from the *Quarterly Census of Employment and Wages* (also referred to as ES-202 data) to construct an EZ business activity database;[4]

3.   Conducting an EZ business survey to obtain business activity data not included in the *Quarterly Census of Employment and Wages*; and

4.   Constructing a demographic and socio-economic database on the EZs.

Phase I of the project involved generating digitized GIS maps of the EZs. As demonstrated in Figure 1, the EZs are not coterminous with government jurisdiction boundaries (county or municipal boundaries) or U.S. Census geographic units of analysis (Metropolitan Statistical Areas, or census tracts, blocks, or block groups). As a result, the digitized maps of the EZs would allow OFMA staff to isolate street addresses located in the EZs. This process would serve as the necessary first step to isolating EZ businesses in the ES-202 employer database.

OFMA staff utilized ArcView GIS software (version 3.2) and U.S. Census Bureau 2002 TIGER/Line files. The TIGER/Line files include various geographic features such as roads, railroads, rivers, lakes, jurisdictional boundaries, and boundaries of U.S. Census geography (census tracts, blocks, and block groups). The files also include latitude and longitude location of features, and address ranges for streets. After some basic instruction on using ArcView, OFMA staff produced initial digitized GIS maps of each EZ using physical maps and legal descriptions of the EZs supplied by the Indiana Department of Commerce. Seven fiscal analysts and the fiscal intern produced the initial GIS maps of the EZs over a three to four-week period. GIS specialists from the Legislative Services Agency also assisted by providing guidance and trouble shooting assistance to the map generators. The GIS maps of the EZs identified addresses, streets and roads, jurisdictional boundaries, railroads and waterways, U.S. Census geography, and other geographic information comprising the EZs.

To check the accuracy of the maps, the UEAs agreed to review the maps based on the legal descriptions and their knowledge of their own EZ boundaries. The initial maps were plotted on paper and mailed to the UEAs for feedback. OFMA requested that each UEA review the plotted EZ map and make necessary corrections in pencil and return mail it or, if the map was correct, return mail the map noting that it was correct. A total of 22 UEAs responded with corrections or confirmation that the map was correct, and five UEAs responded by e-mailing OFMA digitized maps already generated for five EZs. Upon receipt of the information from the UEAs, OFMA staff generated the corrected maps complete with census geography.

Phase II of the project involved geocoding the ES-202 employer data. This process isolated economic data applicable only to businesses operating in Indiana's EZs. It was entirely dependent on generating the digitized maps and developing the GIS containing street addresses in the EZs during Phase I of the project. The quarterly ES-202 database contains North American Industry Classification System (NAICS) industry sector codes, employment and wage levels, and physical location addresses for employers.[5] The ES-202 data was provided by the Indiana Department of Commerce to OFMA under a confidential use agreement for purposes of conducting the project. OFMA obtained 3rd quarter (July-September) ES-202 data for three years—1997, 1999, and 2002. OFMA staff determined early on in the project that the GIS mapping work and geocoding the ES-202 data for only one year would require substantial time to complete. Thus, to ensure both the timely completion of the project and that the EZ business database included the most current data, the geocoding process was conducted only with the 3rd quarter 2002 data.

While the mapping phase of the project was important, the geocoding phase represented the most important and fresh component of the project. Sawicki and Flynn (1996), Haque (2001), and Nicholls (2001) outline and demonstrate various ways that public managers employ GIS. Primarily, GIS is employed to provide visual presentations of spatial data (such as streets, roads, highways, utilities, and jurisdictional boundaries) and non-spatial demographic and socio-economic data that have already been geocoded (such as census tract level and block level data). These researchers, however, pay little attention to the process of geocoding and the potential to add information to a GIS via its existing geographic database. Geocoding allows the GIS user to integrate new data into an existing GIS by linking some geographic component (street address, census geography) of the external data to geography embedded in the GIS. Martin (2000) suggests that 80% of government data comprises information that references a specific geographic location. He posits that geocoding this data could provide public managers and policy analysts an important tool to investigate social phenomena and analyze public programs and policies.

The geocoding process matched street addresses of businesses in the ES-202 employer database with street addresses contained in the Tiger/Line files underlying the GIS maps of the EZs. The 3rd quarter 2002 ES-202 database selected for geocoding consisted of almost 154,000 business establishments. The geocoding process generally involved paring the ES-202 files to be matched to the municipality containing the focal EZ, and then checking and cleaning the address data for the selected ES-202 files. Since EZs are limited to a single municipality, the ES-202 files to be geocoded could be batched by the municipality reported as the physical location of the business. As a result, files containing physical location addresses outside the pertinent municipality were eliminated from the start. Since governmental and non-profit entities are not eligible for EZ tax incentives, ES-202 files pertaining to employers from these sectors also were eliminated based on NAICS industry codes.[6]

To optimize the match rate between the ES-202 employer addresses and the TIGER/Line addresses, OFMA staff spent substantial time cleaning the ES-202 file addresses, and adding address information manually when it was missing. Based on the TIGER/Line address formats, format rules were developed for use in cleaning ES-202 address information. For cases where address information was missing or a "P.O. Box" was recorded as an employer's physical location address, relevant address information was obtained via searches using databases such as the *On-line Yellow Pages* and *Reference USA*. Data cleaning was performed by seven fiscal analysts, with a fiscal intern and one fiscal analyst conducting the geocoding. Again, GIS specialists from the Legislative Services Agency provided guidance and trouble shooting assistance with the geocoding. The geocoding process for each municipality containing an EZ ultimately generated match rates of about 80%. This match rate indicates that 80% of the addresses in the ES-202 database from a municipality containing an EZ were successfully geocoded or matched to a TIGER/Line files address (Lowe, 2004). The geocoding results for Fort Wayne and the Fort Wayne EZ are presented in Figure 2, with the white dots representing address matches between the TIGER/Line files and the ES-202 files.

Phase II of the project generated a database of EZ employers in 2002. The employer database for each EZ identified the industry sector of each EZ business, the number of persons employed by each EZ business, and the annualized wage payments made by each EZ business.

Figure 2. Geocoding results for Fort Wayne EZ

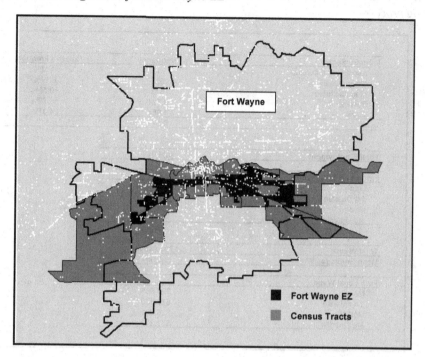

For data analysis purposes, five overarching industry sectors were analyzed: Agriculture and Mining; Construction; Manufacturing; Service; and Trade. Summary employment and wage statistics were derived from the databases for each EZ. State totals for the EZs are presented in Table 1.

The information in Table 1 suggests that the 28 EZs operating in Indiana at the completion of the project contained approximately 6,400 businesses employing about 135,000 workers.[7] The EZ businesses paid an estimated $4.73 billion in annualized wages. The data indicated that EZ businesses were concentrated in the service and trade sectors, with about 56.8% being service businesses and about 24.4% being involved in retail or wholesale trade. Manufacturing businesses constituted about 10.6% of EZ businesses, while construction businesses represented about 8.2%. Because the ES-202 data includes NAICS industry sector codes for each business, employment and wage levels also were derived for each industry sector. Table 2 presents EZ employment and wage levels by the industry sector for the EZs operating at the time the project was completed.

Phase III of the project involved a survey of EZ employers identified in Phase II of the project. The survey was intended to develop business activity information that could not be gleaned from the ES-202 data. Principally, the survey asked firms for annual sales receipts, annual investment expenditures, and current value of real and tangible personal property. The survey also asked questions aimed at revealing the types of incentives EZ firms would likely

Table 1. EZ business census and employment and wage statistics generated by the geocoding process

Industry Sector	Frequency	Relative Frequency
Agriculture & Mining	7	0.11%
Construction	521	8.17%
Manufacturing	673	10.56%
Service	3,621	56.79%
Trade	1,554	24.37%
Total	6,376	

Total Employment	134,915

Firm Level Employment	
Mean	21.2
1st Quartile	2.0
Median	6.0
3rd Quartile	15.0

Total Wages	$4,731,048,692
Mean Employee Wage	$35,067

Firm Level Wage	
Mean	$24,685
1st Quartile	$10,880
Median	$20,391
3rd Quartile	$31,273

Table 2. EZ industry sector employment and wage statistics generated by the geocoding process

	Agriculture & Mining	Construction	Manufacturing	Service	Trade
Total Employment	79	9,300	55,455	50,000	20,081

Firm Level Employment					
Mean	11.3	17.9	82.4	13.8	12.9
1st Quartile	4.0	3.0	5.0	2.0	3.0
Median	7.0	8.0	16.0	5.0	6.0
3rd Quartile	15.0	18.0	44.0	12.0	13.0

	Agriculture & Mining	Construction	Manufacturing	Service	Trade
Total Wages	$2,554,652	$378,345,388	$2,580,036,648	$1,266,236,184	$503,875,820
Mean Employee Wage	$32,337	$40,682	$46,525	$25,325	$25,092

Firm Level Wage					
Mean	$39,389	$27,687	$30,818	$24,031	$22,477
1st Quartile	$24,872	$17,011	$20,669	$9,600	$11,160
Median	$29,469	$26,810	$29,487	$18,200	$18,501
3rd Quartile	$35,025	$36,000	$38,135	$29,236	$28,894

respond to and utilize. The survey instrument was developed by OFMA staff and the Purdue research team, and was tested by the Purdue research team on businesses in the Lafayette, Indiana EZ. Random samples of EZ businesses were selected for the survey. Initially, the survey was conducted via telephone in two EZs. Surveys in the remaining EZs were conducted by fax. The UEA staffs for the remaining EZs faxed questionnaires to selected businesses after contacting them by telephone. The telephone and fax surveys failed to generate sufficient response rates. In total, survey responses were obtained from only 10 of the 29 EZs operating in 2003. The survey response rates for these EZs ranged from about 15% to 20%, well below an adequate response rate of 50%. As a result, the information generated by the survey could not be used to validly represent businesses in the EZs.

Phase IV of the project generated demographic and socio-economic measures of the EZs. The Indiana Business Research Center constructed these measures using *Census 2000* response data contained in *Summary File 1* and *Summary File 3*. The Indiana Business Research Center is an economic research unit of Indiana University. The Indiana Business Research Center is both a *State Data Center* and a *Business and Industry Data Center* under these cooperative programs with the U.S. Census Bureau. While this phase of the project would not generate business activity information regarding the EZs, it was undertaken to enhance the available information describing the EZs. OFMA staff also concluded that the demographic and socio-economic measures could potentially be useful in the event tax relief measures for residents or homeowners in EZs were to be proposed.

OFMA provided the Indiana Business Research Center with copies of the GIS for each EZ. Staff at the Indiana Business Research Center constructed the measures from block level and block group level data. Data allocation rules were employed when block or block group boundaries extended beyond EZ boundaries. Phase IV of the project generated a demographic and socio-economic profile of each EZ. The profiles described the population and household composition, housing stock, and labor force of the EZs, and provided measures of the educational attainment and poverty status of EZ residents.

Current Challenges

The *Enterprise Zone (EZ) Fiscal Impact Project* was an effort by the Office of Fiscal and Management Analysis (OFMA) to assemble a database describing the businesses and business activities occurring in Indiana's EZs. Prior to the completion of the project even a simple count of the businesses operating in Indiana's EZs did not exist. The project was motivated by OFMA's responsibility to estimate the revenue impact of the new tax incentive regime proposed for Indiana's EZs in 2003. The proposed new incentive regime was offered in response to state and local tax restructuring changes enacted in 2002 that were expected to have detrimental effects on the existing EZ tax incentive regime. In summary, the project yielded current information on employment levels, wage levels, and the industry sector of businesses operating in Indiana's EZs. These data ultimately were utilized by OFMA staff to inform the decision making of the legislature regarding potential new elements of the EZ tax incentive regime. The project, however, did not yield all sought after business and economic information on the EZs, including measures of business income, sales, and investment in the EZs. As a result, the project revealed how GIS technology can be utilized effectively to develop economic databases describing localized and idiosyncratic geographic areas for which data is not available. It also showed that researchers must implement this technology with care to ensure that the databases it yields are valid and reliable indicators of the economic activity within the relevant geographic areas.

The four phases of the project successfully identified businesses operating in Indiana's EZs, and assembled a rich database categorizing these businesses by industry sector, and reporting the employment and wage levels of these businesses. The database provided a sufficient source of information to estimate the impact of various wage and job creation tax incentives in the EZs. As to some of the more narrow incentives proposed for the EZs in 2003, the employment data from ES-202 files and the EZ workforce data from *Census 2000* were used as the basis for estimating the potential impact of the job training incentives. What's more, the North American Industry Classification System (NAICS) industry sector information was utilized to estimate the potential impact of the retail merchant's tax incentive providing an additional collection allowance for EZ merchants.

Nonetheless, the EZ business database still only provided a foundation of data to be used in the estimation process. OFMA staff had to assemble or estimate other supplementary economic measures to augment information in the EZ business database. These supplemental measures consisted of growth rates, response rates, and unit cost amounts that were combined with the business count data, or the base employment or wage totals, to derive a tax incentive cost. For example, the fiscal impact estimate for the proposed $1,500 jobs credit depended on two supplementary measures:

1. An estimate of the historic underlying growth rate for employment in each of the EZs to estimate the credits claimed for new jobs that would occur independently of the credit; and

2. An estimate of the wage elasticity of demand for labor to estimate the credits claimed for new jobs created due to the reduction in wage cost from the credit.

Additional supplementary measures included the average job training expenses by industry from survey research conducted by the U.S. Bureau of Labor Statistics, and the average and median retail merchant's collection allowance supplied by the Indiana Department of State Revenue. These supplementary economic measures would have been useless to derive the fiscal impacts of the proposed new incentives without the EZ business database generated as a result of Phase I and Phase II of the project.

It is also important to highlight that the project fell short of the data collection goals initially set by OFMA staff. The project failed to develop measures of sales receipts and income generated by EZ businesses, investment expenditures made by EZ businesses, and fixed assets held by EZ businesses. On the one hand, the EZ business survey conducted in Phase III of the project was an attempt to glean these data using street addresses and telephone numbers of EZ businesses identified in Phase II of the project. Unfortunately, the survey response rates were insufficient to generate valid measures of sales, income, investment, and fixed assets of EZ businesses.

Alternatively, OFMA staff studied the potential efficacy of geocoding information from state individual income tax, corporate income tax, and sales tax returns to derive sales and income measures applicable to EZ businesses. This strategy would match the address reported on the tax return with those already identified in the EZs. Ultimately, the strategy was not pursued because sales and income information is not compiled on these tax returns in a manner that allows the analyst to isolate sales and income that is attributable solely to a business's operations in an EZ. Since business income reported on consolidated corporate income tax returns is an aggregate of the filer corporation's operations in the EZ as well as at locations of other affiliated companies, the income attributable to business operations in the EZ is not determinable. Likewise, retail companies filing sales tax returns may report on a consolidated return basis. Such a return would include sales at a company's stores located throughout Indiana although the return would be submitted from a single address, such as the company's corporate center in Indiana. Thus, the sales data is an aggregate amount attributable to locations besides the EZ location from where the return may have been submitted. Finally, business income flowing through the state's individual income tax system cannot be delineated from other forms of income such as wages, salaries, dividends, or capital gains. This is because computation of the tax begins with the taxpayer's Federal Adjusted Gross Income (AGI), with no reporting of the activities (business or otherwise) that generated the AGI amount. Interestingly, Ventura (1995, p. 461) suggests that "successful use of GIS (by an organization) depends on technical choices and on the ability, capacity, and willingness of (the) organization to absorb and use new forms and quantities of information." Nevertheless, the problems outlined earlier suggest that while geocoding, on its face, presents a comprehensive and effective solution to assembling data for rather unique geographic areas like EZs, pertinent data is not always reported in a manner conducive to timely or effective geocoding. Ultimately, the data availability and time issues were impediments to OFMA generating a more comprehensive EZ business database.

Despite the shortcomings of the project, the resultant EZ business database was a useful tool for OFMA staff to inform policymakers about current conditions in Indiana's EZs and about the potential fiscal impact of various new tax incentives being proposed for the EZs. The extent to which this information affected legislative outcomes, however, is unclear. Potentially, EZ business data and the fiscal analysis conducted with this data augmented a more global and less formal analysis that policymakers were performing vis-à-vis the fiscal constraints they were operating under during this period. The effort to provide new tax incentives for the EZs was initiated during the 2003 legislative session, with the legislation not enacted. At this time, data on the EZs was lacking severely and OFMA staff was unable to place a fiscal impact on any of the proposed incentives. It's quite possible that the lack of fiscal impact information did weigh against the adoption of new EZ tax incentives at this time. With the project completed, legislation was introduced again in 2004 and 2005 proposing a package of EZ incentives similar to that proposed in 2003. In 2005, the General Assembly enacted a new local property tax incentive for the EZs, but did not enact any new state tax incentives. Notwithstanding the available data and fiscal analysis, this outcome may have been shaped by the general fiscal and budgetary pressures present in Indiana (as was the case in most other states) during the 2001-2005 period.[8] It's quite possible that for these reasons policymakers focused on a property tax incentive that would limit fiscal impact to communities with EZs and not generate any state fiscal impact.

References

Haque, A. (2001). GIS, public service, and the issue of democratic governance. *Public Administration Review, 61*(3), 259-265.

IDOC. (Indiana Department of Commerce). (2003). *Indiana enterprise zone program handbook.* Indianapolis, Indiana.

Lowe, S. (2004). *Indiana enterprise zone program: Employment growth and fiscal impact analysis of a job creation tax credit.* Unpublished master's thesis, Purdue University, West Lafayette, Indiana.

Martin, D. E. (2000). Geographic information systems and the public manager. In G. D. Garson (Ed.), *Handbook of public information systems* (1st ed., pp. 535-550). New York, NY: Marcel Dekker, Inc.

NASBO. (National Association of State Budget Officers). (2000). *The fiscal survey of states.* December 2000. Washington, DC.

NASBO. (National Association of State Budget Officers). (2006). *The fiscal survey of states,* June 2006. Washington, DC.

Nicholls, S. (2001). Measuring the accessibility and equity of public parks: A case study using GIS. *Managing Leisure, 6*(4), 201-219.

Sawicki, D. S., & Flynn P. (1996). Neighborhood indicators: A review of the literature and an assessment of conceptual and methodological issues. *Journal of the American Planning Association, 62*(2), 165-183.

Ventura, S. J. (1995). The use of geographic information systems in local government. *Public Administration Review, 55*(5), 461-467.

Endnotes

[1] Prior to 2005, approval and oversight of the EZs was conducted by the Indiana Enterprise Zone Board which was housed in, and supported by the Indiana Department of Commerce. Since then, approval and oversight of the EZs has been conducted by the Indiana Economic Development Corporation which replaced the Indiana Department of Commerce as Indiana's state economic development agency.

[2] The aggregate statistics reported were generated from annual Enterprise Zone Business Registration Reports submitted by incentive recipients to the Indiana Department of Commerce.

[3] A C Corporation is the traditional corporate organization in which investors are able to limit their liability to the total amount of their investment. The C Corporation pays federal and state income taxes on earnings. But, when the earnings are distributed to the corporation's stockholders as dividends, this income is also subject to federal and state income tax imposed on the stockholder's income. An S Corporation also provides for limited liability of investors, but is limited in number and type of stockholders. C Corporations may issue different classes of stock such as common and preferred stock, with the latter providing the investor a greater claim on the corporation's assets than is the case for common stockholders. S Corporations are limited to 75 stockholders and only a single class of stock. However, S Corporation income is not taxed through the corporate income tax. Rather, S Corporation income is taxed under the individual income tax when it is distributed to stockholders. A partnership consists of general partners who manage the business and are equally liable for the businesses' debts. Limited partners have no say in the management of the

business but their liability is limited to the extent of their investment in the business. In addition, partnership income is like S Corporation income only taxed upon distribution to the partners.

[4] The ES-202 Program is a cooperative federal-state program that tabulates at the employer level employment and wage information for workers covered by state and federal unemployment compensation programs.

[5] The North American Industry Classification System (NAICS) is a classification system for collection of business and economic activity data in the United States, Canada, and Mexico. The classification system reports various data on the basis of the following 20 industry sectors: (1) agriculture, forestry, fishing and hunting; (2) mining; (3) utilities; (4) construction; (5) manufacturing; (6) wholesale trade; (7) retail trade; (8) transportation and warehousing; (9) information; (10) finance and insurance; (11) real estate and rental and leasing; (12) professional, scientific, and technical services; (13) management of companies and enterprises; (14) administrative and support and waste management and remediation services; (15) educational services; (16) health care and social assistance; (17) arts, entertainment, and recreation; (18) accommodation and food services; (19) other services except public administration; and (20) public administration. Within these major sectors, data is also classified and reported at lower levels for industry sub-sectors, yet smaller industry groups, and, finally, for particular industries.

[6] Files with the following 2-digit, 3-digit, and 4-digit NAICS codes were eliminated: 624-Social Assistance; 7111-Performing Arts; 712- Museums, Historical Sites, and Similar Institutions; 813-Religious, Grantmaking, Civic, Professional, and Other Similar Organizations; 92-Public Administration.

[7] The EZ in Anderson, Indiana expired at the end of 2003 and is not included in the statistical tables.

[8] The Fiscal Year 1999 year-end General Fund balance totaled about $1.47 billion, with a Rainy Day Fund balance totaling about $525 million (NASBO, 2000). By Fiscal Year 2005, the year-end General Fund balance totaled about $119 million, with the Rainy Day Fund balance totaling $317 million.

Author's Biography

Jim Landers is a Senior Fiscal/Program Analyst for the Indiana Legislative Services Agency. His research interests focus on state and local tax policy and economic development programs and policy. He received his PhD from the School of Public Policy and Management at The Ohio State University. His previous employment includes services as a research analyst for the Arkansas Bureau of Legislative Research and a researcher and legislative drafter for the Ohio Legislative Service Commission.

Chapter XXI

The Techonomic Divide

Alex Pettit, City of Denton, Texas, USA

Anthony Caranna, City of Denton, Texas, USA

Executive Summary

Much has been written on the digital divide, whereby less affluent citizens are (or will be) left out of the "next wave" of progress due to the financial costs prohibiting their participation in the broadband society being formed. Little has been written about the transformation of the electronic payment receipt process, and how participation in e-payment requires a credit card or MasterCard/Visa debit card to complete online transactions. This has the effect of excluding the cash and check-based society from participation, and directly impacts not only the digital divide but also the ROI of these e-payment solutions to the government entity providing them. The City of Denton has worked to address this "techonomic" divide by developing equitability in payment options.

Background

Established in 1857, Denton is the county seat of Denton County, and was named for John B. Denton. John Denton was a lawyer, preacher, and a soldier. His grave is on the courthouse lawn in the center of Denton's historic downtown square. The centerpiece of the downtown square is the old Denton County Courthouse, which was erected in 1896 and restored in 1987. The courthouse contains a museum highlighting historic photographs and artifacts from the city's founding to the present.

Denton is the proud home of two public universities—Texas Woman's University and the University of North Texas, the 3rd largest university in the State of Texas, with a combined enrollment of approximately 40,000 students.

Denton's current estimated population is over 100,000 residents. The city is a full-service municipality, providing electric, water, solid waste, drainage, fiber optic, airport, public transit, ambulance, and traditional public services to residents and businesses in the community. There are 1,237 full-time employees of the city. Forty-three buildings comprise the campus, which are connected with single-mode fiber optic cables, enabling gigabit connectivity from any city facility or from the mall. The city limits encompass 70 square miles, and this is expected to increase with the population. Denton will have over 200,000 residents by 2020.

The City of Denton is a manager/council form of government, whereby the City Council appoints the city manager, city attorney, and municipal court judge. The city manager is responsible for hiring the division managers in the organization and accountable for the smooth operation of city services. A detailed organization chart can be found on the city's Web site www.cityofdenton.com.

The city has embraced the practice of outcome management from the Carver Governance model. Outcomes define where the city is going, what will be accomplished, for whom and at what cost over the next several years. Several outcome statements have been defined and can be found in the department-specific strategic plans or white papers on the city's Web site.

These outcome statements have been defined to the detail the council wants to describe them, and focus on the aspects of the organization that come into direct and continuous contact with the citizens. As an internal service provider, the key to success for Technology Services is to partner with our stakeholders to understand, achieve, and if possible to enhance the desired outcomes.

One of these areas where Technology Services has been able to better understand and enhance the desired outcomes has been in the development of e-government solutions. In response to a directive from the City Council, facilitation for electronic access to government services were developed and deployed beginning in 1999. After only a year's worth of data, it became apparent that our electronic payment processing was impacted by both demographic preferences and the famous "digital divide". The concept of the "digital divide" was first espoused by Larry Irving, who, as a technology advisor to the Clinton Administration, pointed out how socio-economic differences between communities impact the way computers and the Internet are utilized. In more specific terms, less affluent citizens are (or will be) left out of the "next wave" of progress due to the financial costs prohibiting their participation in the broadband society being formed. Little has been written about the transformation of the electronic payment receipt process, and how participation in e-payment requires a credit card or MasterCard/Visa debit card to complete online transactions. This has the effect of excluding the cash and check-based society from participation, and directly impacts not only the digital divide but also the Return On Investment (ROI) of these e-payment solutions to the government entity providing them.

The city began providing Web, interactive voice response (IVR), and kiosk payment services through a single technology solution in September of 2000. Evolution of these services and the impact of adding check readers, cash readers, and location of devices will be discussed and data presented showing that the digital divide is more apparent in the methods of payment than in the access to the services. Should public policy wish to address the digital divide, equitability in payment options must be achieved and is factually demonstrated by our statistics.

Architecture of the solution, presenting a media-independent structure (kiosk, IVR, Web, and ultimately handheld) interface that homogenizes multiple sources into a consistent look and feel to any access point will be diagramed and explained. Associated statistics demonstrating user acceptance (or rejection) will be presented and explained, and our inferences drawn to the digital divide will be explored. Finally, the impact of these anomalies on the ultimate ROI of these products will be presented, and what impact this has on our continued development of online solutions will be presented.

Setting the Stage

Information retrieval and access continues to change the face of the public-sector services environment. Timely and accurate information impacts all facets of the customer service experience regardless which service the citizen, patron, rate payer, tax payer, or visitor to our city interacts. This is easy to state and often cited as the sole justification to e-government expenditures.

The e-government initiative in the city is more than providing existing services through electronic media. Rather, it is the transformational engine providing the departments the opportunity to re-define the fundamental elements of service and citizen support, the relationship between the city and the citizens, and the expansion of the reach of our services to citizens who would not receive these benefits and services otherwise. Traditionally, Technology Services has operated as an internal service provider to city departments, but the advent of e-government has created an interface between the technology and the citizenry on behalf of the outward-facing departments. It is this interface that is the vehicle through which Technology Services comes into direct contact with the citizens.

This opportunity to re-define services to citizens was recognized by city staff in 1998, and was refined by a citizen committee into a series of outcome statements for online services. These outcome statements represented the expectations of the populous, as voiced through the citizen committee, and provided the initial public recommendations for the city's e-government direction.

In 1999, the city began working with vendors to develop integrated online bill-payment solutions. A framework for these services was designed and incorporated the following key elements: all solutions are required to provide both voice and thin-client access; applications must conform to support our existing multi-layered security design; all solutions must update in real time our existing back-office database systems using Open Data Base Connections (ODBC) or XML connections and support existing Application Program Interfaces (API) constructs of the applications; and the services offered had to be sufficiently varied to ensure they were accessible to the public, the technology could not be a barrier to access (Americans with Disabilities Act Section 407 compliance to ensure support for the disabled, telephone access, public kiosk access, and online Web access).

Through this architecture, several commercial products have been designed. All support account inquiry, payment, real-time update, and access from Web, kiosk, or telephone. We rolled out the services one at a time, beginning with municipal court fines on both the Web and the phone. We then rolled out the tax payment service, the utility billing service, and finally the building permitting and inspection scheduling service. We expected that the media preference would be 50/50, with half of the payments and inquiries for whichever specific service coming in by telephone, and half through the Web. With two universities, we expected many college students or their parents to avail themselves of the Web services, and local residents to prefer the telephone services. We expected that there would be a shift over time from the telephone access to the Web access, and considered not deploying a kiosk for self-service customers. We deployed our first public kiosk solution in 2001 in the lobby of the police department, expecting municipal court ticket payers would utilize the device.

By 2002, there was sufficient data to perform a meaningful analysis of the transaction behaviors and look at trends and preferences. We found that some services tend to favor one media over another. Specifically, municipal court transactions and queries are primarily performed by telephone. At that time, we concluded that the technology most readily available to the citizen when they wish to resolve a ticket is their cell phone. We tuned the municipal court system to support more incoming phone calls, and extended the time-out (or hang-up) delay to allow for cell phone's tendency to go into and out of service areas and not drop the call. On the other hand, we found that tax payments and queries are almost exclusively done via the Web. This reflects the technology available to the citizen when they are paying their taxes is their home computer. We have removed most of the telephone capability for the tax system to better deploy this resource to where it is most needed. All Web and telephone collection statistics can be found in the charts in Figures 1 and 2. These anomalies will be explored and explanations offered in the next section.

The most interesting statistics were with the kiosk. The kiosk we placed in August 2002 in the lobby of the police department will only accept credit cards. The device cost $7,000, and by January 2003 it was apparent that it would be several years before this service reached a break-even point on just collection amounts. We viewed this as a failure, but we were uncertain of the underlying cause. We left the device up, and suspended the kiosk program indefinitely.

The City of Denton has operated a storefront (City Hall in the Mall) in the local mall since 1988, primarily to facilitate collections of utility fees and taxes. Contractually, the city must keep the storefront staffed during mall hours of operation. Employees were stretched beyond their traditional 8-5 jobs to make sure there was someone at the mall until 9 or 10 p.m. and on the weekends. Although 60% of our in-person payments for utility services come in at the mall, the overtime and shift-differential costs were significantly eating into our revenue stream. When approached, the mall operator (Simon Properties) agreed to reduce our required hours of operation if a kiosk service were available to provide collection services for bill payment.

Figure 1. Total number of transactions processed by department

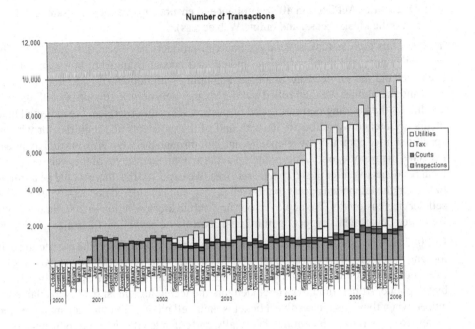

Figure 2. Total dollar value of transactions processed by department

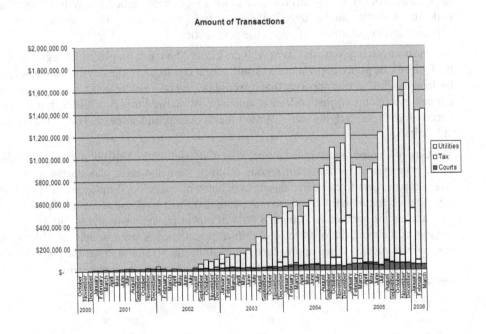

Figure 3. Comparison of Web, IVR, and kiosk utilization

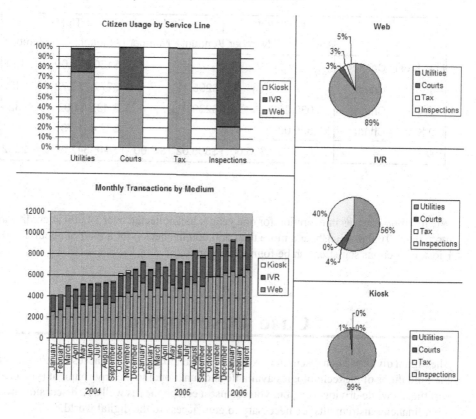

We studied the transactions that were taking place at the mall, and found that the majority of them were done by cash or check, and not by credit card. Often, two people who shared utility expenses would present themselves and one would pay by cash and the other by check. Most of these people had received a disconnect notice, letting them know that if they did not remit a payment to the city immediately the electricity would be cut off to their residence. Many of these people historically only pay when they receive a disconnect notice, and often can only pay by either cash or check.

We have labeled this the techonomic divide. Although this group has a need for immediacy, they cannot participate in e-government because they do not have the required media for payment (a credit card). If we were going to reduce the hours of the City Hall in the Mall, we would need to accommodate the needs of these people or face their complaints at our council meetings and in the newspaper.

We found a device that would accept cash, check, and credit cards for payment. We needed to be able to read the routing number off the check, to recognize real from phony money, and to provide a receipt to the user that would assure them that their services would not be discontinued the next day. This device was $15,000.

Figure 4. Kiosk statistics

		CITATION		TAX		UTILITIES	
		Amount	Number	Amount	Number	Amount	Number
Mall Kiosk	Cash					$130,233.00	1119
	Check			$295.11	1	$272,223.73	1102
	Charge	$3,080.00	18	$239.91	1	$ 43,444.02	320
PD Kiosk	Charge	$3,525.00	17			$ 2,441.79	21
Total		$6,605.00	$35.00	$535.02	$ 2.00	$448,342.54	2562

When this device was in operation for one year, it had collected over $4,000 in credit cards, more than $10,000 in cash, and more than $60,000 in checks, for a total of about $75,000. Kiosk collections statistics can be found in Figure 4.

Case Description

The digital divide is not a discussion exclusive to broadband Internet access. It also includes the limitations of the technologies available and functional in the environment (you cannot surf the net while driving a car, but you can use a cell phone) as well as a discussion around what financial instruments are necessary to gain access to the digital world.

Our conclusion was that some services have a natural proclivity for one media over another, and that many people are excluded from participating in online services, as they do not possess a debit/credit card to perform the transaction.

This conclusion may seem to be obvious. But it is still unclear how great of an impact this has on the digital community. Beginning in October 2000, we initiated online collections processing for our municipal court. We provided four telephone lines to support telephone support, and from the same Microsoft server we provided the Web services. In this manner, we have a single code source to manage. Modifications to the code result in changes to all systems simultaneously. Using Teleworks technology, we designed the IVR solution to "read" the Web pages to a phone-in customer. We next added building inspections scheduling, tax collections, and finally utility billing. Both phone and Web services were available at the same time for each service, and the hardware was upgraded to accommodate this architecture.

What we found was that, despite our efforts, not all services were reaching all citizens. We initially believed this was due to inherent differences (or preferences) in media with the associated service. Initially, our municipal court statistics demonstrated that interactions by telephone were more than double the interactions by Web. Over time, however, this imbalance has shifted somewhat to reflect closer to a 60/40 split of Web versus IVR usage, as seen in Figure 1. One of our findings with regards to court fine payments over the IVR was that the majority of incoming calls were numbers assigned to cell phones. We concluded that the many municipal court violations are being addressed by the person with the technology available to them in the vehicle—a cell phone. We found that this same disparity was obvious in our building inspections scheduling (10 to 1 in favor of the phone), and concluded that the technology available at a building site is usually a cell phone. On the other side, we found that property tax queries and payments heavily favor the Web, with no payments received through the IVR solution. We believe this reflects the environment where taxes are calculated, most usually at a desk where a PC is available for use. We will expect to see changes to the payments as changes come to the technology in use (broadband wireless should impact building inspection scheduling, for instance). But this did not explain our kiosk usage variances.

In our 1995 Technology Services Plan, it was decided to budget for the development of a public kiosk solution. The project plan was a budget of $30,000 and no specifics on what need a kiosk was to fulfill and for whom. At the time, the majority of municipal public kiosks were devoted to provide information to tourists and citizens. This was similar to what the first generation of online Web services provided—static information about people, some history, points of interest, calendars of events, and announcements. Fairfax County, Virginia was and continues to be the pioneer of these informational kiosks—http://www.fairfaxcounty. gov/dit/kiosk.htm. This design for the kiosks was to take our Web site and make it available from a walk-up device, thereby helping to bridge the digital divide. It was believed that we could accomplish this with only hardware and minimal modification to the city's Web page as it currently existed. As the plan started to form, it was envisioned that information kiosks would be placed in the three City Hall facilities, at the three libraries, and four of the parks and recreation locations to provide access to the residents.

We purchased a kiosk as a development platform from IBM in 2000, which had a touch screen, a keyboard, a roller-ball mouse, an infrared reader, a receipt printer, an Ethernet port, and a podium that fixed all of it in place (see Figure 5). The device runs Windows NT 4.0 SP 6, which would support an Internet Explorer browser and would be configured only to browse the city's Web site. The touch screen or the roller ball could be used to navigate the site. We purchased this device for $6,000.

From analyzing our Web usage statistics, it became apparent that our Web site users were not looking for general information about the city, but rather specific questions or information that they were seeking. When we first began our Web presence there was only the main site URL publicized, and the vast majority of Web traffic originating from the parent site. We recognized early on that the trend was away from a central site (or lead portal) and toward direct page requests to destinations below the city's main page. From our statistics for the month of April 2000 (see Figure 6), you can see that 40% of the Web site visits (the first two index sites listed represent views on the front page of the city's Web site) originate from the top of the page, with the remaining 60% of the visits going directly to a sub page of the site. By November 2000 (see Figure 7), this has dropped to 31%.

This trend was partially by design. Each organization in the city wanted to have a distinct and unique presence, within some overall rules on consistency and uniformity for all city sites. Unique URL's were reserved, including www.dentonpolice.com, www.dentonparks. com, and www.dentonfire.com, to name a few. This tended to negate the centralized portal concept, where a generic front end would direct the user to the pages they were interested in visiting. As a result of this shift in Web site design, it was no longer practical to utilize the kiosk as a walk-up device for navigating the city's informational portal.

Figure 5. IBM kiosk

Figure 6. April 2000 Web usage statistics

Statistics Report for cityofdenton.com

Monthly Site Activity Analysis

Analysis for the Month of April, 2000

Total pages tracked during period: 1,244

Total page views recorded: 161,645

The average number of views per page: 129.94

Top 5 most commonly accessed pages during period:

	Page Views	Percentage of all traffic
/index.html	67,862	41.98
/hr/index.html	15,818	9.78
/hr/job.html	13,007	8.05
/communiuty.html	4,873	3.02
/directory.html	3,956	2.45

Figure 7. November 2000 Web usage statistics

Statistics Report for cityofdenton.com

Monthly Site Activity Analysis

Analysis for the Month of November, 2000

Total pages tracked during period: 2,261

Total page views recorded: 178,943

The average number of views per page: 79.14

Top 5 most commonly accessed pages during period:

	Page Views	Percentage of all traffic
/index.html	56,202	31.41
/hr/job.html	7,148	3.99
/search.html	6,340	3.54
/police.html	2,637	1.47
/agenda.html	1,378	1.15

We considered putting the department specific page as the lead page for every kiosk (a kiosk placed in a parks and recreation facility would default to the Denton parks Web page, for instance). However, in the spring of 2001, the city received a grant to deploy PC's for public Internet access at our recreation centers, libraries, and other public facilities. These were configured to default to the city's home page on boot, and although the devices can go to other sites, the presence of these public-access computers eliminated the need for an informational kiosk.

A new purpose for the kiosk had to be defined. After several months, it was decided to try the device as a self-service payment solution for city services. At the time, only the municipal court module was generating receipts in any great amount, so this seemed to be the most logical starting point. The courts and police share one end of a city facility, with a common lobby open 24 hours a day, staffed by a duty officer. Often, people would come to the police department and ask where they could pay their traffic tickets. If after normal business hours (past 5 pm), the officer behind the desk would refer them to the kiosk in the lobby to make their payments. We made the necessary programming adaptations to the e-payment system ($24,000 for the municipal court software) and deployed our kiosk in August of 2002. In the first five months of operations, we had 65 citation views (the kiosk was used to check on the status of a traffic citation), but only two payments were received. When compared to the IVR and Web receipts for municipal courts, this seemed very unusual. We tried improved signage, put notifications on municipal court statements, and moved the device to a more prominent location in the PD lobby, but nothing increased the transaction volume of the device.

In December 2002, the city's Utility Customer Services Department approached us for a kiosk solution for the City Hall in the Mall presence. Over 60% of all in-person payments are received at the mall for utility payments, however to have a presence in the mall requires the city storefront to be open during mall hours. This necessitated staffing the mall offices from 11am M-F until 6pm, Saturdays from 9am to 8pm, and Sundays from noon until 8pm. Simon Properties, who operates our mall in Denton, agreed to let us reduce the hours of operation 8 to 6 M-F and 9 to 4 Saturdays if we had a kiosk that could accept payments and place it outside the facility in the mall. This would eliminate overtime, shift differentials, and a great deal of staffing difficulties the Customer Services Department was having. Even if the kiosk collected nothing it would still pay for itself in the personnel savings alone.

We studied the transaction data of the pay-in-person demographic, and found that the vast majority of them paid either by cash, check, or a combination of payments. As mentioned earlier, the City of Denton is home to two universities, and many of those students share apartments and houses throughout the city. Often, they split the utility payment between two or more residents. When they come to pay the utility bill, one will often pay with a check while the other will pay with cash. In order for the kiosk to support transactions of this nature, it would be necessary for it to have the ability to accept cash and checks as well as credit cards.

The only available device that would accept all three forms of payments was the NCR kiosk (see Figure 8). However, to support the other interfaces required modifications to the application. This device and the programming modifications brought our total investment

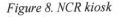

Figure 8. NCR kiosk

in the kiosk solution to just over $100,000. In salary savings, it would take us over a year and a half to recover our investment.

The kiosk went "live" on March 1, 2003 when the City Hall in the Mall moved to their new location. Since that date, the device has collected $449,515.77, 90% through either cash or check. We've noted that for municipal court fines (citations), the dollar amount collected is the same at either kiosk, and payment by check has not made an impact. Kiosks also do not seem to be popular options for property tax payments.

Utility bills are the big story for the second kiosk. The PD lobby device collects as many utility payments (21) as municipal court payments (17), although the dollar amount is larger on court collections.

This is obviously a significant improvement over the IBM device, and has contributed not only in reduction of hours of operation but also in reducing the labor associated with acceptance of an in-person payment. There are several potential causes for the differences in collection amounts, but the collections in check and cash stand out so much that there is obviously something else in play.

Current Challenges Facing the Organization

This is the "techonomic divide" we have identified. All of the utility bill collections done by the kiosk at the mall are performed after staffing hours. For reference, please view Figure 4—Kiosk Statistics.. Although more than 22 million has been collected online through ether Web or IVR for the utility, these are exclusively MasterCard or Visa transactions. People with credit cards find using the phone or Web a more appealing alternative than the paying at the kiosk, which is to be expected.

But there are still a large number of transactions with kiosk services. To boost self-service, the kiosk with check and cash acceptance has made the difference. Some future developments would be to adapt the IVR and Web services to accept electronic check (given a check routing number, we could debit the bank account automatically similar to credit services), replacement of the IBM kiosk with an NCR kiosk, or the placement of an NCR kiosk outside the City Hall East location where our Customer Services Department is based. How to best service the cash paying customer base is currently under study.

In recent developments, the city has elected to discontinue acceptance of credit cards in face-to-face transactions, and only accept payment by credit card through the self-service kiosks, over the Web, or through the IVR. This change is being instituted in order to allow the city to levy a convenience fee for the use of credit cards, and reduce that burden to the city budget by putting it back on the cardholder. In order to go forward with this change, it will be necessary to place the credit-card processing kiosks in areas traditionally serviced as face-to-face transactions, and re-educate the citizenry on the change. How this will impact the way people pay their bills is still under speculation. From a technical standpoint, it also significantly impacts the operation of the NCR kiosk at the Mall, due to the fact that the mall kiosk will no longer be able to accept cash, checks, and credit cards if the use of a credit card would result in an additional fee to the user. Under the guidelines set forth by the credit card companies, it is in violation of the merchant agreement to charge a customer extra because of their choice of payment. In order that customers not be penalized for their right to choose what payment method they wish to use, all payment types available to a customer through a specific transaction medium must be equal. Because cash and checks make up the largest volume of the mall kiosk's transactions, it is expected that the credit card payment option will be removed, so as to preserve the cash and check processing. However, this will necessitate the addition of a second kiosk, one that will accept only credit cards (and the associated convenience fees), in order to allow the customers to continue to pay in that manner if they choose.

References

Carver, J. (n.d.). *The Carver policy governance model.* Retrieved July 8, 2006, from http://www.carvergovernance.com/model.htm

Zachman, J. A. (1987). A framework for information systems architecture. *IBM Systems Journal, 26*(3), 276-292.

Authors' Biographies

Alex Pettit is the Chief Technology Officer and member of the leadership team for the City of Denton. Alex provides technical direction to the various city departments, including public safety, utility services, and financial accounting. His team is responsible for all system implementations, security, and both the tactical and strategic planning for technology solutions and services. During his tenure with the City of Denton, Mr. Pettit and his department have earned several awards and have been recognized by groups such as Government Technology and the Public Technology Institute for the innovative use of technology in government. He received the Technology Leadership Award for 2004 from Public Technology Institute, received a Best of Texas award for Demonstrated Leadership in Management of IT in 2005, and the 2004 Premier Award for the innovative use of technology for historical records preservation.

Anthony Caranna is currently the Solutions Architect and Telecommunications Manager for the City of Denton, where he heads a team of technical specialists, programmers, and project managers who implement and maintain new systems and technologies for the city government. Recent major projects include disaster recovery and business continuity planning, integrated enterprise e-government solutions, development of an integrated user authentication and security model, design of a hierarchical storage management and multi-tiered storage architecture solution, and implementation of an enterprise-wide digital document imaging and management system. Mr. Caranna has a BS in engineering technology from the University of North Texas, and has been with the City of Denton since 1995.

About the Editor

Bruce Rocheleau is a professor of political science in the Division of Public Administration at Northern Illinois University. He has been doing research and contributing publications concerning governmental information management since the early 1980s. He recently authored the book *Public Management Information Systems*. He has published numerous articles, chapters, and monographs related to governmental information management.

Index

advocacy groups 250
aerospace and technology 127
affordable housing initiatives 24
AFHCAN (Alaska Federal Health Care
        Access Network) 201, 205,
        211, 214
    cart 214
    data 211, 212
    listed cost reduction 212
    literature 206, 208
    mandate 206
    mission 205
    network 210
    office 210
    organization 210
    pilot study 209
    project office 206
    report 207, 213
    sites 205
    software 208, 214
    system 214
    WAN 213
    Web site 207, 212
AFHCP (Alaska Federal Health Care
        Partnership) 205, 214
    mandate 205
AG Consulting 132
agency
    CIOs 172, 243
    commissioner 250
    home page 235
    missions 232
    newsletters 167
    participation 232
    partners 169
    rollout 12
    security officers 232
    staff participation 18
    Web pages 240
    Web sites 234, 235, 237,
    238, 239, 243
    Webmaster 236, 242
agency-based
    CSM 18
    data centers 231
agency-by-agency 2
agency-level priorities 235
aggregated demand 134
AGI amount 311
aging services 127
agricultural marketing cooperative 38
Agriculture and Mining 307
Agriculture, Trade and Consumer
        Protection 14
air
    access 205
    evacuation 211
    medical evacuation 204
    travel 204
airfare 212
airport 127, 315
Alaska
    Native beneficiaries 205
    Native Health System 205
    Native Lands Settlement Act
    (ANCSA) 203
    Native Medical Center

(ANMC) 203, 205
    Native organizations 204
    Native Tribal Health Consor-
    tium (ANTHC) 205
    Regional Hospital 203
    Telehealth Advisory Com-
    mission (ATAC) 205
    Telemedicine Testbed Project
    (ATTP) 204
Alaska-based telecommunications car-
        riers 209
Alaskan
    Indian Services 204
    Natives 202, 205, 209
Albany, NY 247
alcohol beverage taxes 300
Aleut 203
Alexa
    Internet Traffic Rankings
    224
    Web site rankings 225
Allen County, Indiana 304
Allstate 21
alphabetical list of the state agencies
        237
alternative
    business model 223
    governance model 265
    hosting providers 162
    minimum tax 34
Alutiiq 203
ambulance 315
    rescue service 82
    service fees 82
American Federation of State, County
        and Municipal Employees
        (AFSCME) 131
American people 158
American Red Cross 249
American Telemedicine Association
        President's Awards for the
        Advancement of Telemedi-
        cine 213
Americans with Disabilities Act Sec-
        tion 407 compliance 317
Amoco 70
amusement park 25
analysis 298
analyst programmer 115
ANCHOR 249, 253
    initiative 253
Anchorage, Alaska 203, 204, 206,
        209, 211
Animal Control 182
Ankara Metropolitan Municipality Web
        site 225
ANMC (Alaska Native Medical Cen-
        ter) 211, 214
annexation agreements 293
anniversary event 171
announcements 321
annual
    assessment activities 181
    budget planning time 62
    budget process 30, 63
    consensus revenue forecast-
    ing process 300

employment 302
fiscal budget 82
funding 112
funding for the UEAs 301
investment expenditures 307
maintenance 86
maintenance fee 268
materials budget 167
OMB business case 174
operating budget 71
sales receipts 307
support costs 73
tactical marketing plan 168
tax incentive 301
turnover rate for dispatch-
    ers 278
antennas 264
ANTHC (Alaska Native Tribal Health
        Consortium) 215
antibiotics 212
Anti-Diphtheria serum 203
Anti-Outsourcing Model of IT Service
        Delivery 29
antiquated e-mail system 25
anti-virus updates 40
applicable
    acceptance criteria and speci-
    fications 149
    functional requirements 149
application 9
    base 7
    development 26, 237, 239
    development and support 3
    of e-government 226
    performance 100
    program interfaces (API)
    316
    programs 118
    servers 99
approval hierarchies 85
approvers 87
arbitration 150
ArcGIS 290
Architecture Committee 30
Arctic Circle 202
ArcView 305
    GIS software 305
area of public administration 219
art 203
articulated business strategies 7
artists' colony 32
ask a question 182
assembly 238
assessed value 197
assessment 129
    value of property 197
asset
    database 107
    inventories 184
    management process 101,
    102
    management systems 94
assistant county auditor 144
associated convenience fees 326
association newsletters 169
AT&T 70, 162, 180
    Alascom 204, 206, 209

V

"vanilla" 132
VA records system 214
vacation benefits 267
value
    of sharing information 249
    proposition 156, 165, 169
valve 94
vanilla approach 133
VA (Veterans' Administration) 215
vehicle registration 238
vendor 242
    and product evaluation
    process 143
    information 87
    personnel 149
    service contracts 3
vendor's
    chief executive officer 150
    director 149
    failings 154
    project manager 149
    proposed changes 151
verification process 149
Veterans 168
    Administration usage of carts
    214
    Affairs 204
vetting process 243
VHF Simulcast Fire Paging System
    269
vice president 115
Vice President Al Gore 33
video
    otoscope 211, 214
    production 28
    Web casts 34
videoconferencing 33
    equipment 211
    services 33
Vignette® 163
    Enterprise Content Manage-
    ment System 163
village 218-220, 223
    clinics 203, 204, 207, 211
    council 209
    of Butler, Wisconsin 275
    of North Hudson 258
    police forces 36
    residents 209
virtual
    archives 34
    corporation 38
    private network (VPN)
    technology 268
    servers 53
    work groups 38
viruses 150
Visa transactions 325
visibility 142
VISIO for visualization and discussion
    291
visioning 58
visitation statistics 165
visual
    feedback 212

    presentations of spatial data
    306
visualization 289
vital signs monitor 207
voice
    access 316
    over IP (VoIP) 278
    over IP (VoIP) telephonics
    258
    over IP Phone Calls 278
    telephone network 204
    XML 39
voice/long-distance networks 3
VoIP 278
    9-1-1 279
    calls 278
    in Southeastern Wisconsin
    278
    phone service 278
    phone users 278
    use 278
voluntary participation and commit-
    ment 248
volunteer fire departments 257
Volunteers of America 248
Vonage 278
Vons 127
Vrakas, Dan 260

W

Wachs, Joel 128
    Chief of Staff 128
wages 311
    and employment levels 304
    and job creation tax incen-
    tives 310
    elasticity 310
    information 313
    levels 298, 307, 309
    payments 306
    statistics 307
    totals 302, 310
walk-in service 242
walk-up device 321
WAN (Wide-Area Network) 215
    links 213
warehouse
    consolidation 133
    manager 130
warehoused agreements 282
warehousing 131
warranties by the vendor 149
Washington Mutual 127
Washington, D.C.
    buses 170
    subway system 170
wastewater 179
    collection 92
    collection and treatment 127
    treatment 82, 293
water 179, 315
    and power utility 127
    and sewage treatment 282
    and wastewater GIS asset
    database 101
    and Wastewater Sales 69, 93

    and wastewater system GIS
    databases 96
    and Wastewater Utility 69,
    93
    and Wastewater Utility-Water
    93
    distribution 92
    Distribution and Collection
    Division 94
    distribution feature 105
    distribution system GIS
    database 94
    main 94
    main break 99
    meter 106
    Operations 100, 102-103,
    105, 107-108
    Operations Division 94, 103,
    105
    Operations Division Manager
    95, 107-108
    Operations Division staff
    field inventory 97
    Operations Division work-
    flow 101
    Operations Division's budget
    manager 106
    Operations GIS data 108
    Operations Manager 95
    Operations staff 97, 99-101,
    103, 108
    Operations Utility Specialist
    107
    Operations' work processes
    104
    pumps 93
    related amenities 82
    shut-off 99
    system GIS map 106
    treatment plant 82
    Utility 93, 95, 102, 105
    Utility Civil Engineering 105
    utility engineering 103
    Utility management 104
    Utility's Civil Engineering
    Division staff 97
    Utility's Water Operations
    Division 102
"waterfall" approach to software devel-
    opment 30
water/wastewater
    GIS data 103
    system management 100
Watson Furniture Group Gold 269
Waukesha County, Wisconsin 9, 256-
    257, 259, 263-264, 269, 279
    Communications Center
    (WCC) 256-257, 259
    Geographic Information
    System (GIS) 268
    Land Information System
    Division 268
    municipalities 260
    Technical College 263
Waukesha Freeman newspaper 264
WCC 256, 264, 267, 272, 278
    effort 259